2

DEADPOOL

SAMURAI

STORY BY SANSHIRO KASAMA   ART BY HIKARU UESUGI

DEADPOOL SAMURAI

2

CONTENTS

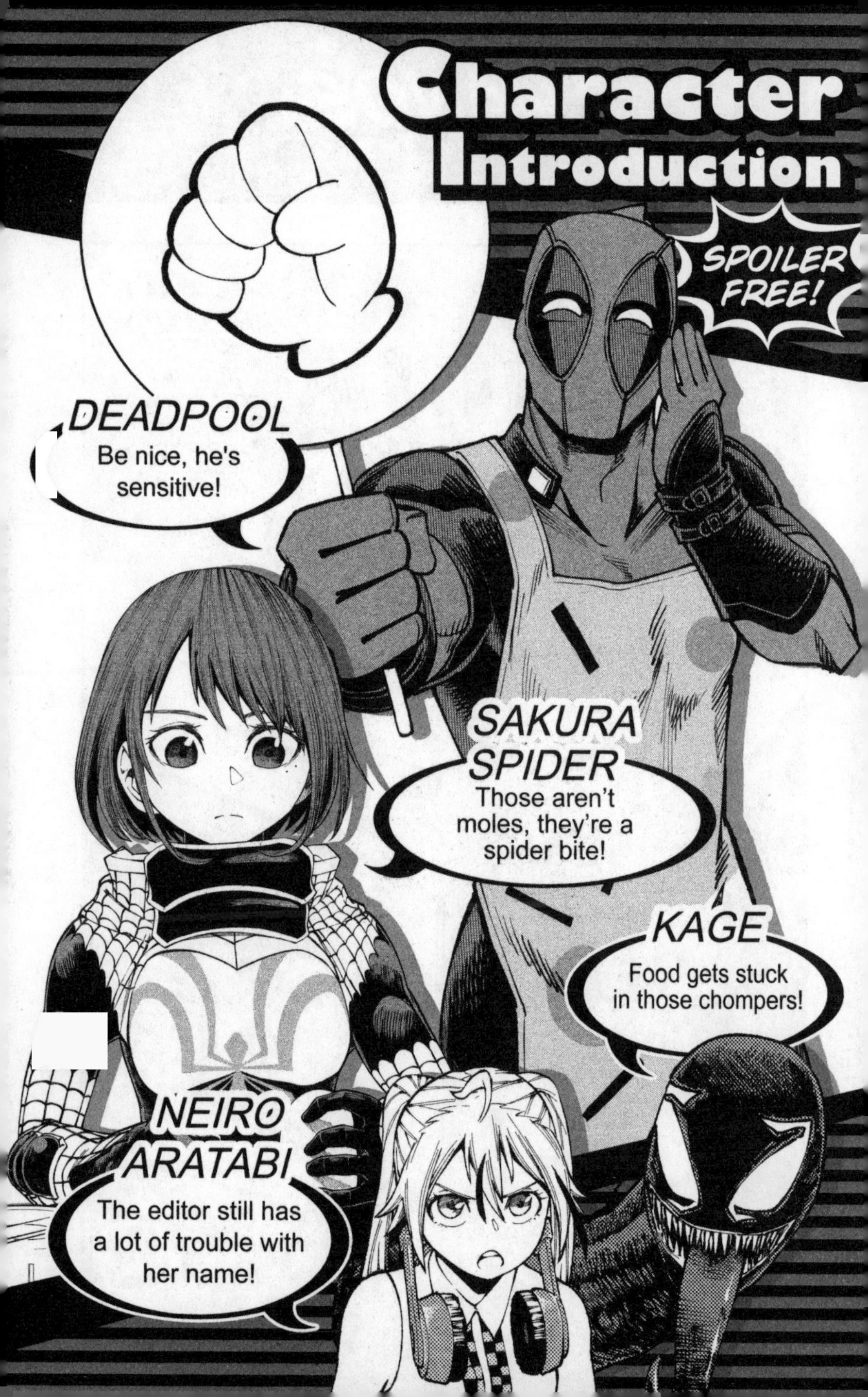
Character Introduction
SPOILER FREE!
DEADPOOL
Be nice, he's sensitive!
SAKURA SPIDER
Those aren't moles, they're a spider bite!
KAGE
Food gets stuck in those chompers!
NEIRO ARATABI
The editor still has a lot of trouble with her name!

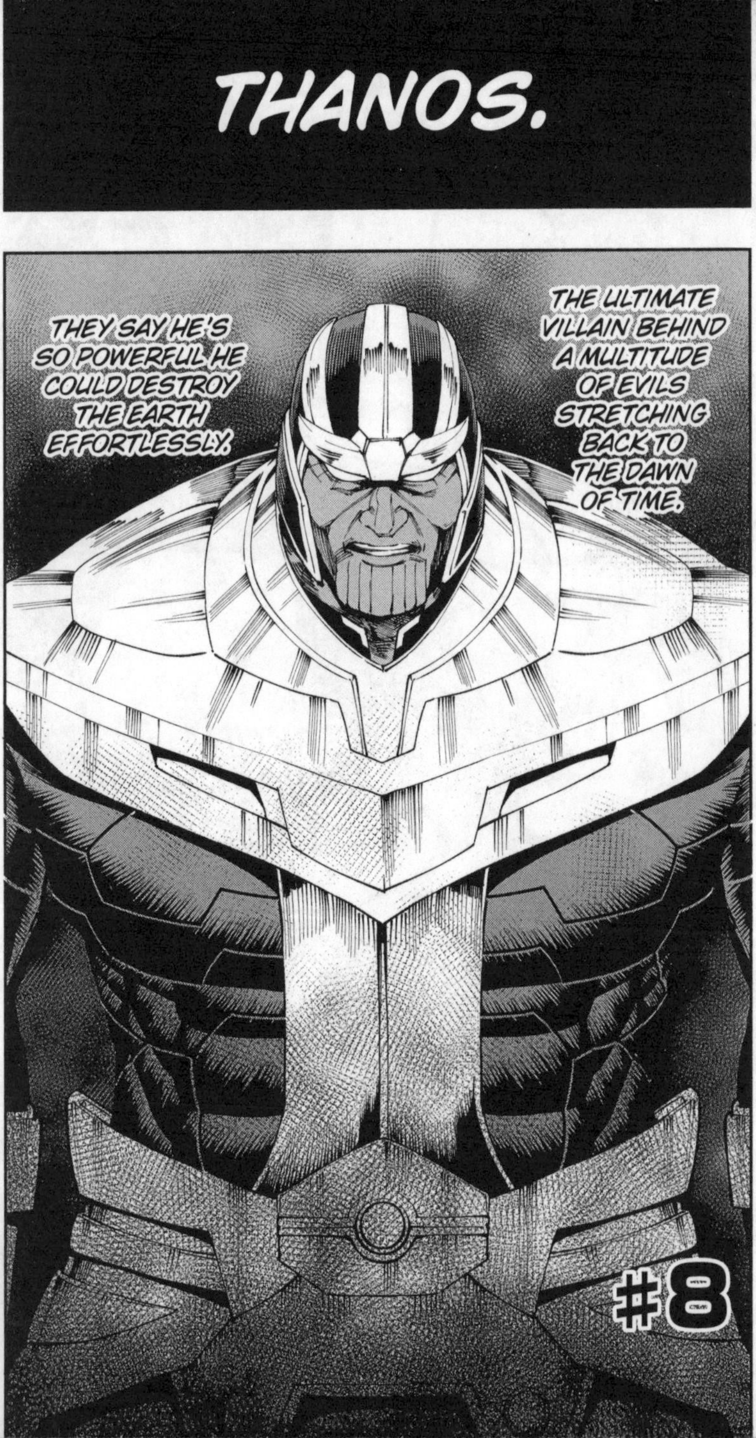
THANOS.
THE ULTIMATE VILLAIN BEHIND A MULTITUDE OF EVILS STRETCHING BACK TO THE DAWN OF TIME.
THEY SAY HE'S SO POWERFUL HE COULD DESTROY THE EARTH EFFORTLESSLY.
#8

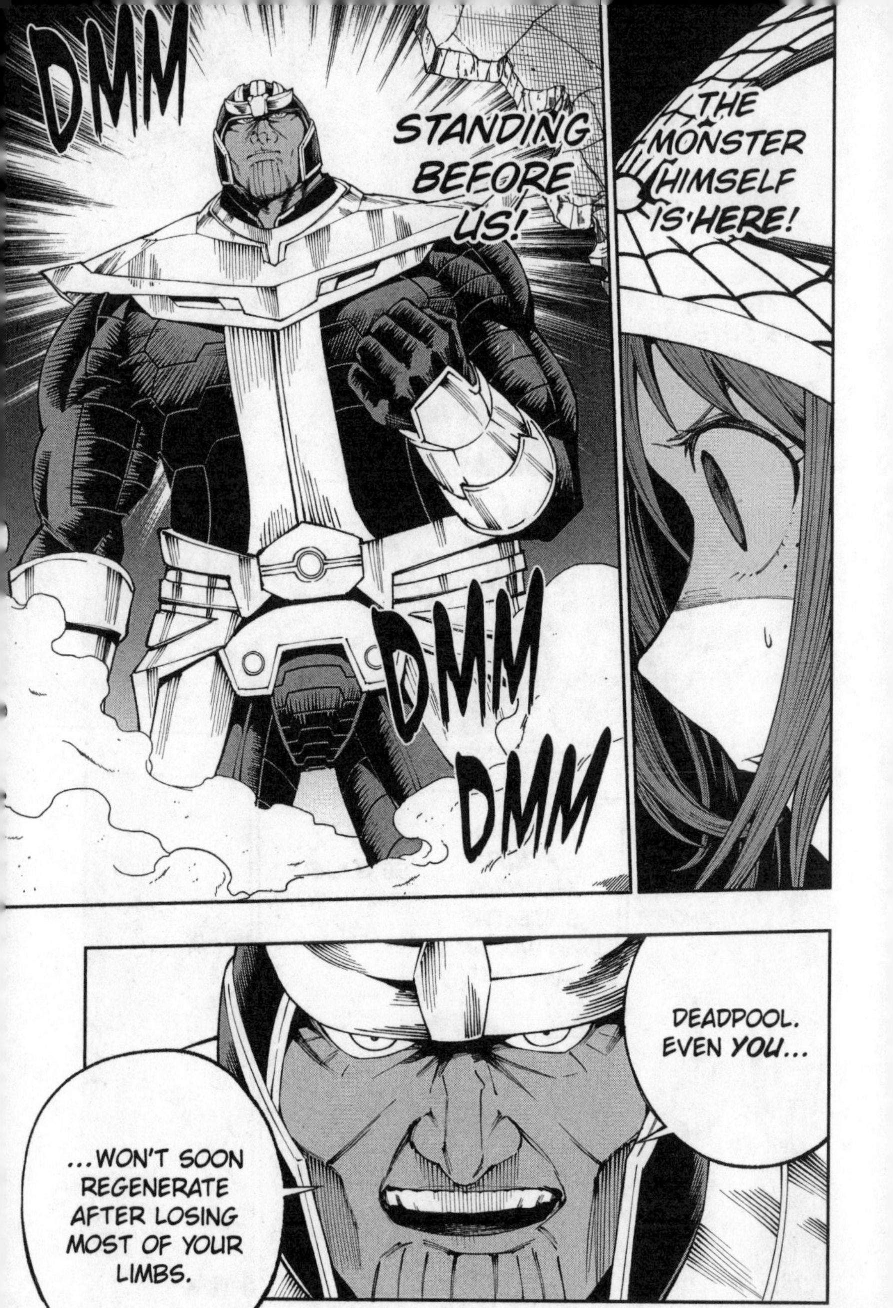
THE MONSTER HIMSELF IS HERE!
DMM
STANDING BEFORE US!
DMM
DMM
DEADPOOL. EVEN *YOU*...
...WON'T SOON REGENERATE AFTER LOSING MOST OF YOUR LIMBS.

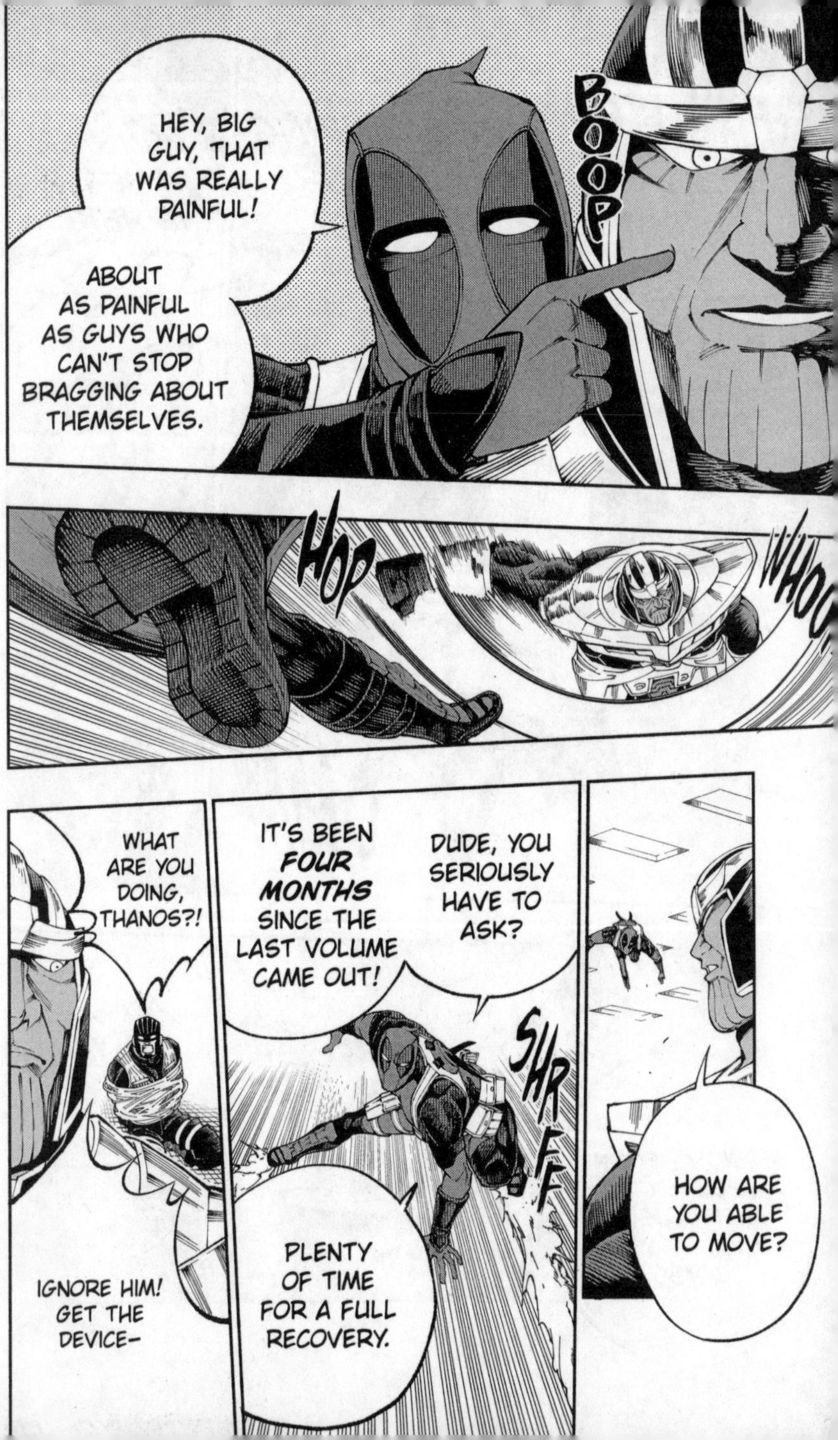
BOOP
HEY, BIG GUY, THAT WAS REALLY PAINFUL!
ABOUT AS PAINFUL AS GUYS WHO CAN'T STOP BRAGGING ABOUT THEMSELVES.
HOP
HOW ARE YOU ABLE TO MOVE?
DUDE, YOU SERIOUSLY HAVE TO ASK?
IT'S BEEN ***FOUR MONTHS*** SINCE THE LAST VOLUME CAME OUT!
SHRFFF
PLENTY OF TIME FOR A FULL RECOVERY.
WHAT ARE YOU DOING, THANOS?!
IGNORE HIM! GET THE DEVICE–

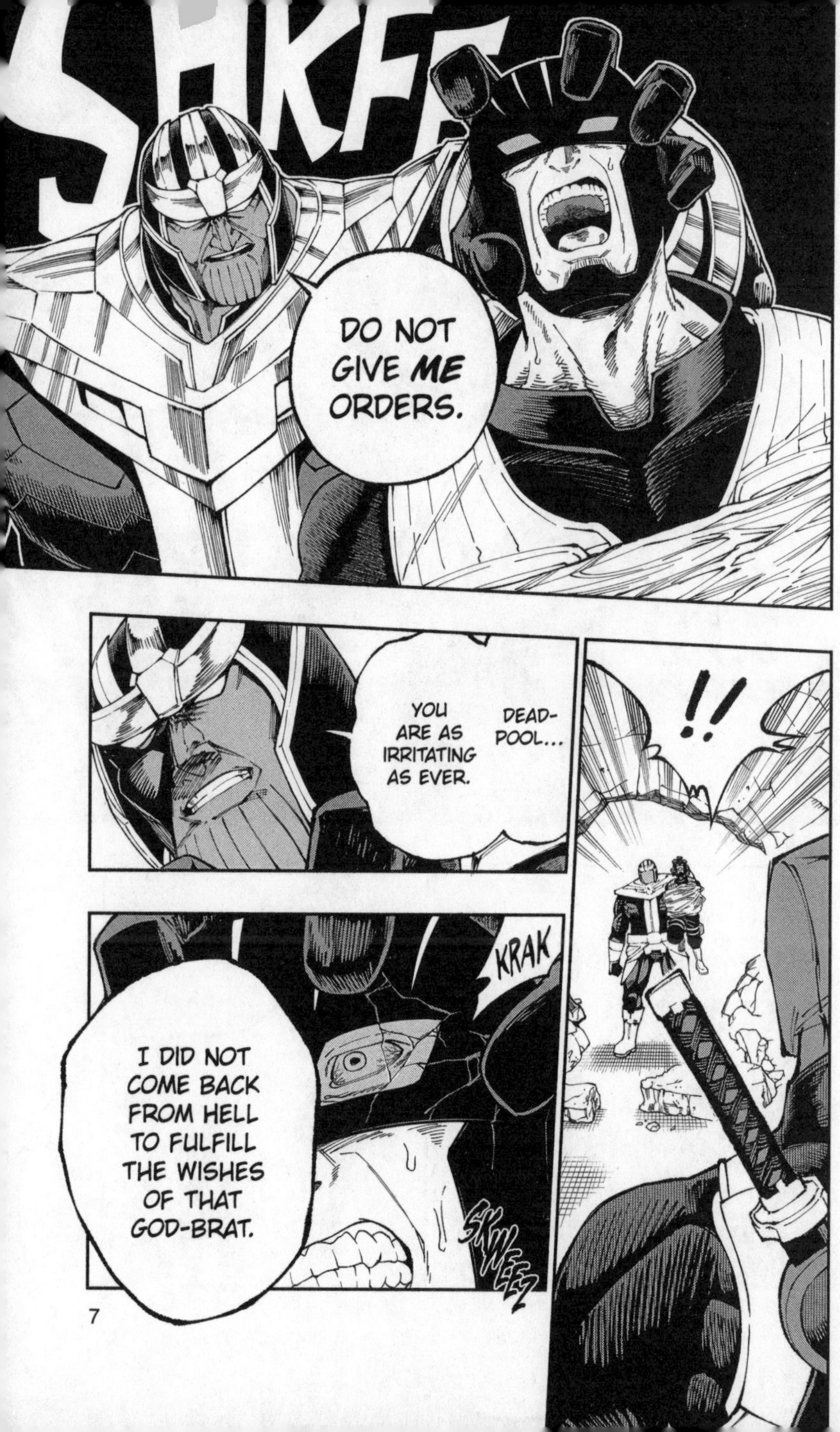
SHKFF
DO NOT GIVE ME ORDERS.
!!
DEADPOOL... YOU ARE AS IRRITATING AS EVER.
KRAK
I DID NOT COME BACK FROM HELL TO FULFILL THE WISHES OF THAT GOD-BRAT.
SKWEEZ

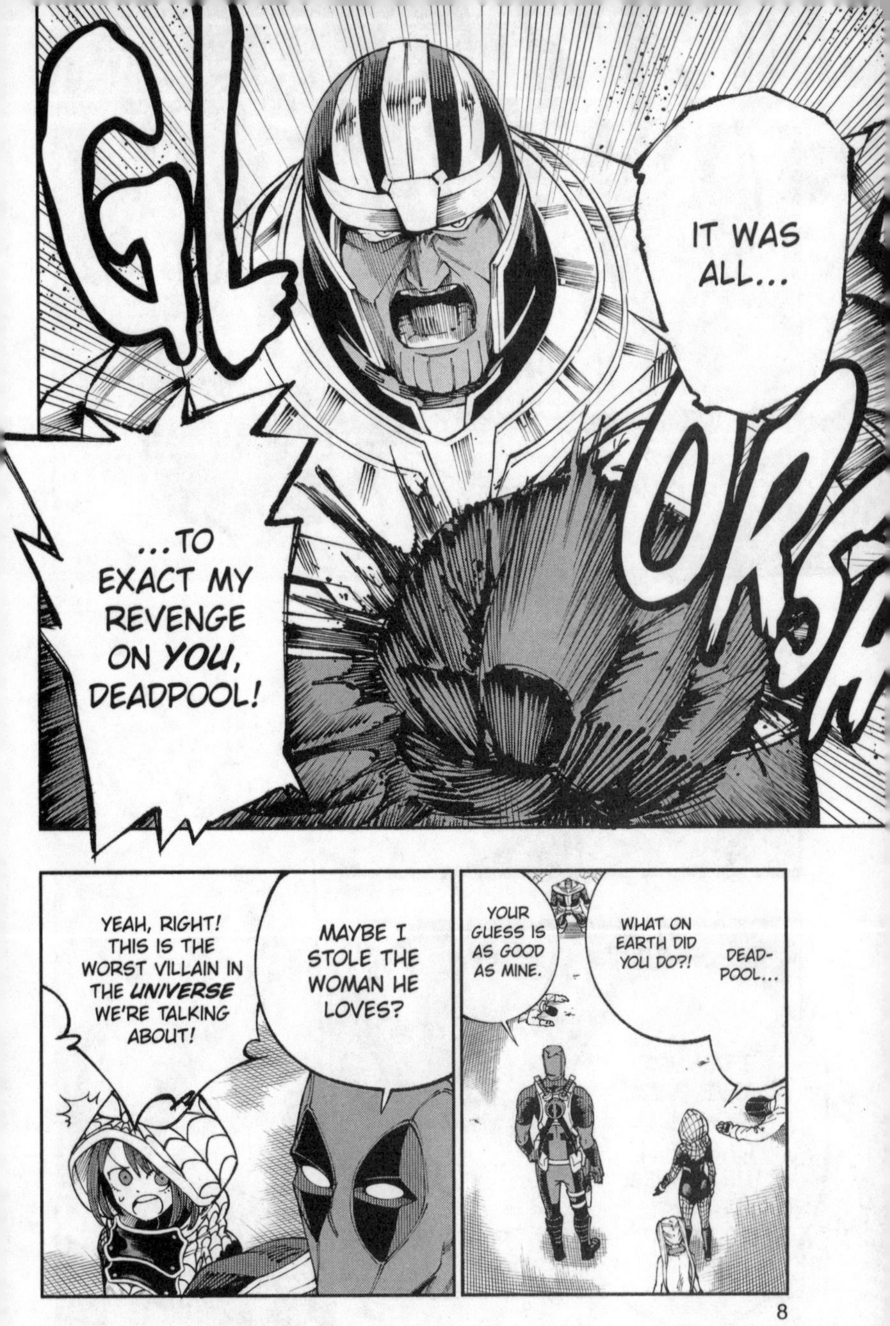
IT WAS ALL...
GL
...TO EXACT MY REVENGE ON *YOU*, DEADPOOL!
DEAD-POOL...
WHAT ON EARTH DID YOU DO?!
YOUR GUESS IS AS GOOD AS MINE.
MAYBE I STOLE THE WOMAN HE LOVES?
YEAH, RIGHT! THIS IS THE WORST VILLAIN IN THE *UNIVERSE* WE'RE TALKING ABOUT!

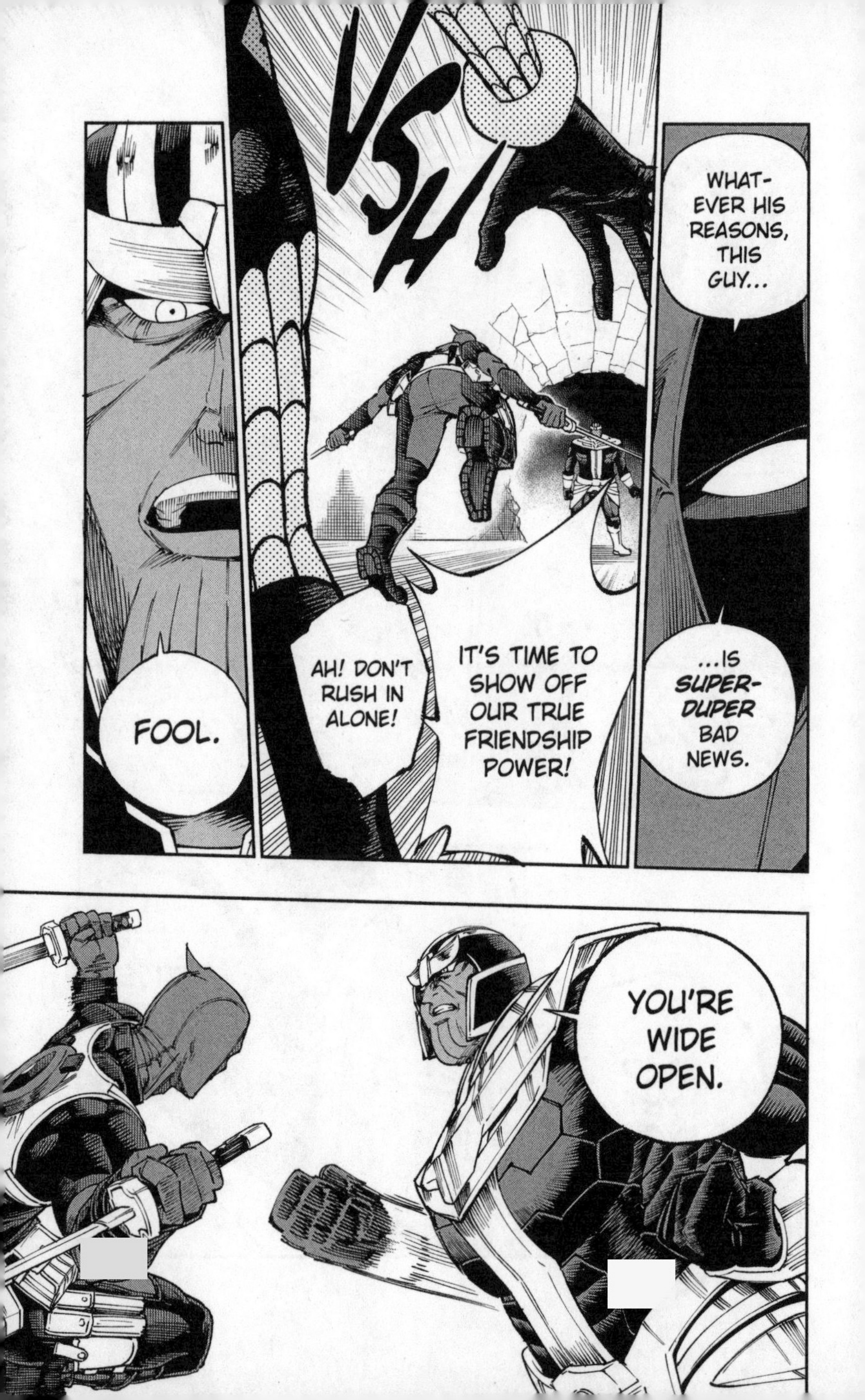
WHAT-EVER HIS REASONS, THIS GUY...
...IS SUPER-DUPER BAD NEWS.
VSH
IT'S TIME TO SHOW OFF OUR TRUE FRIENDSHIP POWER!
AH! DON'T RUSH IN ALONE!
FOOL.
YOU'RE WIDE OPEN.

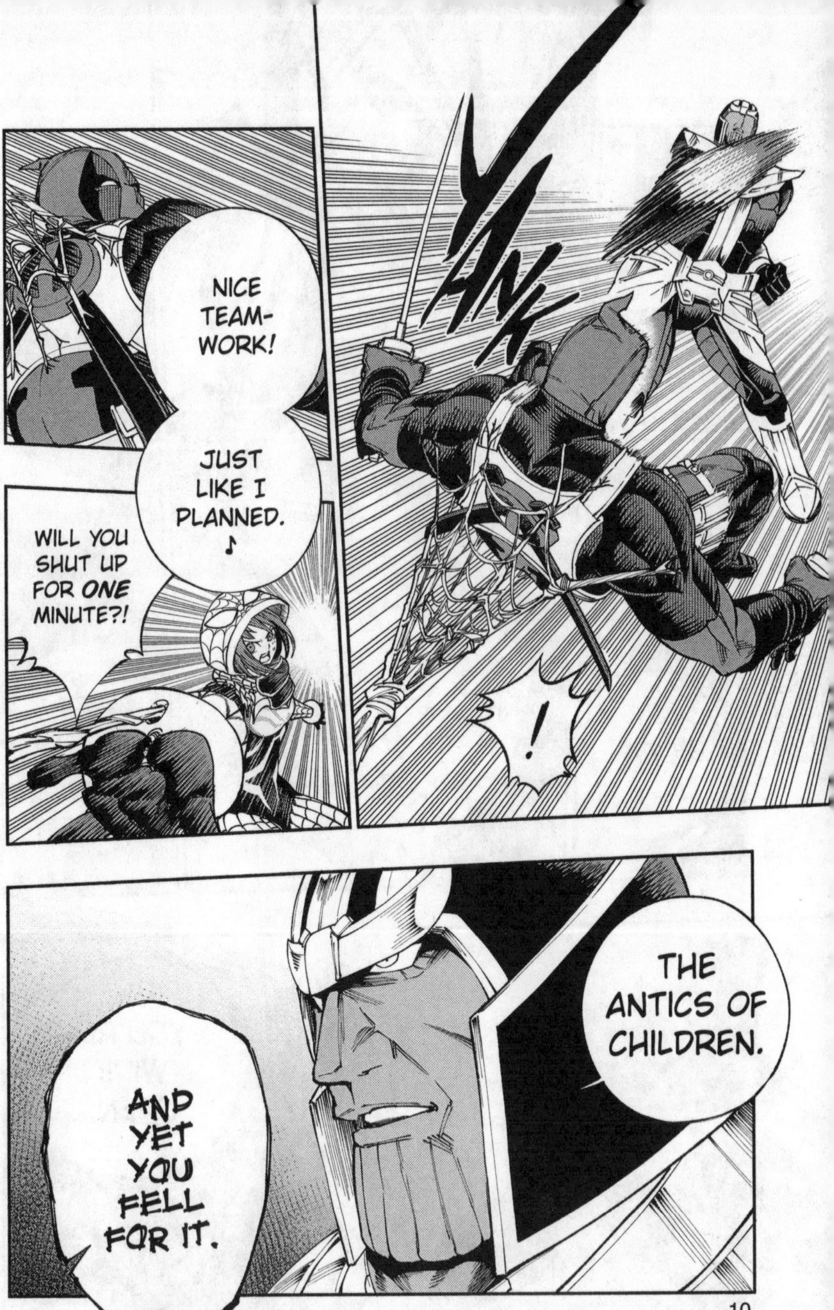
YANK
!
NICE TEAM-WORK!
JUST LIKE I PLANNED. ♪
WILL YOU SHUT UP FOR ONE MINUTE?!
THE ANTICS OF CHILDREN.
AND YET YOU FELL FOR IT.

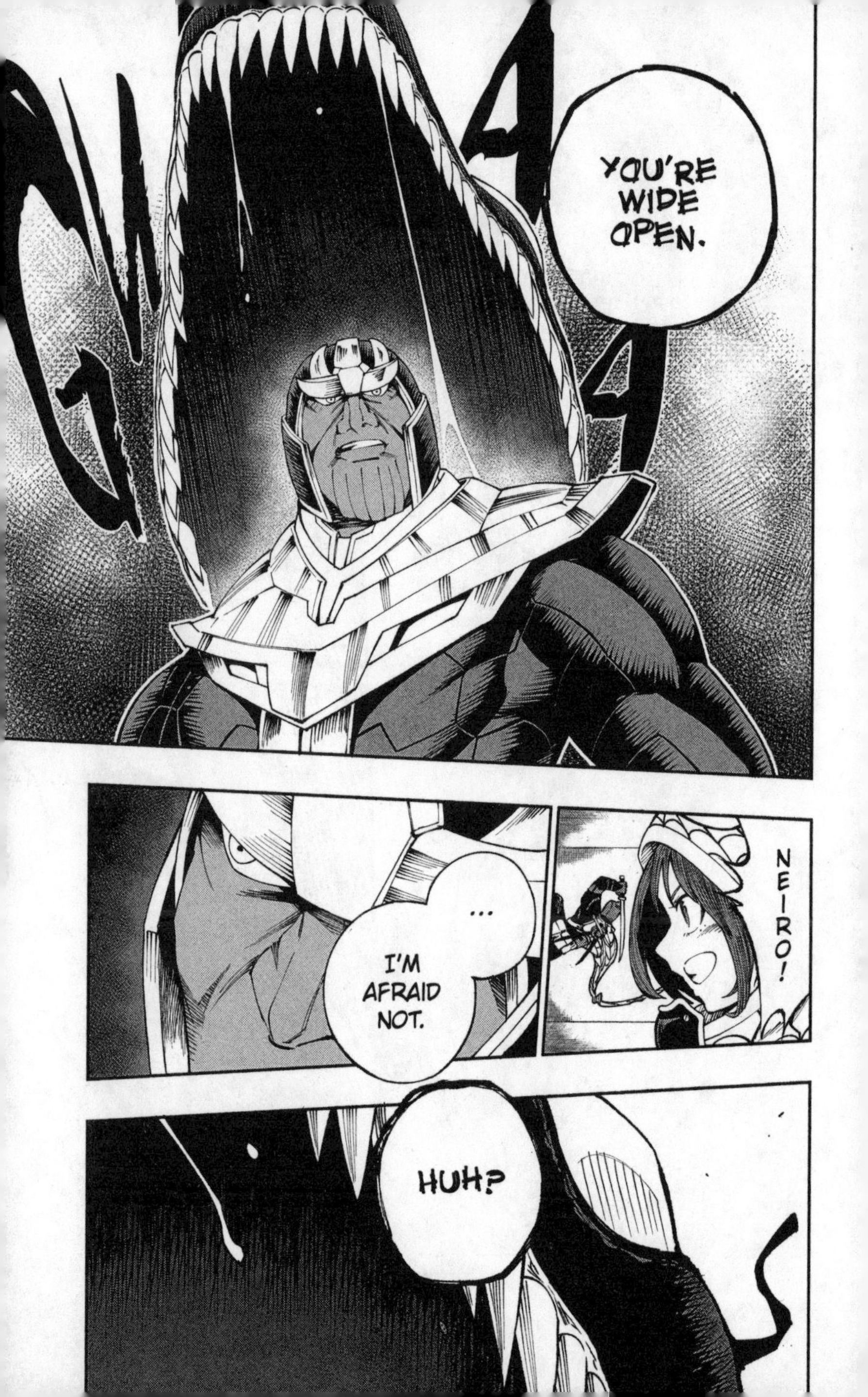
YOU'RE WIDE OPEN.
NEIRO!
...
I'M AFRAID NOT.
HUH?

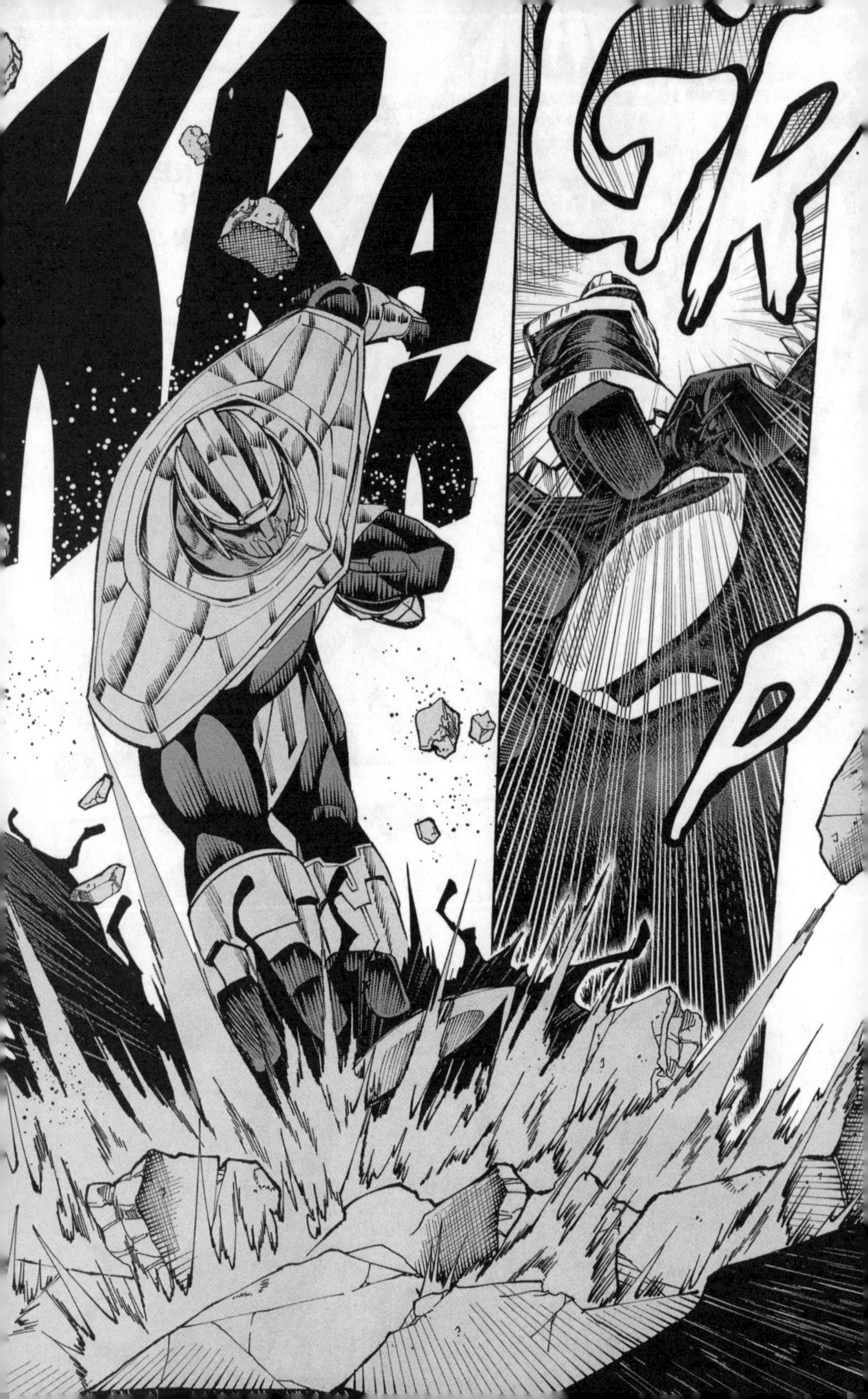
KRAK

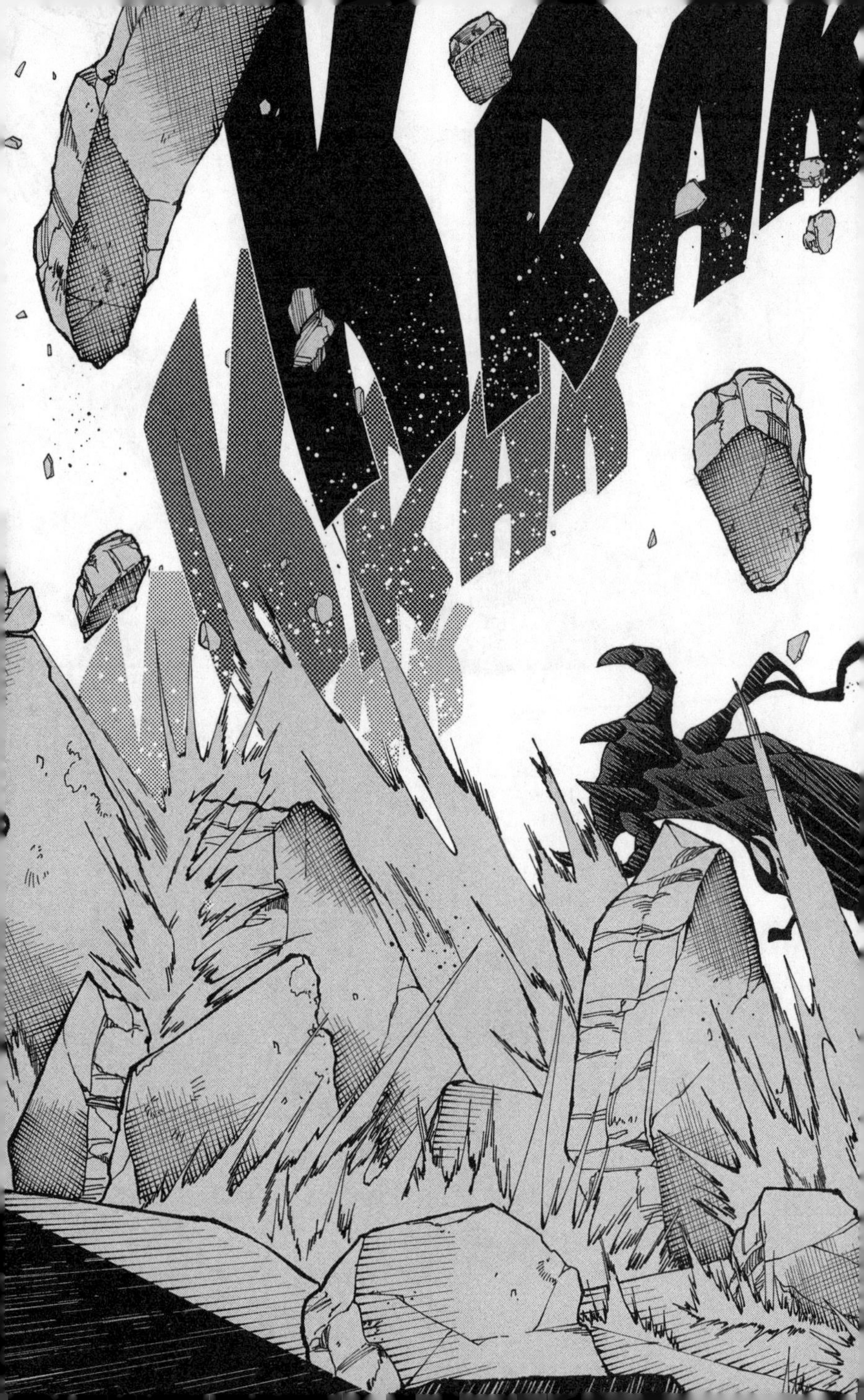
KRAK
KRAK

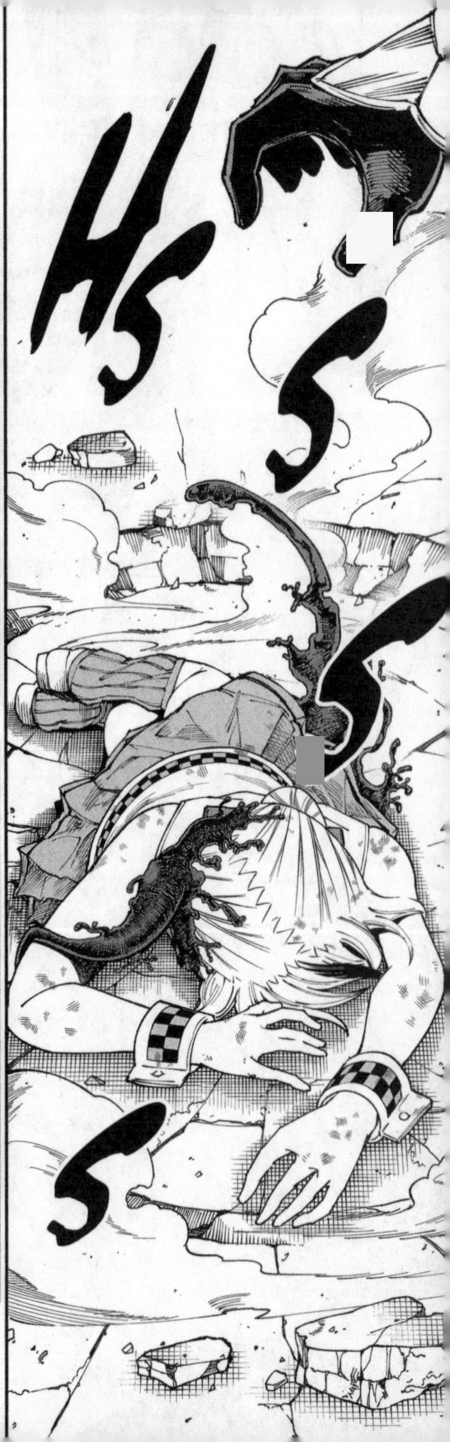
HSSSS

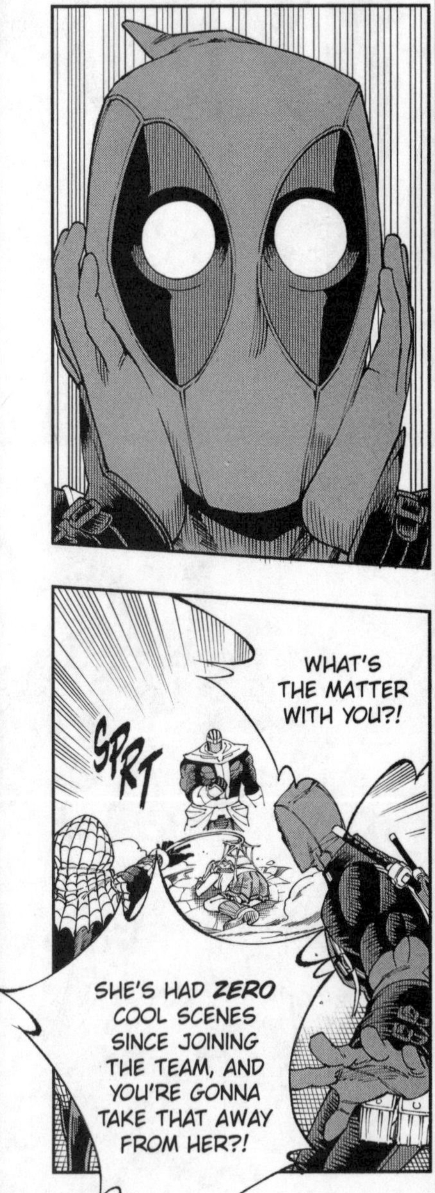
WHAT'S THE MATTER WITH YOU?!
SPRT
SHE'S HAD **ZERO** COOL SCENES SINCE JOINING THE TEAM, AND YOU'RE GONNA TAKE THAT AWAY FROM HER?!

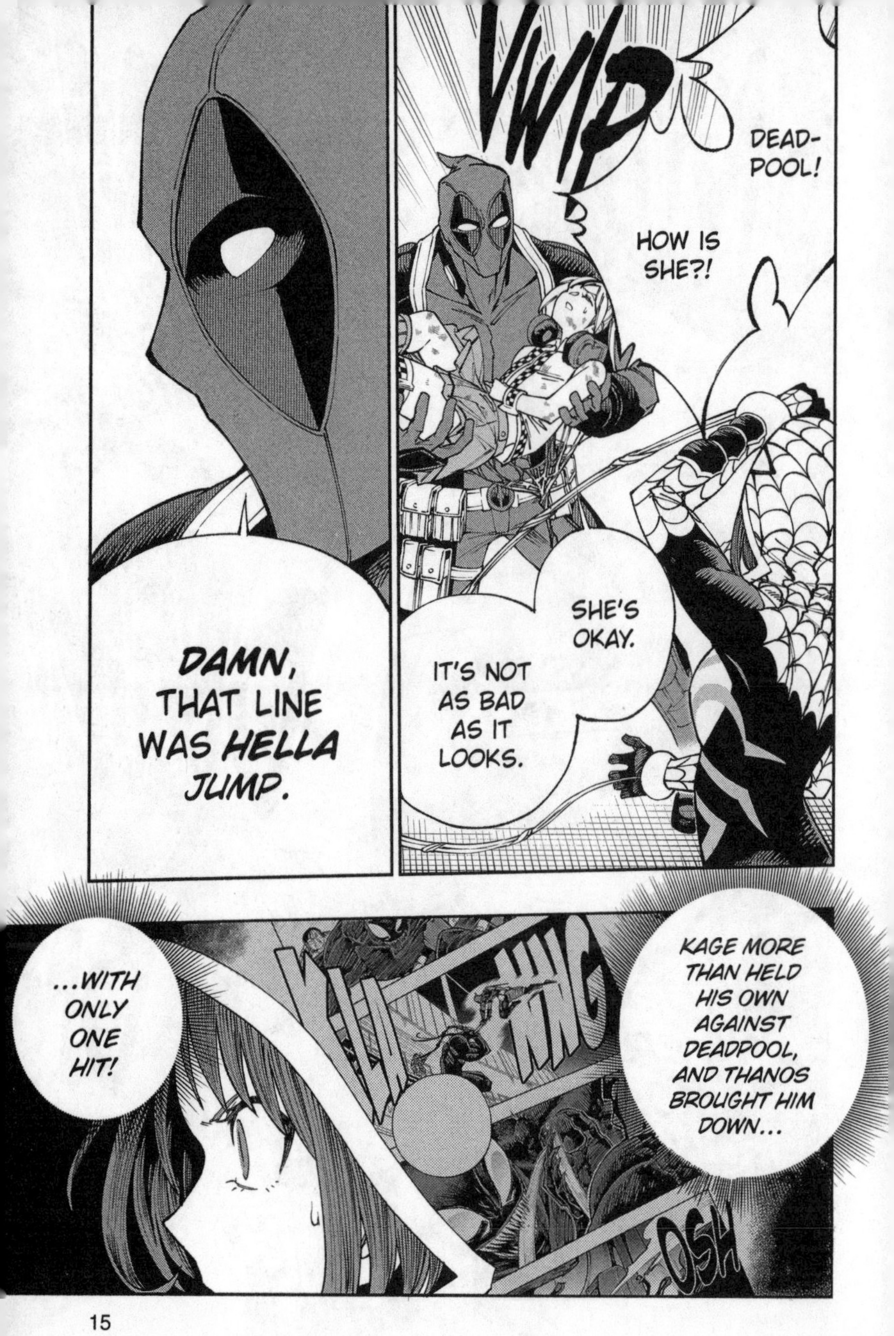
VWIP
DEAD-POOL!
HOW IS SHE?!
SHE'S OKAY.
IT'S NOT AS BAD AS IT LOOKS.
DAMN, THAT LINE WAS HELLA JUMP.
KAGE MORE THAN HELD HIS OWN AGAINST DEADPOOL, AND THANOS BROUGHT HIM DOWN...
...WITH ONLY ONE HIT!
OSH

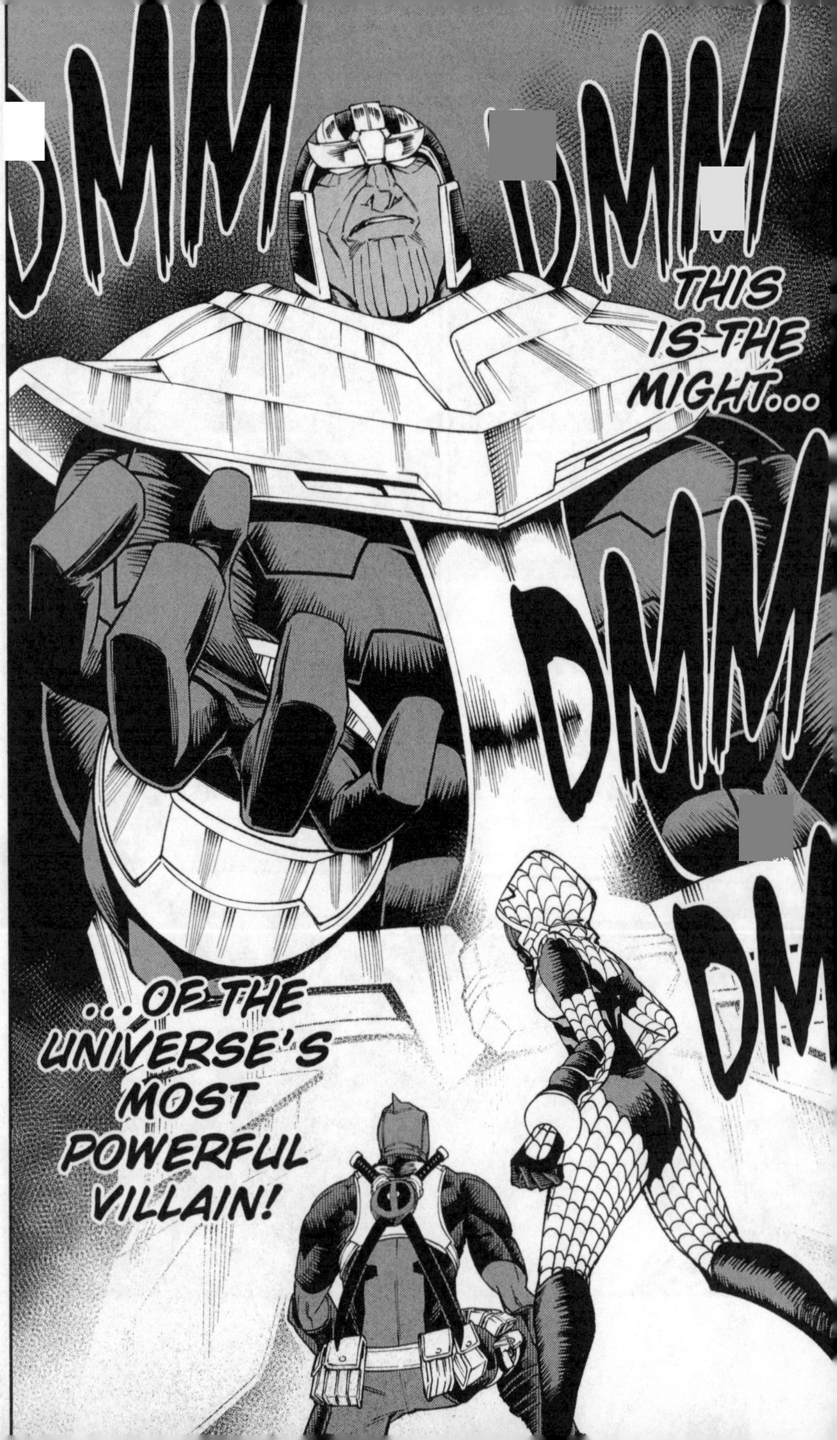
DMM
DMM
THIS IS THE MIGHT...
DMM
DM
...OF THE UNIVERSE'S MOST POWERFUL VILLAIN!

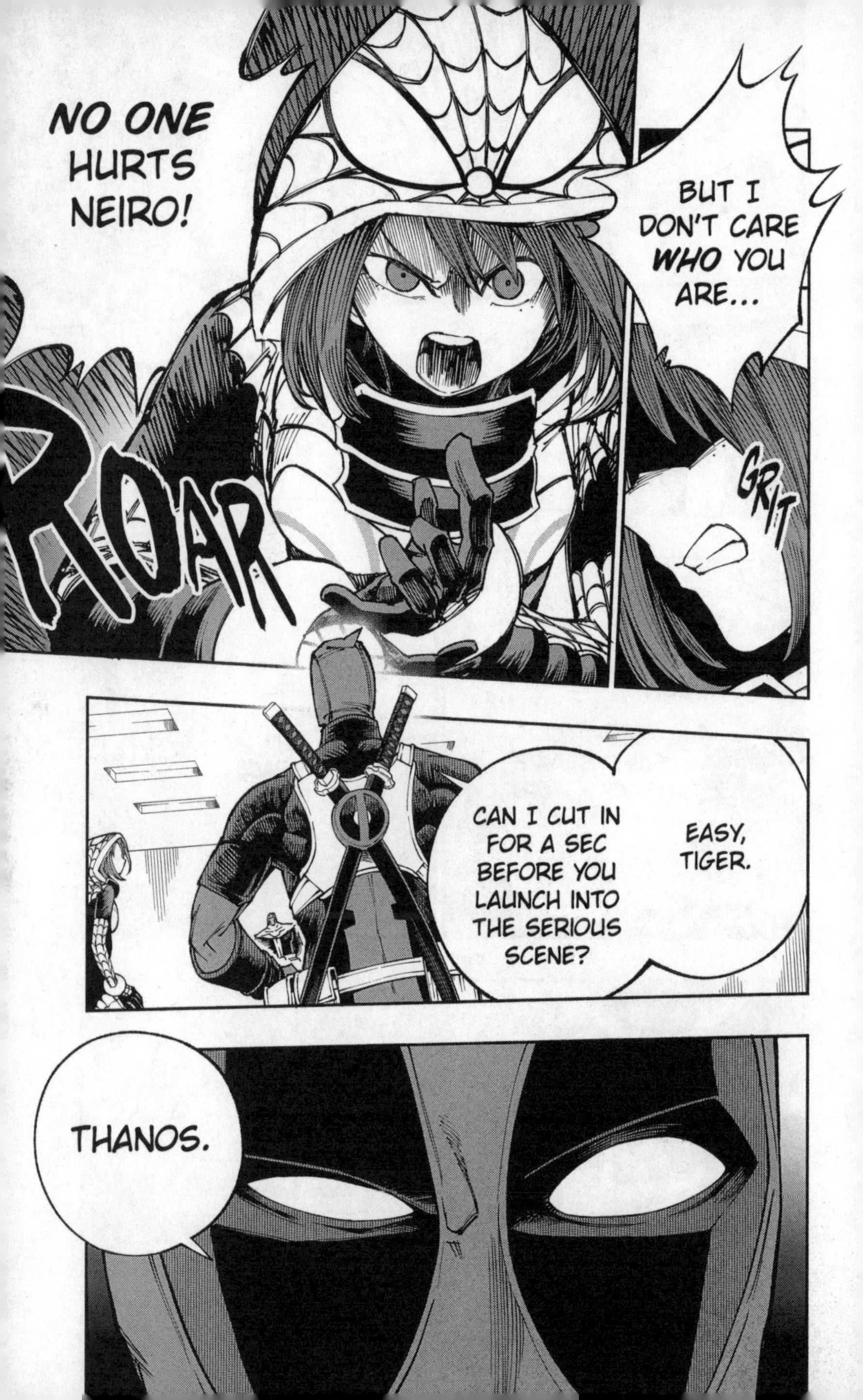
BUT I DON'T CARE **WHO** YOU ARE...
NO ONE HURTS NEIRO!
GRIT
ROAR
EASY, TIGER.
CAN I CUT IN FOR A SEC BEFORE YOU LAUNCH INTO THE SERIOUS SCENE?
THANOS.

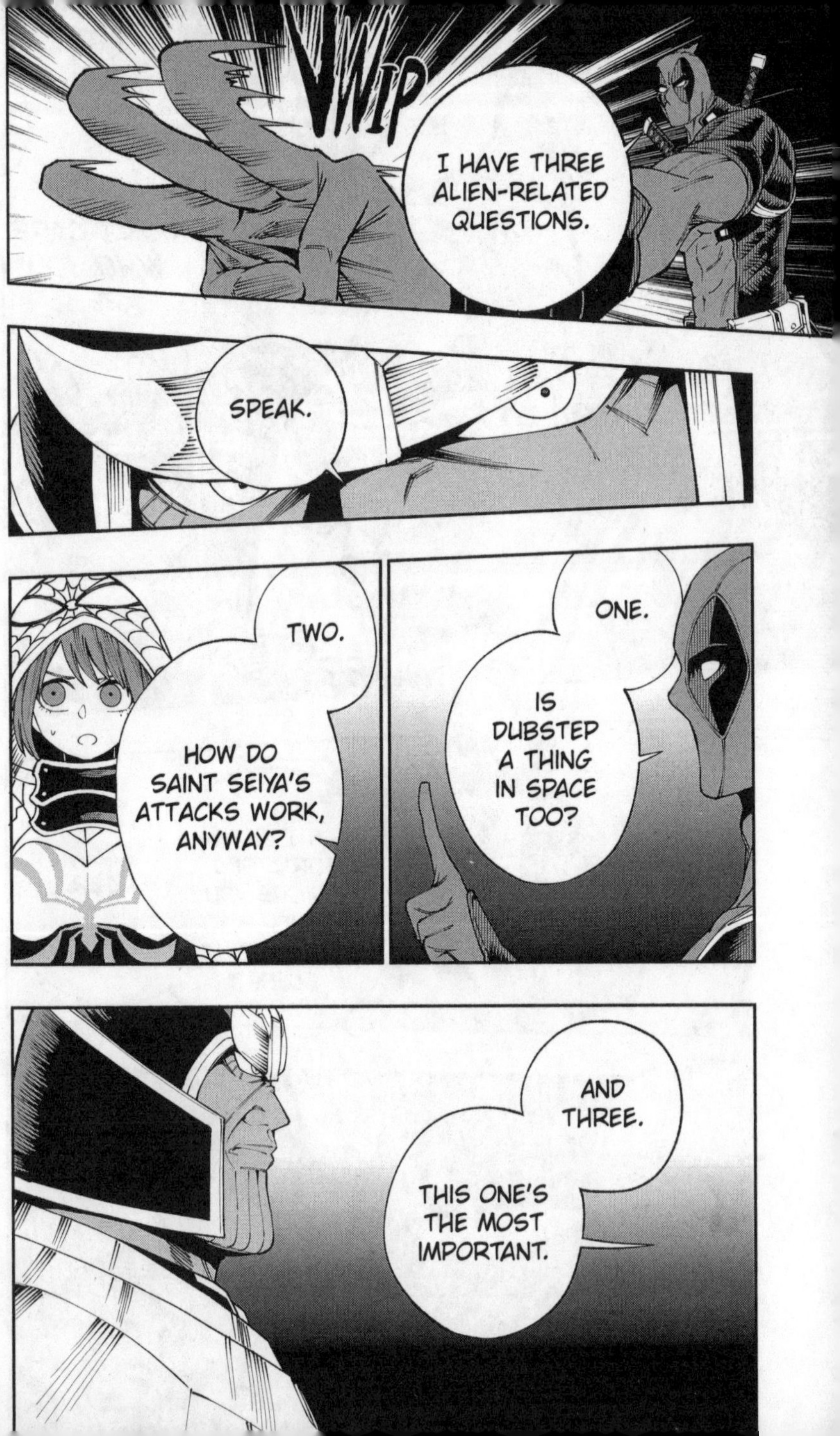
VWIP
I HAVE THREE ALIEN-RELATED QUESTIONS.
SPEAK.
ONE.
IS DUBSTEP A THING IN SPACE TOO?
TWO.
HOW DO SAINT SEIYA'S ATTACKS WORK, ANYWAY?
AND THREE.
THIS ONE'S THE MOST IMPORTANT.

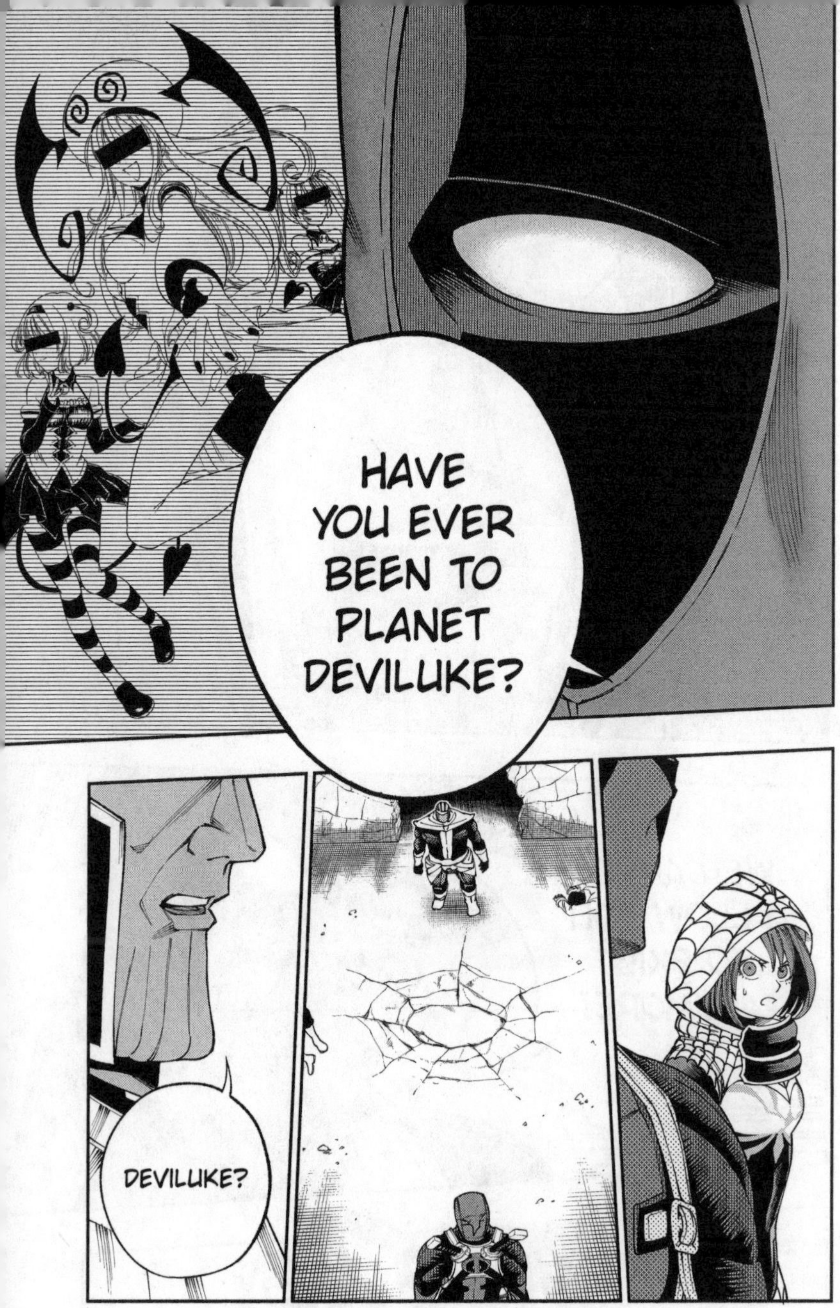
HAVE YOU EVER BEEN TO PLANET DEVILUKE?
DEVILUKE?

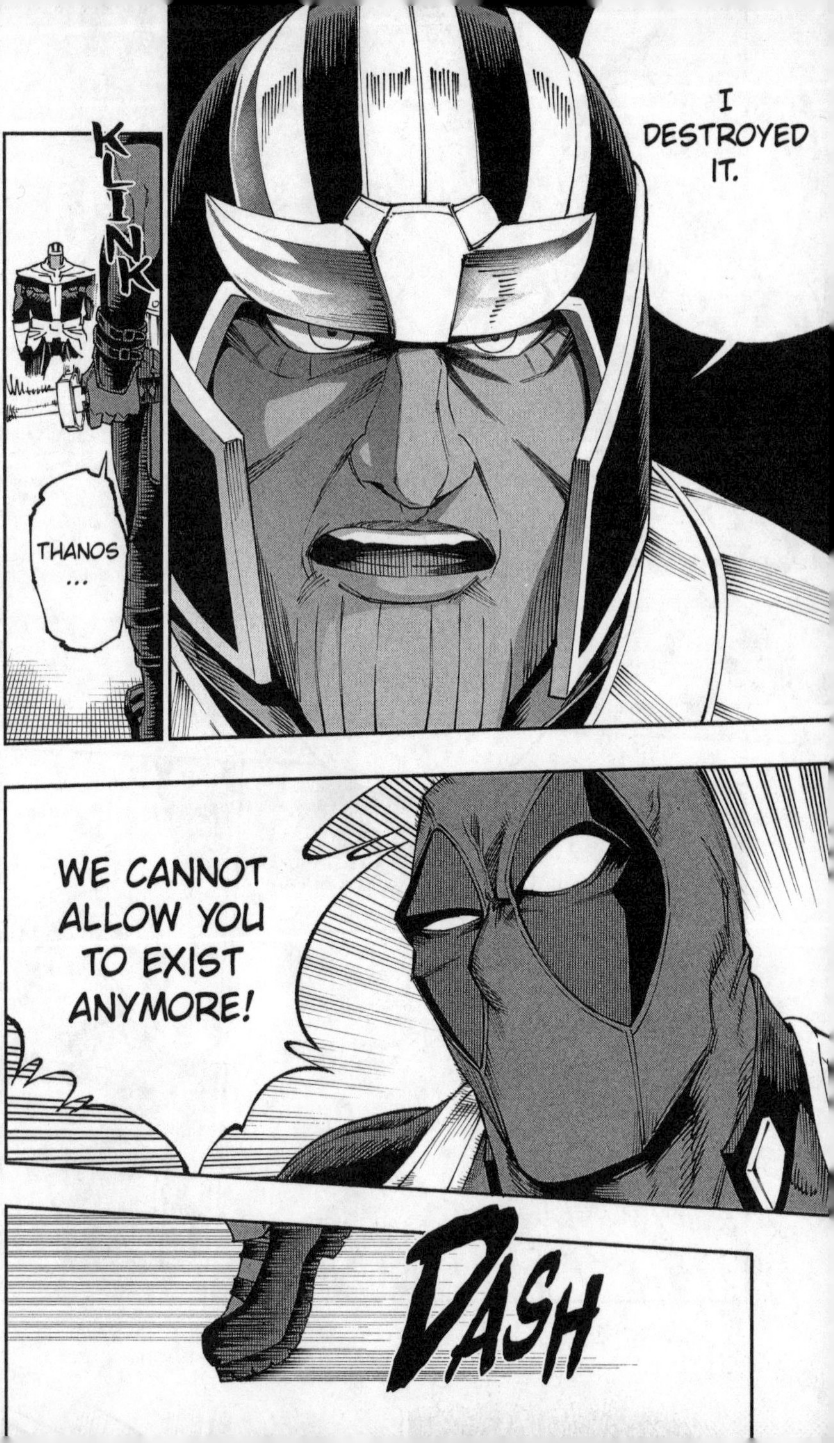
I DESTROYED IT.
KLINK
THANOS ...
WE CANNOT ALLOW YOU TO EXIST ANYMORE!
DASH

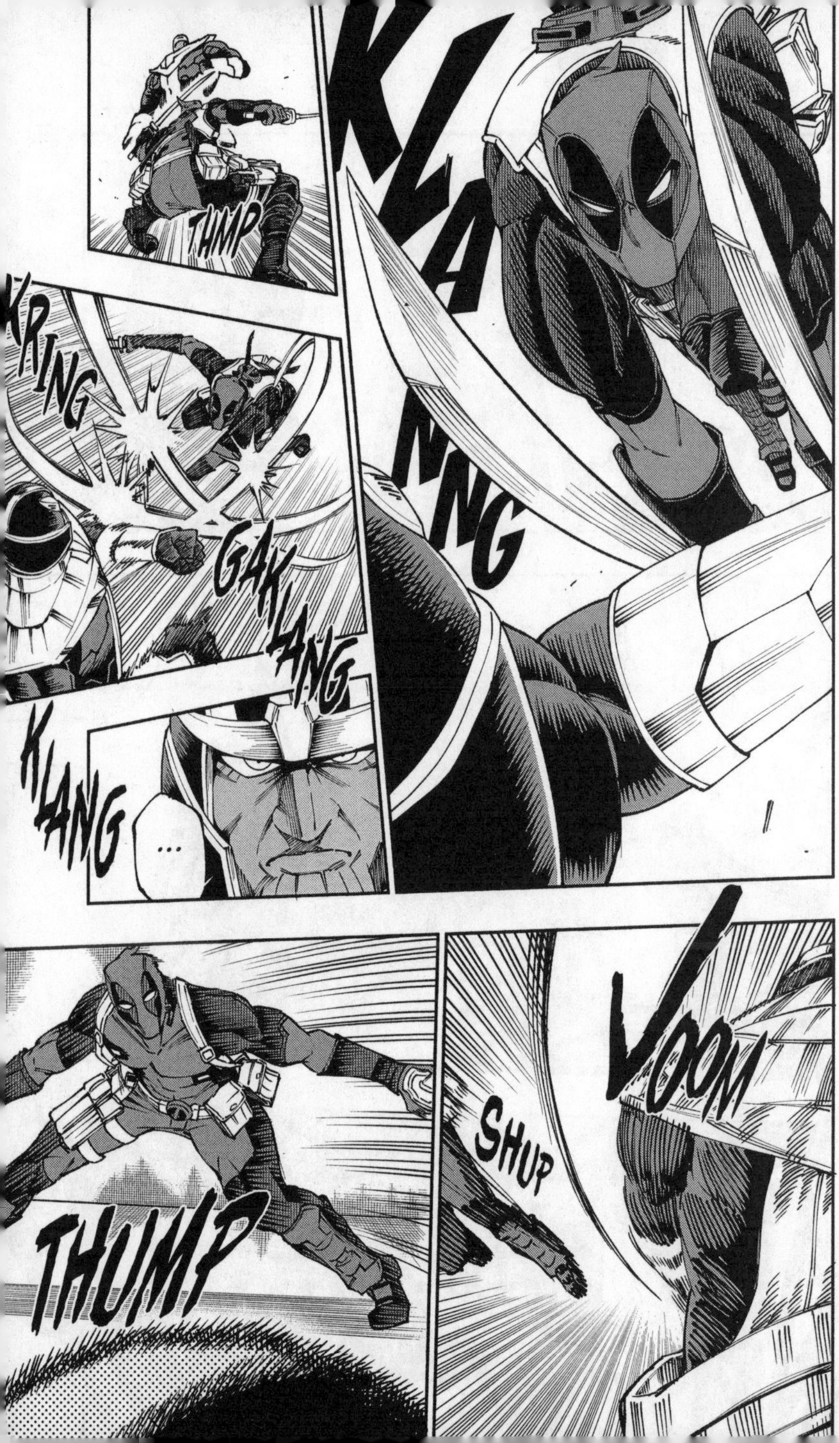
KLANNNG
THMP
KRING
GAKLANG
KLANG
...
VOOM
SHUP
THUMP

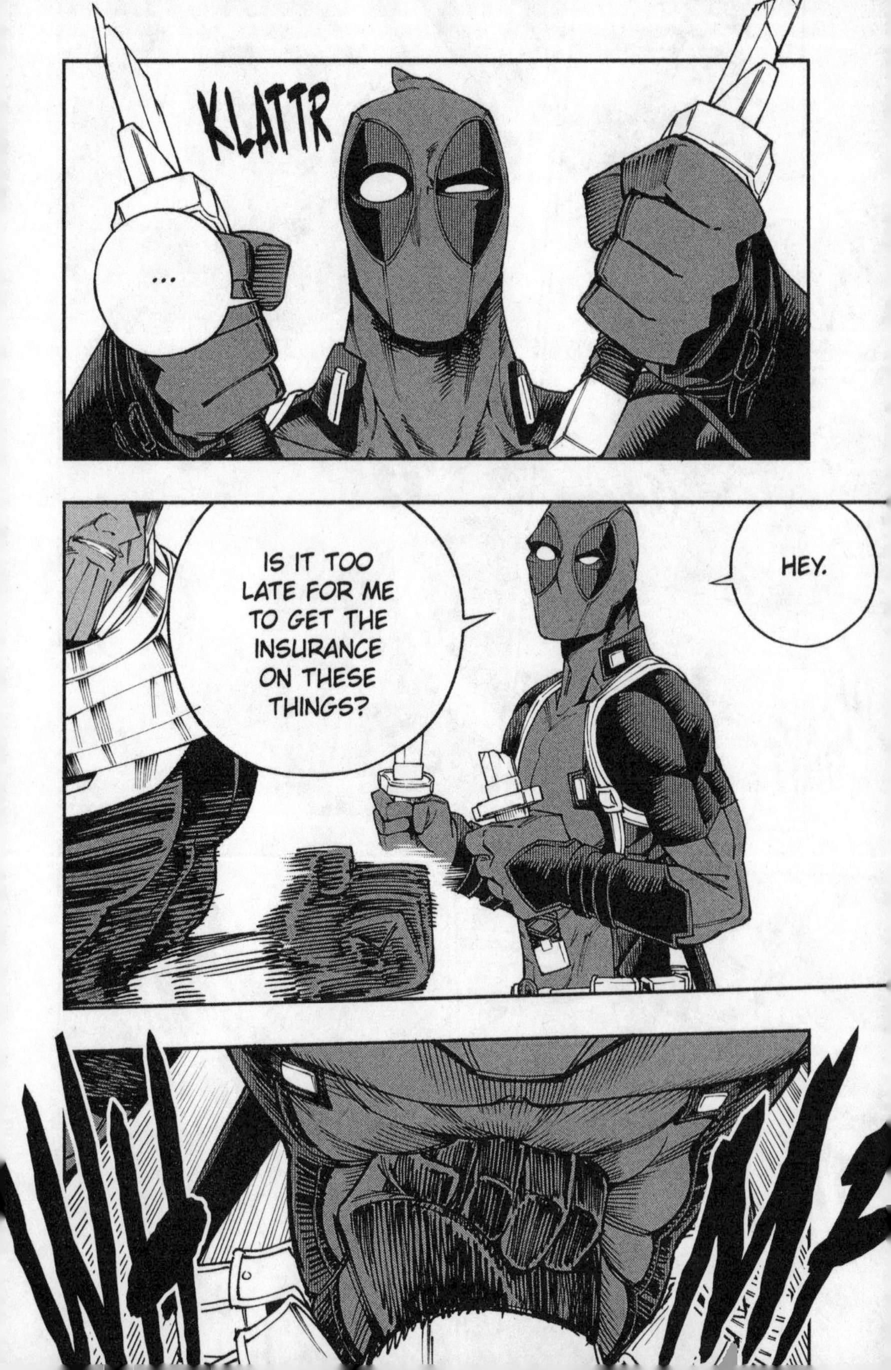
KLATTR
...
HEY.
IS IT TOO LATE FOR ME TO GET THE INSURANCE ON THESE THINGS?

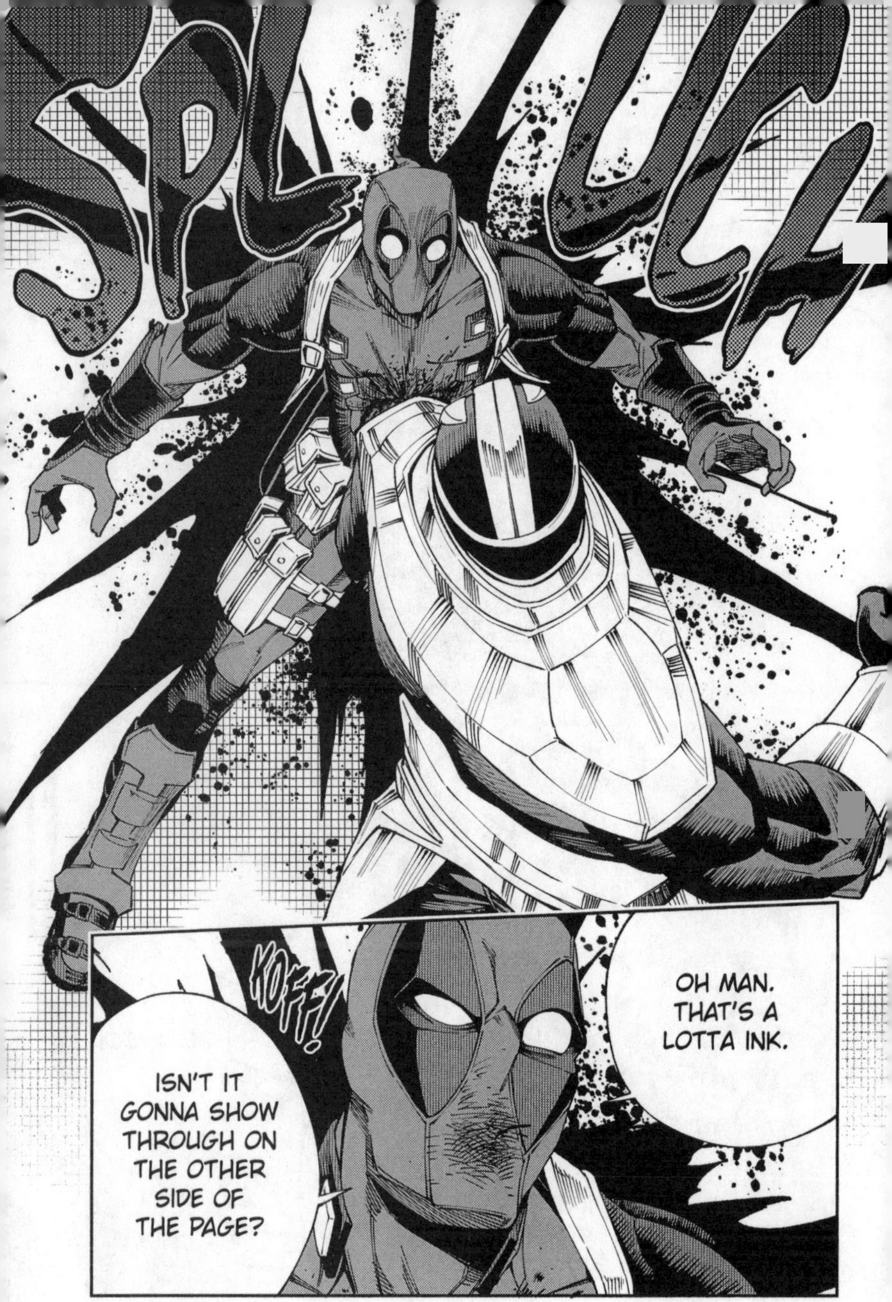
SPLUCH
OH MAN. THAT'S A LOTTA INK.
KOFF!
ISN'T IT GONNA SHOW THROUGH ON THE OTHER SIDE OF THE PAGE?

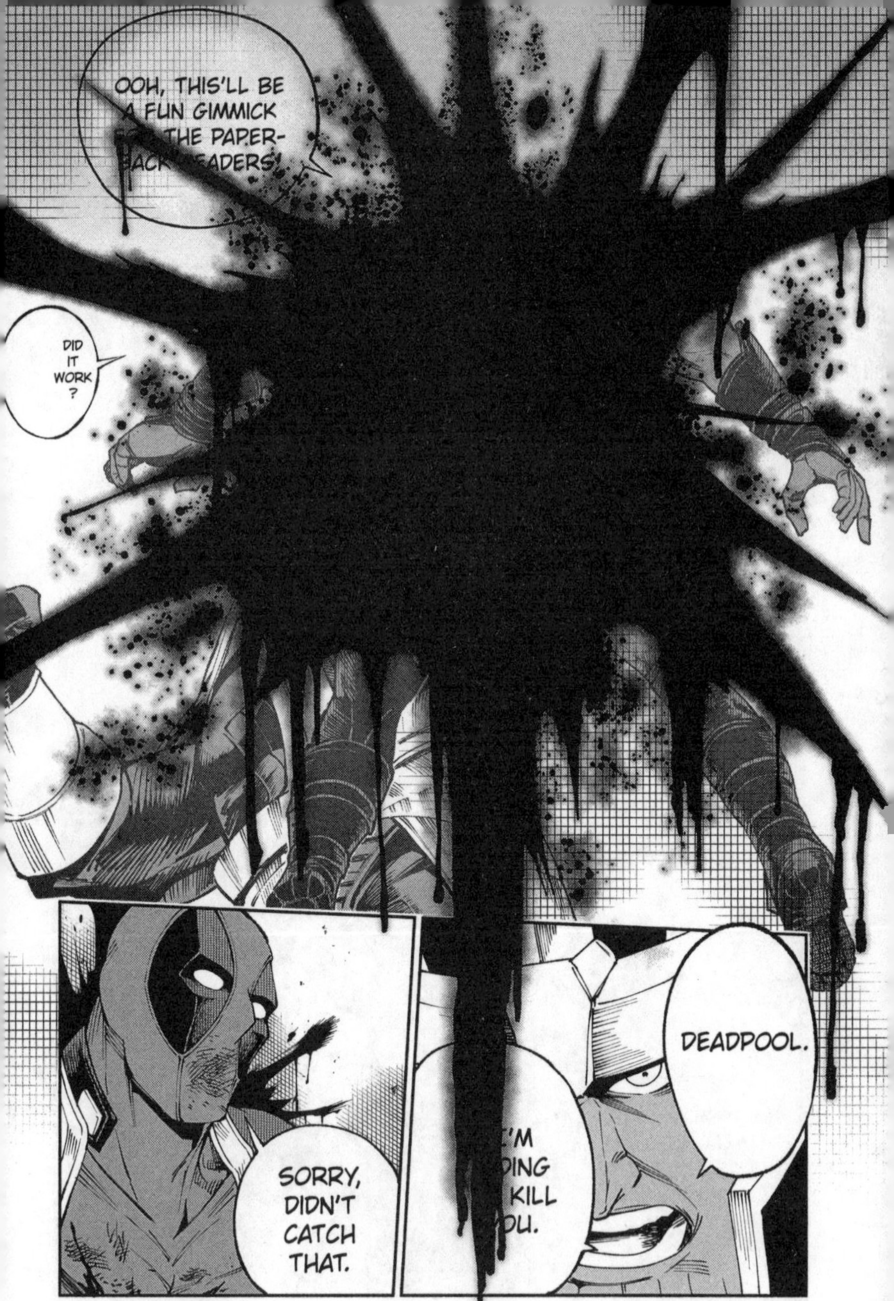
OOH, THIS'LL BE A FUN GIMMICK THE PAPER- ACK EADERS!
DID IT WORK?
DEADPOOL.
'M DING KILL OU.
SORRY, DIDN'T CATCH THAT.

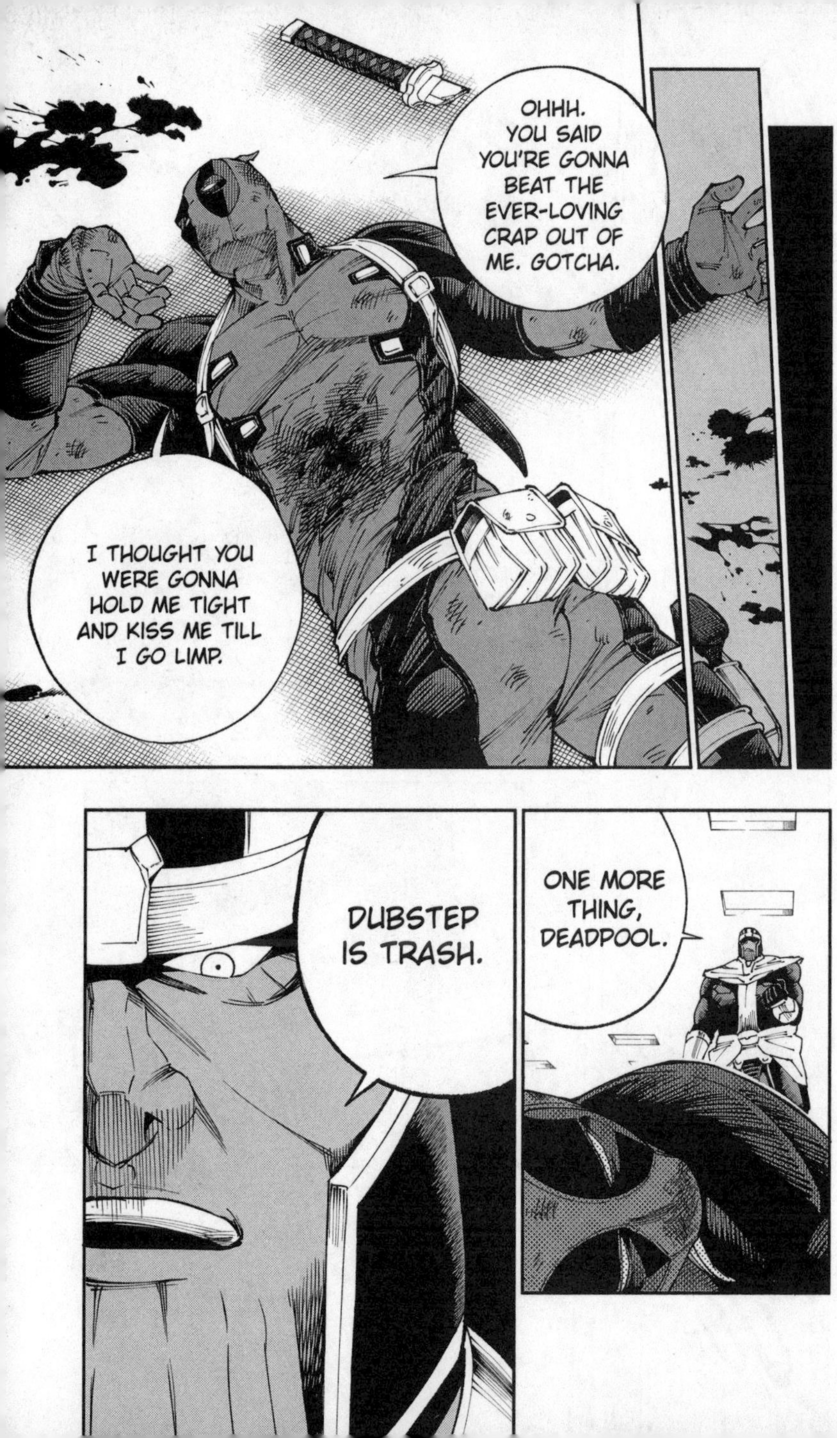
OHHH. YOU SAID YOU'RE GONNA BEAT THE EVER-LOVING CRAP OUT OF ME. GOTCHA.
I THOUGHT YOU WERE GONNA HOLD ME TIGHT AND KISS ME TILL I GO LIMP.
ONE MORE THING, DEADPOOL.
DUBSTEP IS TRASH.

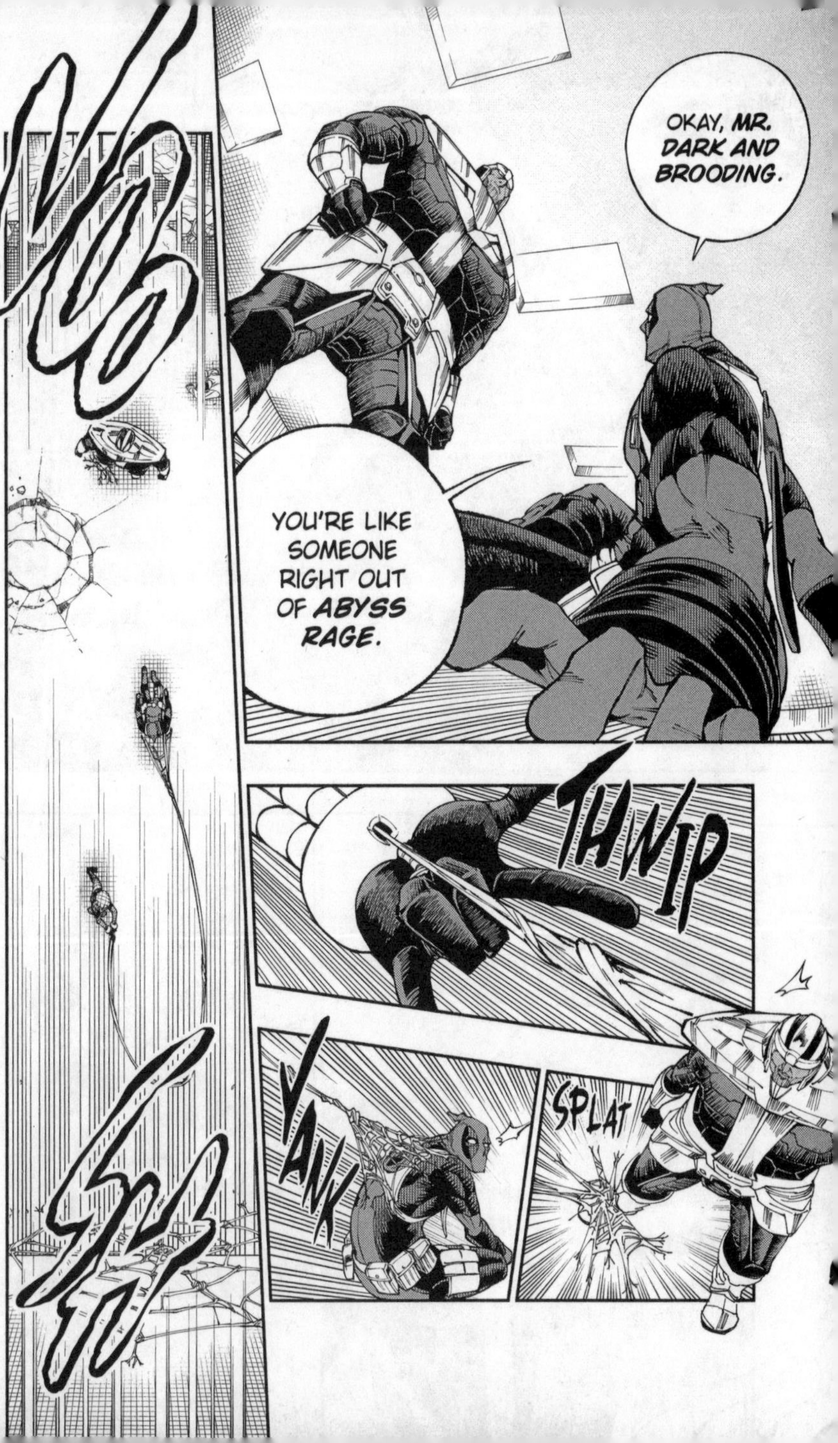
OKAY, MR. DARK AND BROODING.
YOU'RE LIKE SOMEONE RIGHT OUT OF ABYSS RAGE.
THWIP
SPLAT
YANK

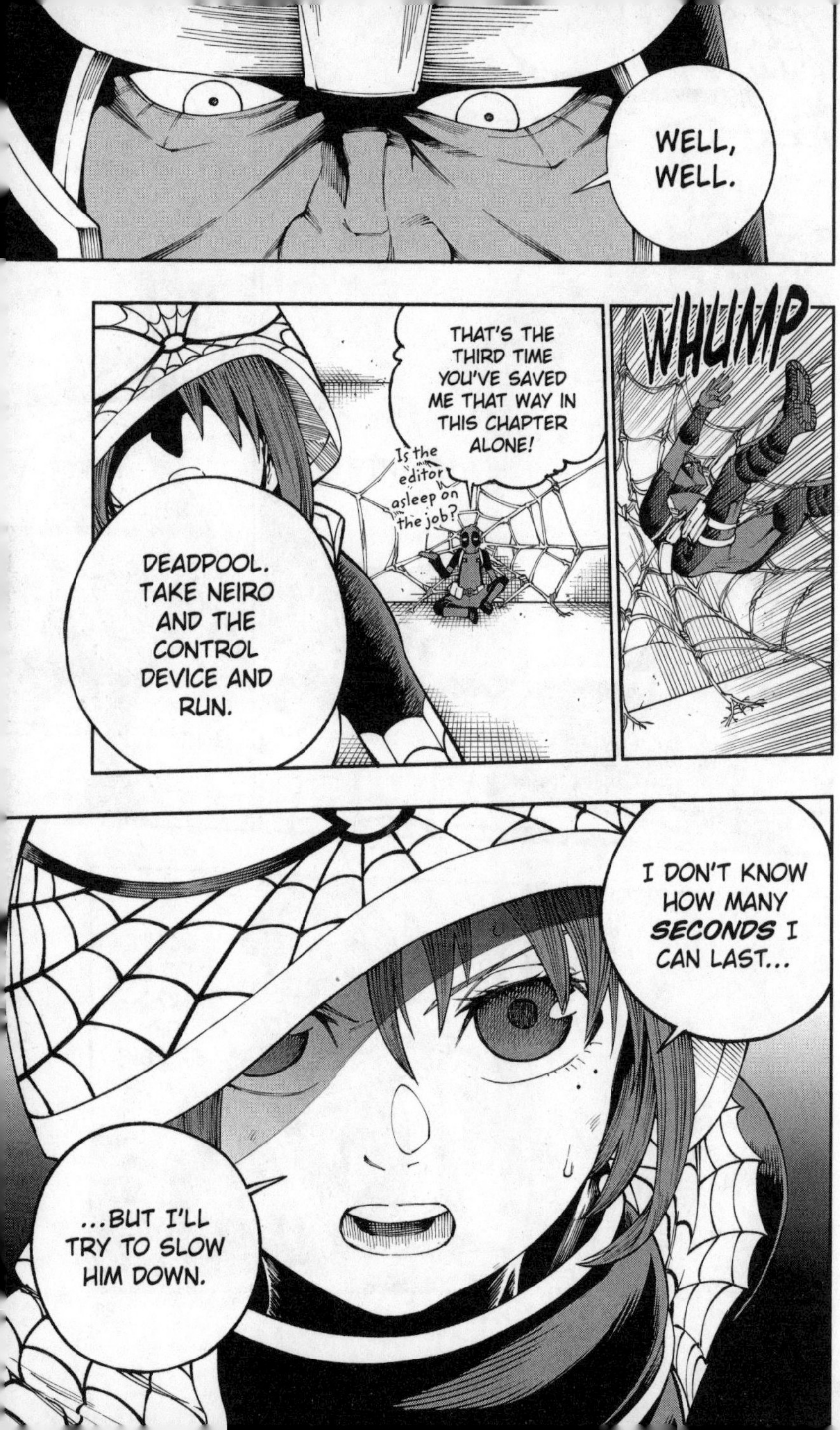
WELL, WELL.
WHUMP
THAT'S THE THIRD TIME YOU'VE SAVED ME THAT WAY IN THIS CHAPTER ALONE!
Is the editor asleep on the job?
DEADPOOL. TAKE NEIRO AND THE CONTROL DEVICE AND RUN.
I DON'T KNOW HOW MANY SECONDS I CAN LAST...
...BUT I'LL TRY TO SLOW HIM DOWN.

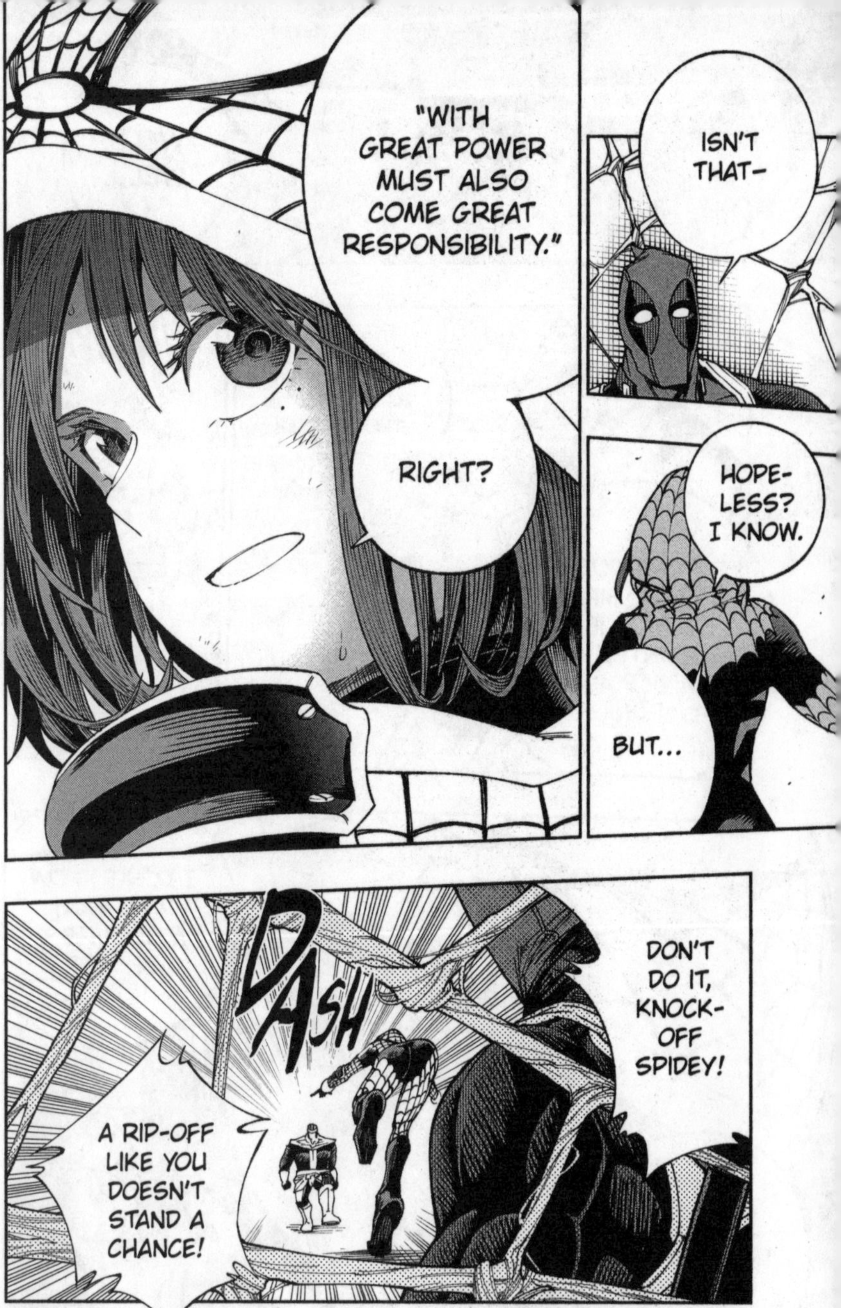
ISN'T THAT-
HOPE-LESS? I KNOW.
BUT...
"WITH GREAT POWER MUST ALSO COME GREAT RESPONSIBILITY."
RIGHT?
DON'T DO IT, KNOCK-OFF SPIDEY!
DASH
A RIP-OFF LIKE YOU DOESN'T STAND A CHANCE!

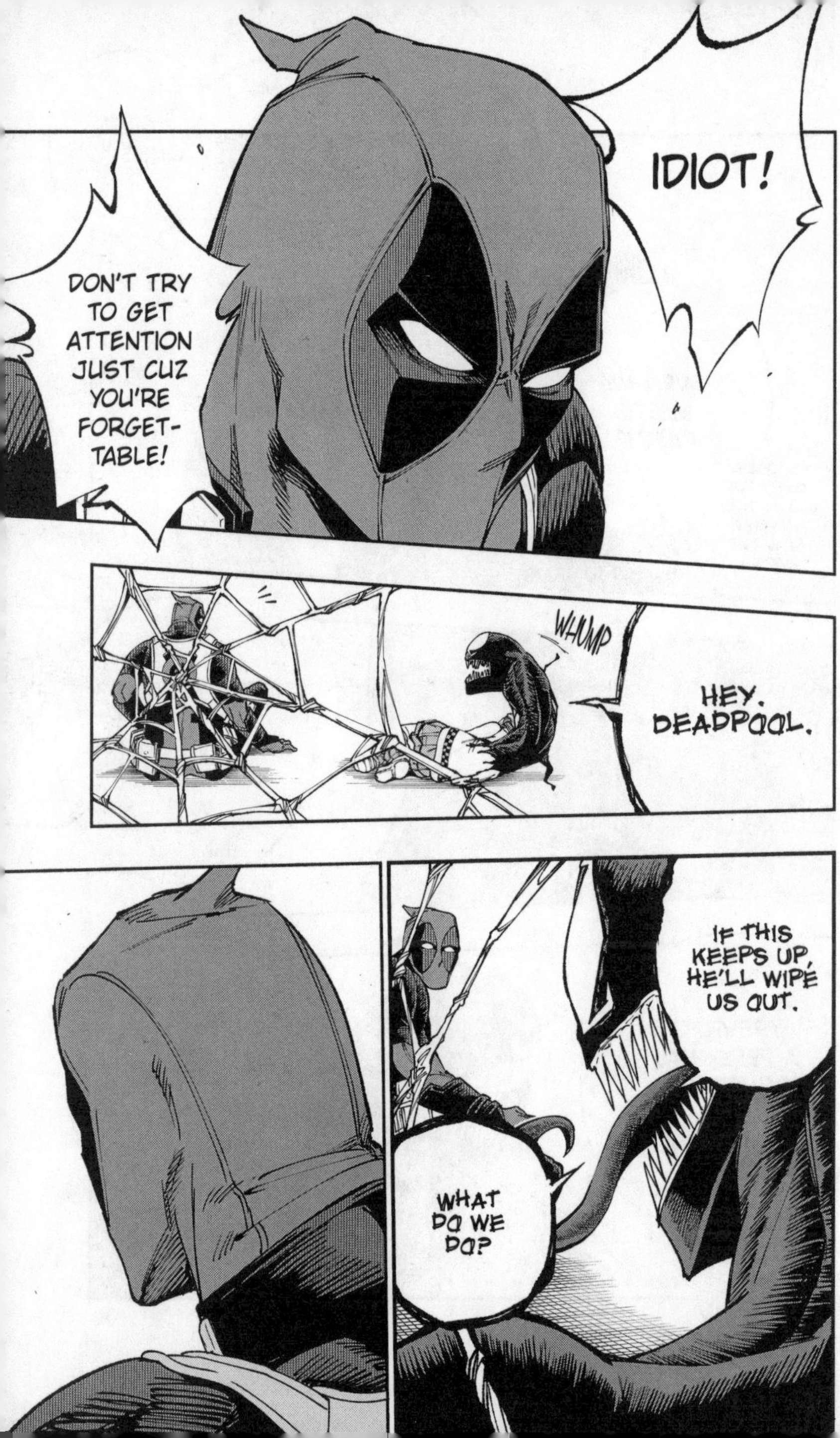
IDIOT!
DON'T TRY TO GET ATTENTION JUST CUZ YOU'RE FORGET-TABLE!
WHUMP
HEY. DEADPOOL.
IF THIS KEEPS UP, HE'LL WIPE US OUT.
WHAT DO WE DO?

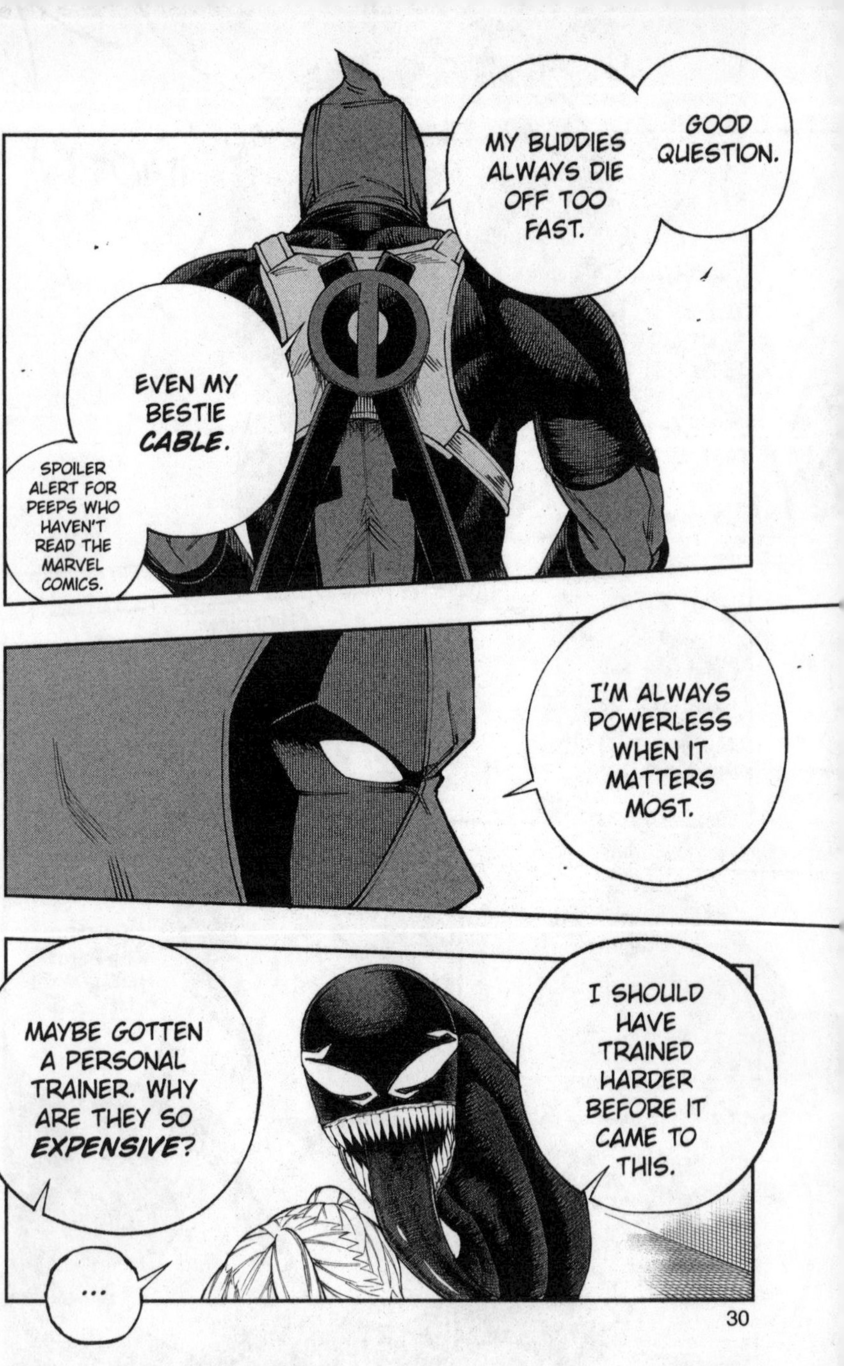
GOOD QUESTION.
MY BUDDIES ALWAYS DIE OFF TOO FAST.
EVEN MY BESTIE *CABLE*.
SPOILER ALERT FOR PEEPS WHO HAVEN'T READ THE MARVEL COMICS.
I'M ALWAYS POWERLESS WHEN IT MATTERS MOST.
I SHOULD HAVE TRAINED HARDER BEFORE IT CAME TO THIS.
MAYBE GOTTEN A PERSONAL TRAINER. WHY ARE THEY SO *EXPENSIVE*?
...

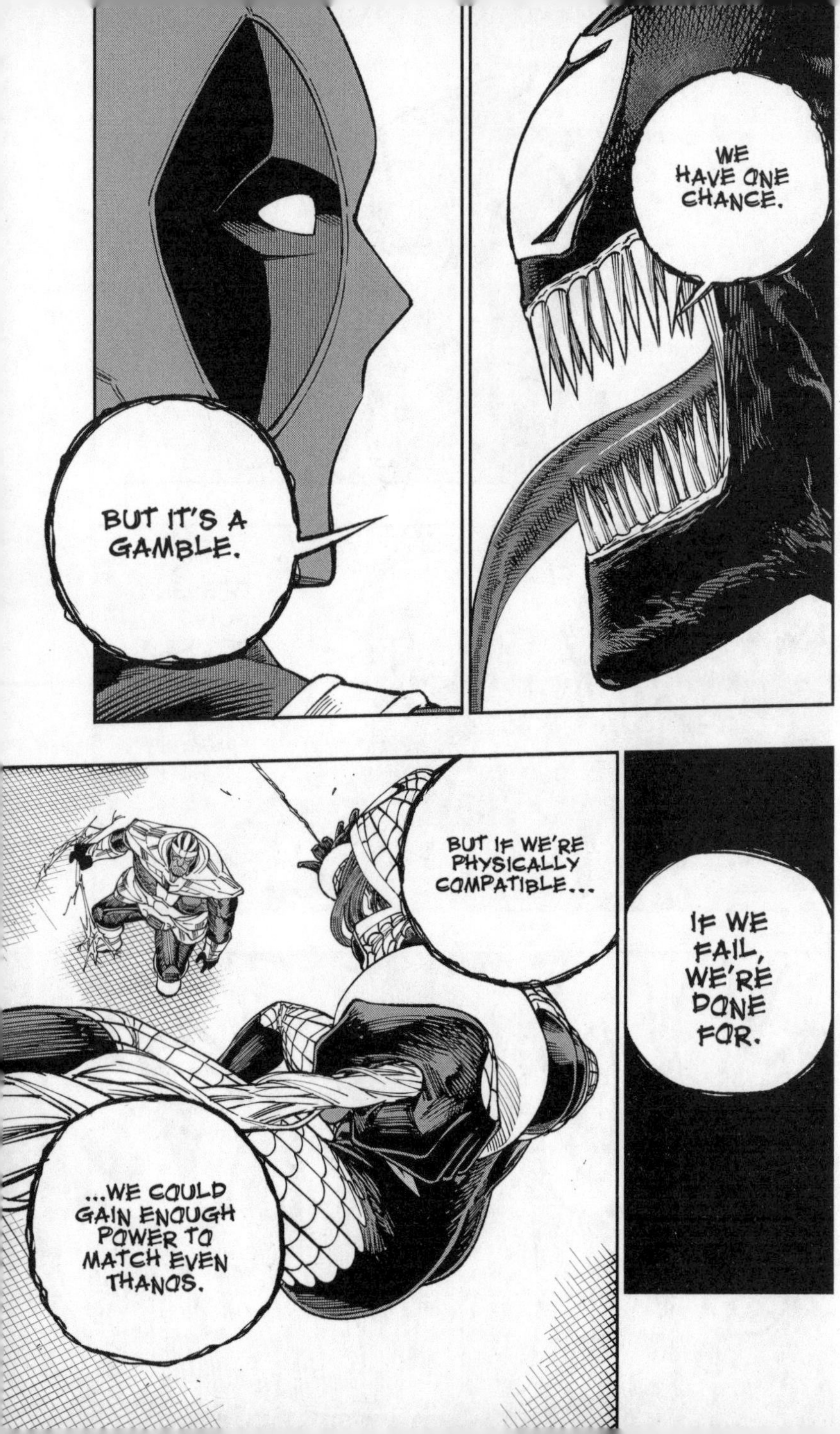
WE HAVE ONE CHANCE.
BUT IT'S A GAMBLE.
IF WE FAIL, WE'RE DONE FOR.
BUT IF WE'RE PHYSICALLY COMPATIBLE...
...WE COULD GAIN ENOUGH POWER TO MATCH EVEN THANOS.

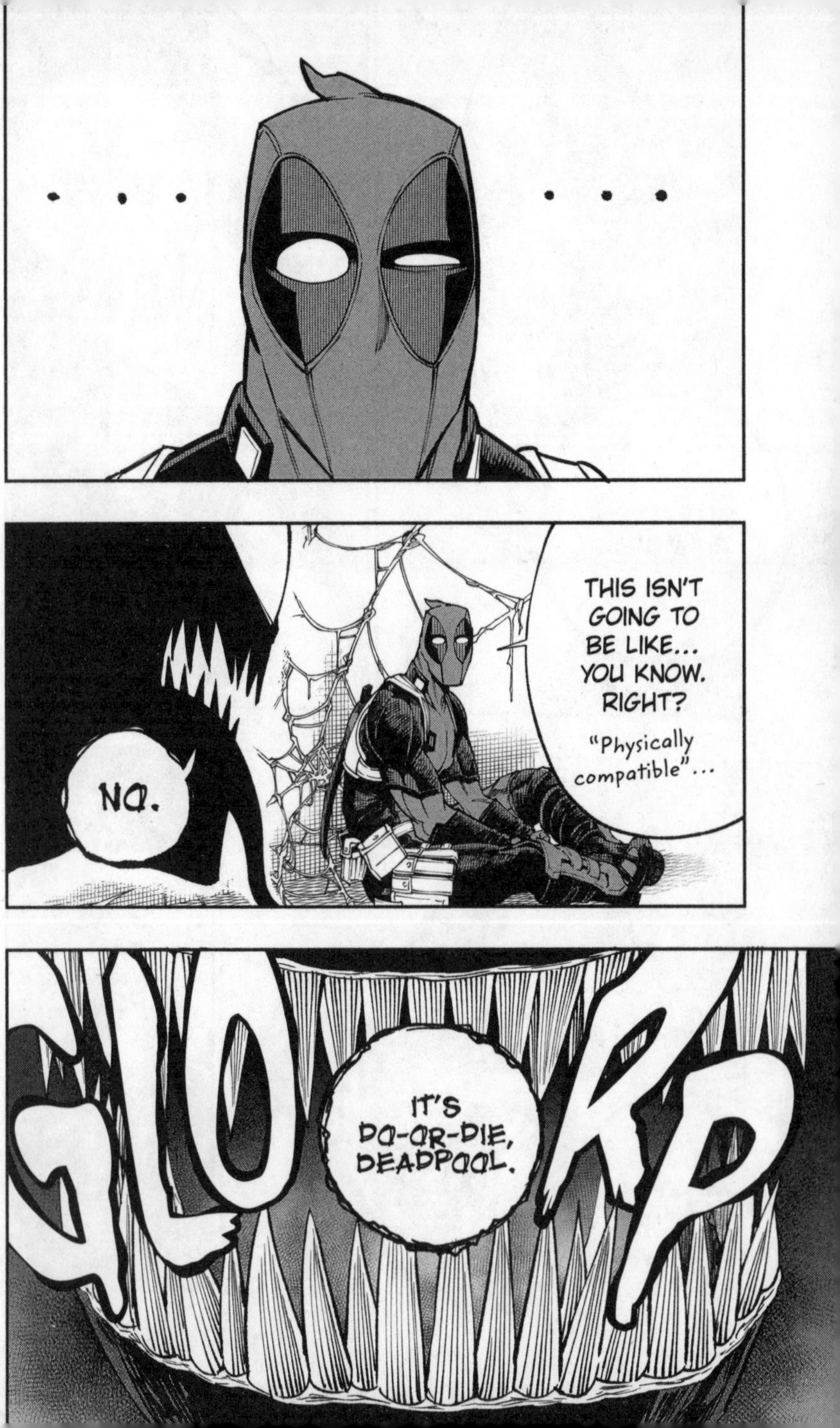
. . .
. . .
THIS ISN'T GOING TO BE LIKE... YOU KNOW. RIGHT?
"Physically compatible"...
NO.
IT'S DO-OR-DIE, DEADPOOL.

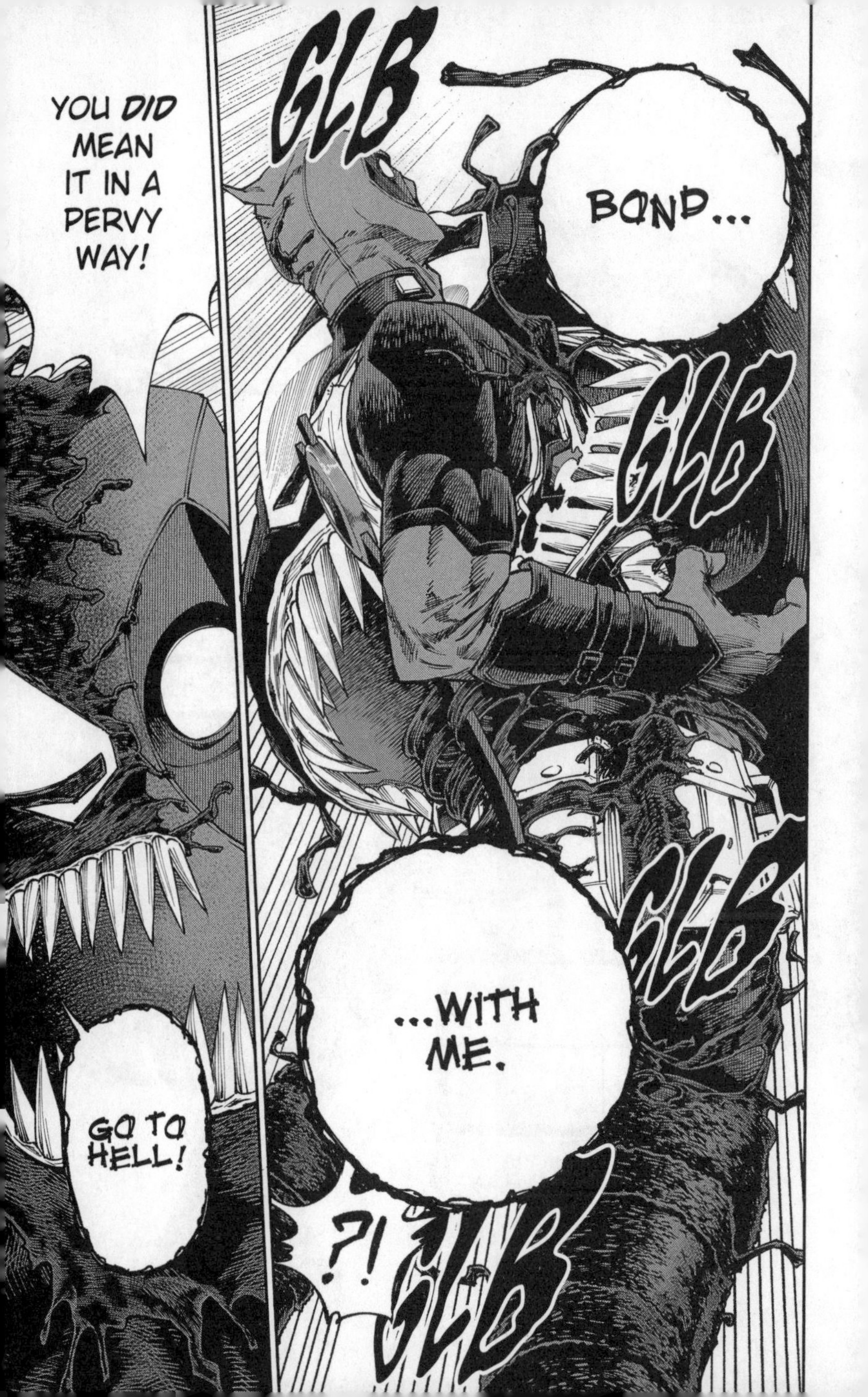
GLB
BOND...
GLB
GLB
...WITH ME.
?!
GLB
YOU DID MEAN IT IN A PERVY WAY!
GO TO HELL!

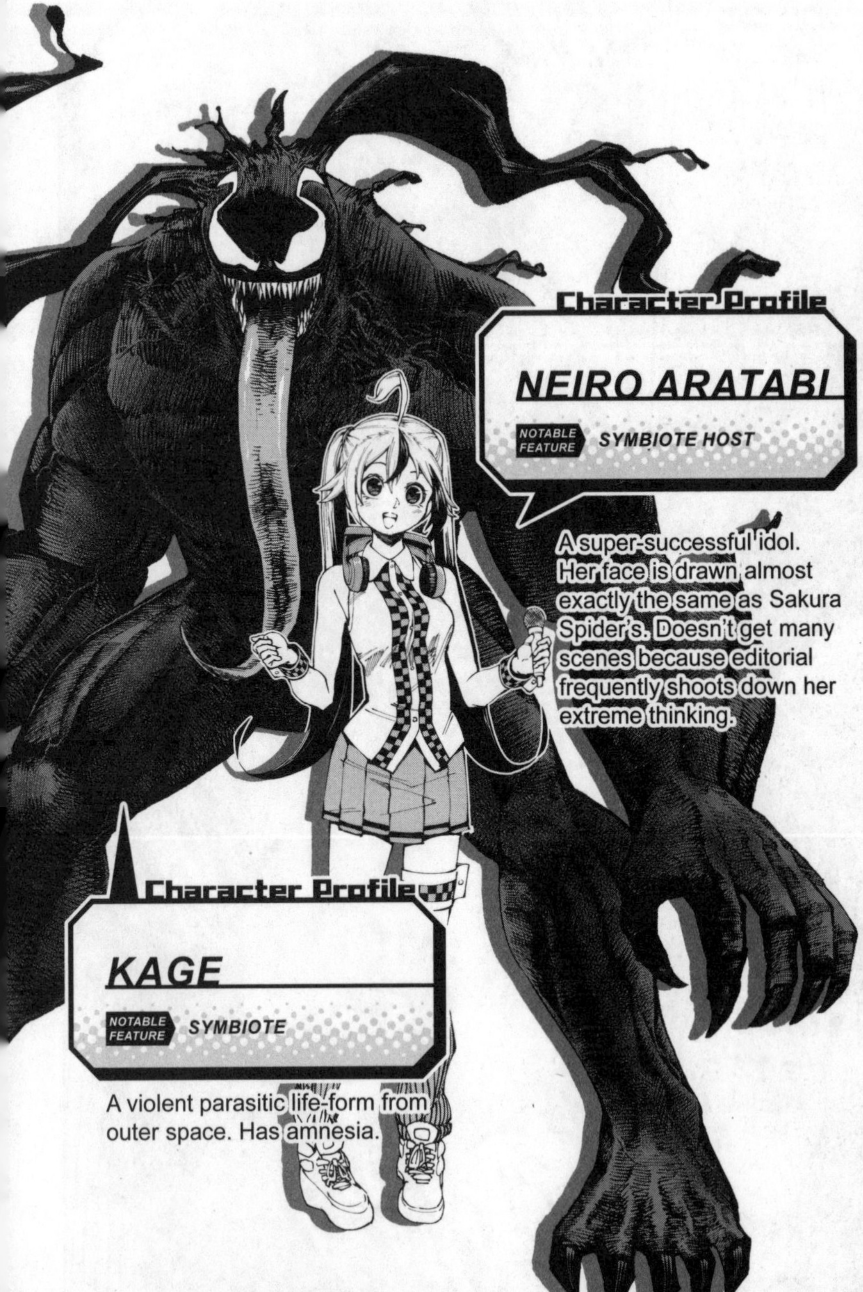
Character Profile
NEIRO ARATABI
NOTABLE FEATURE
SYMBIOTE HOST
A super-successful idol. Her face is drawn almost exactly the same as Sakura Spider's. Doesn't get many scenes because editorial frequently shoots down her extreme thinking.
Character Profile
KAGE
NOTABLE FEATURE
SYMBIOTE
A violent parasitic life-form from outer space. Has amnesia.

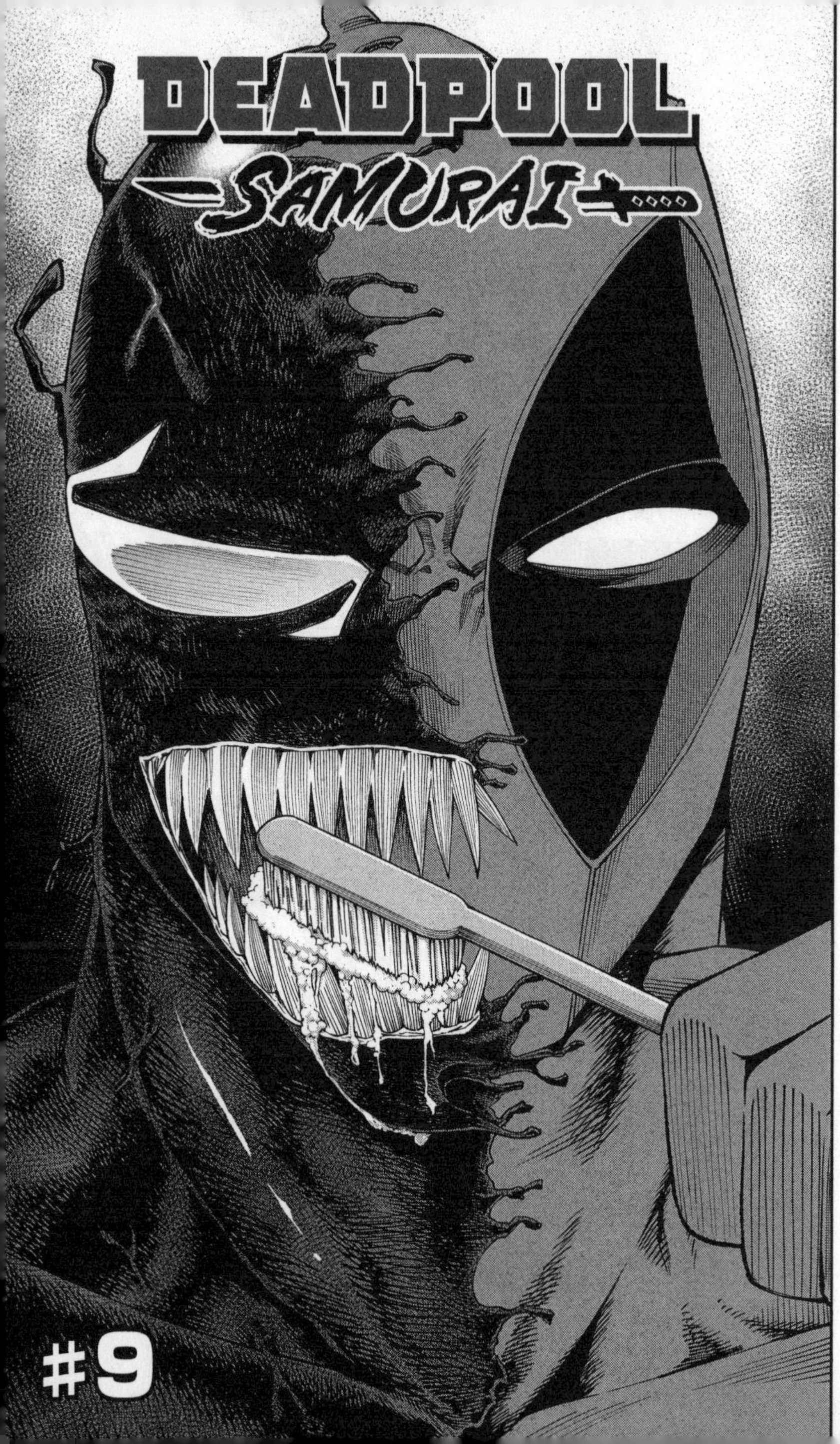
DEADPOOL
SAMURAI
#9

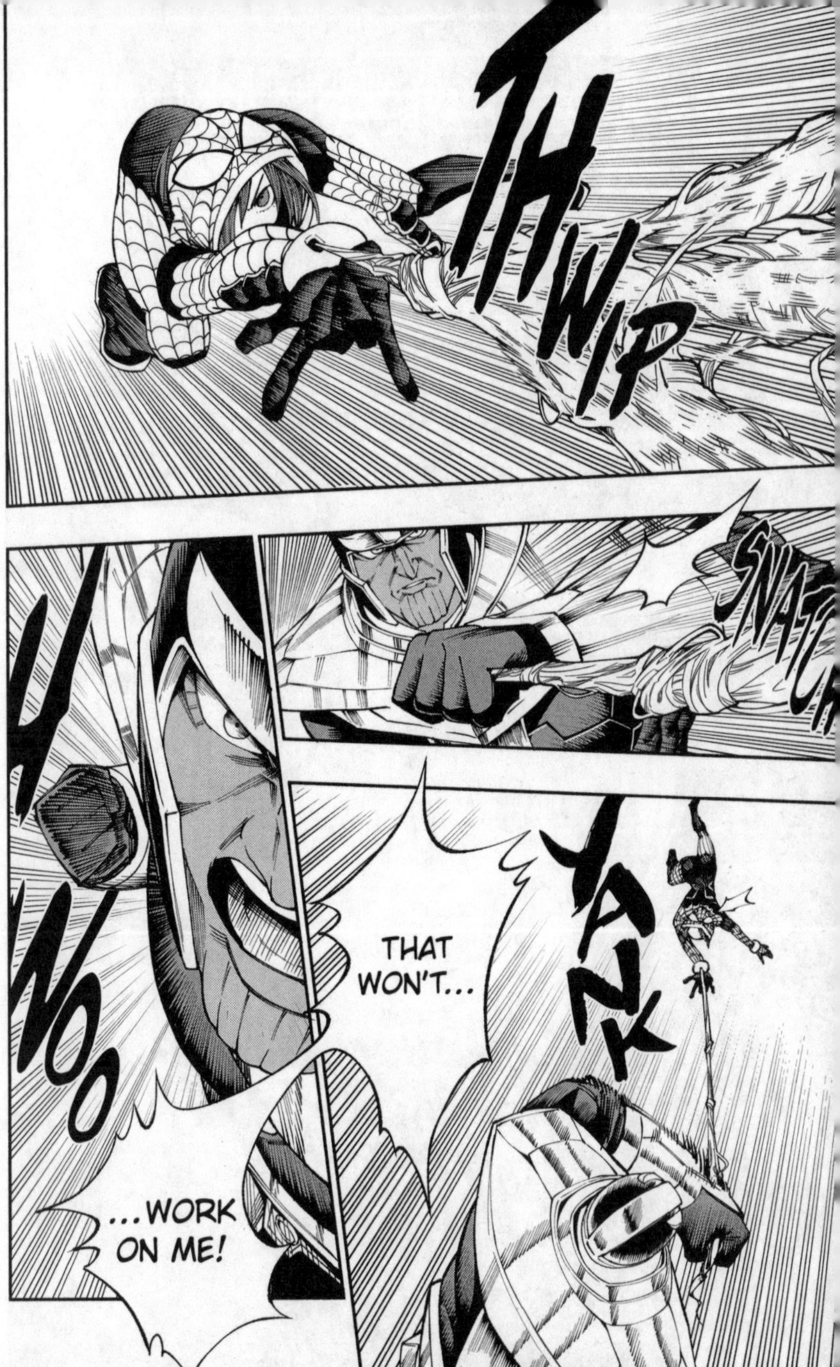
THWIP
SNATCH
YANK
THAT WON'T...
...WORK ON ME!

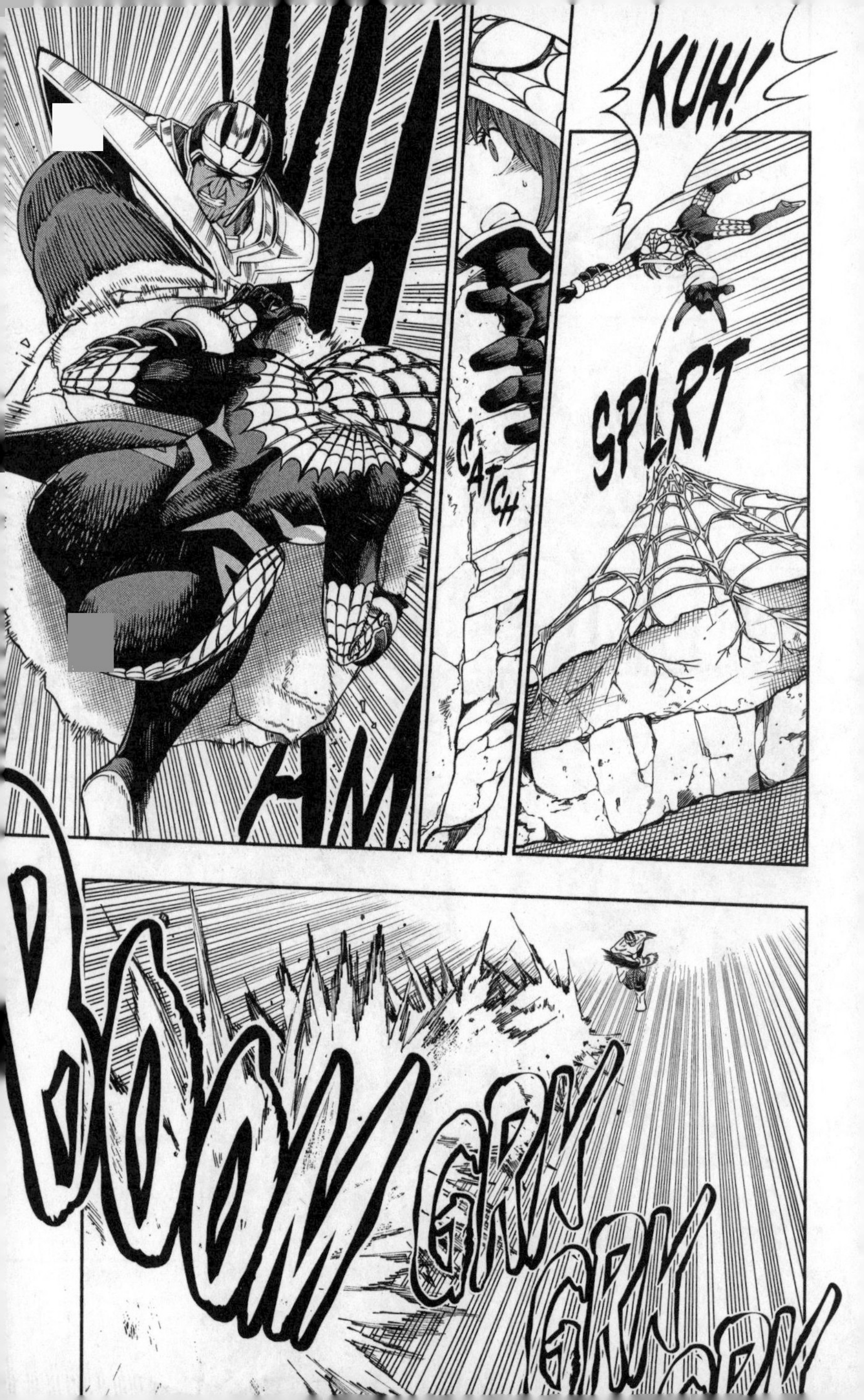
KUH!
SPLRT
CATCH
BOOM

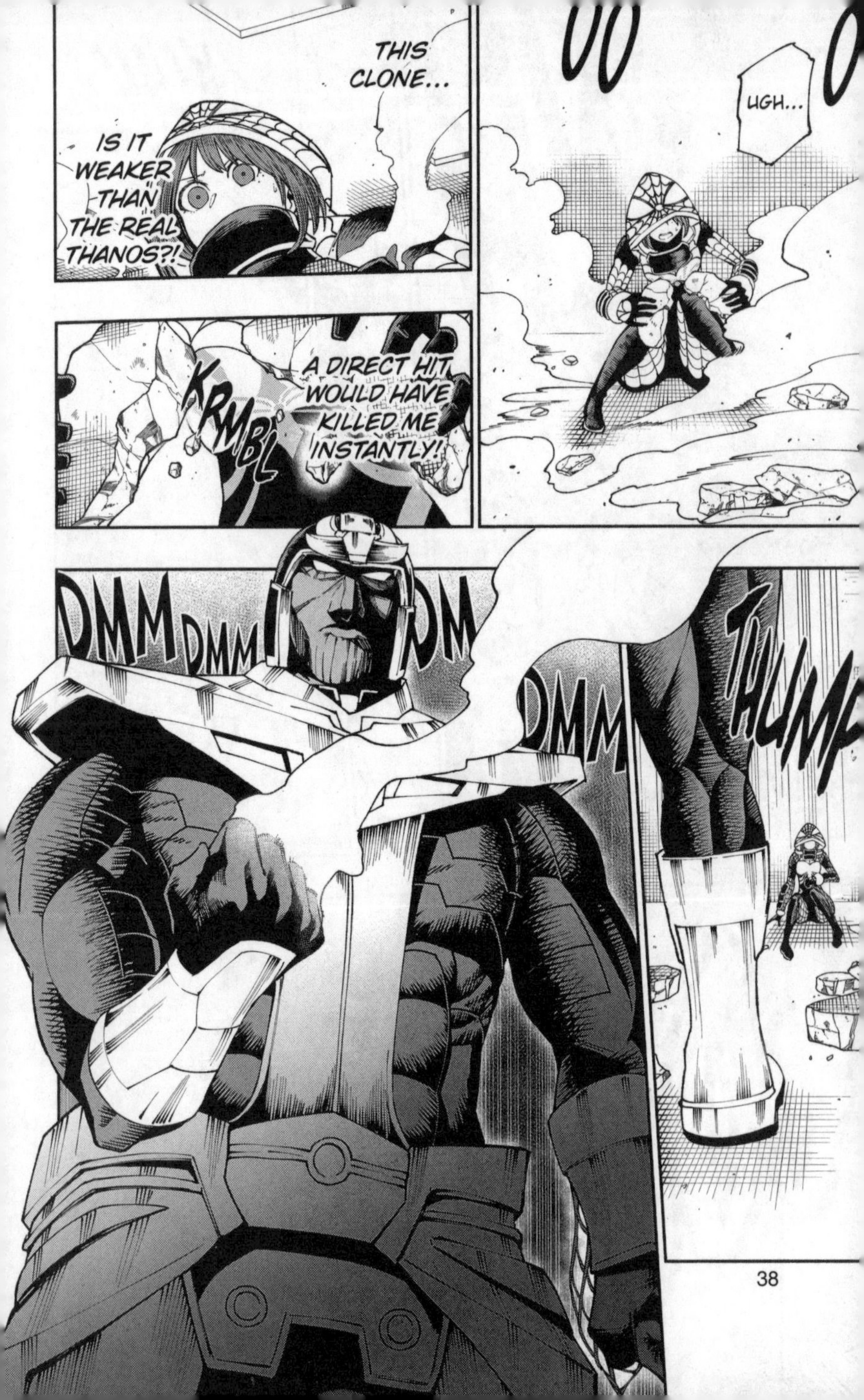
UU
O
UGH...
THIS CLONE...
IS IT WEAKER THAN THE REAL THANOS?!
A DIRECT HIT WOULD HAVE KILLED ME INSTANTLY!
KRMBL
THUM
DMM
DM
DMM DMM

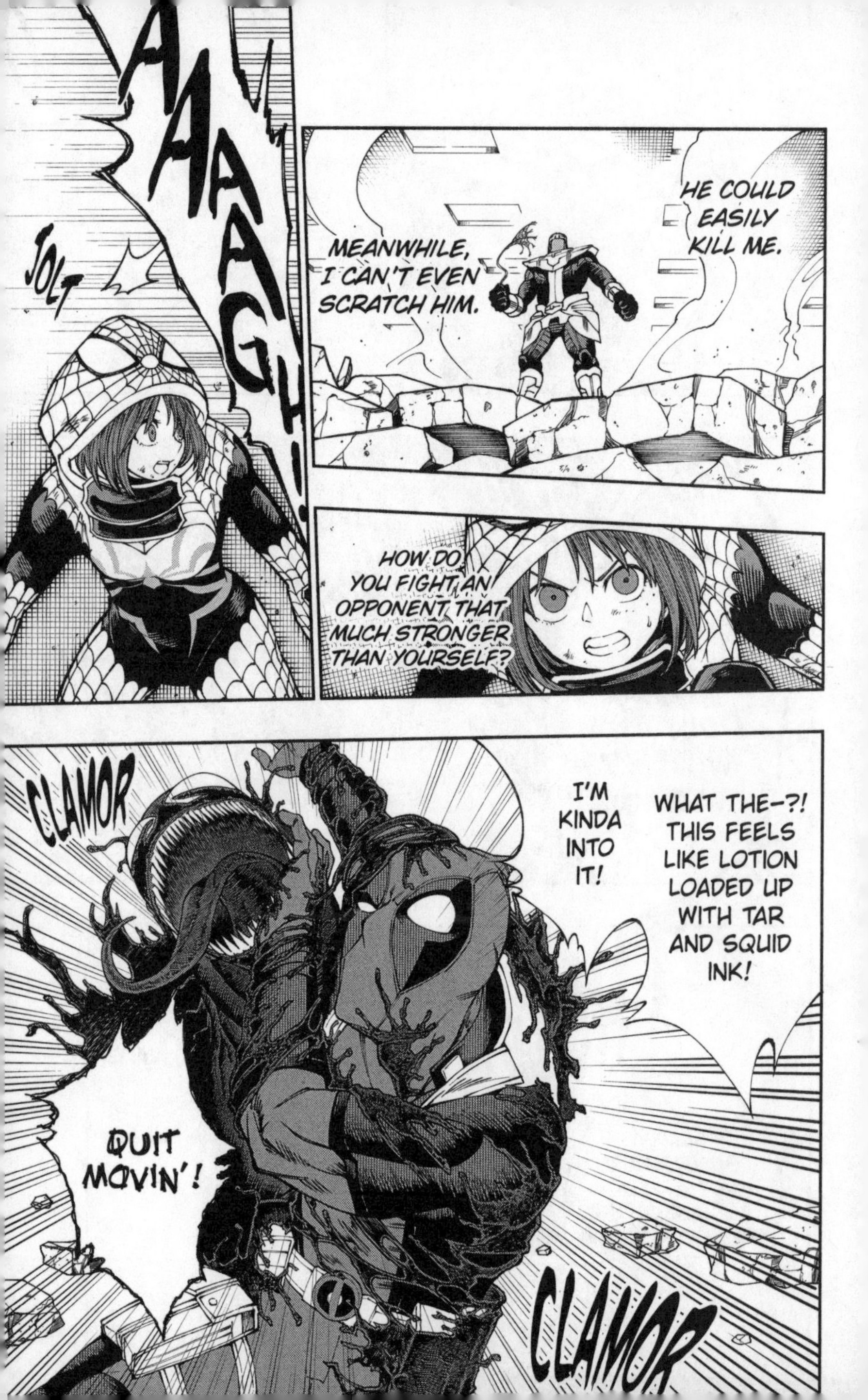
HE COULD EASILY KILL ME.
MEANWHILE, I CAN'T EVEN SCRATCH HIM.
HOW DO YOU FIGHT AN OPPONENT THAT MUCH STRONGER THAN YOURSELF?
AAAAGH!
JOLT
WHAT THE-?! THIS FEELS LIKE LOTION LOADED UP WITH TAR AND SQUID INK!
I'M KINDA INTO IT!
CLAMOR
QUIT MOVIN'!
CLAMOR

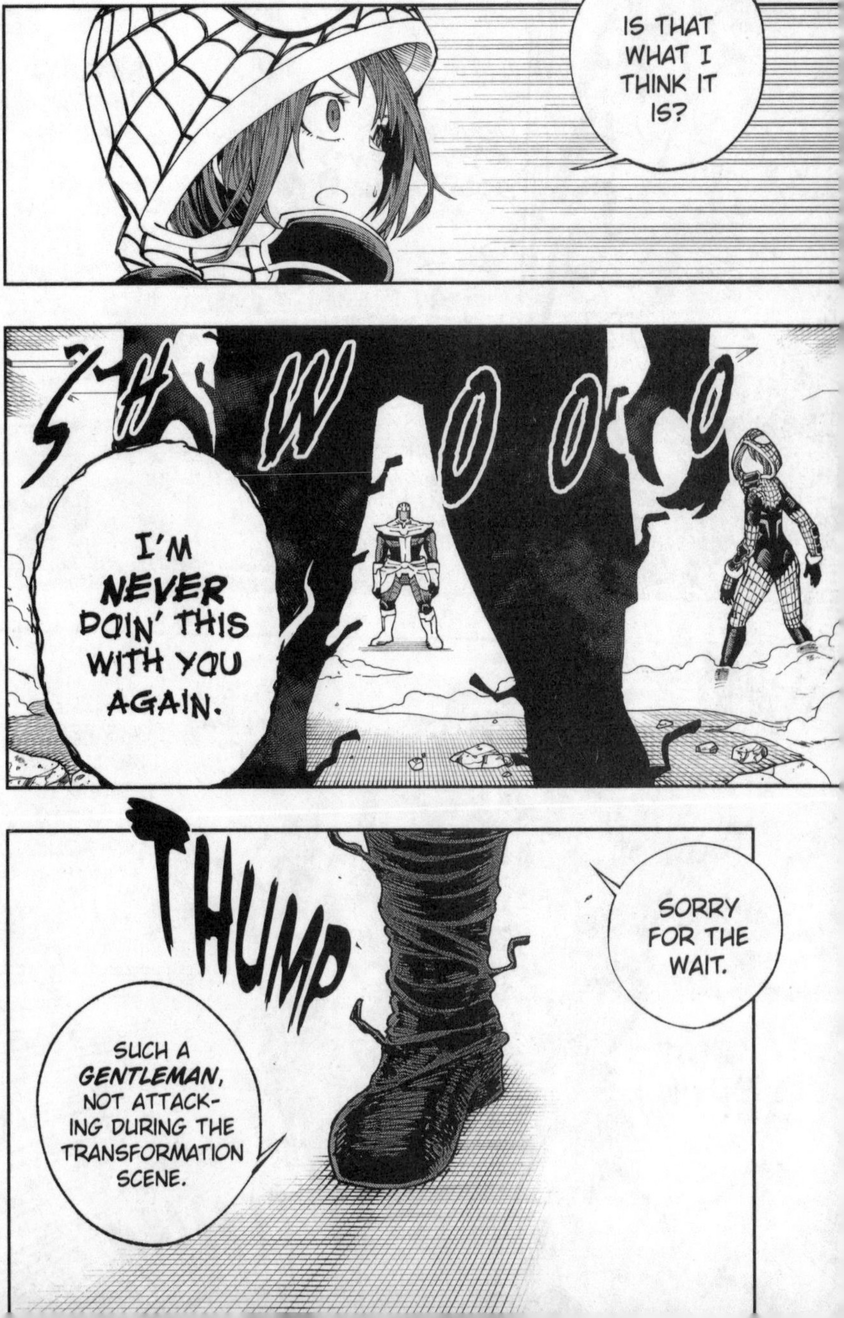
IS THAT WHAT I THINK IT IS?
SHWOOOO
I'M NEVER DOIN' THIS WITH YOU AGAIN.
THUMP
SORRY FOR THE WAIT.
SUCH A GENTLEMAN, NOT ATTACK-ING DURING THE TRANSFORMATION SCENE.

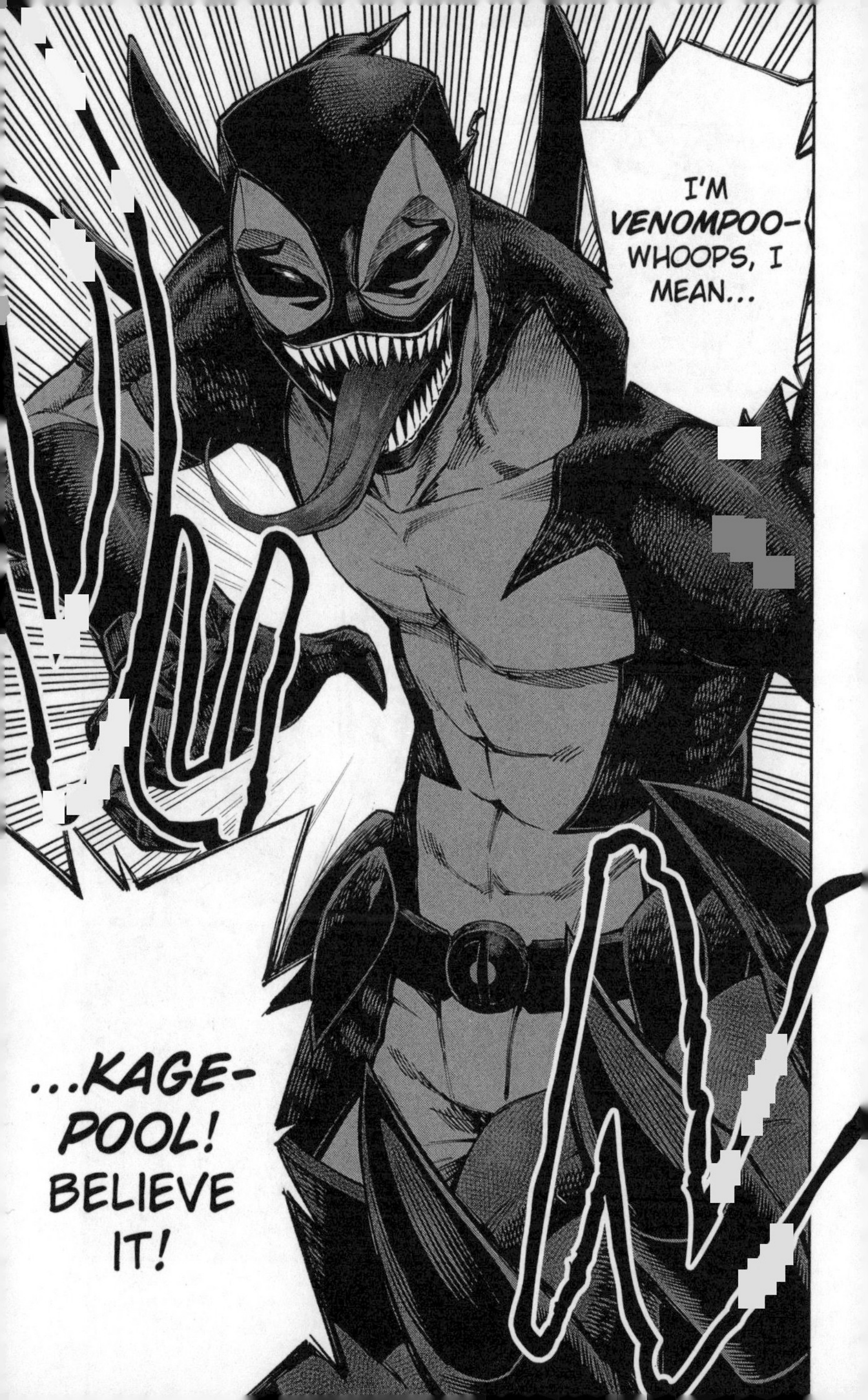
I'M *VENOMPOO-* WHOOPS, I MEAN...
...KAGE-POOL! BELIEVE IT!

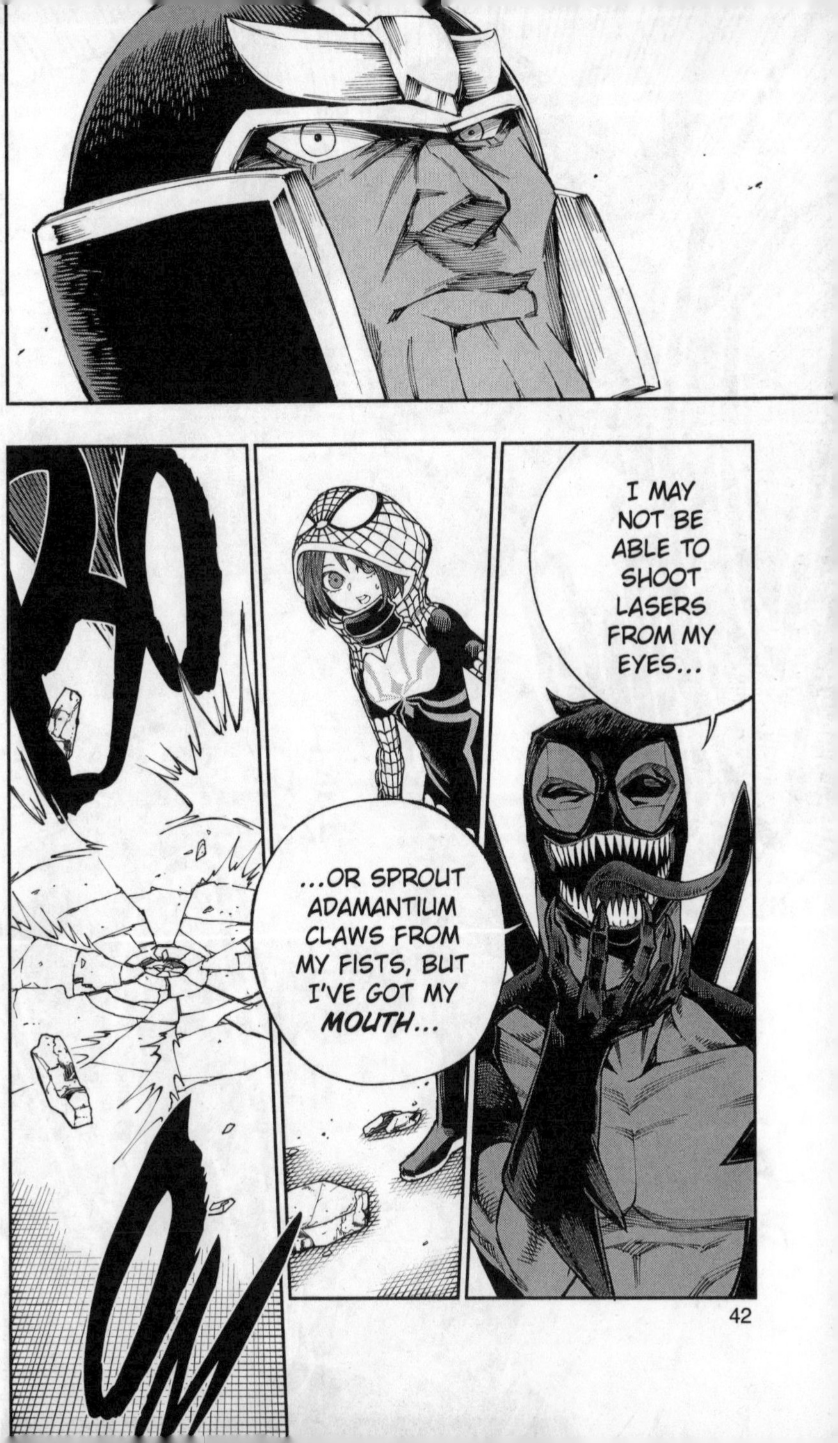
I MAY NOT BE ABLE TO SHOOT LASERS FROM MY EYES...
...OR SPROUT ADAMANTIUM CLAWS FROM MY FISTS, BUT I'VE GOT MY *MOUTH*...

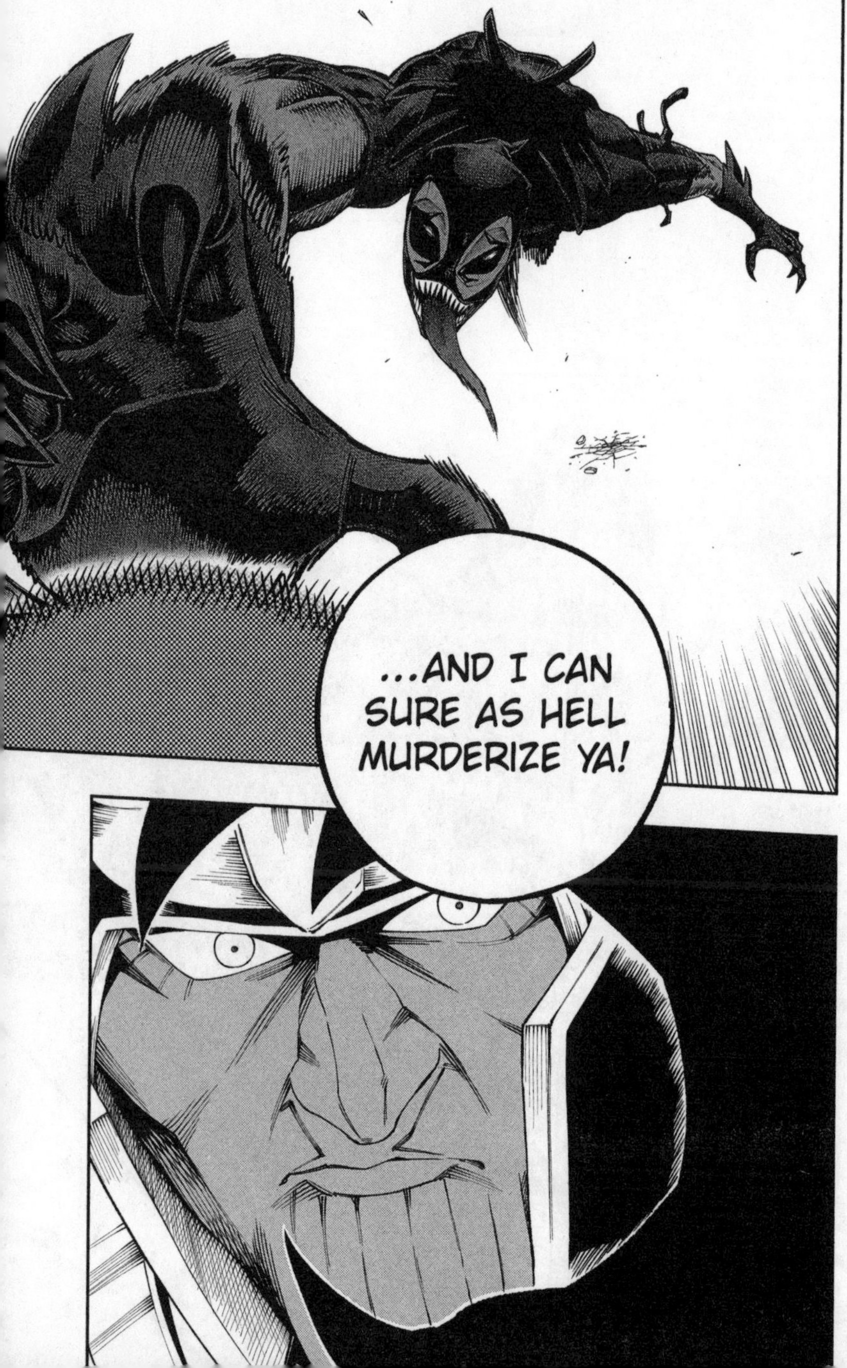
...AND I CAN SURE AS HELL MURDERIZE YA!

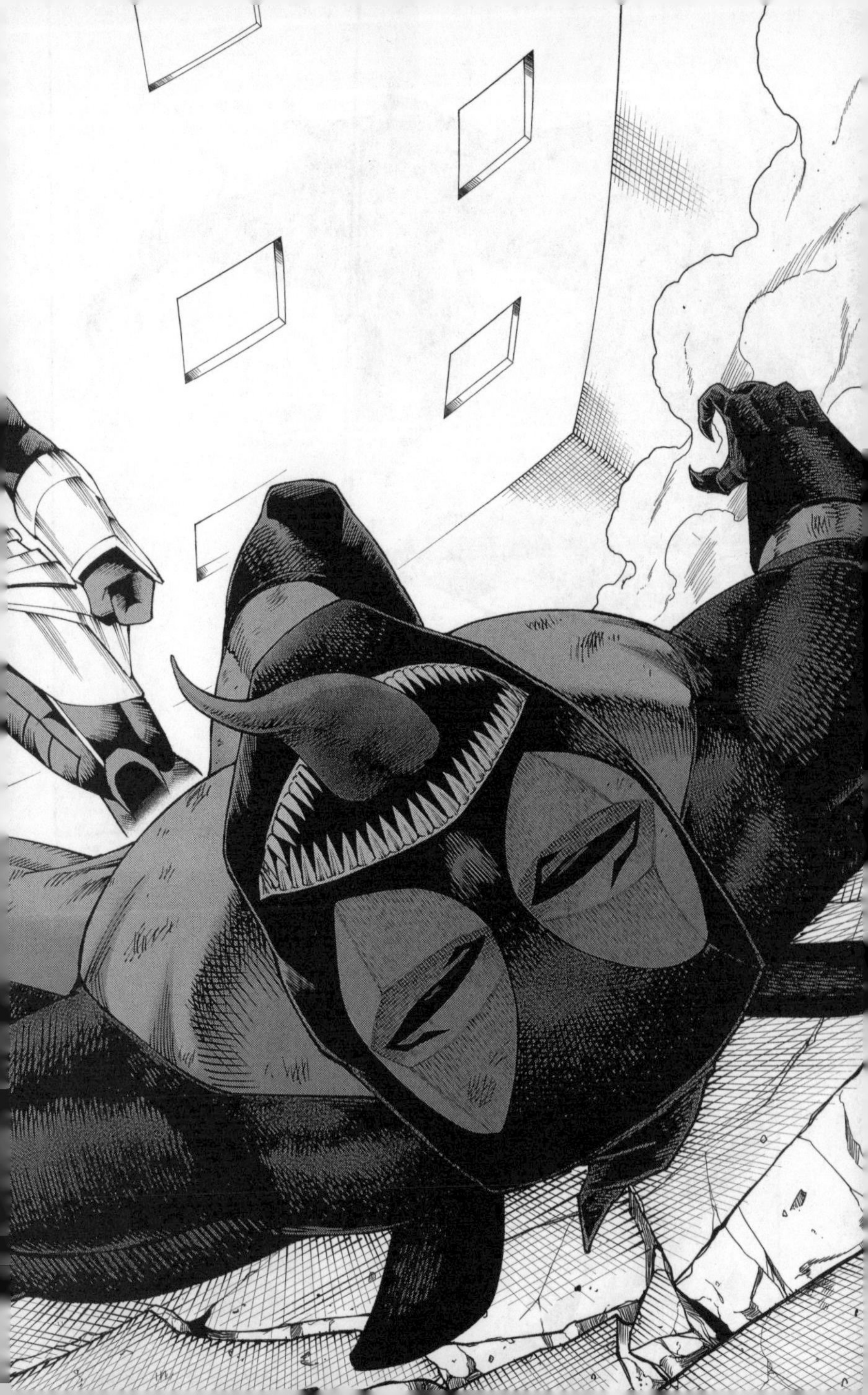

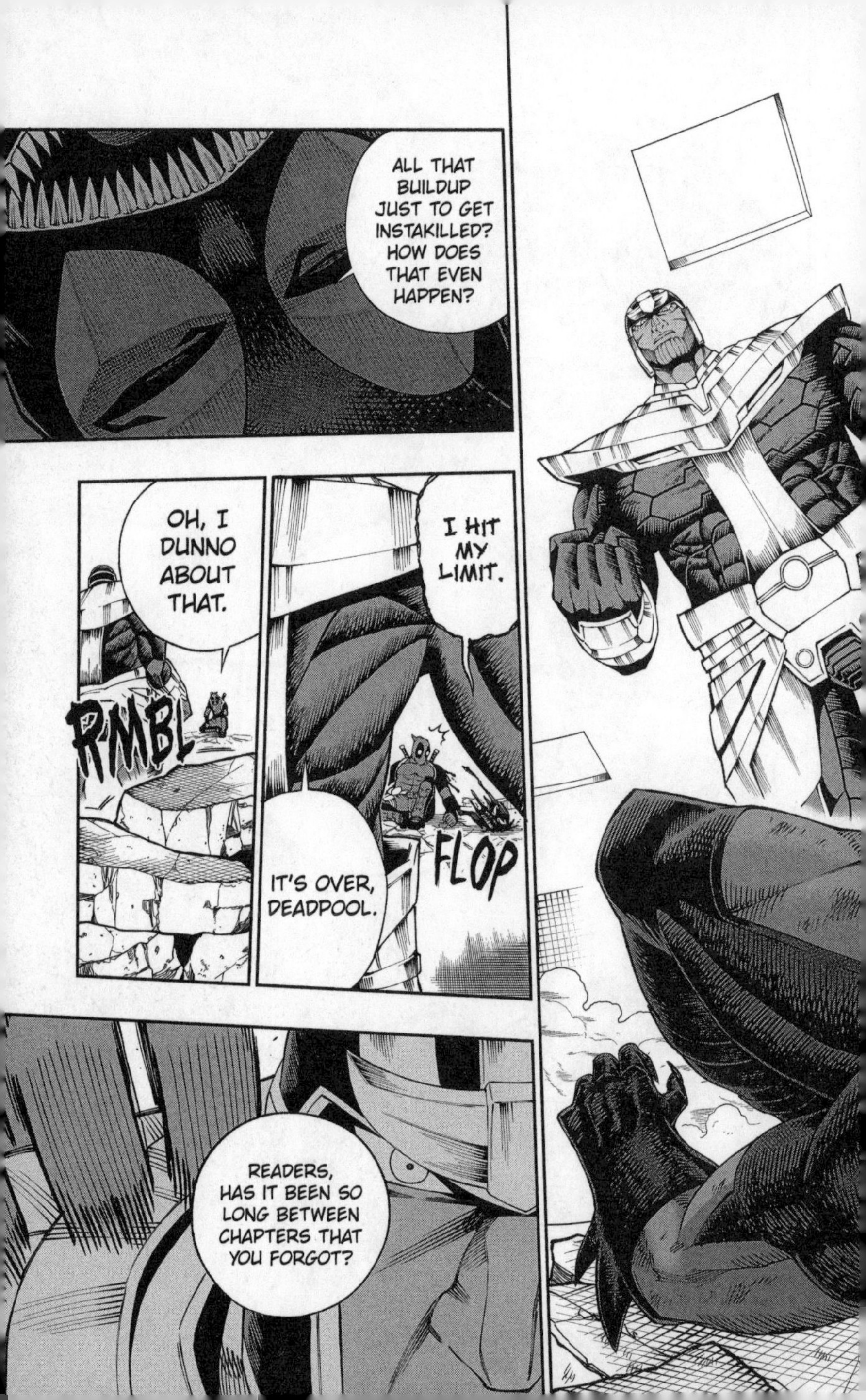
ALL THAT BUILDUP JUST TO GET INSTAKILLED? HOW DOES THAT EVEN HAPPEN?
I HIT MY LIMIT.
IT'S OVER, DEADPOOL.
FLOP
OH, I DUNNO ABOUT THAT.
RMBL
READERS, HAS IT BEEN SO LONG BETWEEN CHAPTERS THAT YOU FORGOT?

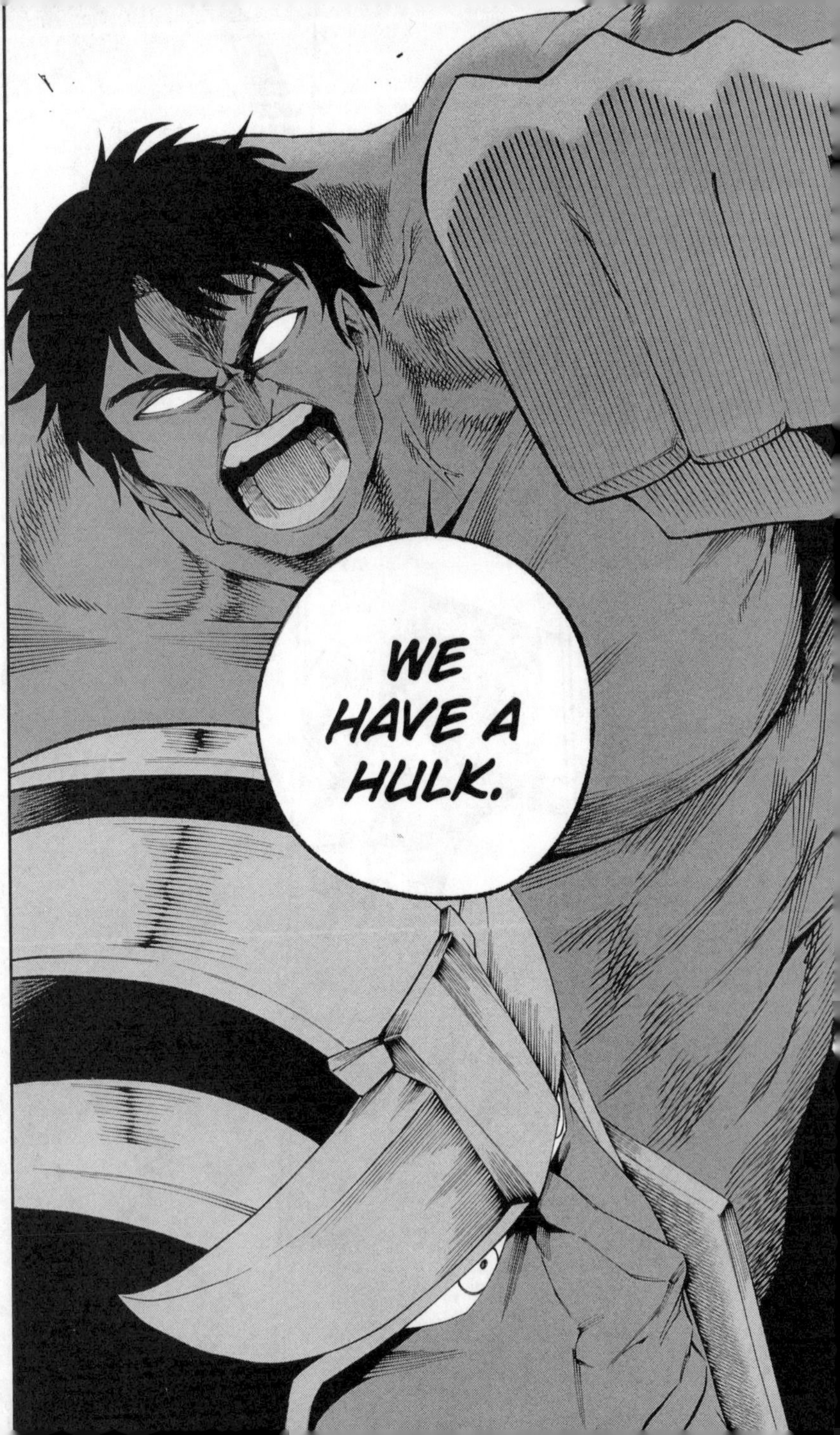
WE HAVE A HULK.

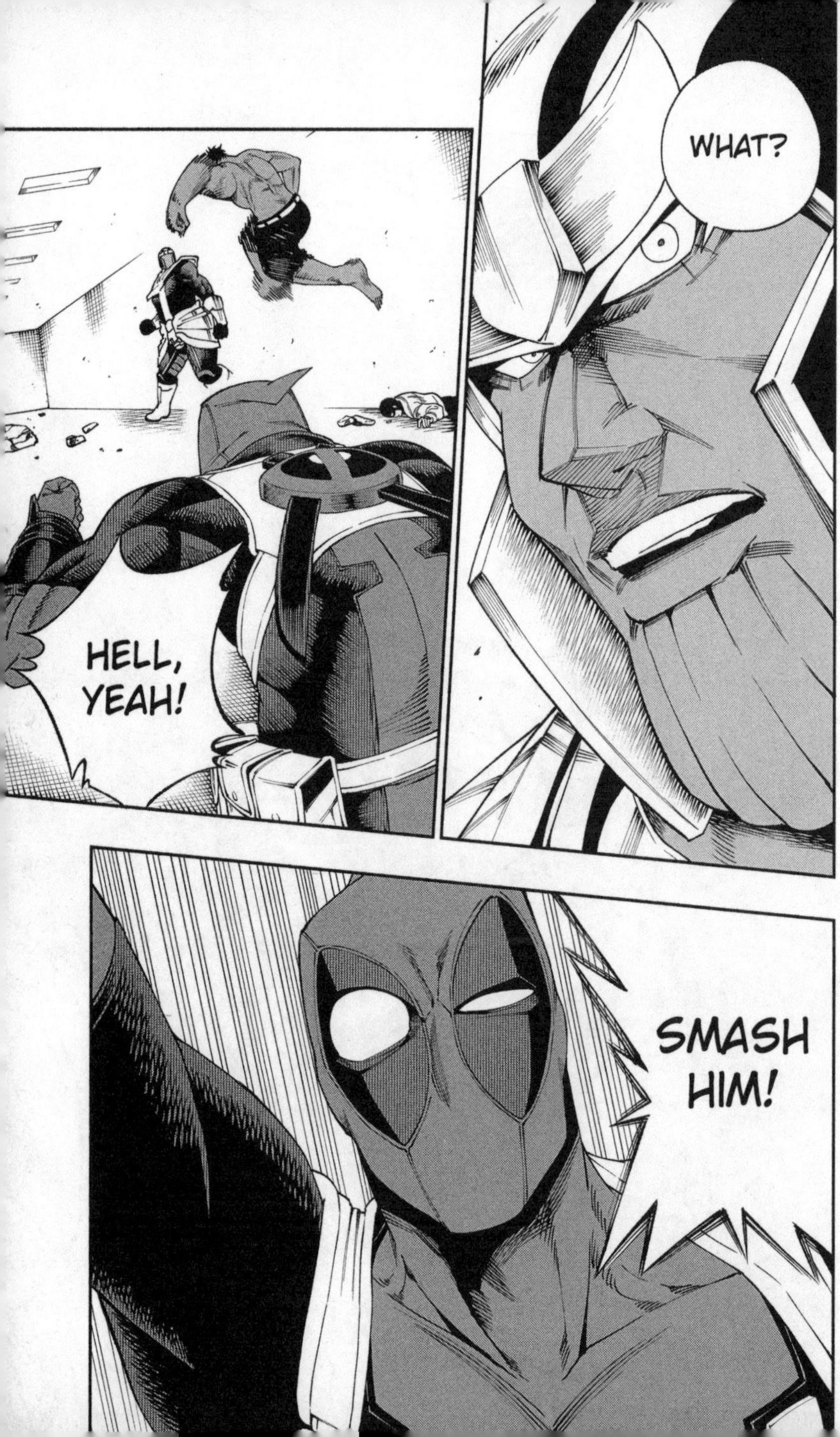
WHAT?
HELL, YEAH!
SMASH HIM!

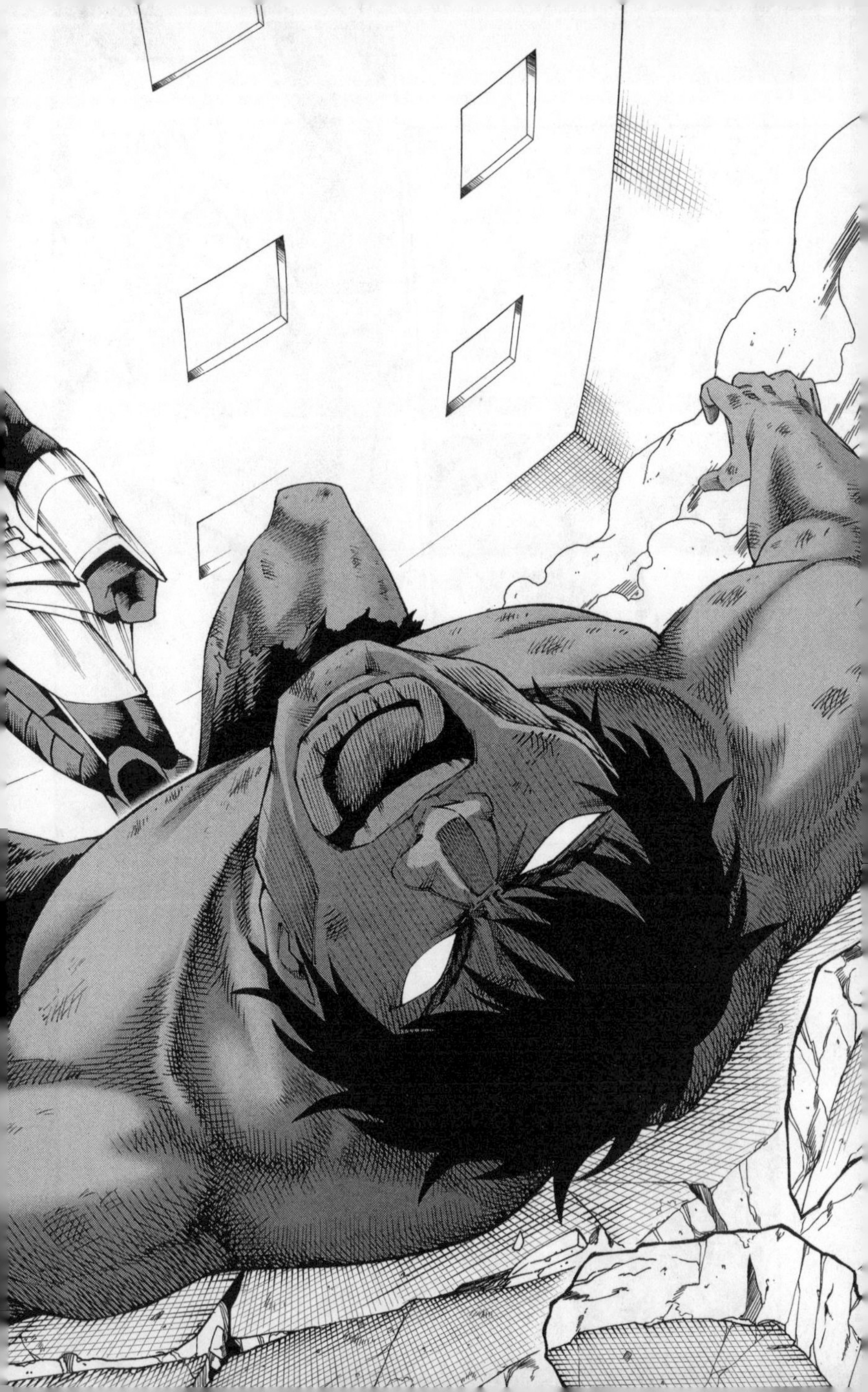

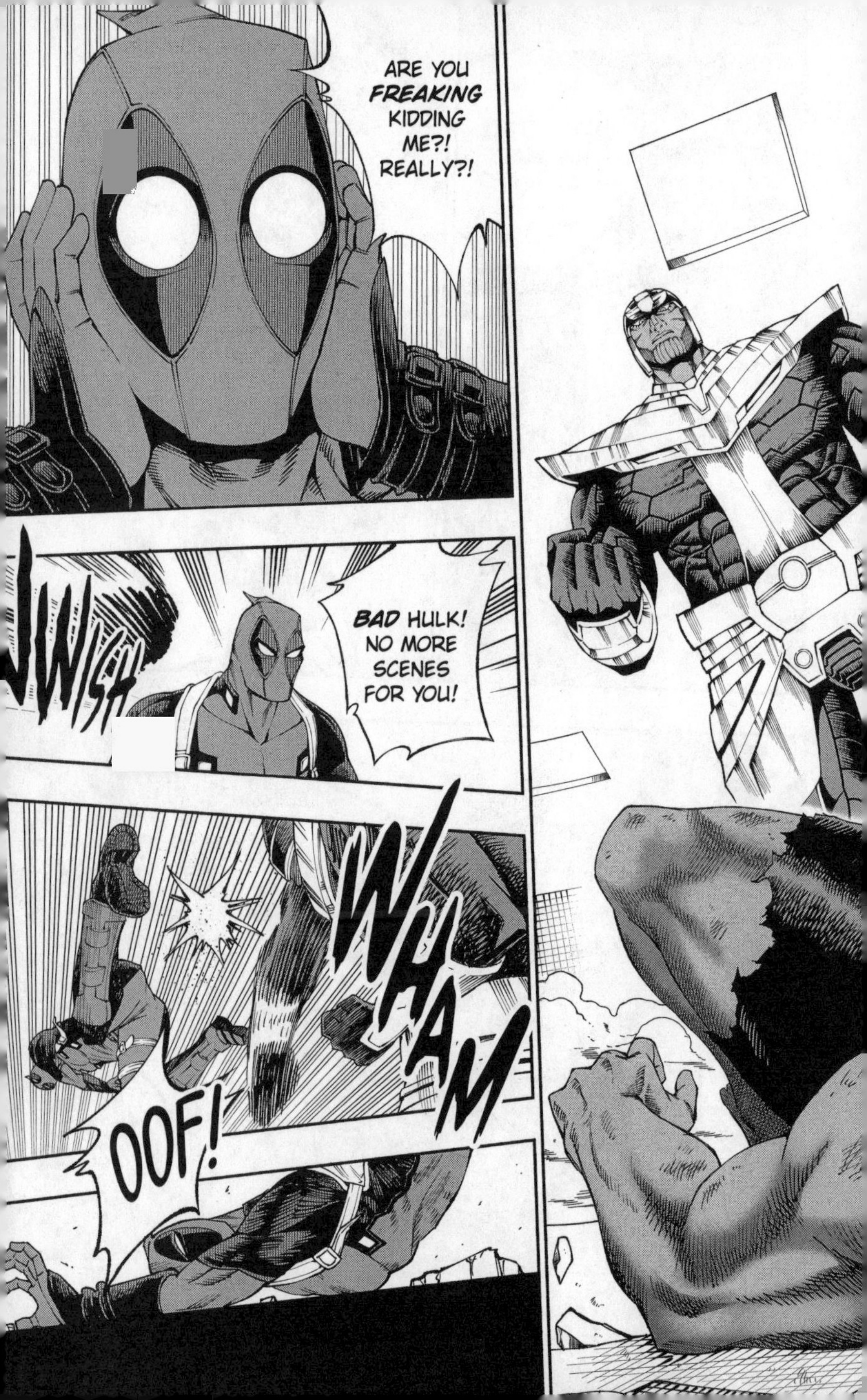
ARE YOU *FREAKING* KIDDING ME?! REALLY?!
BAD HULK! NO MORE SCENES FOR YOU!
JWISH
WHAM
OOF!

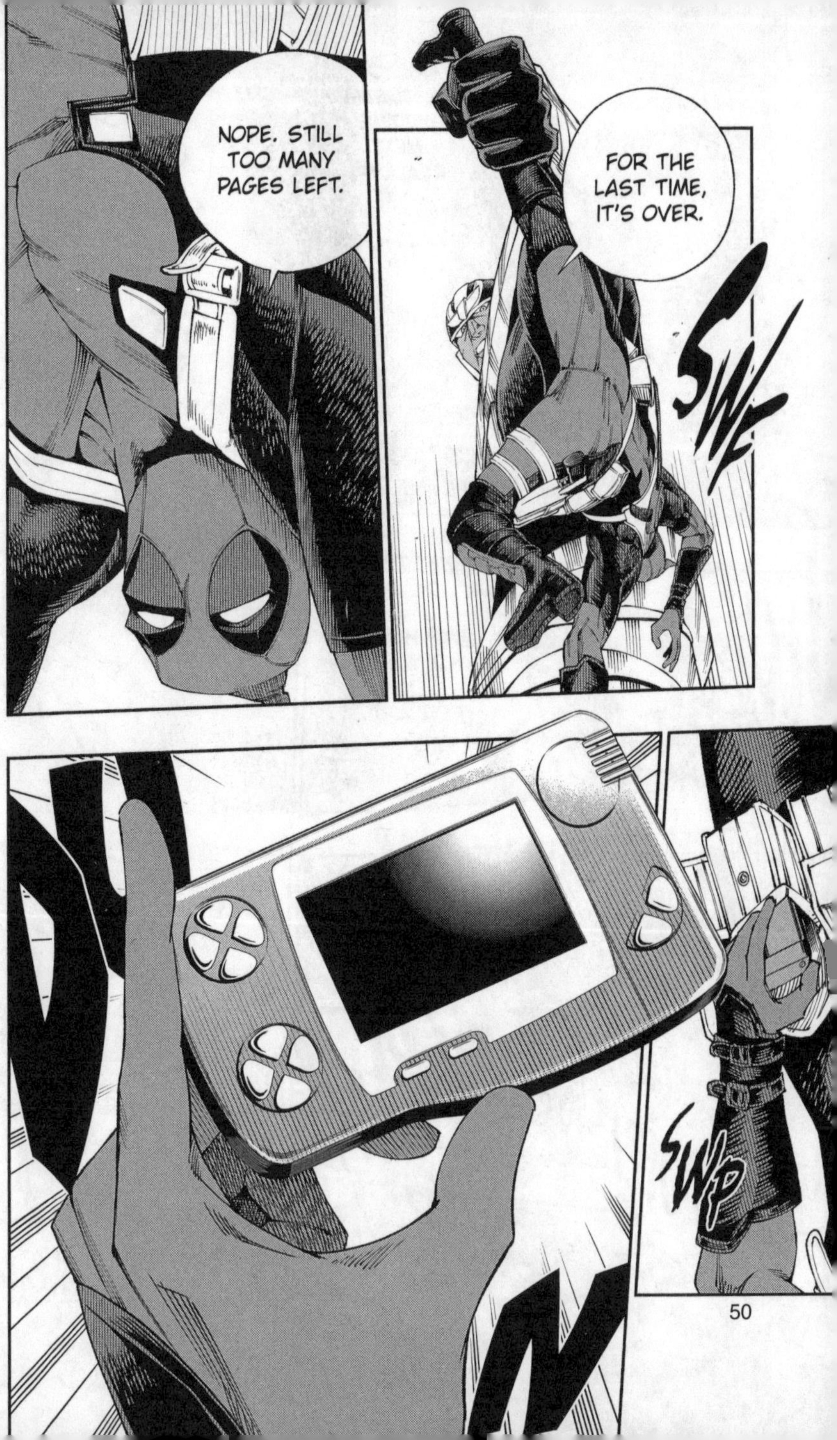
FOR THE LAST TIME, IT'S OVER.
NOPE. STILL TOO MANY PAGES LEFT.
SWP

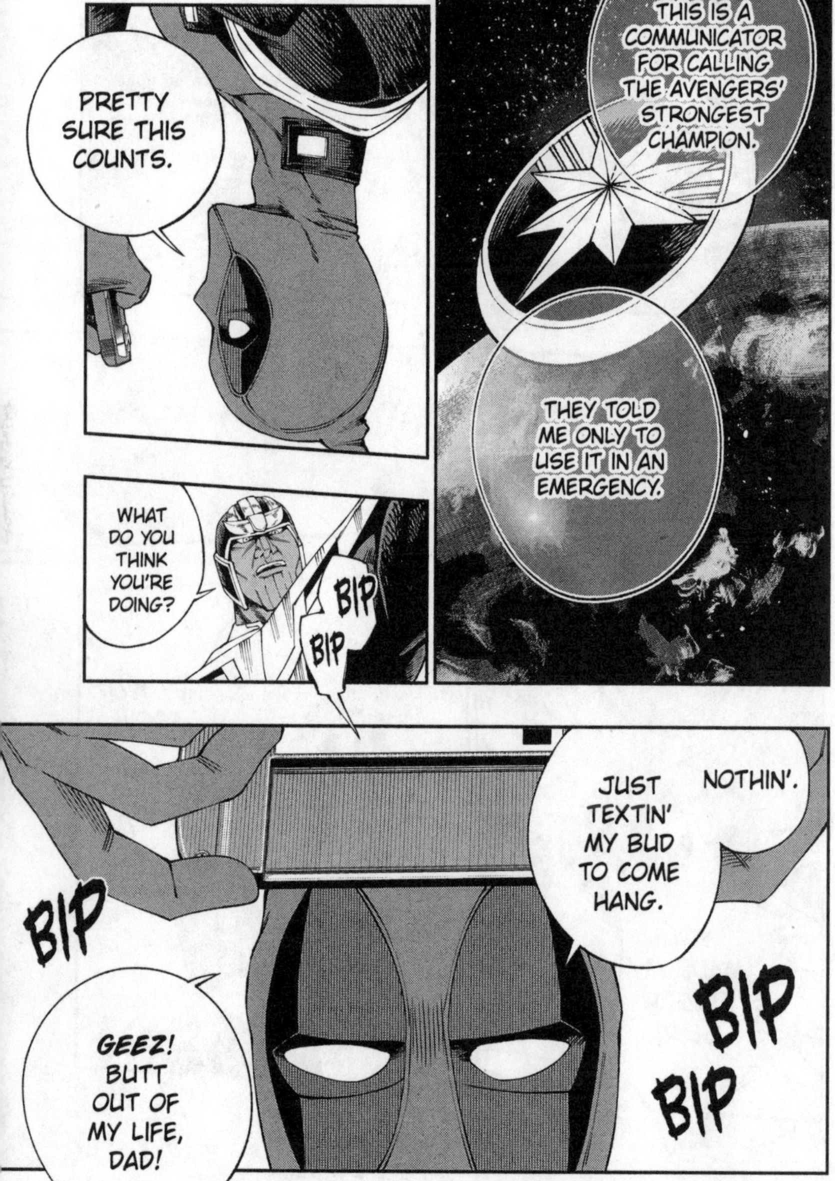

THIS IS A COMMUNICATOR FOR CALLING THE AVENGERS' STRONGEST CHAMPION.
THEY TOLD ME ONLY TO USE IT IN AN EMERGENCY.
PRETTY SURE THIS COUNTS.
WHAT DO YOU THINK YOU'RE DOING?
BIP
BIP
NOTHIN'.
JUST TEXTIN' MY BUD TO COME HANG.
BIP
BIP
BIP
GEEZ! BUTT OUT OF MY LIFE, DAD!

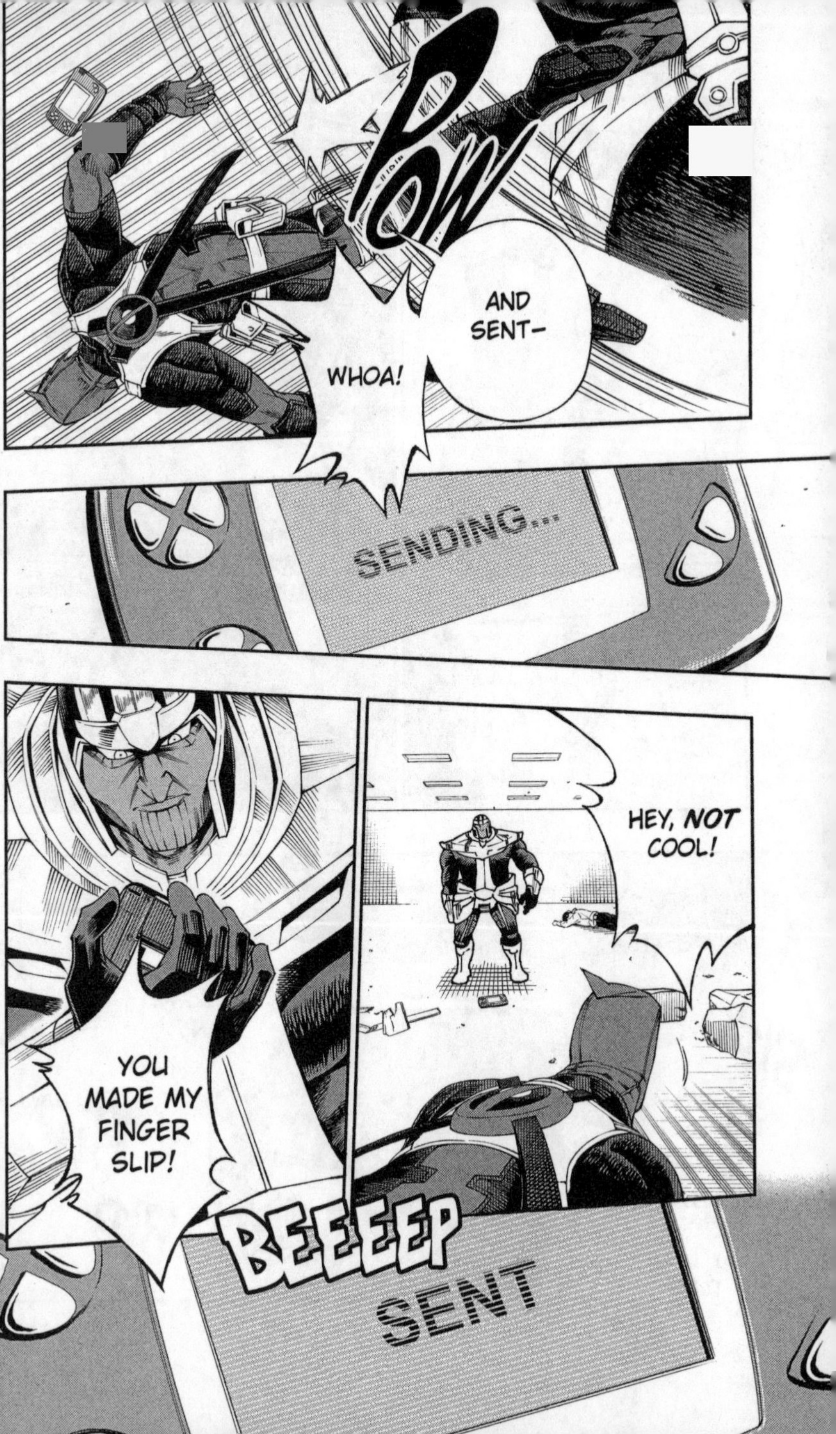
POW
AND SENT–
WHOA!
SENDING...
HEY, *NOT* COOL!
YOU MADE MY FINGER SLIP!
BEEEEP
SENT

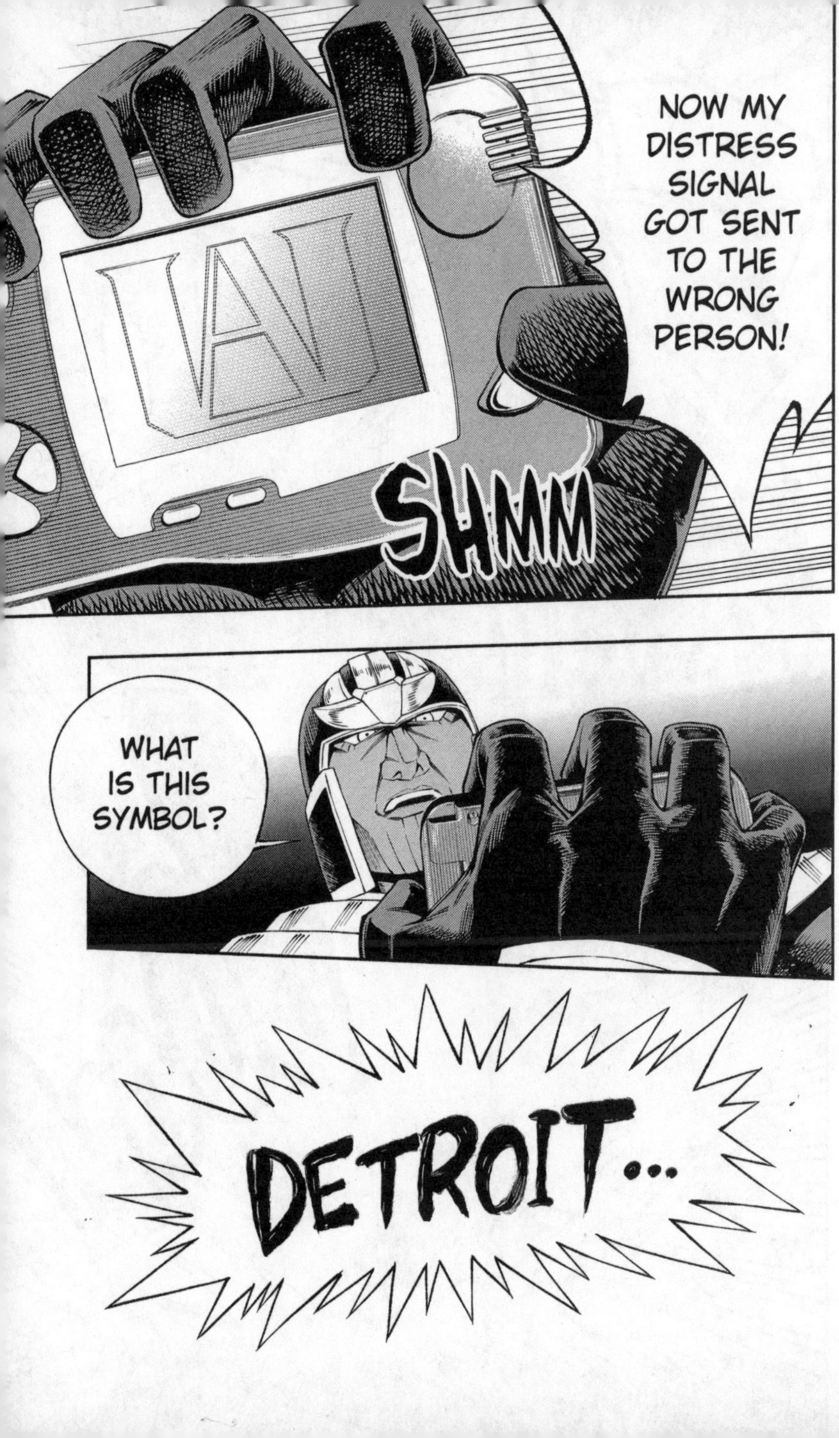
NOW MY DISTRESS SIGNAL GOT SENT TO THE WRONG PERSON!
SHMM
WHAT IS THIS SYMBOL?
DETROIT...

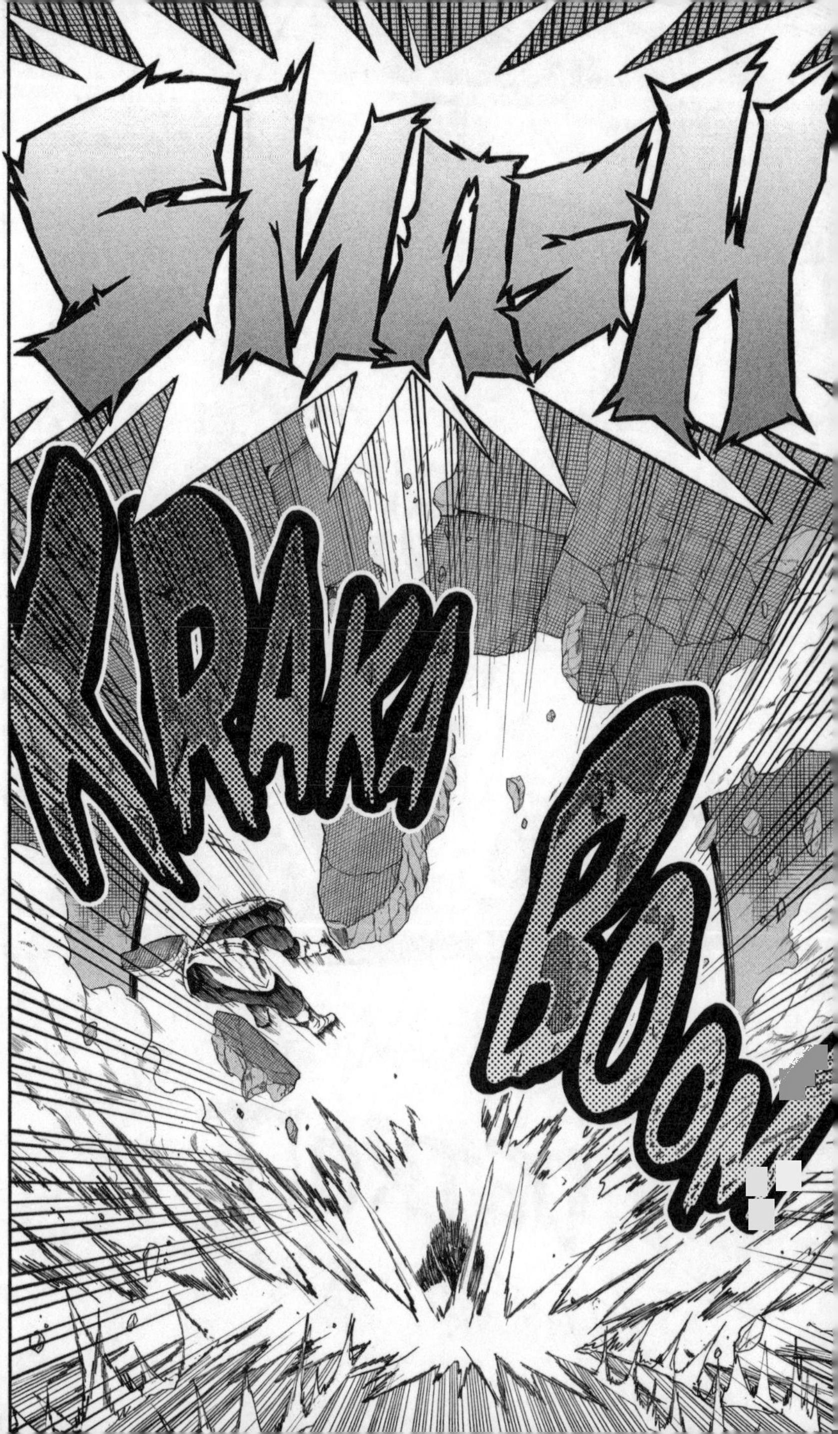
SMASH
KRAKA
BOOM!!

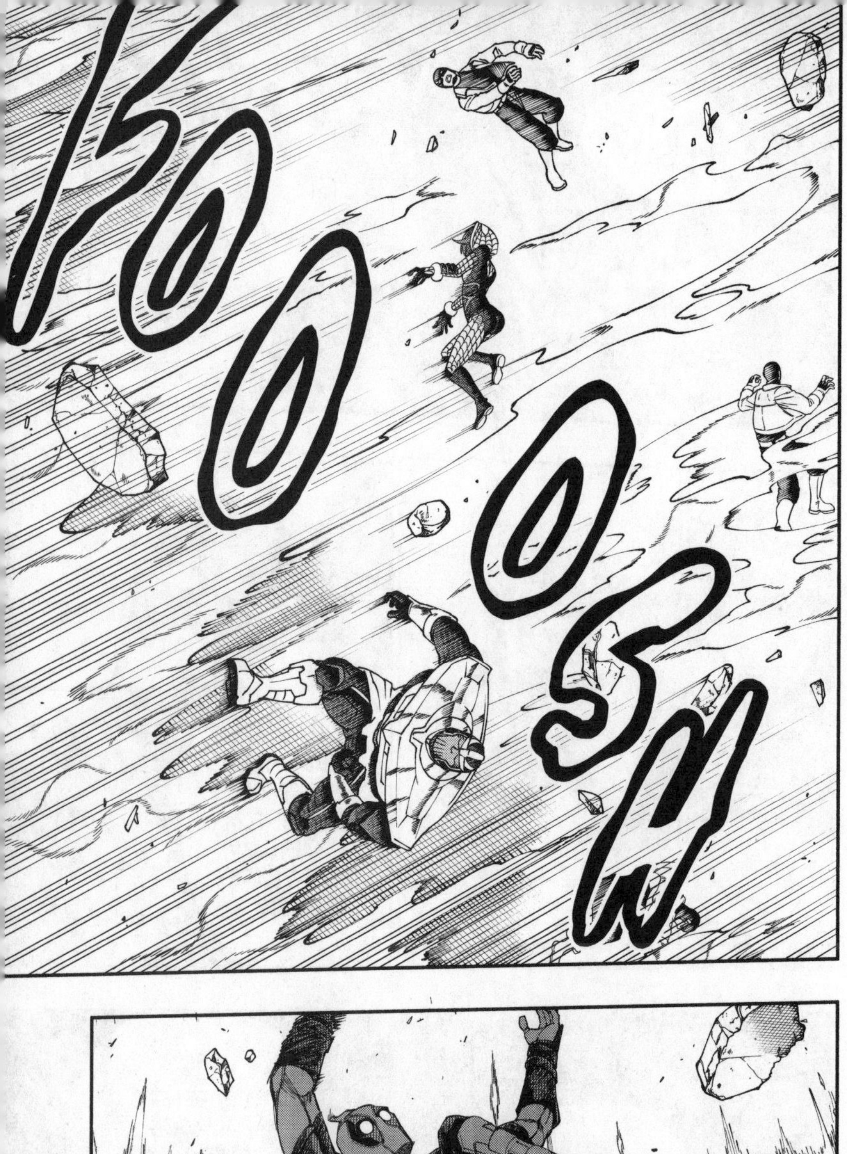
KOOOOSH
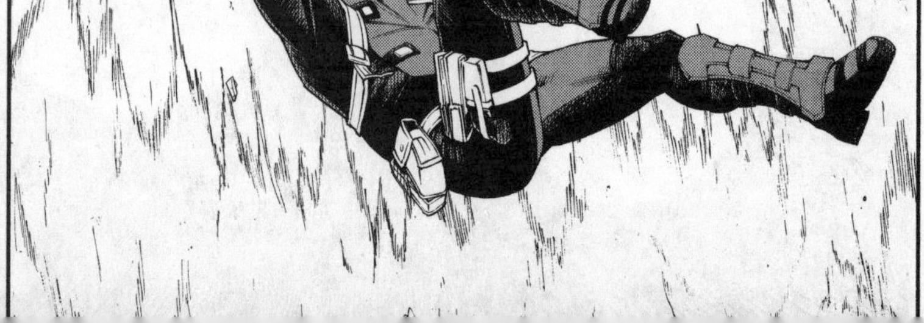

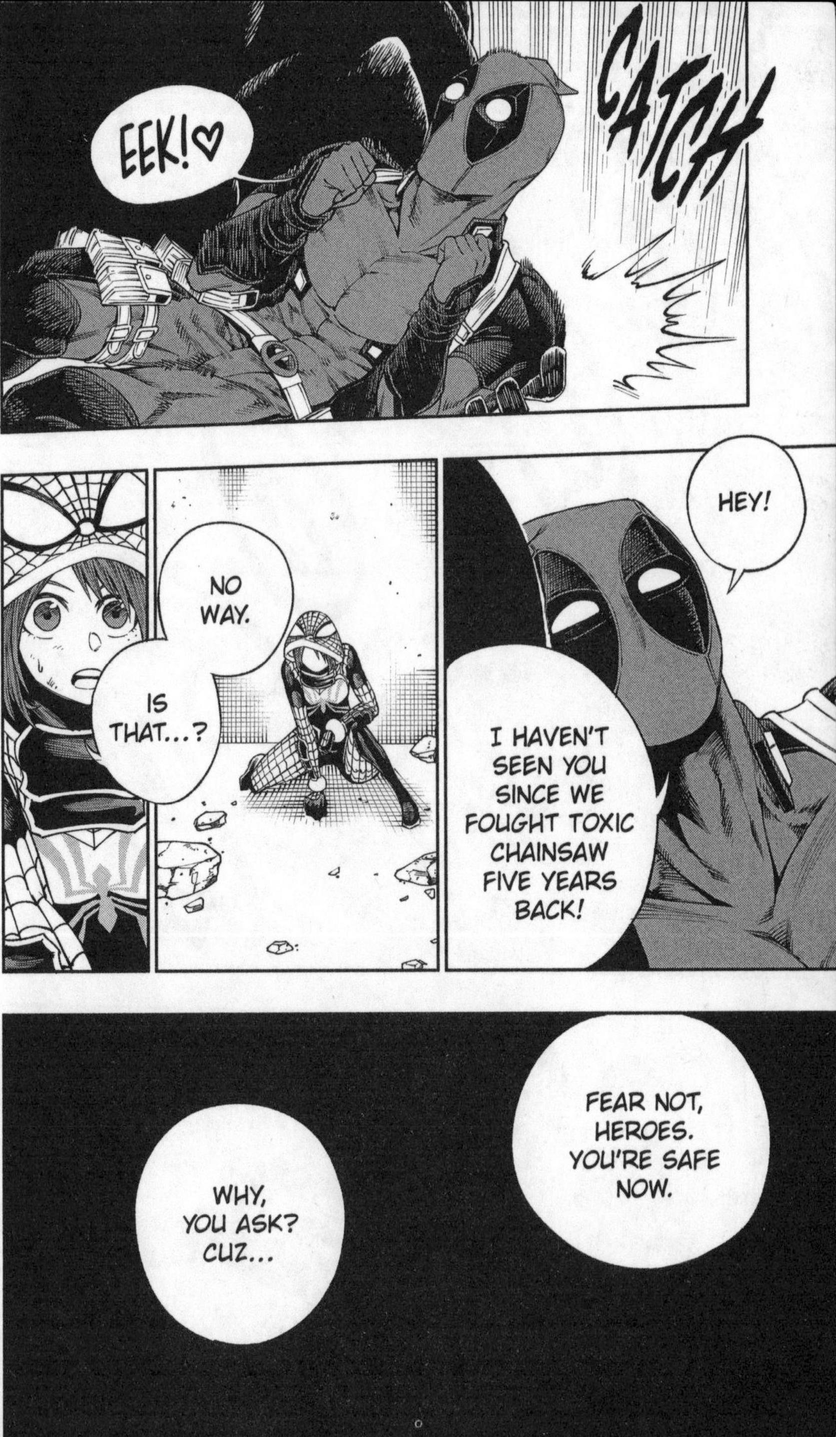
CATCH
EEK!♡
HEY!
I HAVEN'T SEEN YOU SINCE WE FOUGHT TOXIC CHAINSAW FIVE YEARS BACK!
NO WAY.
IS THAT...?
FEAR NOT, HEROES. YOU'RE SAFE NOW.
WHY, YOU ASK? CUZ...

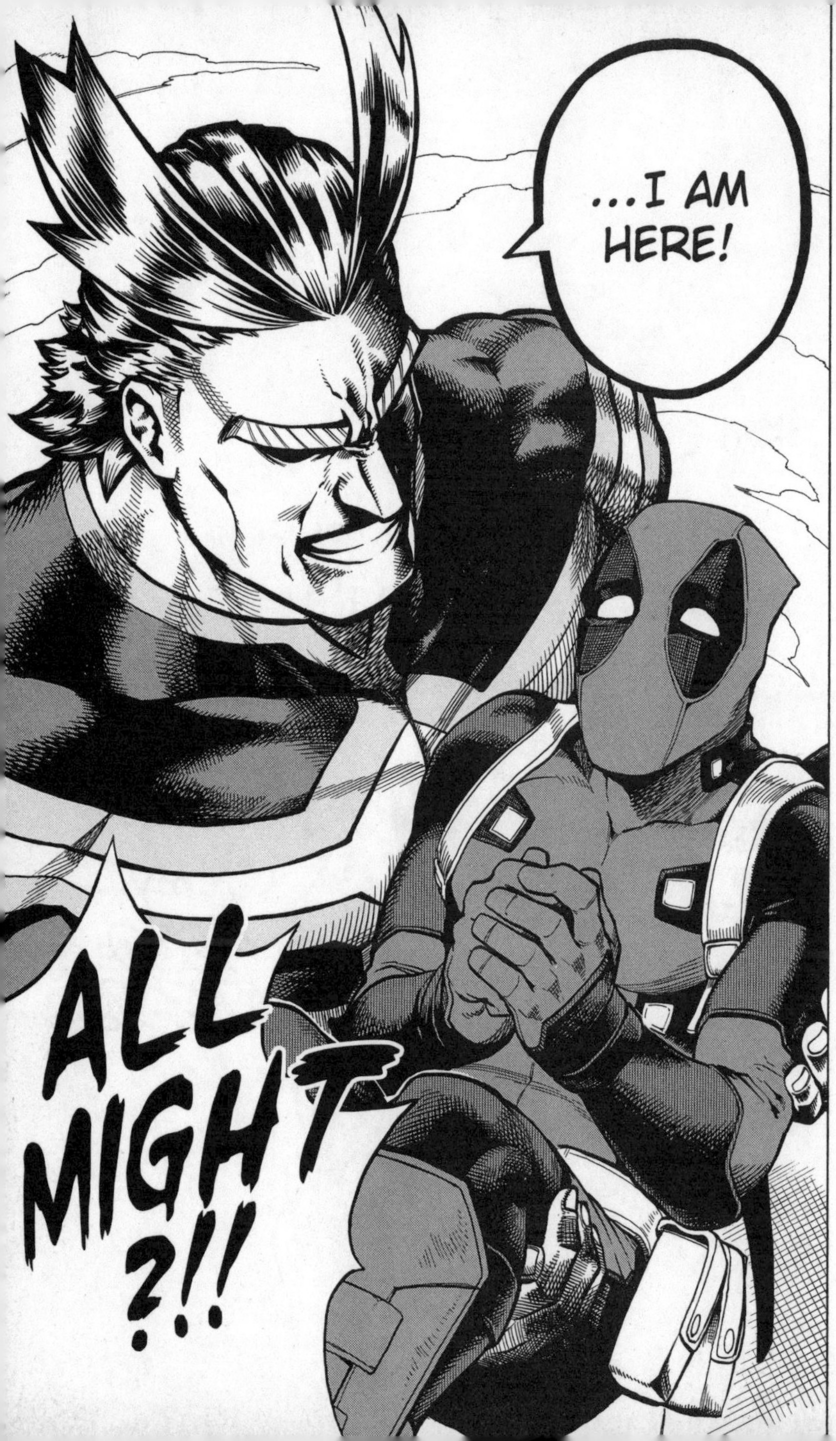
...I AM HERE!
ALL MIGHT ?!!

Kohei Horikoshi—

Thank you so much for writing!

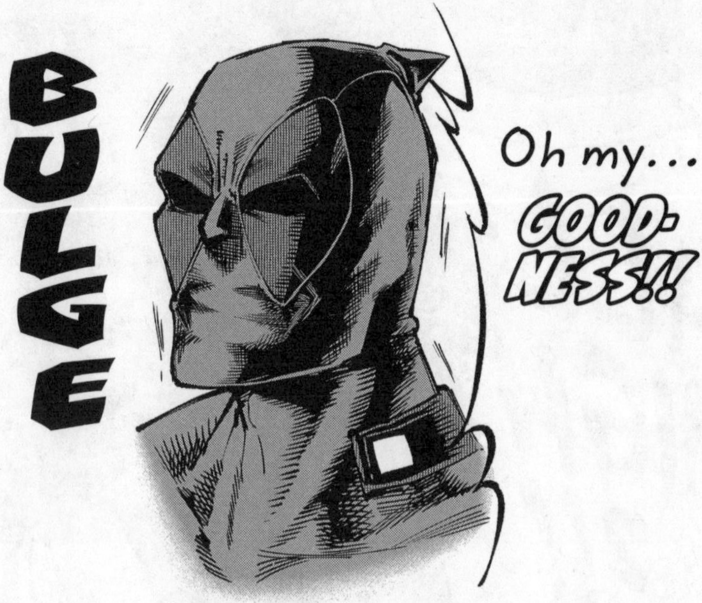
BULGE
Oh my...
GOOD-NESS!!

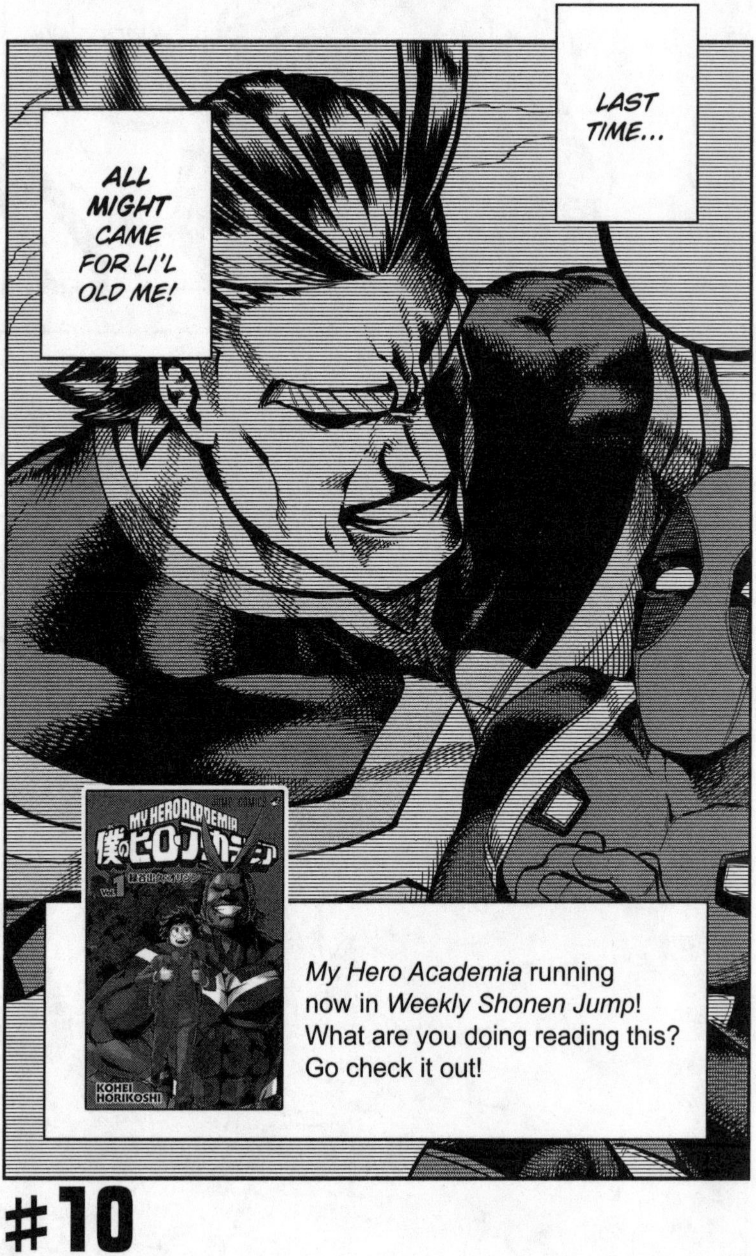
LAST TIME...
ALL MIGHT CAME FOR LI'L OLD ME!
MY HERO ACADEMIA
Vol.1
KOHEI HORIKOSHI
My Hero Academia running now in *Weekly Shonen Jump*! What are you doing reading this? Go check it out!

#10

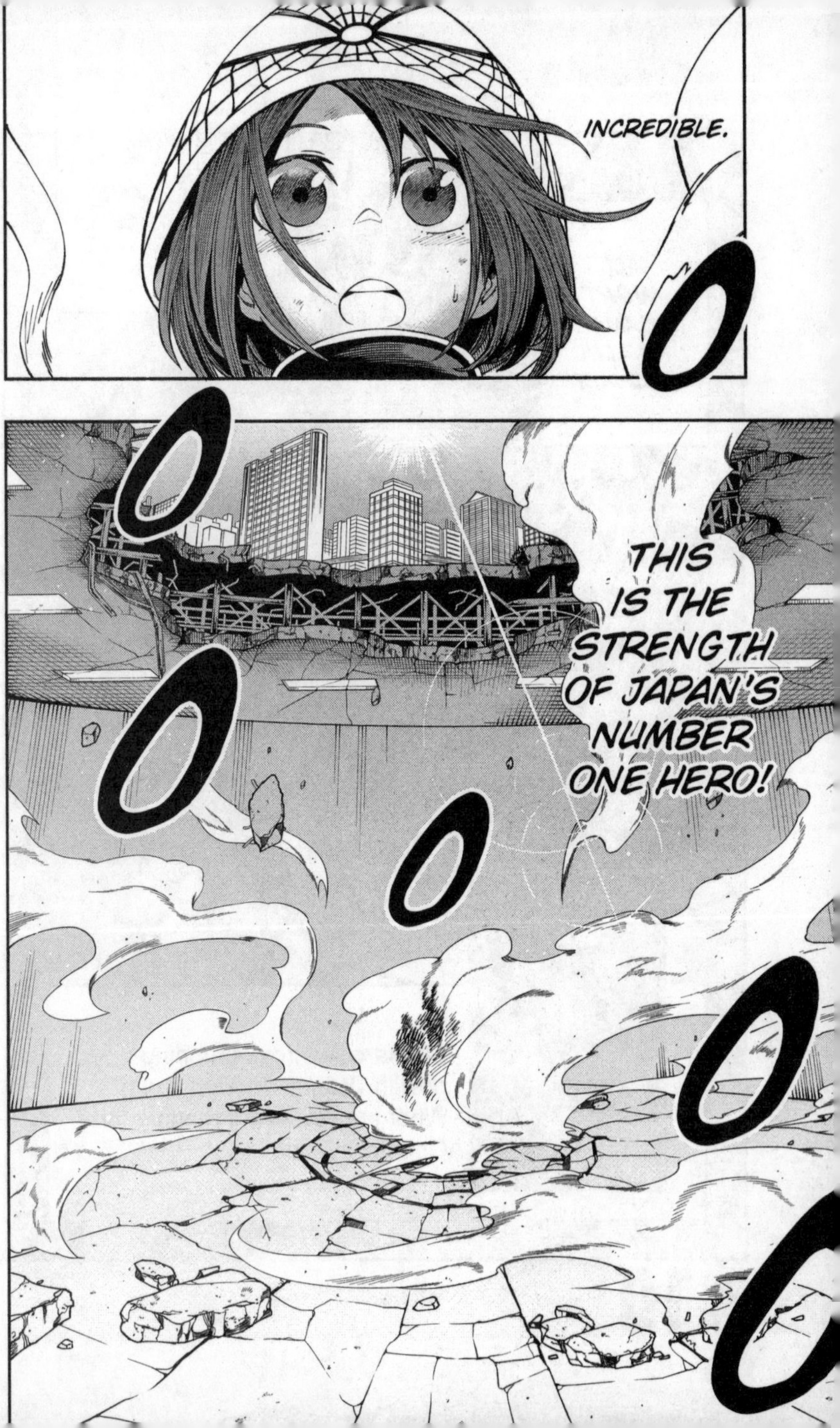
INCREDIBLE.
THIS IS THE STRENGTH OF JAPAN'S NUMBER ONE HERO!

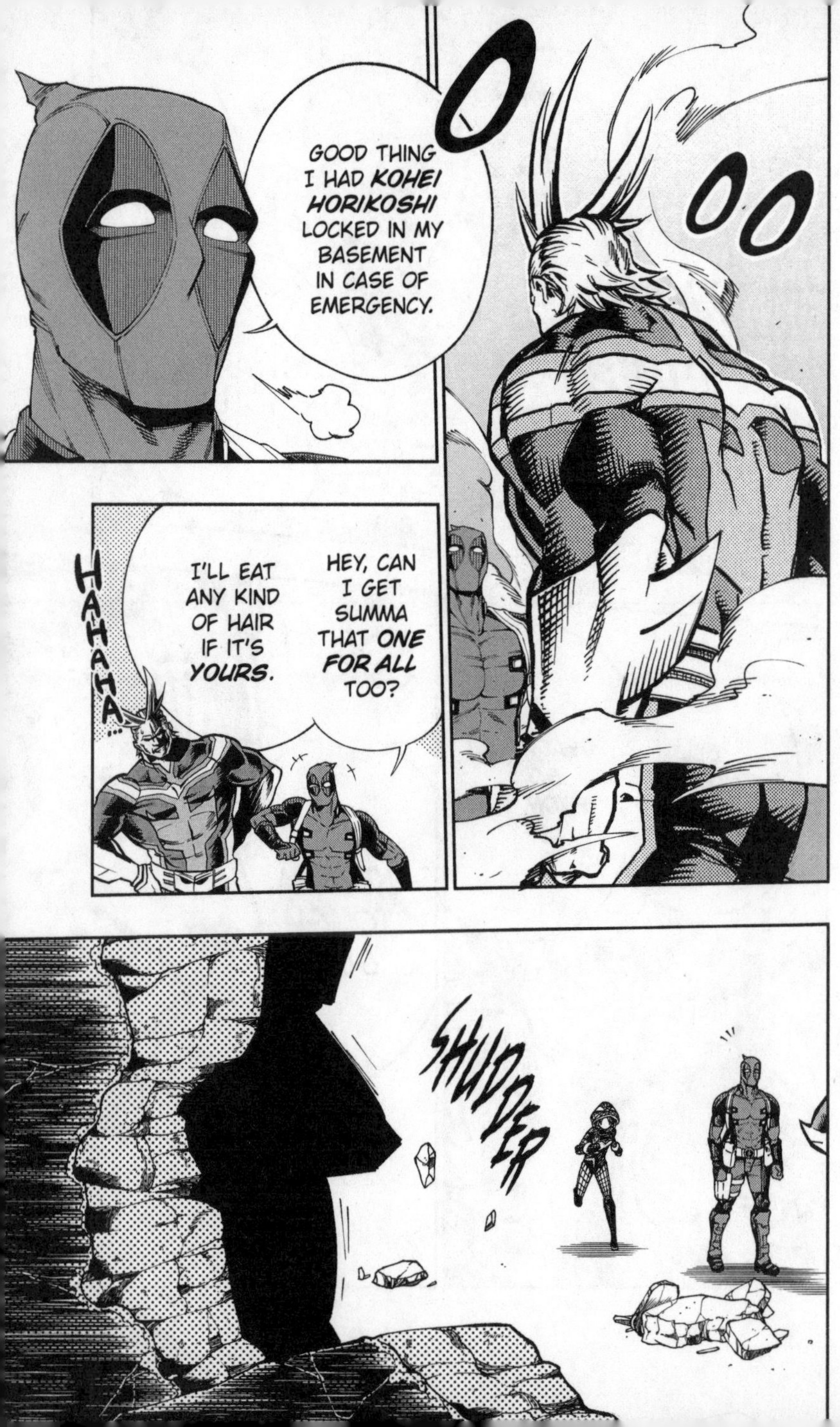
OOO
GOOD THING I HAD KOHEI HORIKOSHI LOCKED IN MY BASEMENT IN CASE OF EMERGENCY.
HEY, CAN I GET SUMMA THAT ONE FOR ALL TOO?
I'LL EAT ANY KIND OF HAIR IF IT'S YOURS.
HAHAHA...
SHUDDER

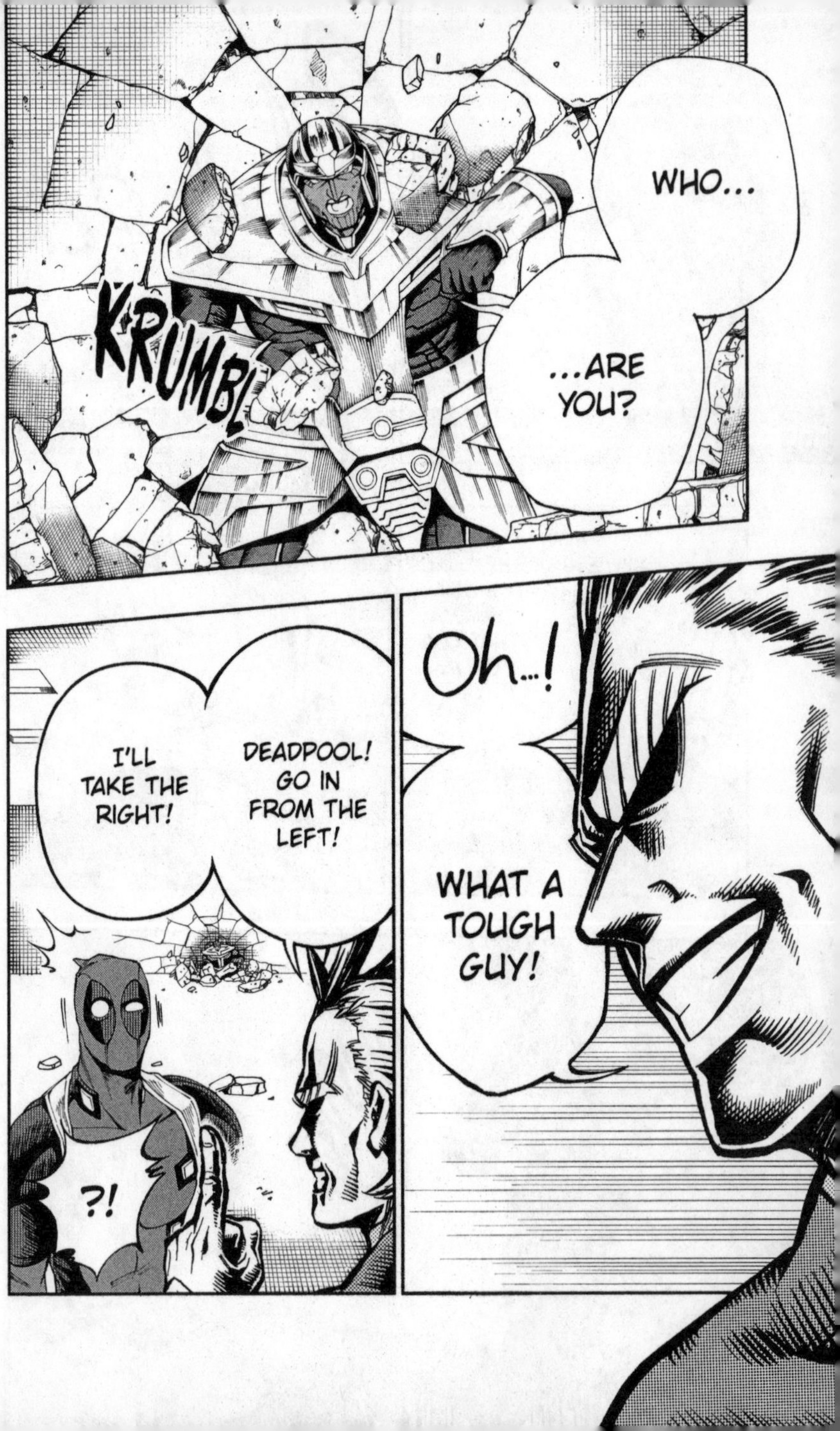
KRUMBL
WHO...
...ARE YOU?
Oh...!
WHAT A TOUGH GUY!
DEADPOOL! GO IN FROM THE LEFT!
I'LL TAKE THE RIGHT!
?!

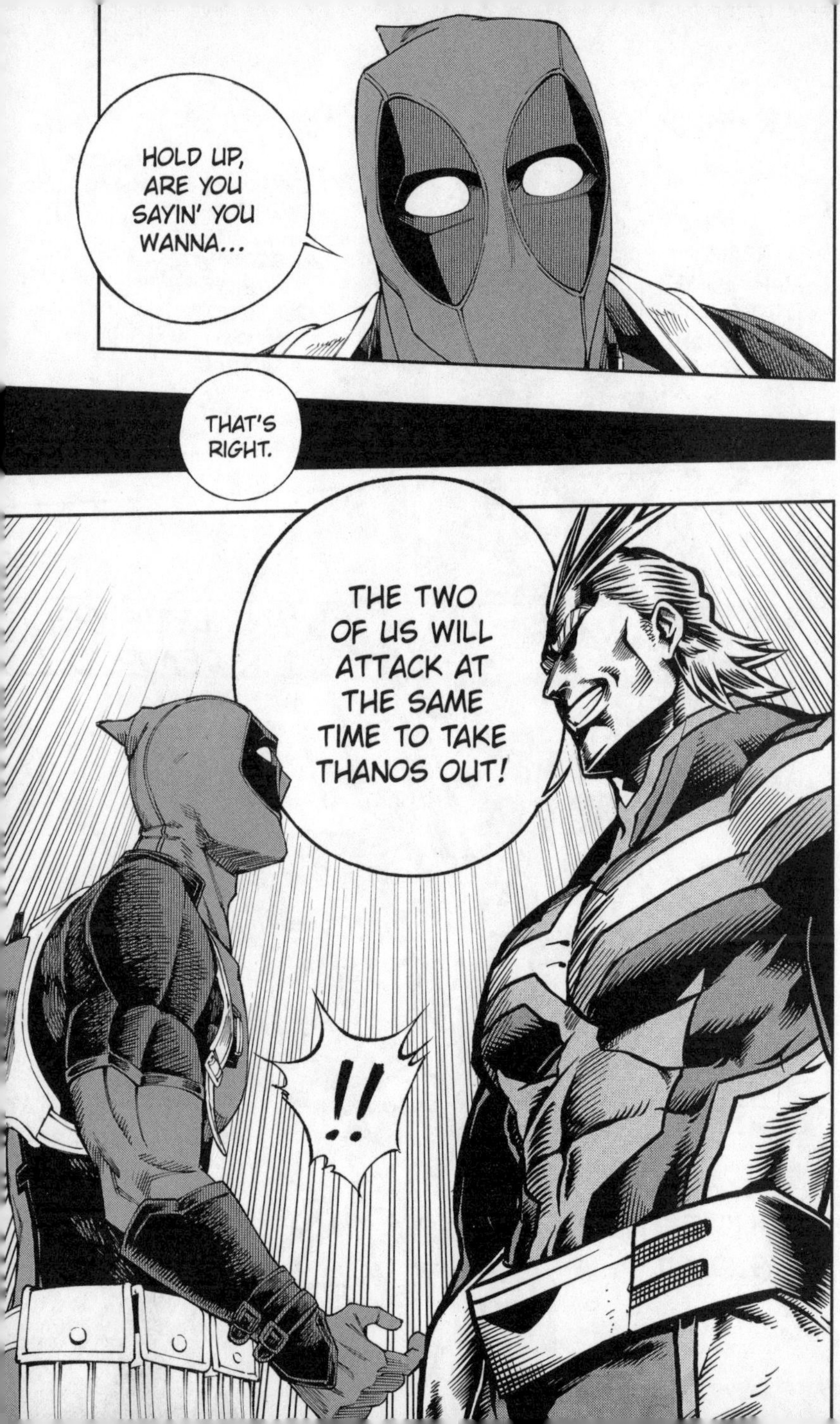
HOLD UP, ARE YOU SAYIN' YOU WANNA...
THAT'S RIGHT.
THE TWO OF US WILL ATTACK AT THE SAME TIME TO TAKE THANOS OUT!
!!

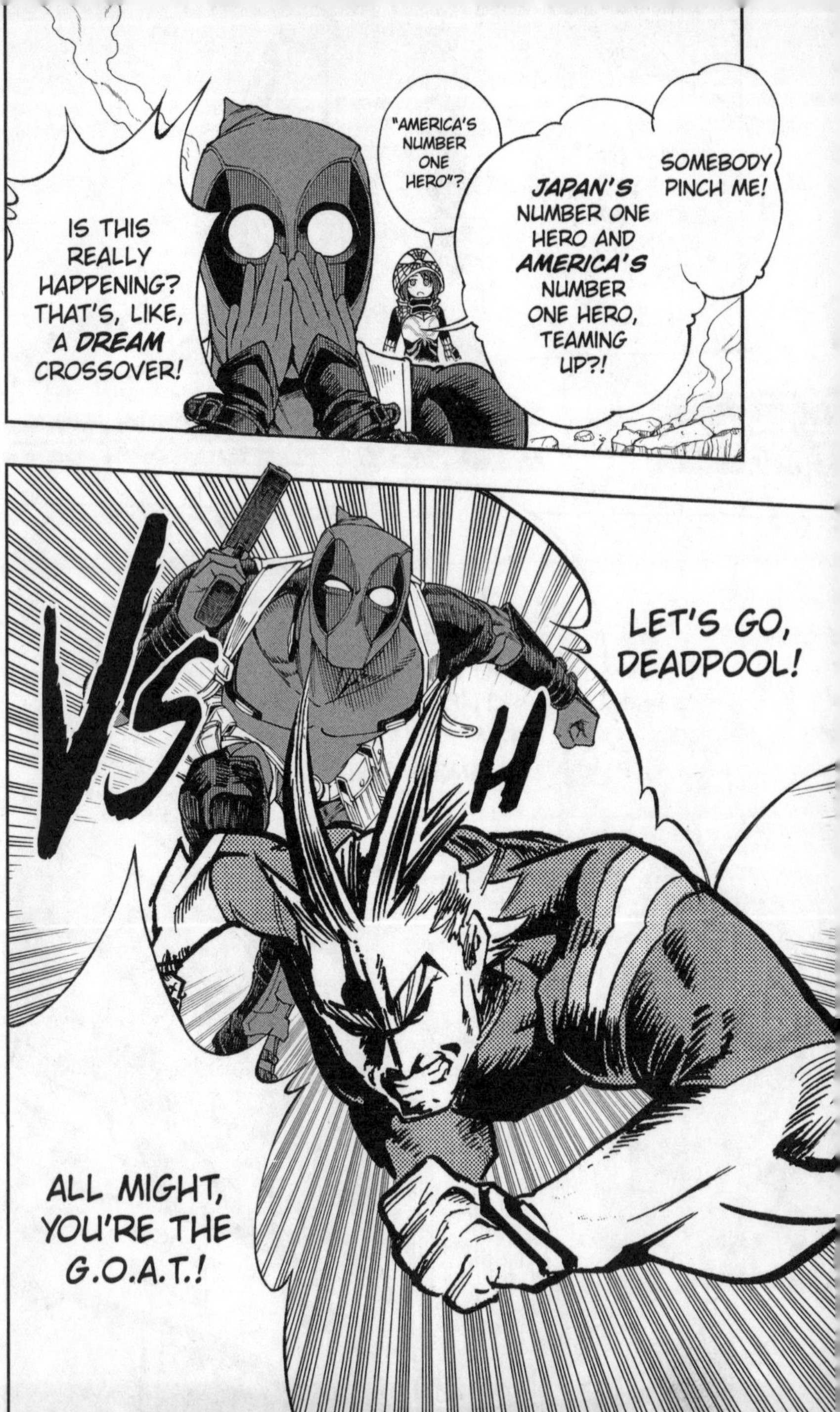
SOMEBODY PINCH ME!
JAPAN'S NUMBER ONE HERO AND AMERICA'S NUMBER ONE HERO, TEAMING UP?!
"AMERICA'S NUMBER ONE HERO"?
IS THIS REALLY HAPPENING? THAT'S, LIKE, A DREAM CROSSOVER!
LET'S GO, DEADPOOL!
VSH
ALL MIGHT, YOU'RE THE G.O.A.T.!

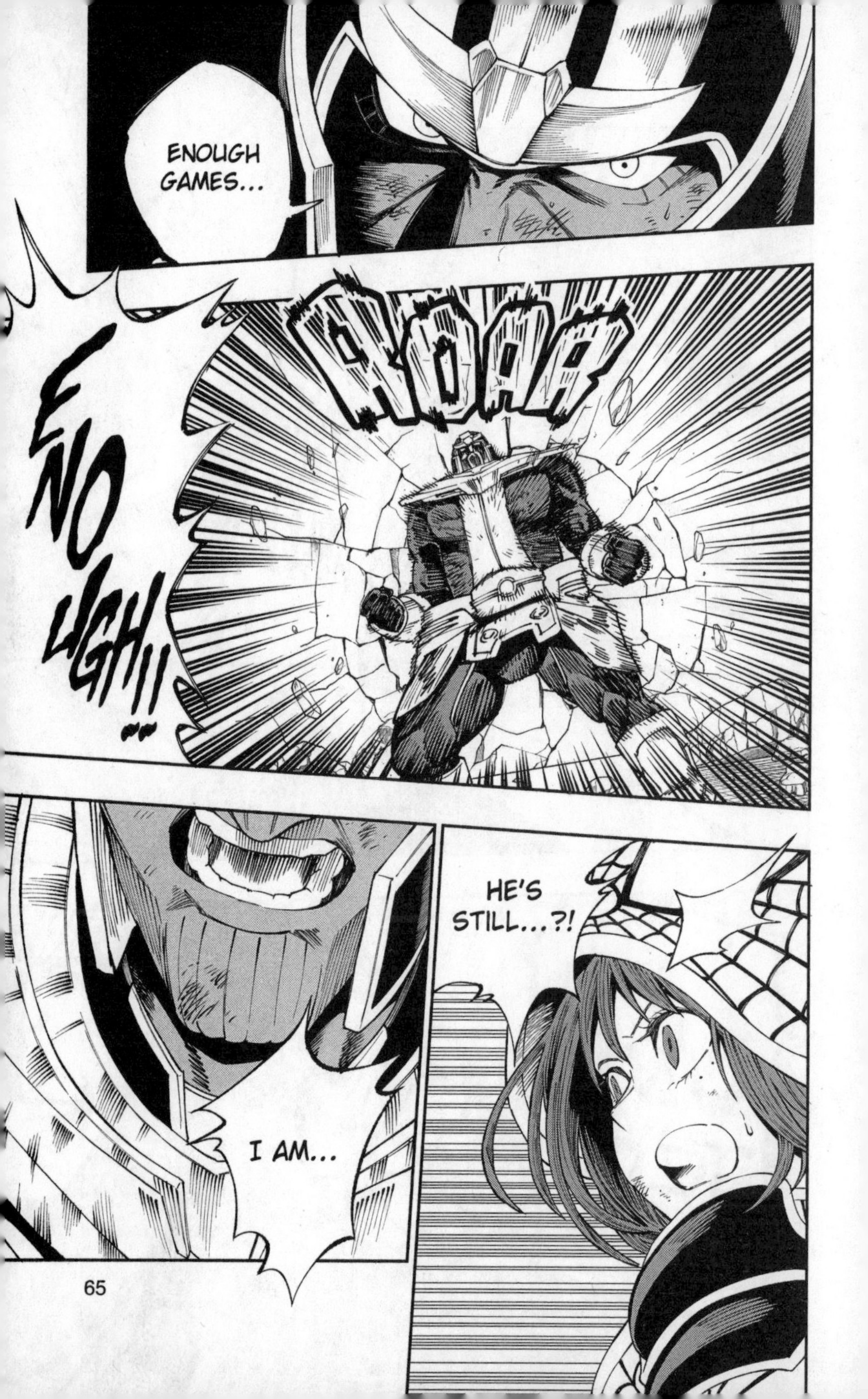
ENOUGH GAMES...
ROAR
ENOUGH!!
HE'S STILL...?!
I AM...

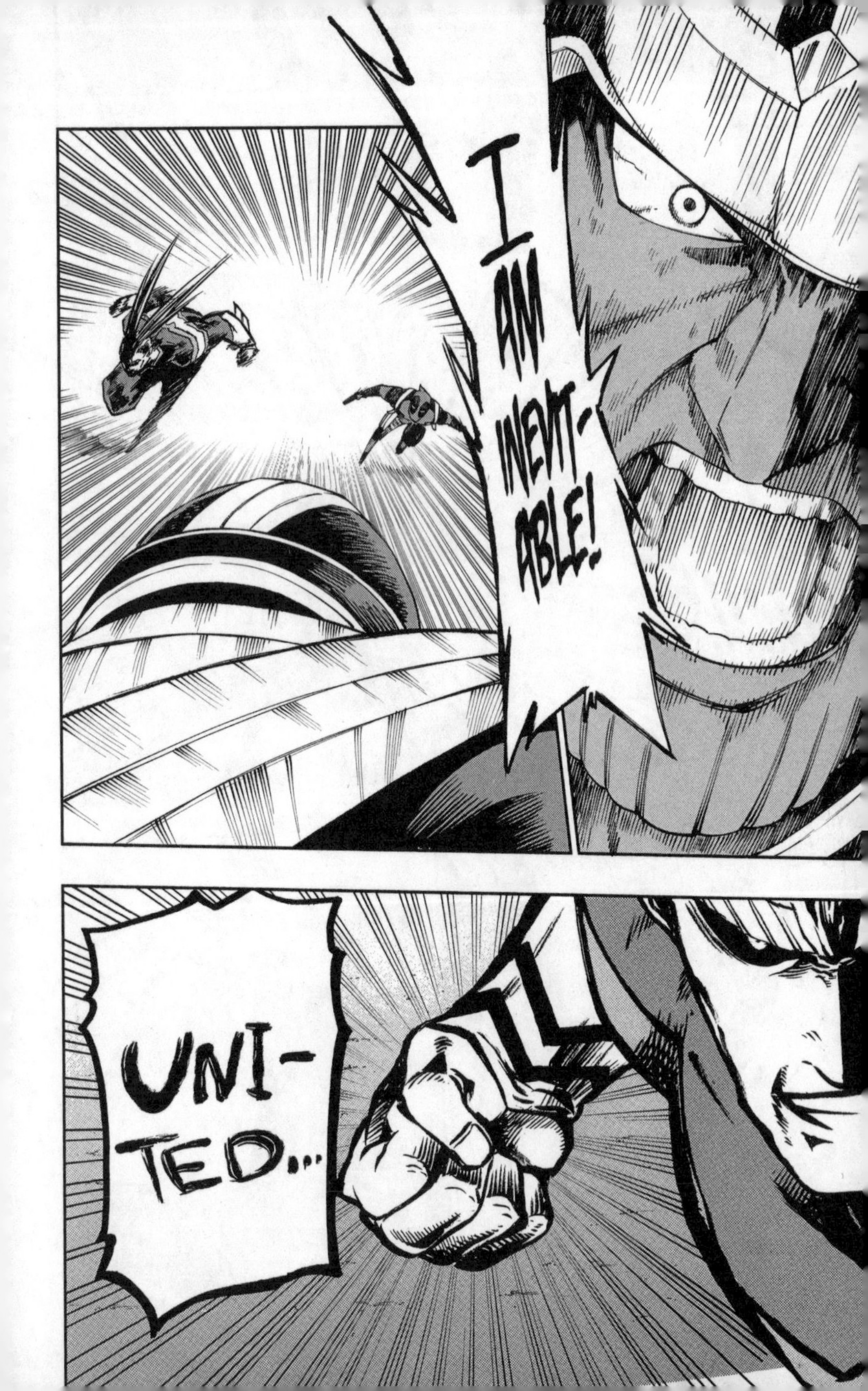
I AM INEVIT-ABLE!
UNI-TED...

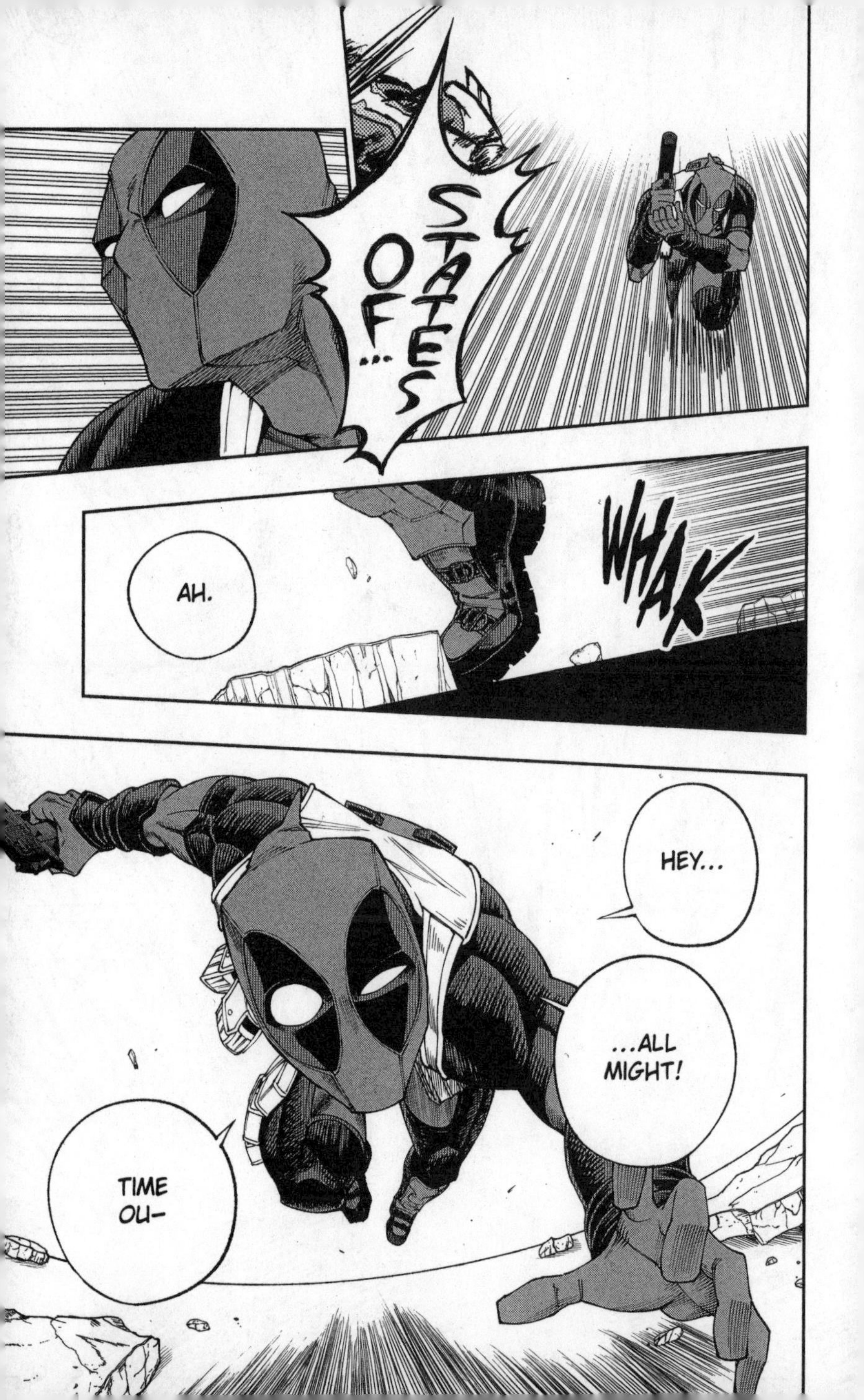
STATES OF...
WHAK
AH.
HEY...
...ALL MIGHT!
TIME OU-

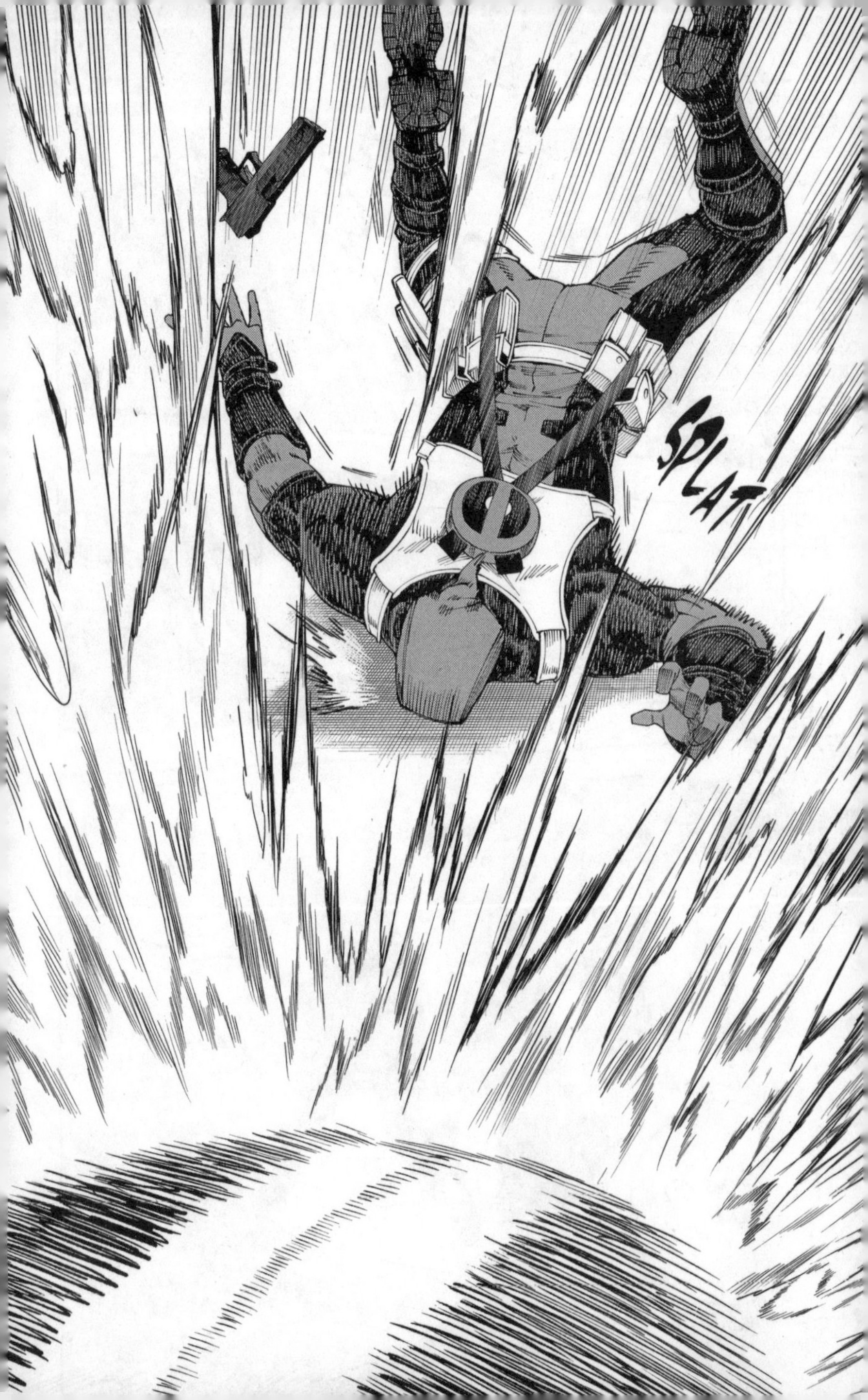
SPLAT

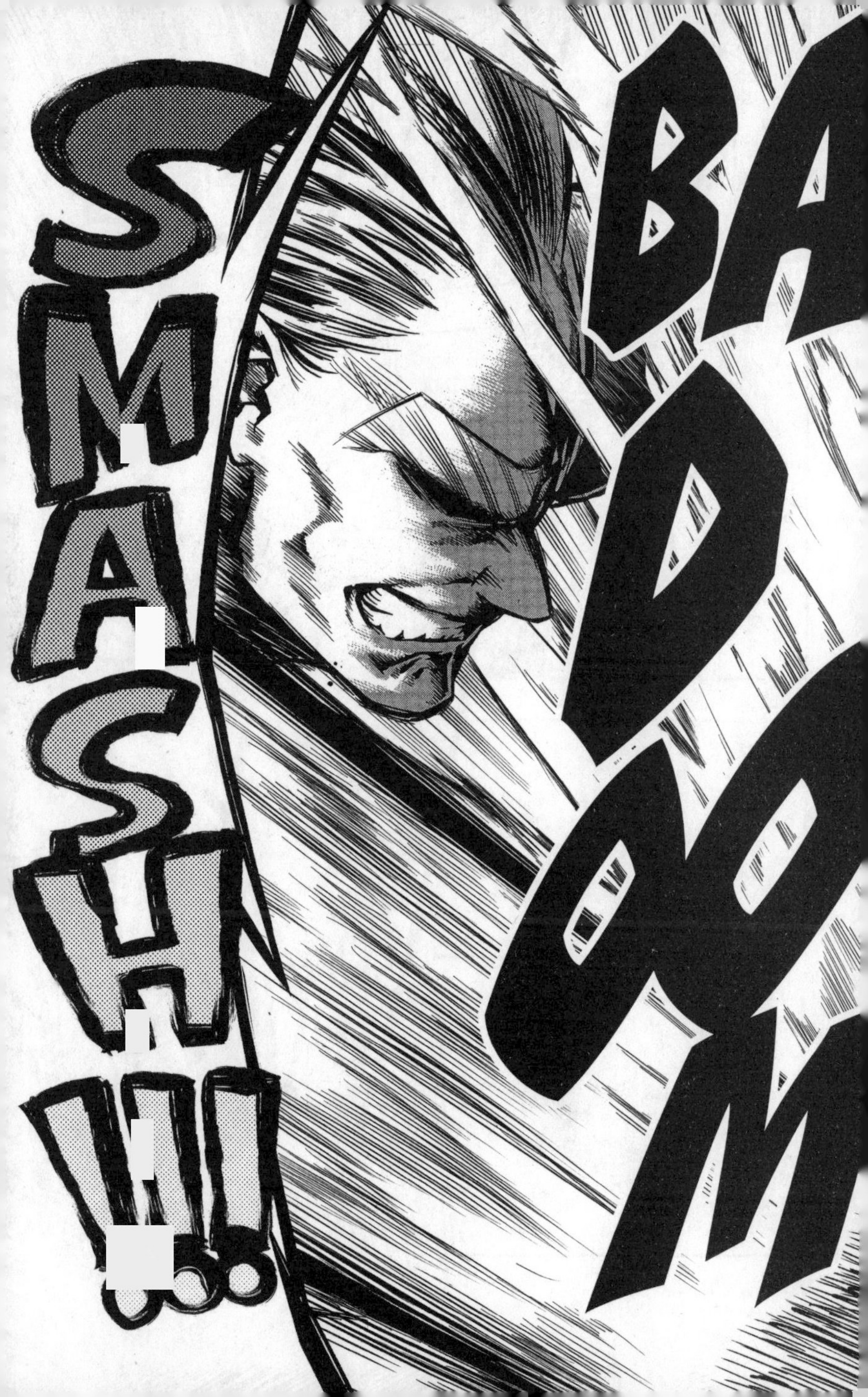
SMASH!!

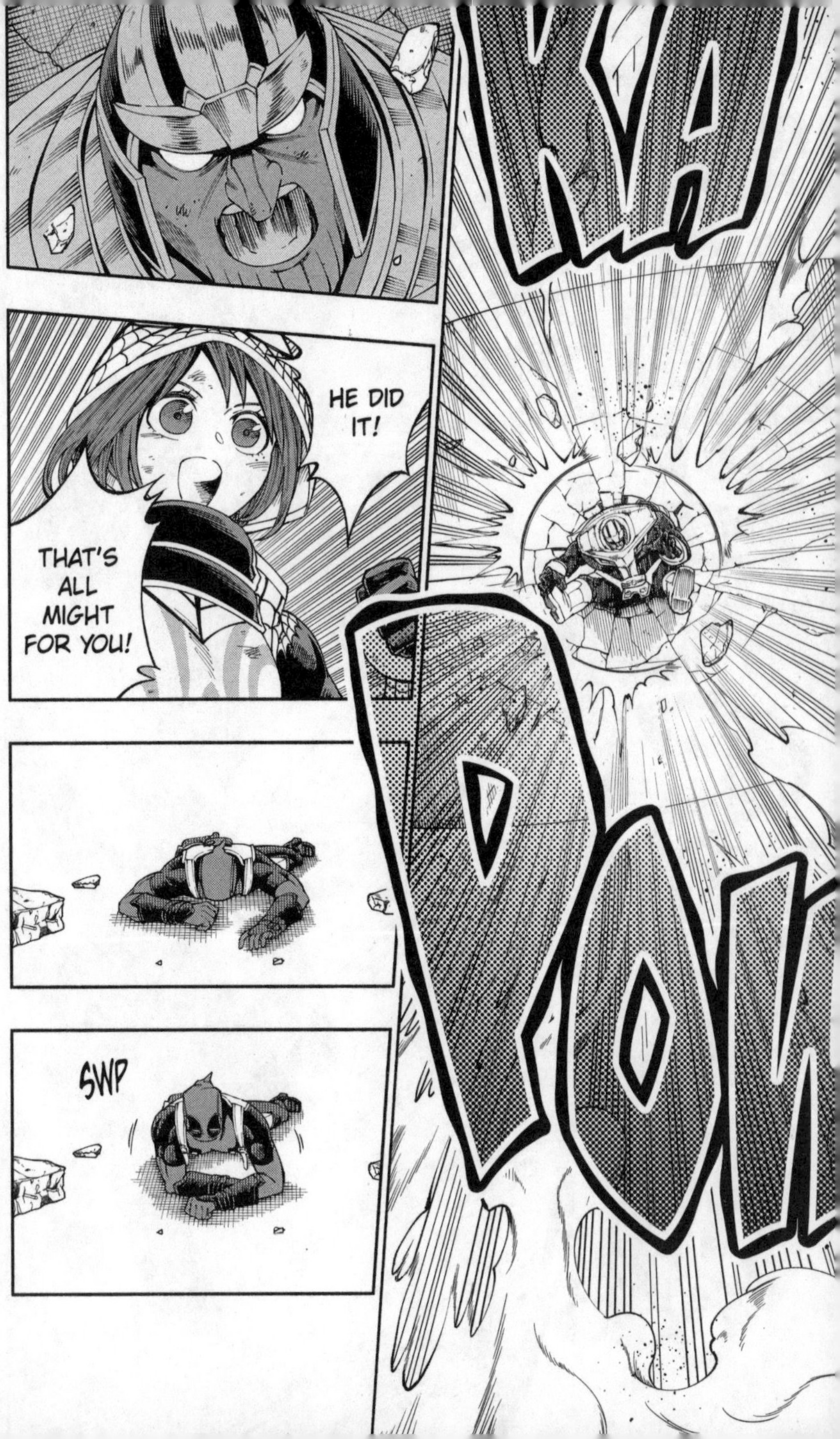
HE DID IT!
THAT'S ALL MIGHT FOR YOU!
SWP

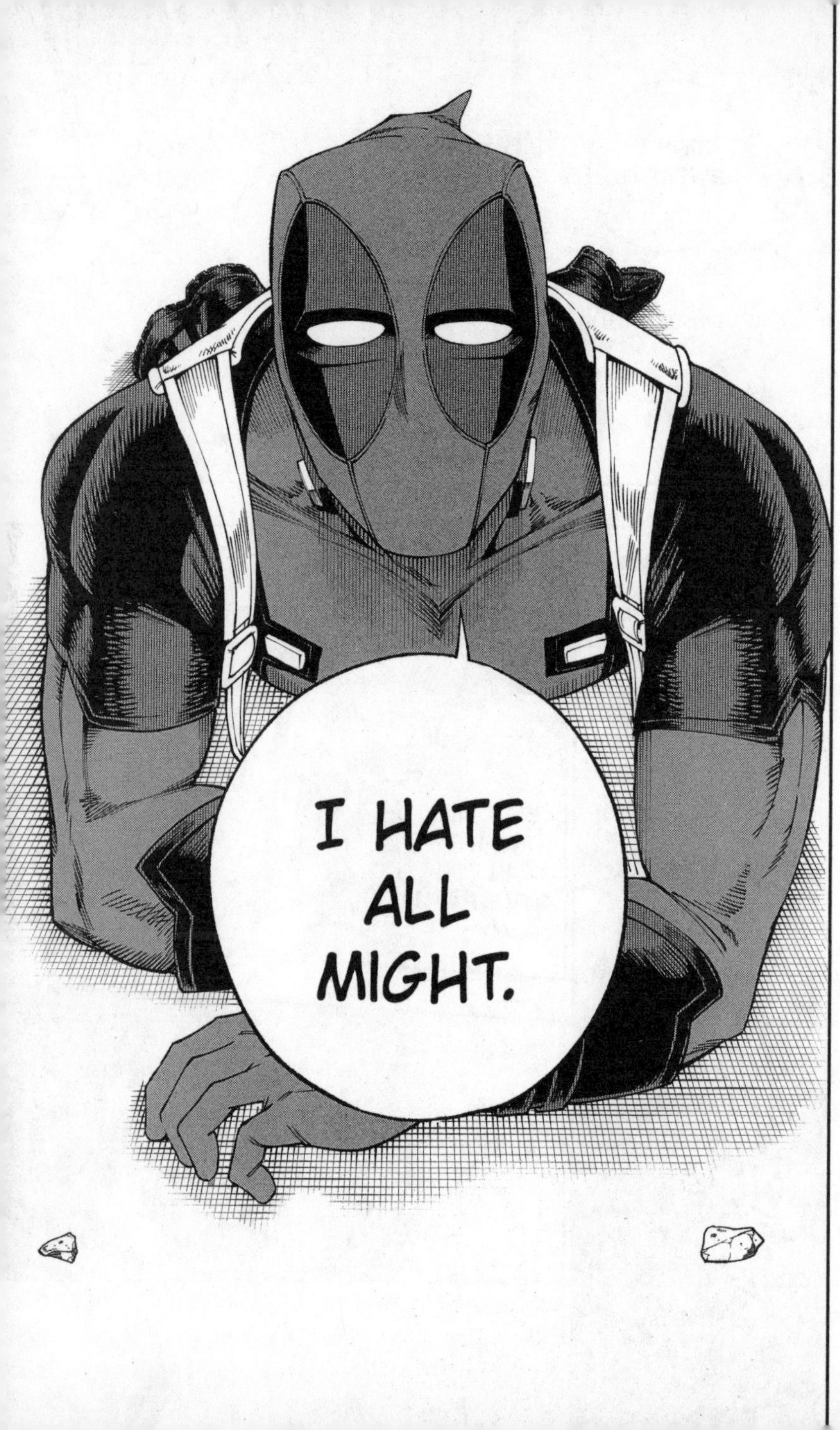
I HATE ALL MIGHT.

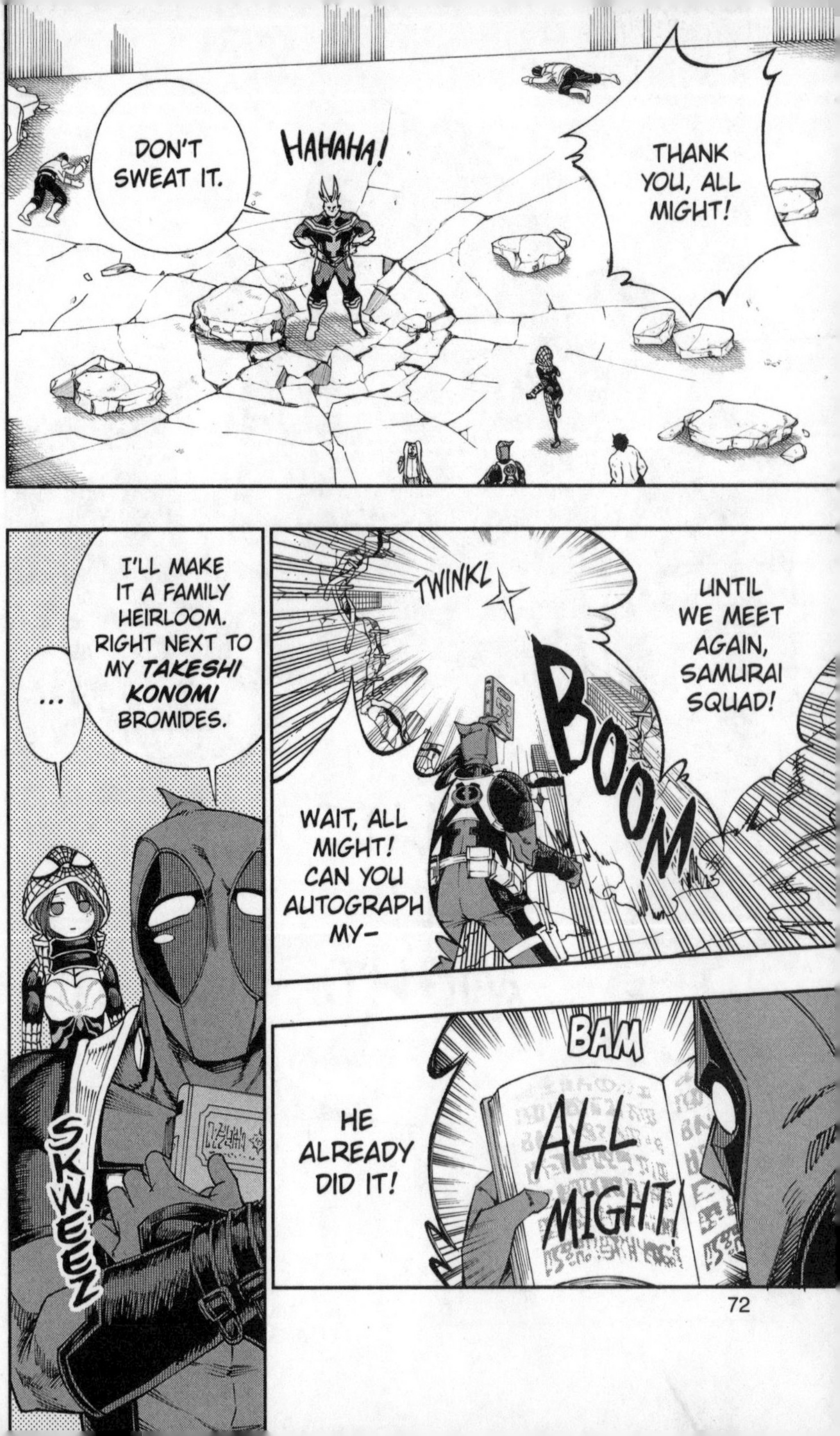
THANK YOU, ALL MIGHT!
HAHAHA!
DON'T SWEAT IT.
UNTIL WE MEET AGAIN, SAMURAI SQUAD!
TWINKL
BOOM
WAIT, ALL MIGHT! CAN YOU AUTOGRAPH MY–
BAM
ALL MIGHT!
HE ALREADY DID IT!
I'LL MAKE IT A FAMILY HEIRLOOM. RIGHT NEXT TO MY *TAKESHI KONOMI* BROMIDES.
...
SKWEEZ

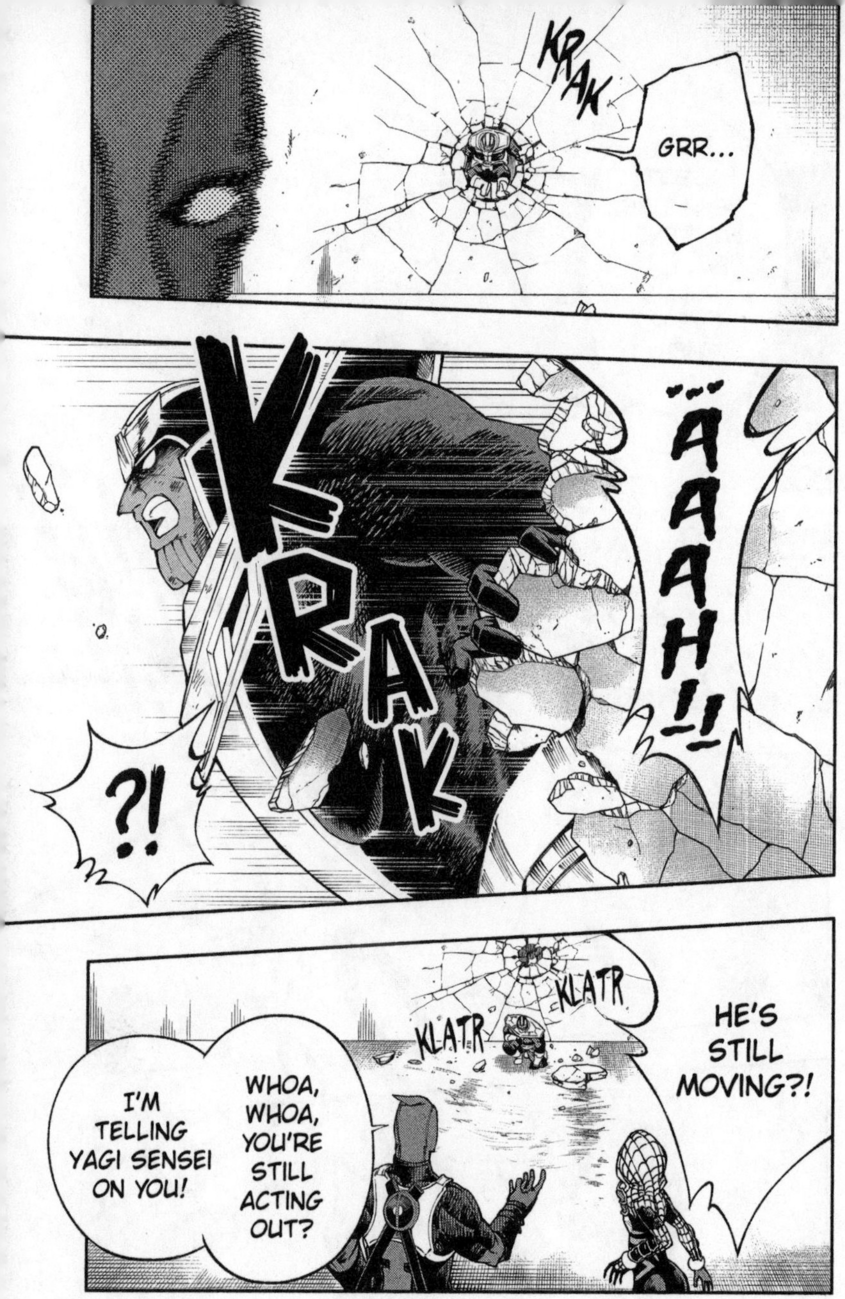
KRAK
GRR...
ÄAAH!!
KRAK
?!
HE'S STILL MOVING?!
KLATR
KLATR
WHOA, WHOA, YOU'RE STILL ACTING OUT?
I'M TELLING YAGI SENSEI ON YOU!

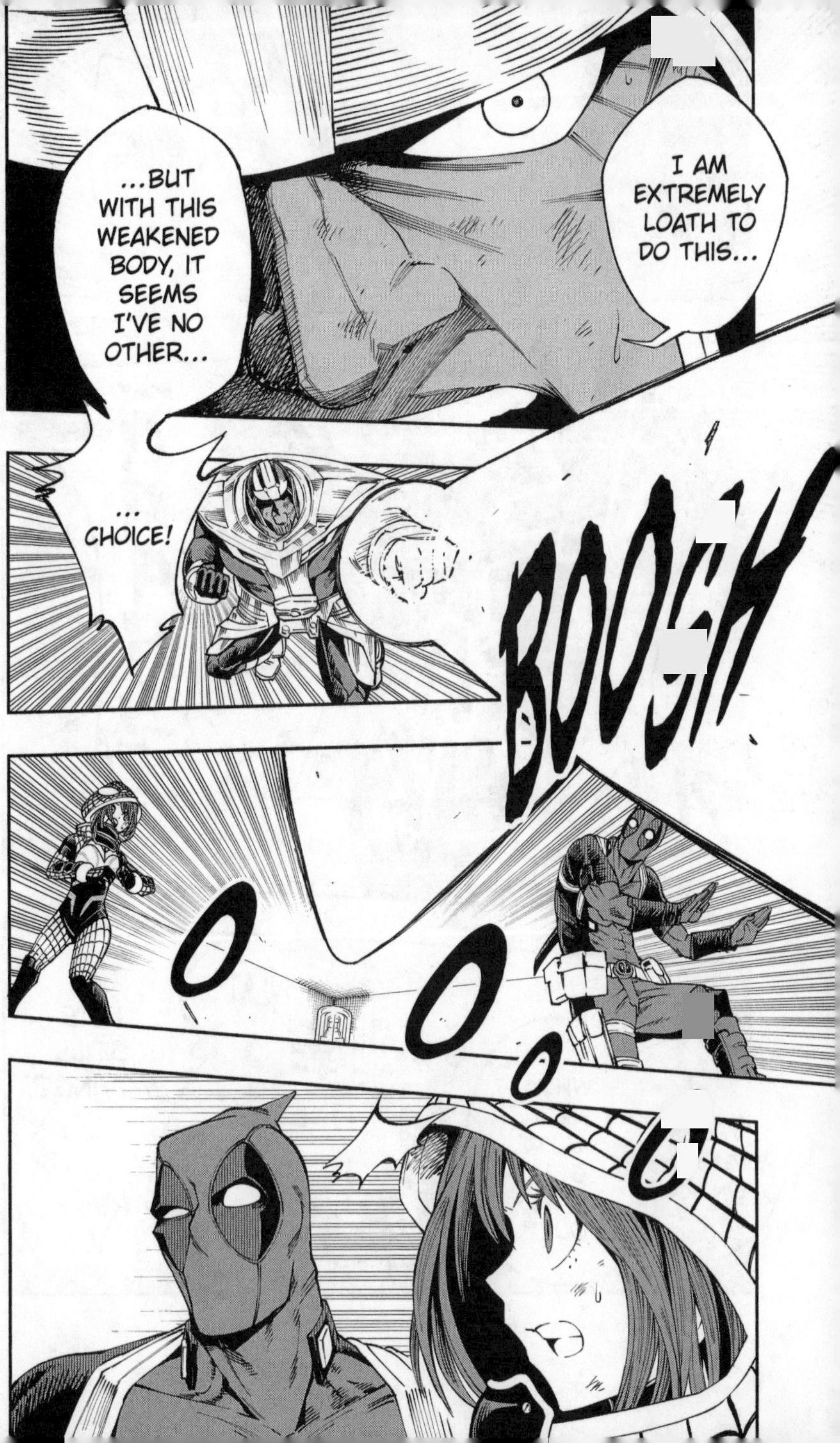
I AM EXTREMELY LOATH TO DO THIS...
...BUT WITH THIS WEAKENED BODY, IT SEEMS I'VE NO OTHER...
...CHOICE!
BOOSH

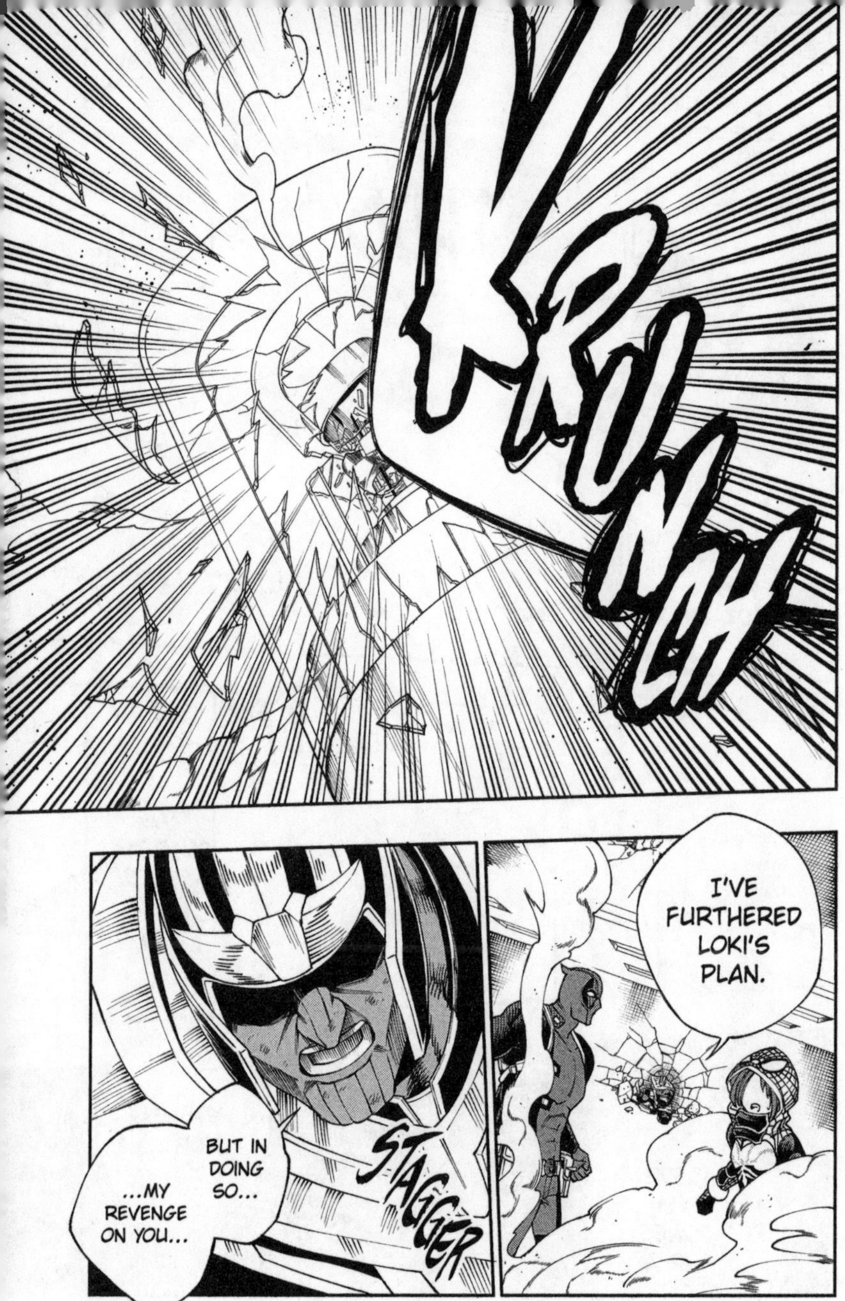
KRUNCH
I'VE FURTHERED LOKI'S PLAN.
BUT IN DOING SO...
...MY REVENGE ON YOU...
STAGGER

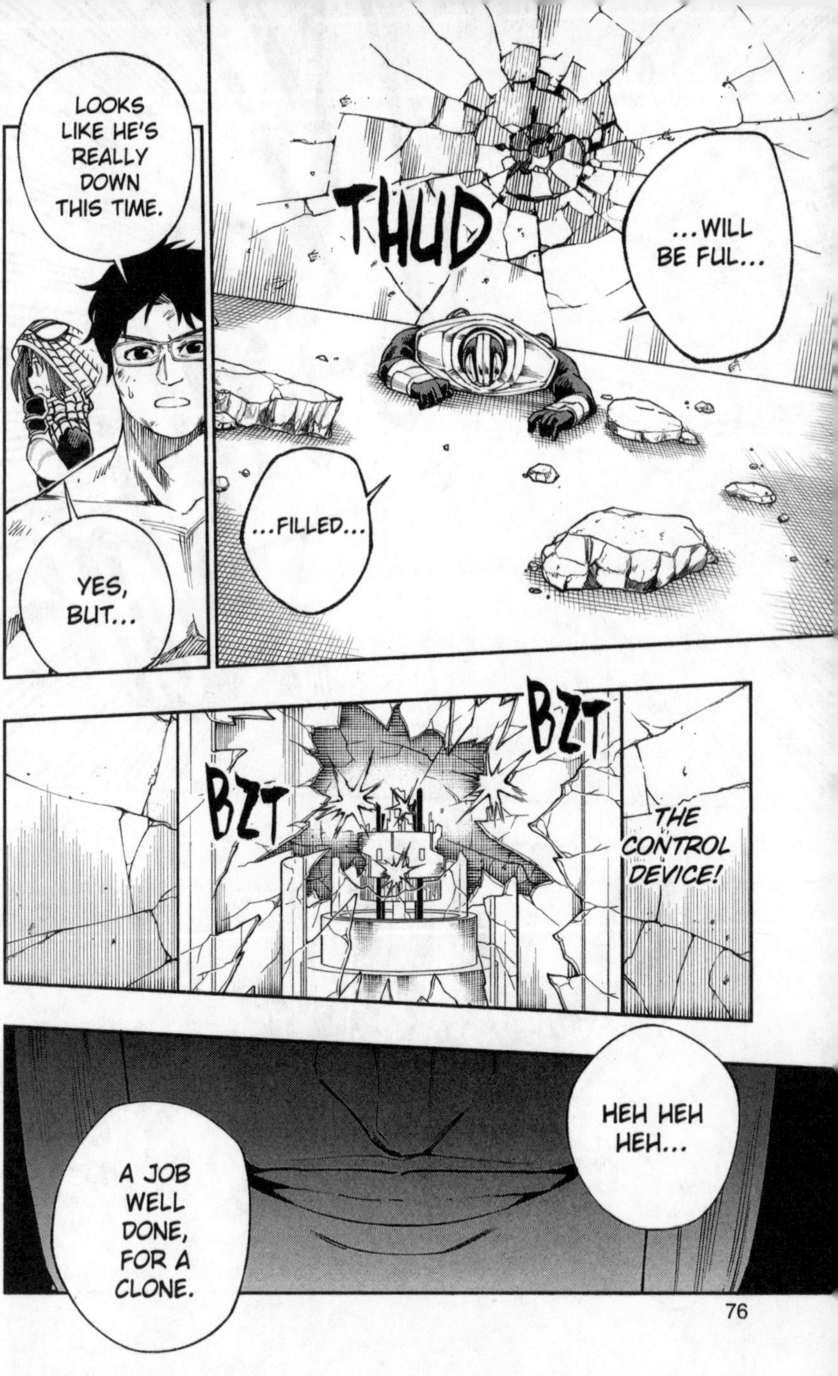
...WILL BE FUL...
THUD
...FILLED...
LOOKS LIKE HE'S REALLY DOWN THIS TIME.
YES, BUT...
THE CONTROL DEVICE!
BZT
BZT
HEH HEH HEH...
A JOB WELL DONE, FOR A CLONE.

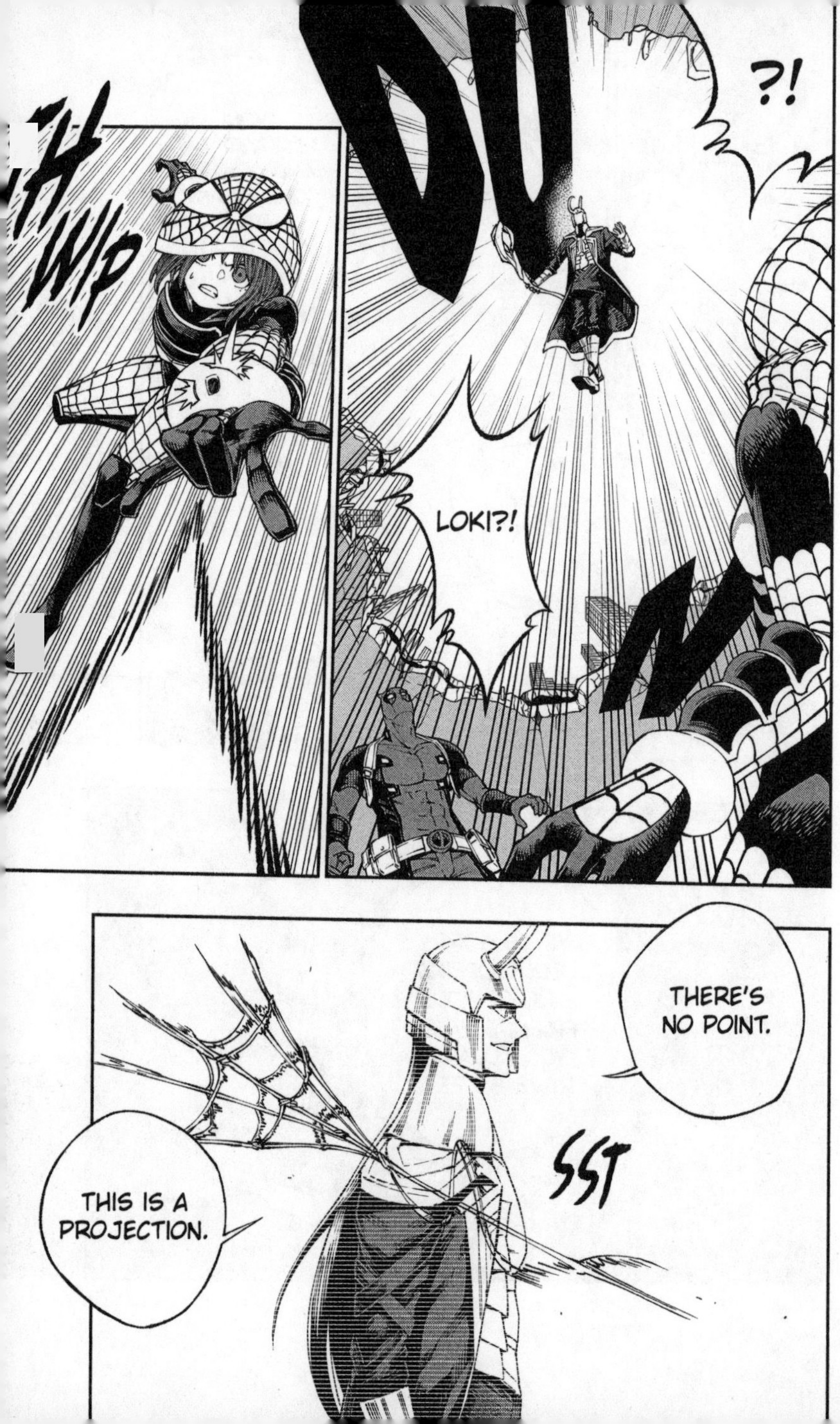
?!
LOKI?!
THWIP
THERE'S NO POINT.
SST
THIS IS A PROJECTION.

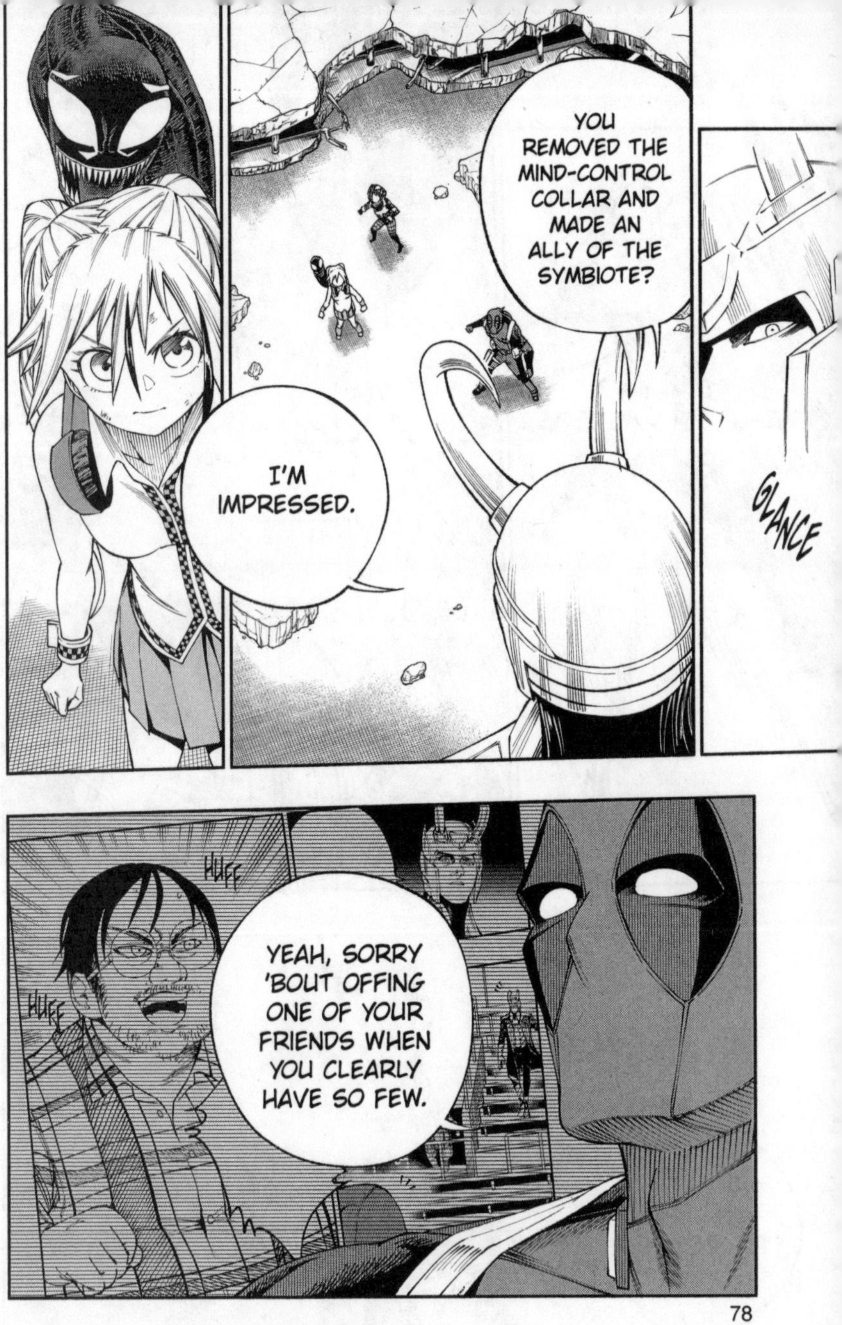
GLANCE
YOU REMOVED THE MIND-CONTROL COLLAR AND MADE AN ALLY OF THE SYMBIOTE?
I'M IMPRESSED.
YEAH, SORRY 'BOUT OFFING ONE OF YOUR FRIENDS WHEN YOU CLEARLY HAVE SO FEW.
HUFF
HUFF

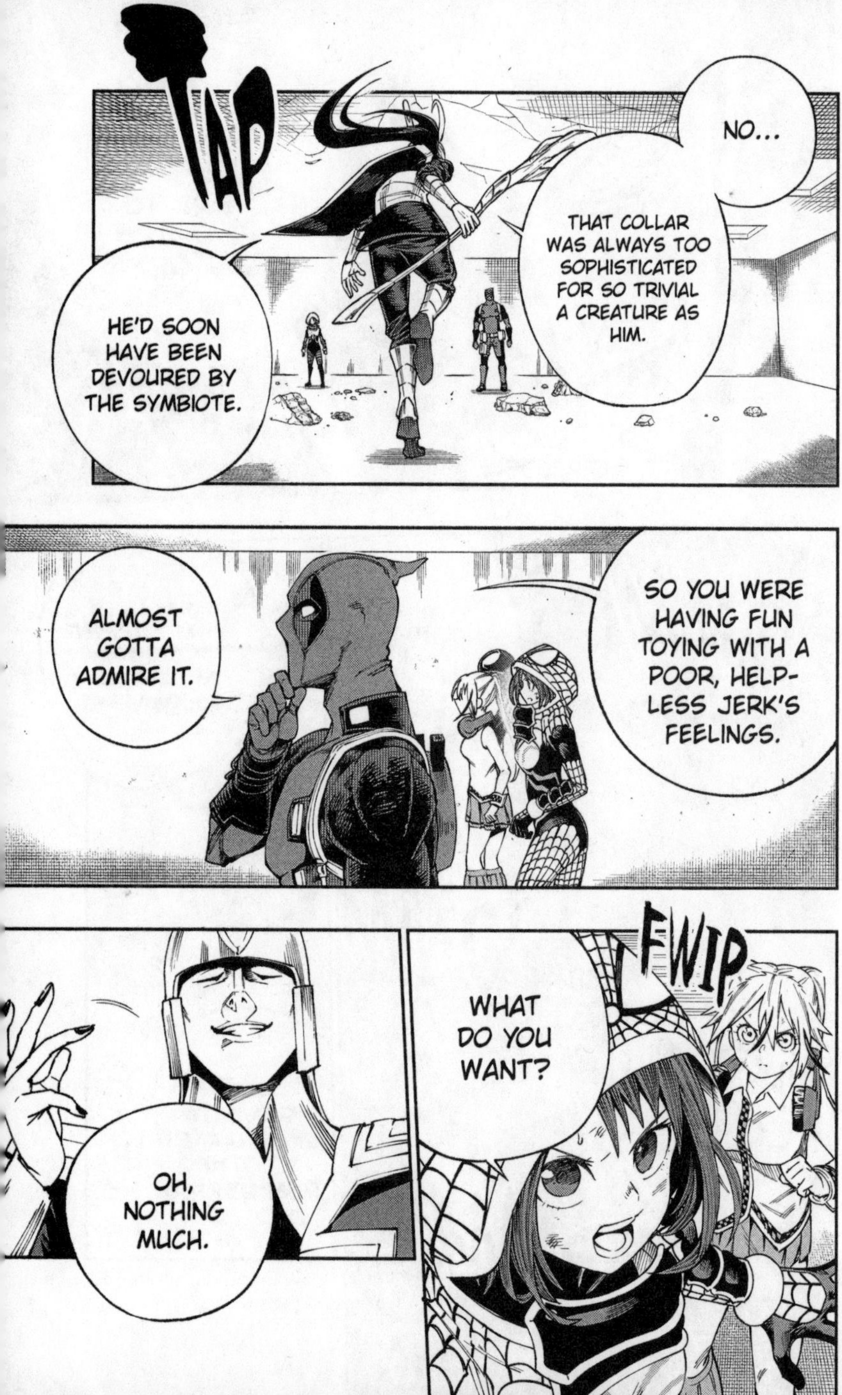
NO...
THAT COLLAR WAS ALWAYS TOO SOPHISTICATED FOR SO TRIVIAL A CREATURE AS HIM.
TAP
HE'D SOON HAVE BEEN DEVOURED BY THE SYMBIOTE.
SO YOU WERE HAVING FUN TOYING WITH A POOR, HELP-LESS JERK'S FEELINGS.
ALMOST GOTTA ADMIRE IT.
FWIP
WHAT DO YOU WANT?
OH, NOTHING MUCH.

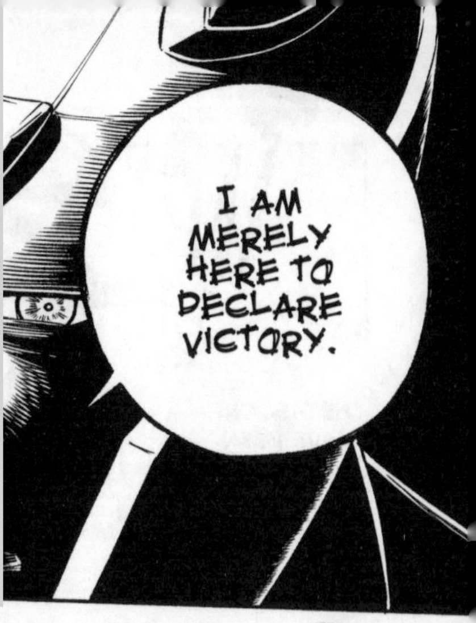
I AM MERELY HERE TO DECLARE VICTORY.

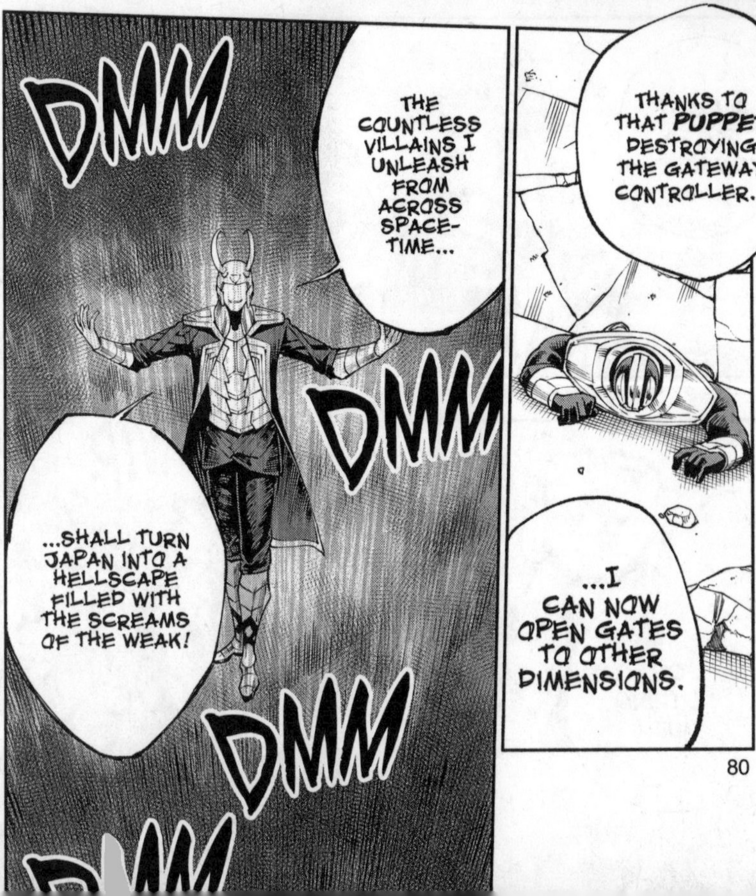
THANKS TO THAT **PUPPET** DESTROYING THE GATEWAY CONTROLLER...
...I CAN NOW OPEN GATES TO OTHER DIMENSIONS.
DMM
THE COUNTLESS VILLAINS I UNLEASH FROM ACROSS SPACE-TIME...
DMM
...SHALL TURN JAPAN INTO A HELLSCAPE FILLED WITH THE SCREAMS OF THE WEAK!
DMM

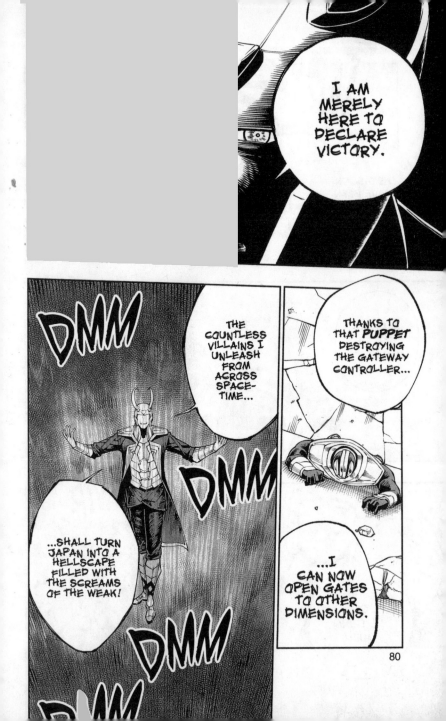

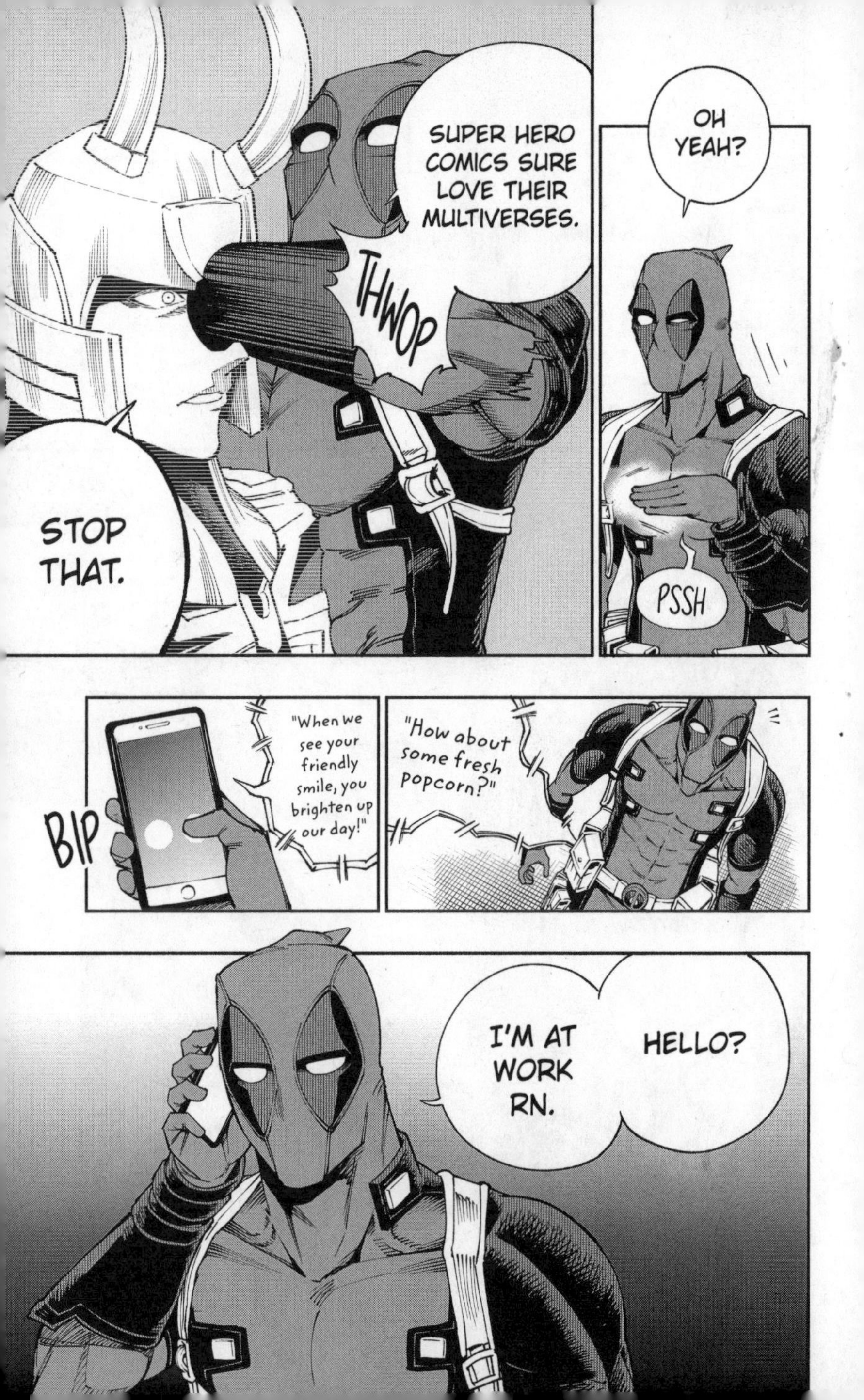
OH YEAH?
PSSH
SUPER HERO COMICS SURE LOVE THEIR MULTIVERSES.
THWOP
STOP THAT.
"How about some fresh popcorn?"
"When we see your friendly smile, you brighten up our day!"
BIP
HELLO?
I'M AT WORK RN.

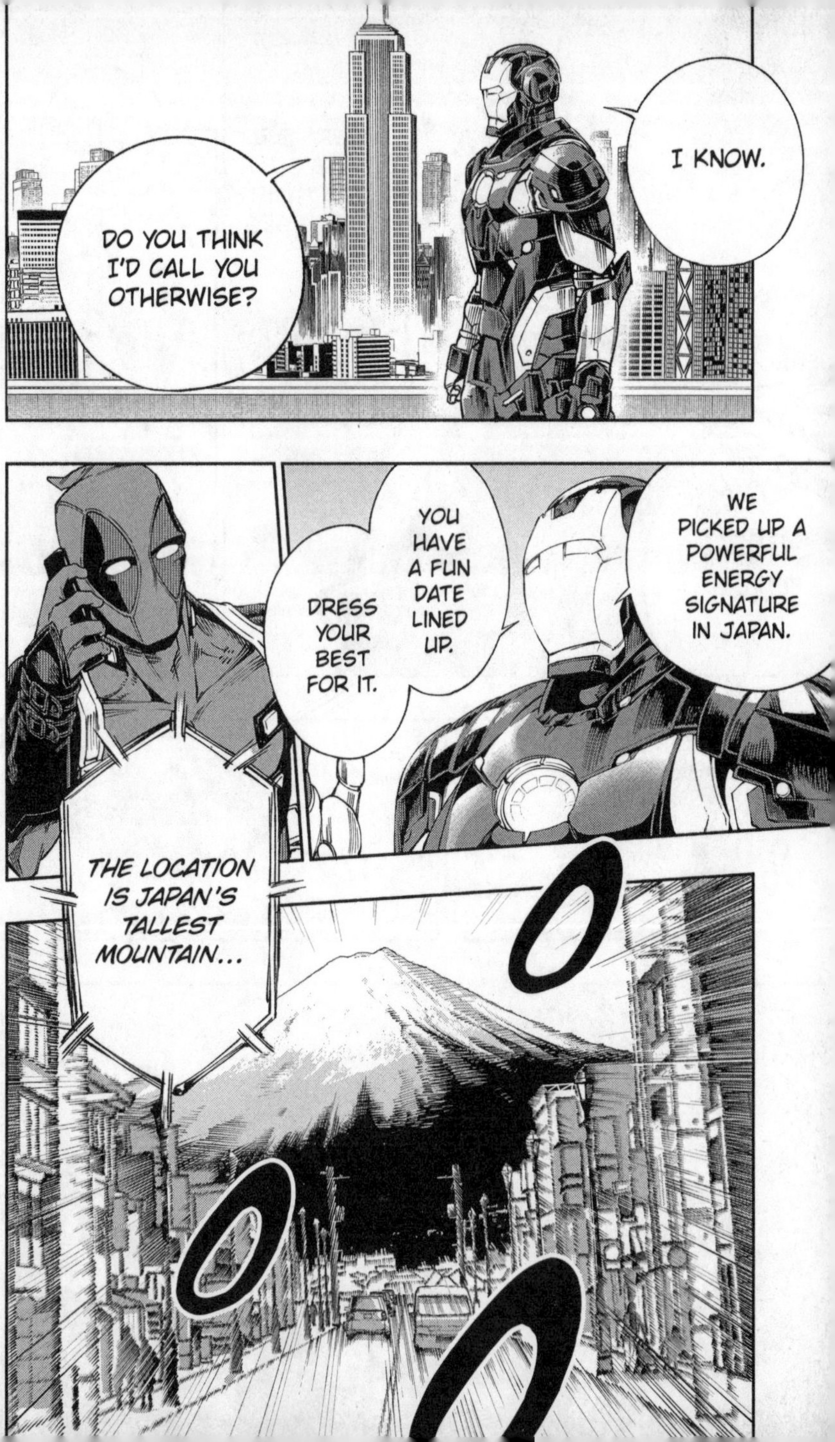
I KNOW.
DO YOU THINK I'D CALL YOU OTHERWISE?
WE PICKED UP A POWERFUL ENERGY SIGNATURE IN JAPAN.
YOU HAVE A FUN DATE LINED UP.
DRESS YOUR BEST FOR IT.
THE LOCATION IS JAPAN'S TALLEST MOUNTAIN...

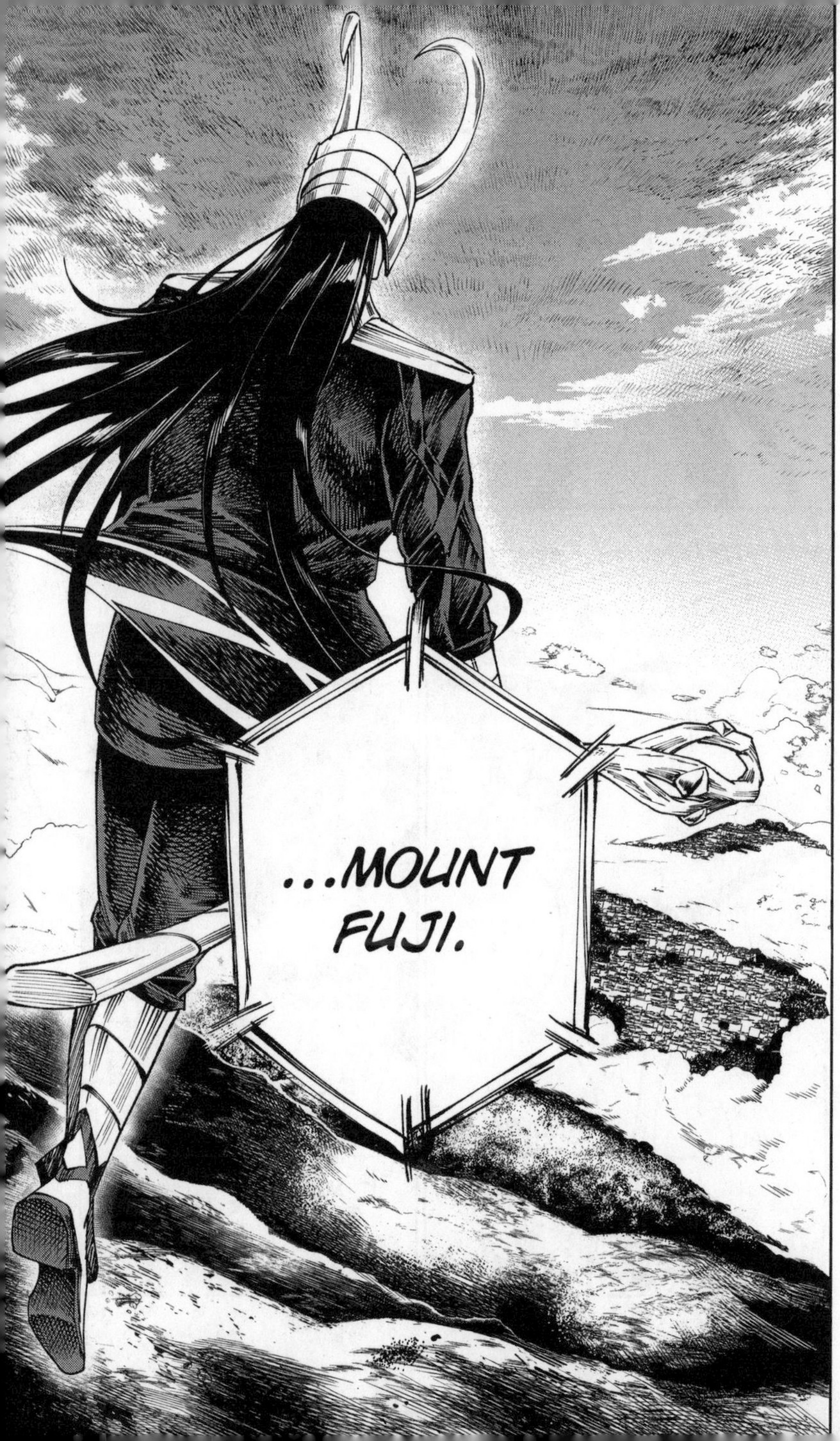
...MOUNT FUJI.

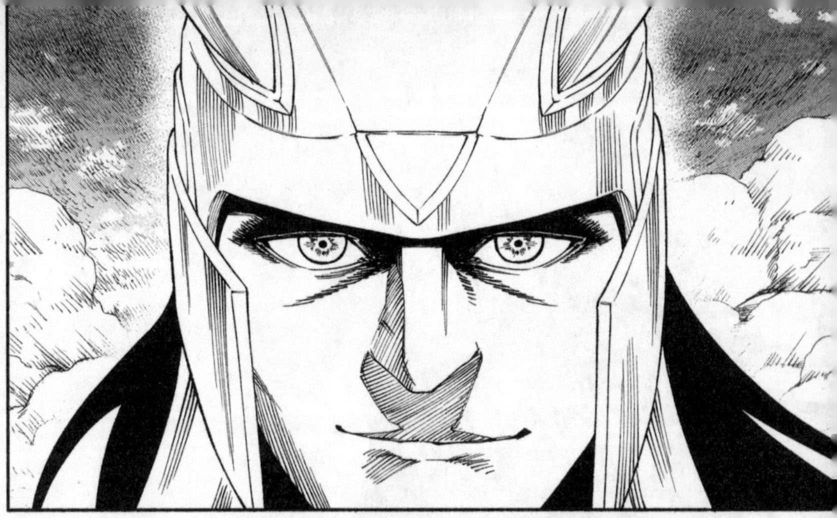

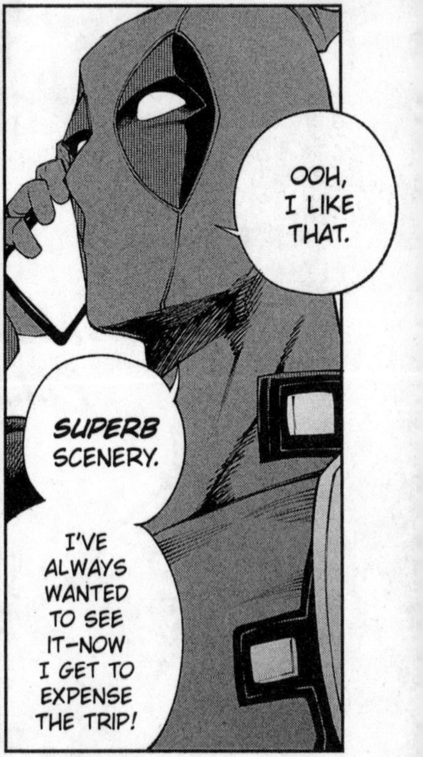
OOH, I LIKE THAT.
SUPERB SCENERY.
I'VE ALWAYS WANTED TO SEE IT—NOW I GET TO EXPENSE THE TRIP!

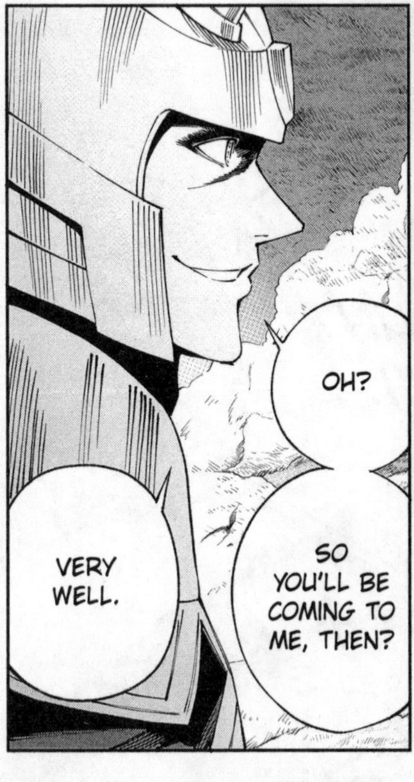
OH?
SO YOU'LL BE COMING TO ME, THEN?
VERY WELL.

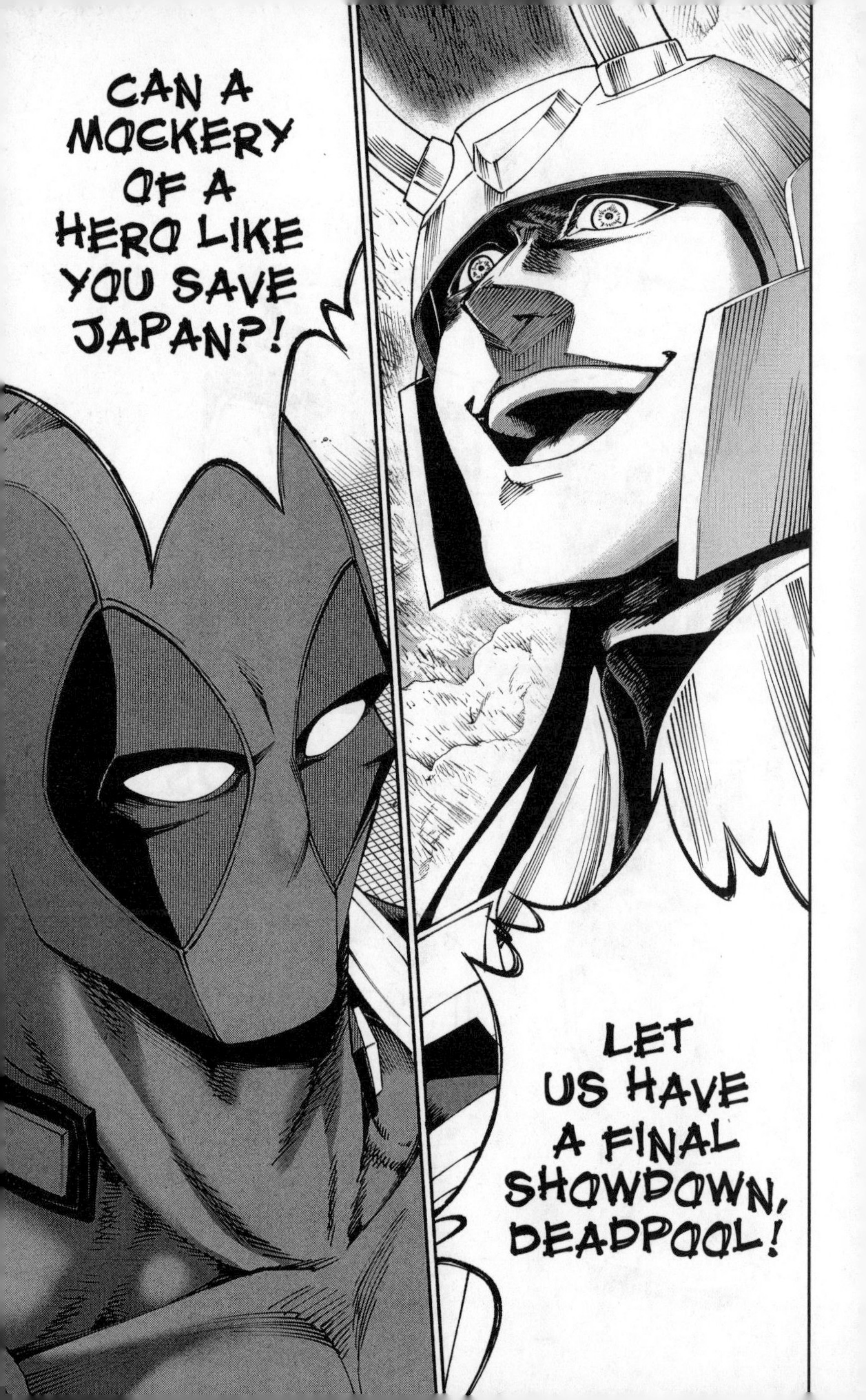
CAN A MOCKERY OF A HERO LIKE YOU SAVE JAPAN?!
LET US HAVE A FINAL SHOWDOWN, DEADPOOL!

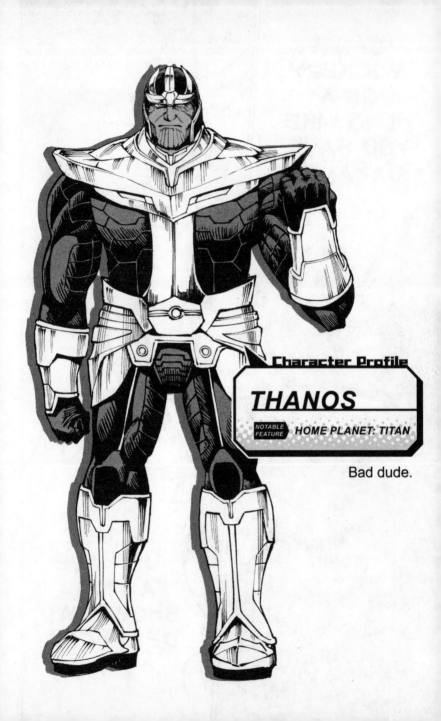

Character Profile

THANOS

NOTABLE FEATURE **HOME PLANET: TITAN**

Bad dude.

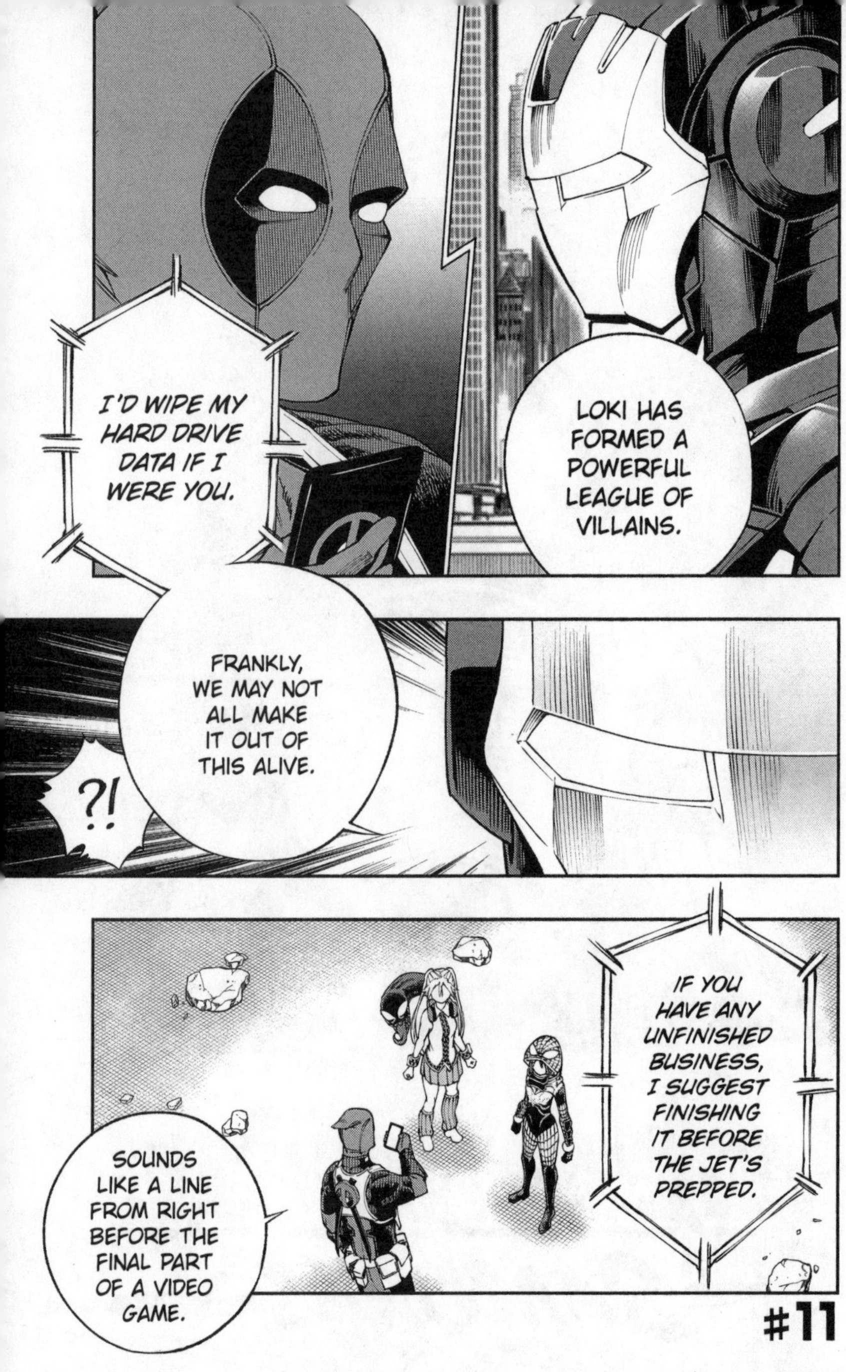
LOKI HAS FORMED A POWERFUL LEAGUE OF VILLAINS.
I'D WIPE MY HARD DRIVE DATA IF I WERE YOU.
FRANKLY, WE MAY NOT ALL MAKE IT OUT OF THIS ALIVE.
?!
IF YOU HAVE ANY UNFINISHED BUSINESS, I SUGGEST FINISHING IT BEFORE THE JET'S PREPPED.
SOUNDS LIKE A LINE FROM RIGHT BEFORE THE FINAL PART OF A VIDEO GAME.

#11

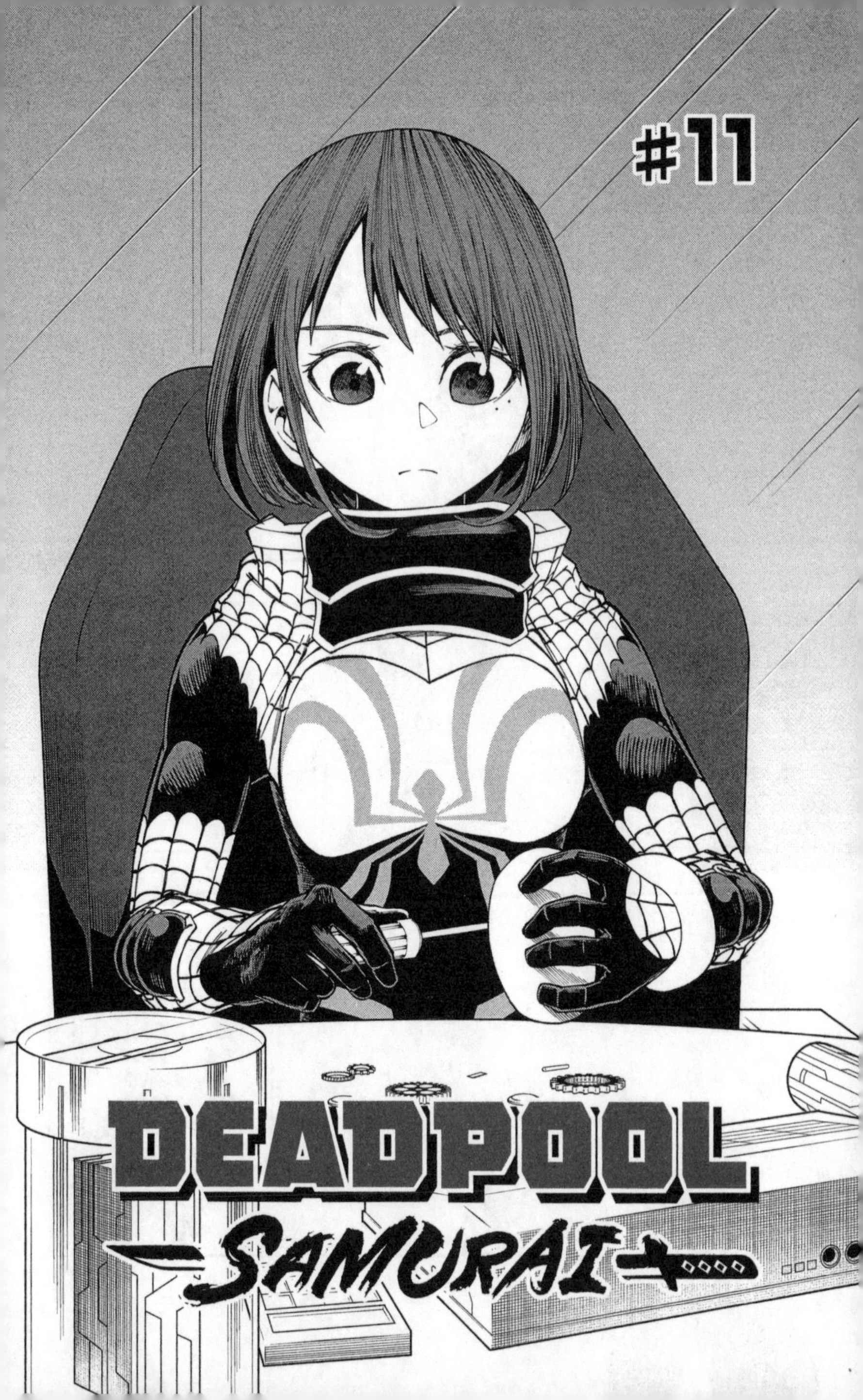
#11
DEADPOOL
SAMURAI

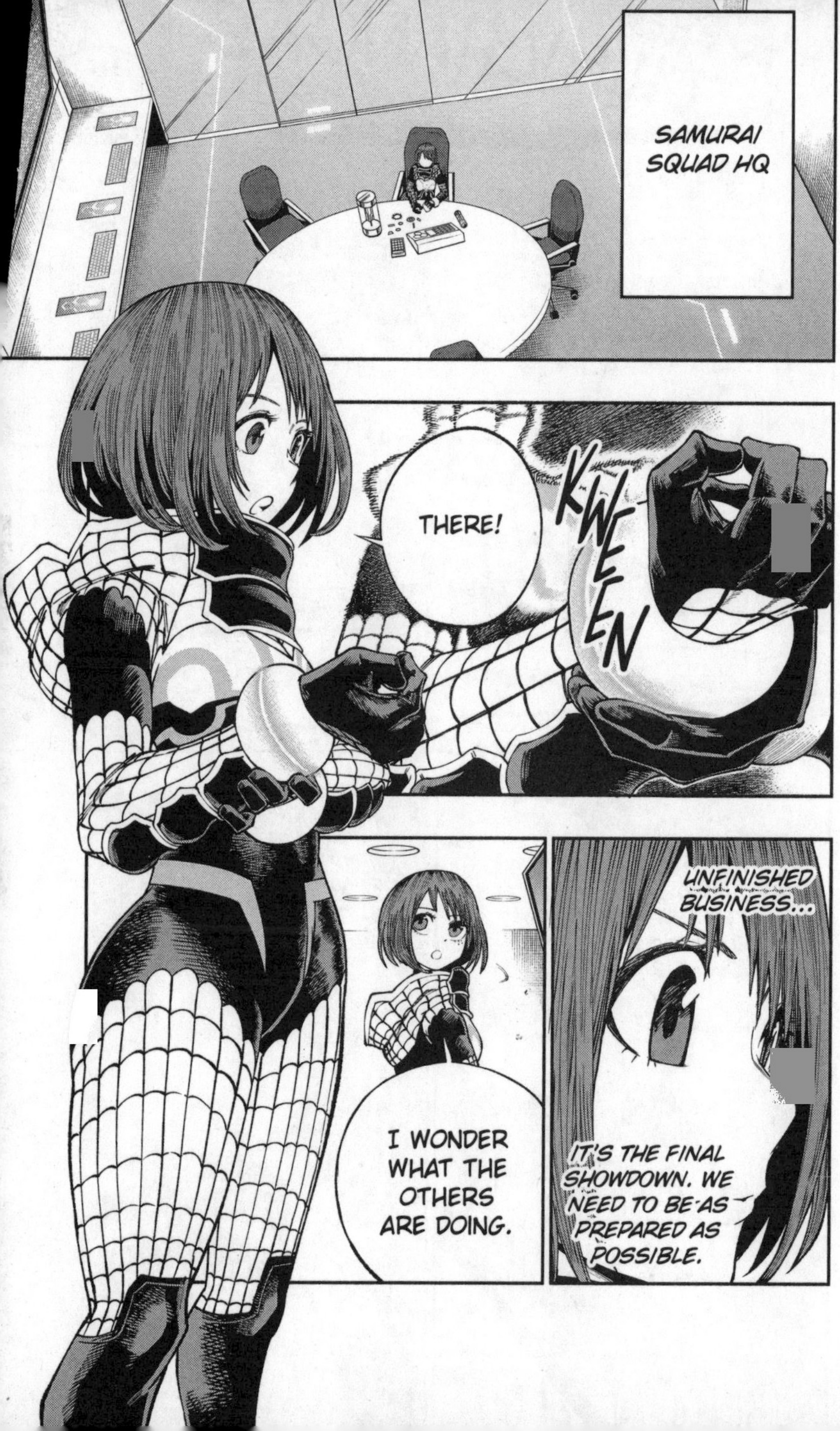
SAMURAI SQUAD HQ
KWEEN
THERE!
UNFINISHED BUSINESS...
IT'S THE FINAL SHOWDOWN. WE NEED TO BE AS PREPARED AS POSSIBLE.
I WONDER WHAT THE OTHERS ARE DOING.

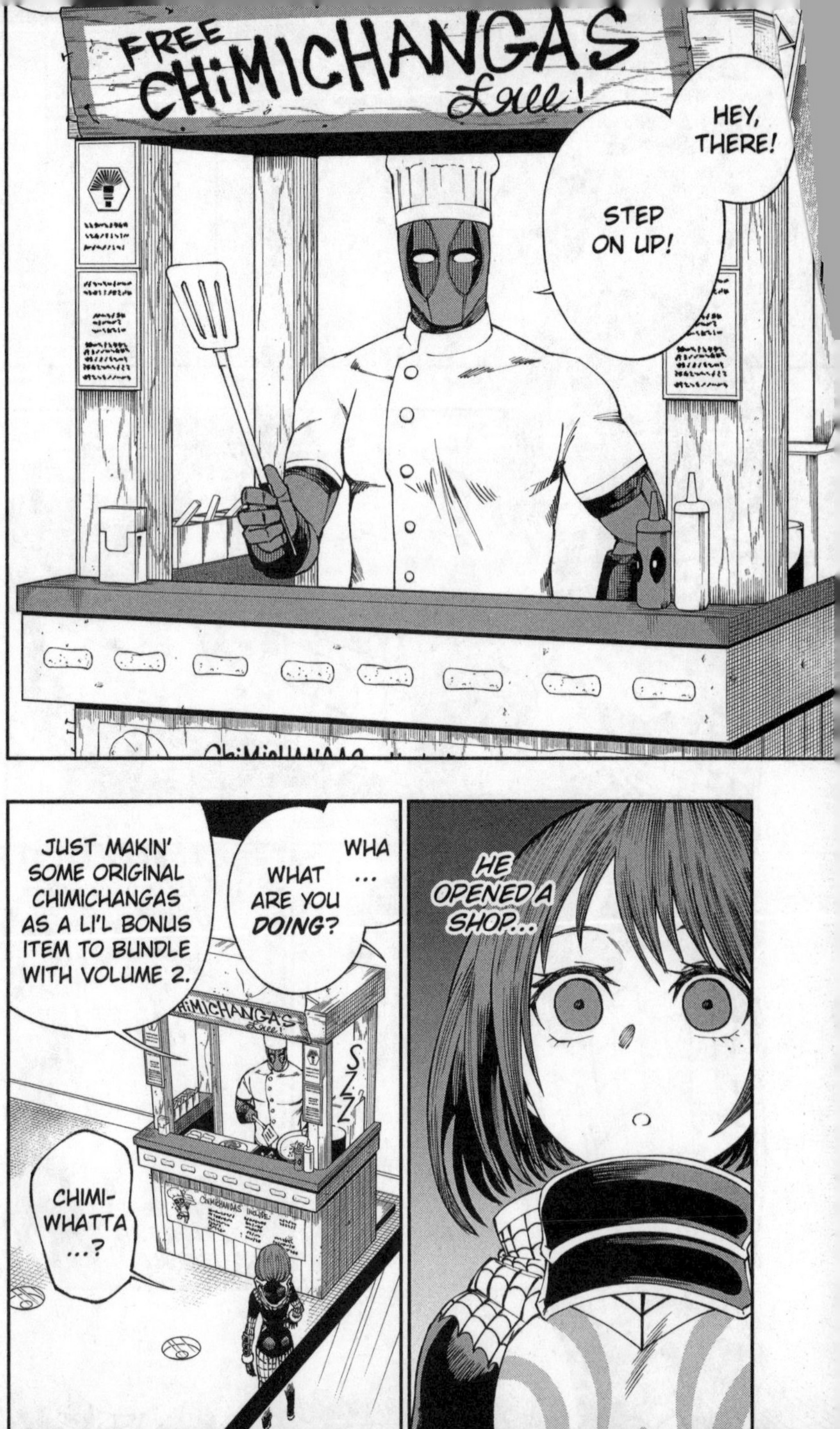
FREE CHiMiCHANGAS Free!
HEY, THERE!
STEP ON UP!
HE OPENED A SHOP...
WHA ...
WHAT ARE YOU *DOING*?
JUST MAKIN' SOME ORIGINAL CHIMICHANGAS AS A LI'L BONUS ITEM TO BUNDLE WITH VOLUME 2.
CHiMICHANGAS Free!
SZZZ
CHIMI-WHATTA ...?

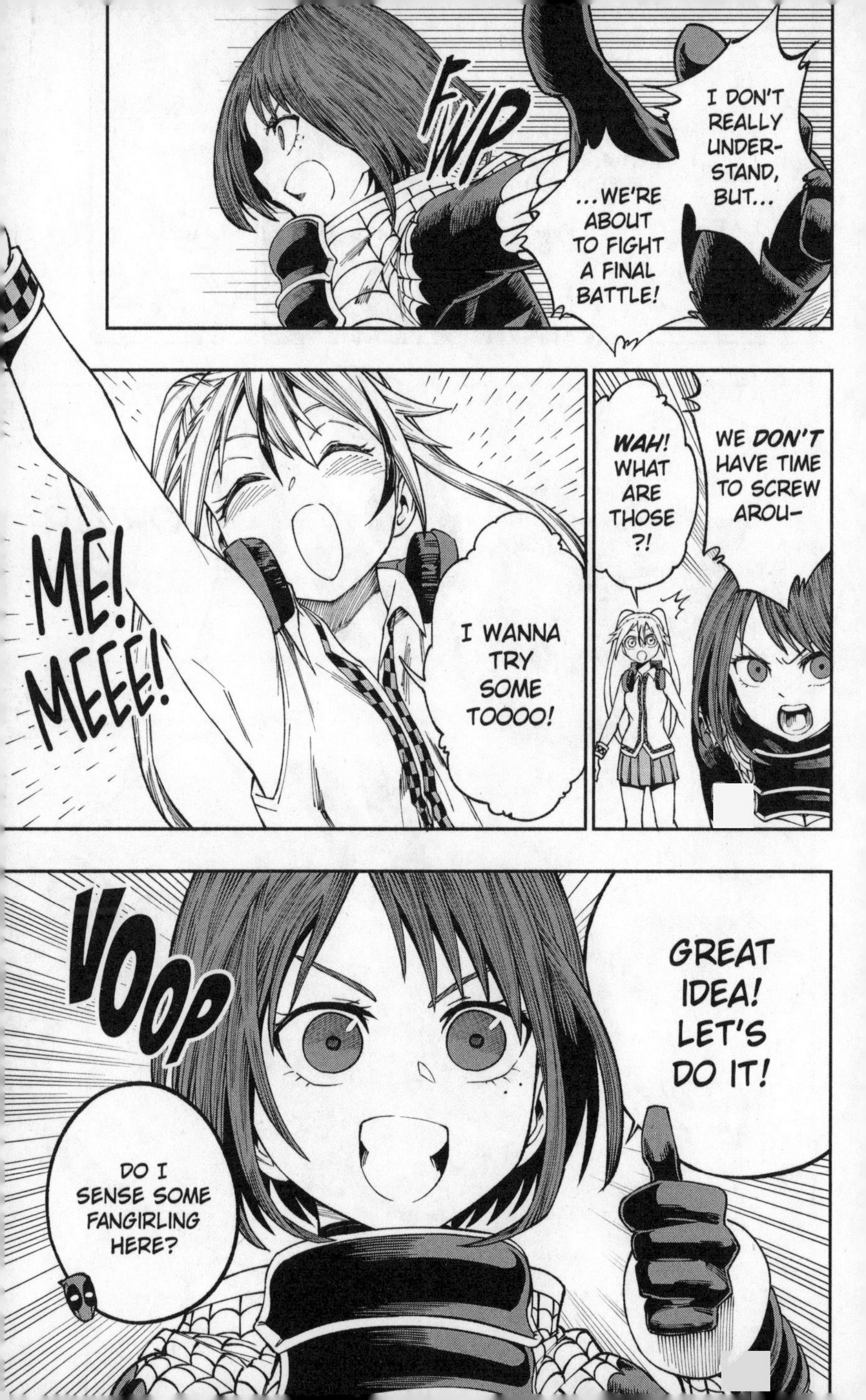
I DON'T REALLY UNDER-STAND, BUT...
...WE'RE ABOUT TO FIGHT A FINAL BATTLE!
FWIP
WE DON'T HAVE TIME TO SCREW AROU-
WAH! WHAT ARE THOSE ?!
I WANNA TRY SOME TOOOO!
ME! MEEE!
GREAT IDEA! LET'S DO IT!
VOOP
DO I SENSE SOME FANGIRLING HERE?

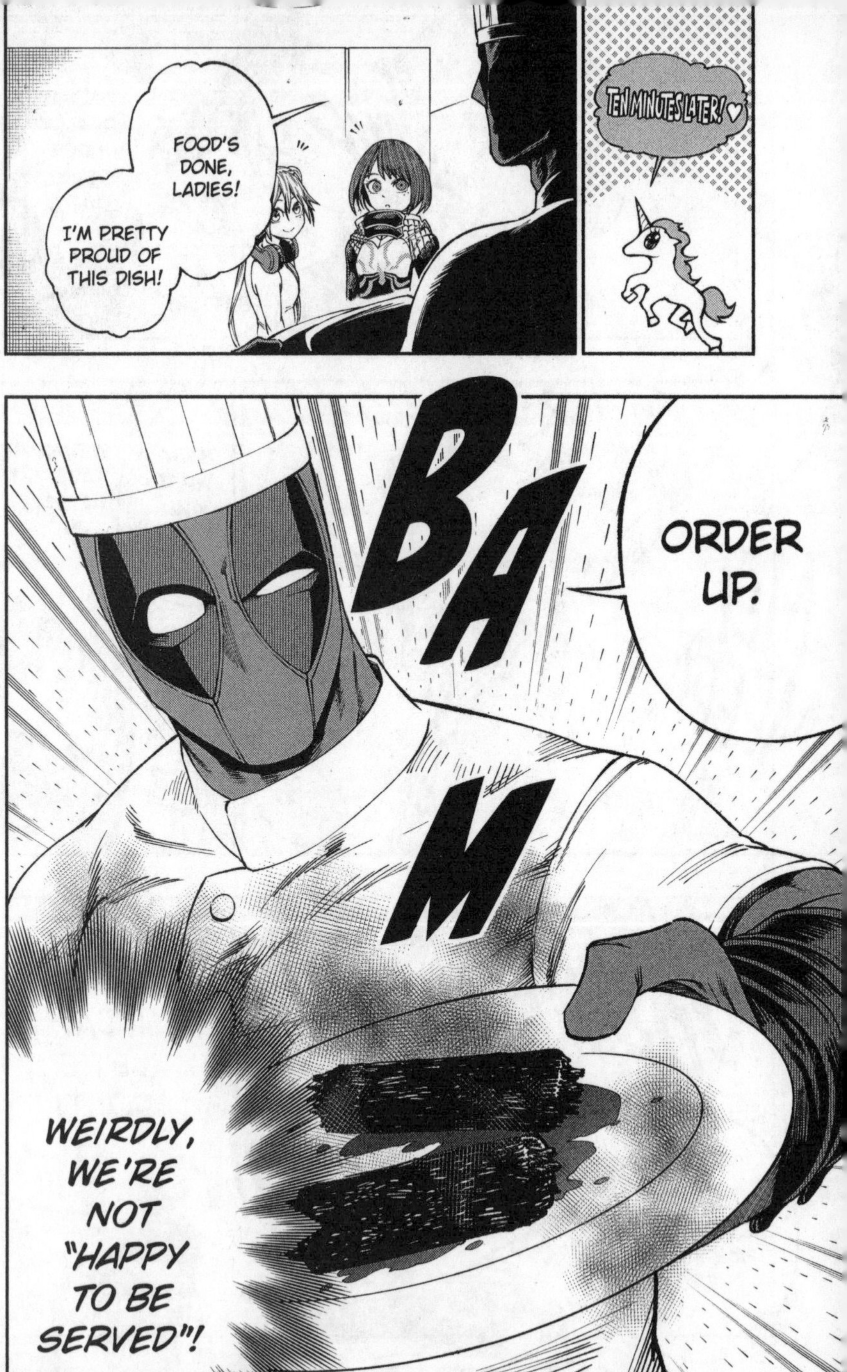
TEN MINUTES LATER! ♥
FOOD'S DONE, LADIES!
I'M PRETTY PROUD OF THIS DISH!
ORDER UP.
BAM
WEIRDLY, WE'RE NOT "HAPPY TO BE SERVED"!

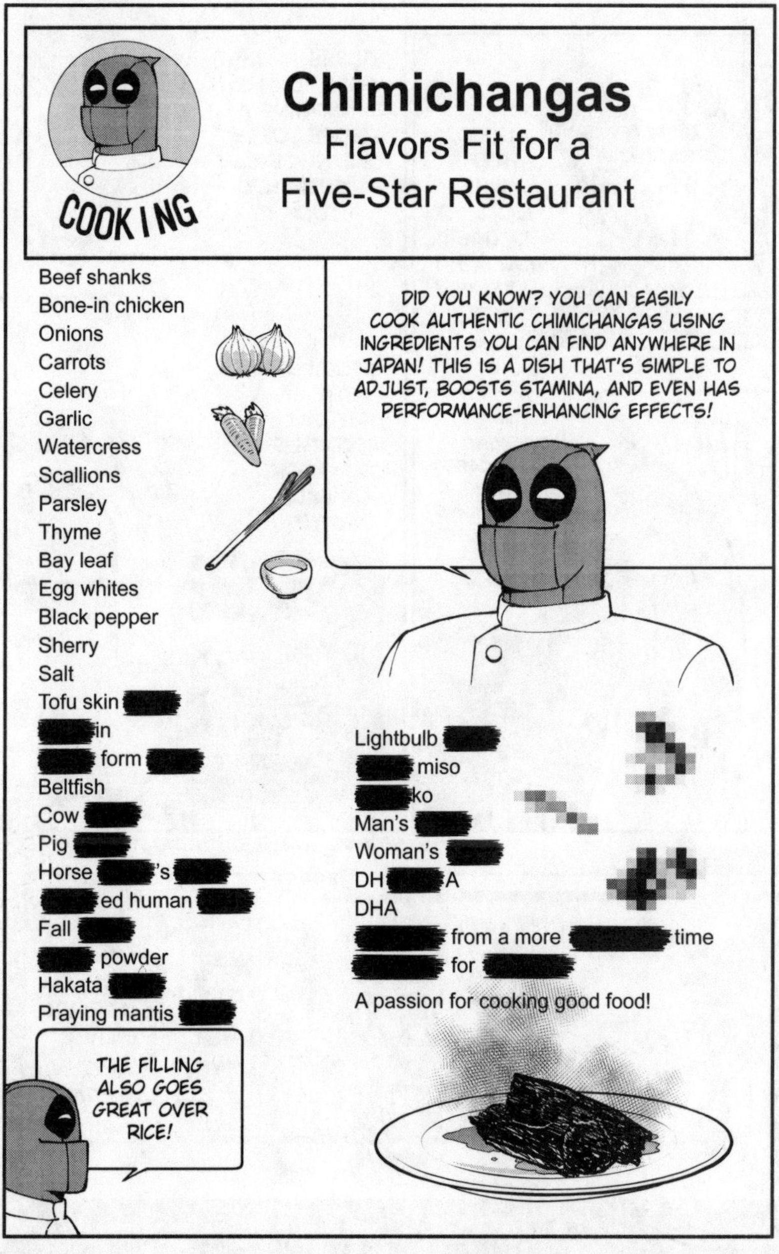
COOKING
Chimichangas
Flavors Fit for a
Five-Star Restaurant
DID YOU KNOW? YOU CAN EASILY COOK AUTHENTIC CHIMICHANGAS USING INGREDIENTS YOU CAN FIND ANYWHERE IN JAPAN! THIS IS A DISH THAT'S SIMPLE TO ADJUST, BOOSTS STAMINA, AND EVEN HAS PERFORMANCE-ENHANCING EFFECTS!
Lightbulb [redacted]
[redacted] miso
[redacted]ko
Man's [redacted]
Woman's [redacted]
DH[redacted]A
DHA
[redacted] from a more [redacted]time
[redacted] for [redacted]
A passion for cooking good food!
Beef shanks
Bone-in chicken
Onions
Carrots
Celery
Garlic
Watercress
Scallions
Parsley
Thyme
Bay leaf
Egg whites
Black pepper
Sherry
Salt
Tofu skin [redacted]
[redacted]in
[redacted] form [redacted]
Beltfish
Cow [redacted]
Pig [redacted]
Horse [redacted]'s [redacted]
[redacted]ed human [redacted]
Fall [redacted]
[redacted] powder
Hakata [redacted]
Praying mantis [redacted]
THE FILLING ALSO GOES GREAT OVER RICE!

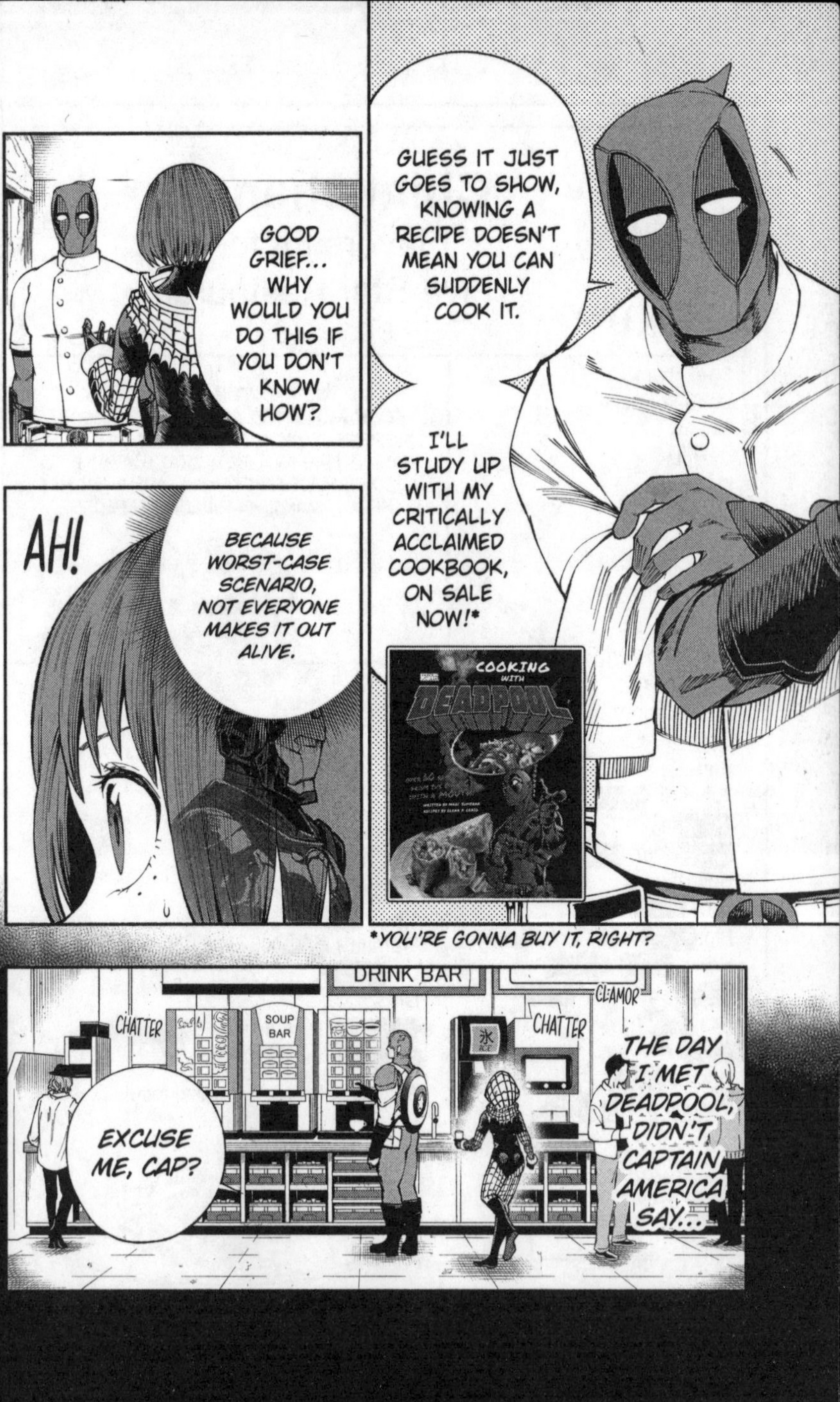
GUESS IT JUST GOES TO SHOW, KNOWING A RECIPE DOESN'T MEAN YOU CAN SUDDENLY COOK IT.
I'LL STUDY UP WITH MY CRITICALLY ACCLAIMED COOKBOOK, ON SALE NOW!*
COOKING WITH DEADPOOL
GOOD GRIEF... WHY WOULD YOU DO THIS IF YOU DON'T KNOW HOW?
AH!
BECAUSE WORST-CASE SCENARIO, NOT EVERYONE MAKES IT OUT ALIVE.
*YOU'RE GONNA BUY IT, RIGHT?
THE DAY I MET DEADPOOL, DIDN'T CAPTAIN AMERICA SAY...
CLAMOR
CHATTER
DRINK BAR
SOUP BAR
CHATTER
EXCUSE ME, CAP?

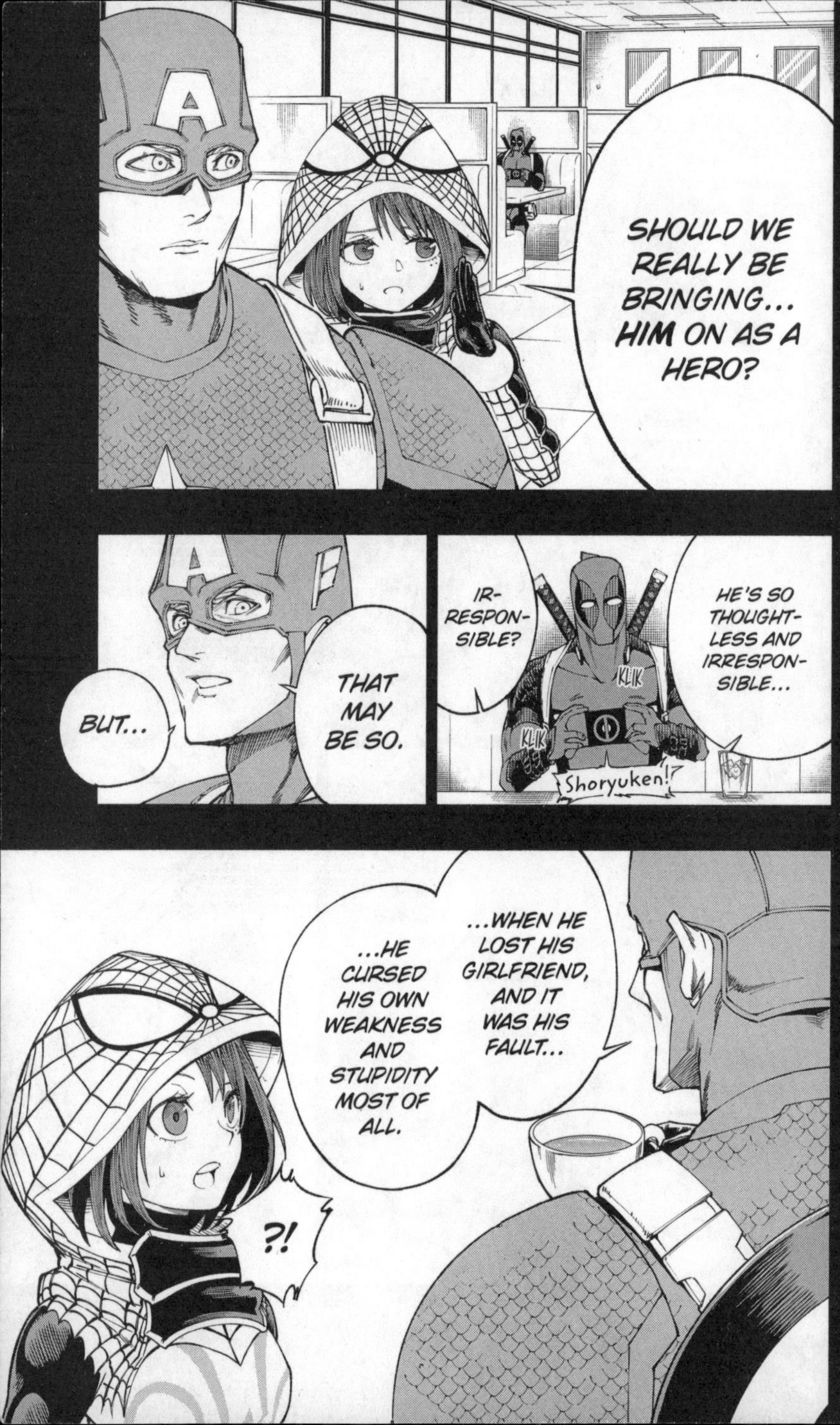
SHOULD WE REALLY BE BRINGING... HIM ON AS A HERO?
HE'S SO THOUGHTLESS AND IRRESPONSIBLE...
IR-RESPONSIBLE?
KLIK
KLIK
Shoryuken!
THAT MAY BE SO.
BUT...
...WHEN HE LOST HIS GIRLFRIEND, AND IT WAS HIS FAULT...
...HE CURSED HIS OWN WEAKNESS AND STUPIDITY MOST OF ALL.
?!

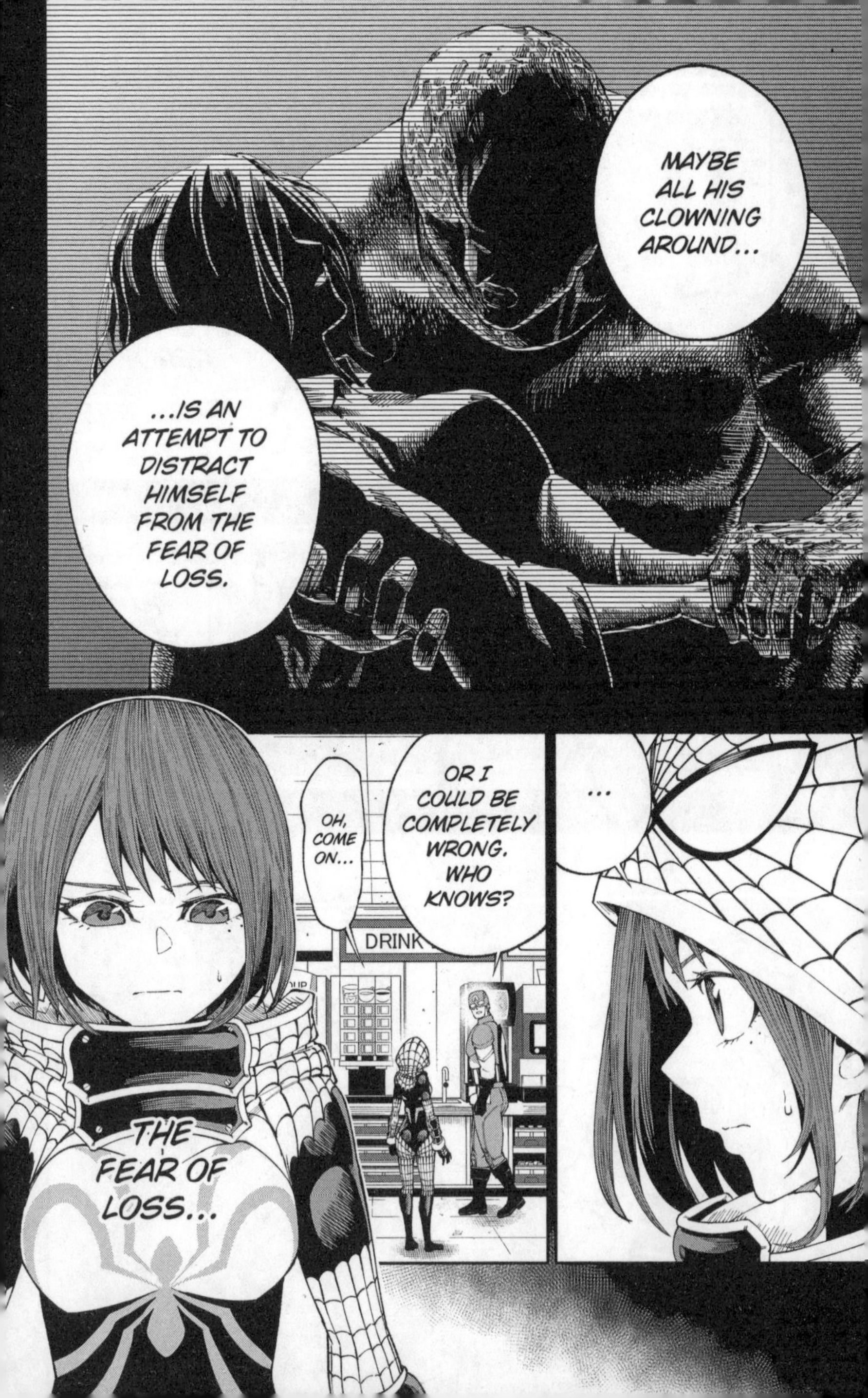
MAYBE ALL HIS CLOWNING AROUND...
...IS AN ATTEMPT TO DISTRACT HIMSELF FROM THE FEAR OF LOSS.
...
OR I COULD BE COMPLETELY WRONG. WHO KNOWS?
OH, COME ON...
DRINK
THE FEAR OF LOSS...

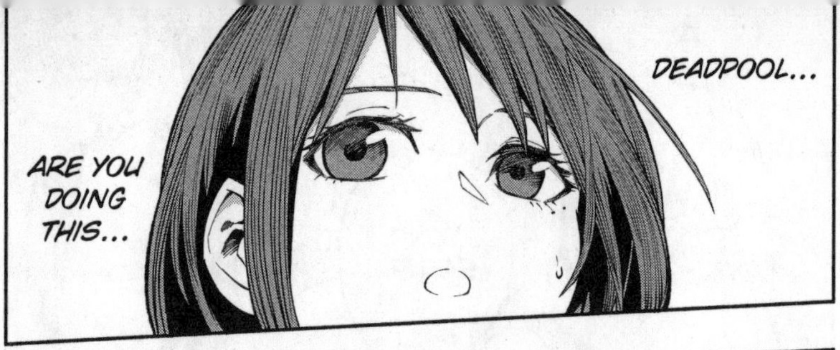
DEADPOOL...
ARE YOU DOING THIS...

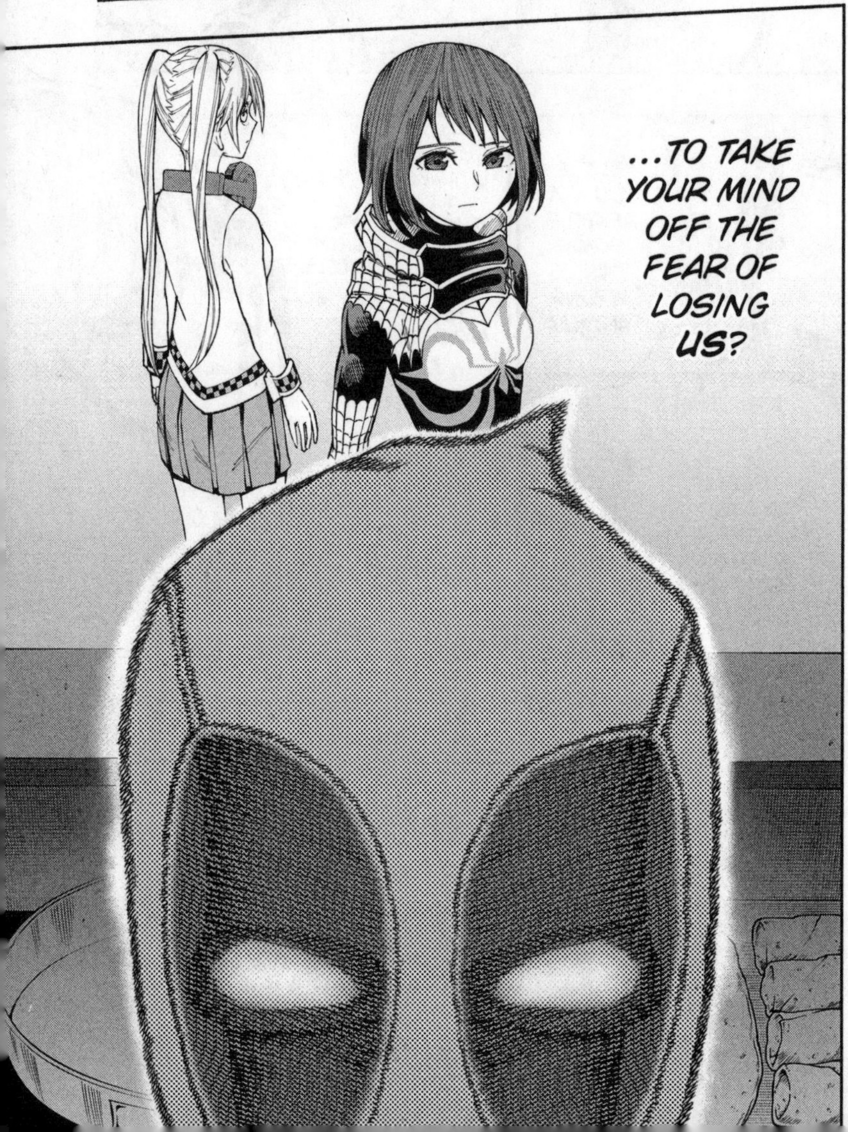
...TO TAKE YOUR MIND OFF THE FEAR OF LOSING US?

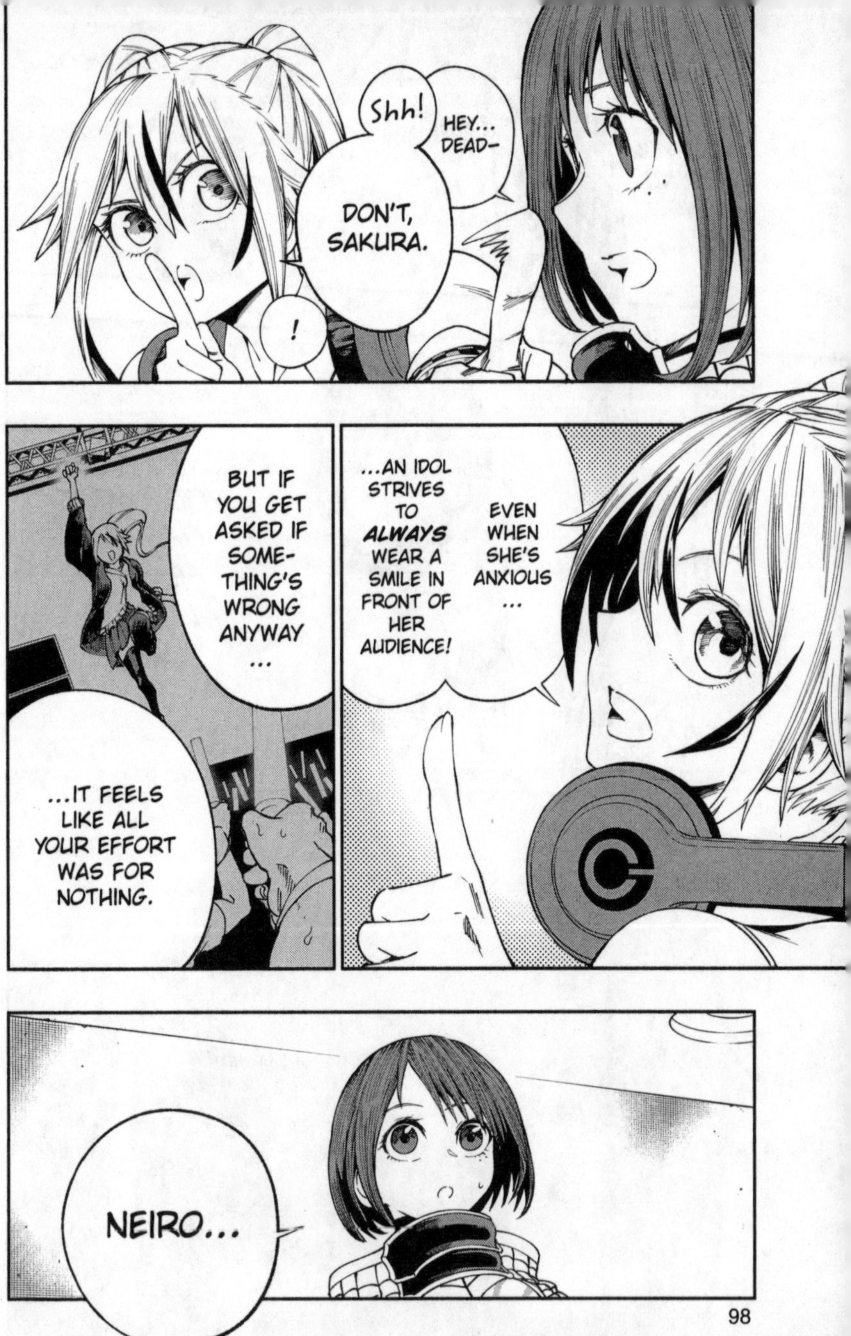
HEY... DEAD-
Shh!
DON'T, SAKURA.
!
EVEN WHEN SHE'S ANXIOUS...
...AN IDOL STRIVES TO ALWAYS WEAR A SMILE IN FRONT OF HER AUDIENCE!
BUT IF YOU GET ASKED IF SOME-THING'S WRONG ANYWAY...
...IT FEELS LIKE ALL YOUR EFFORT WAS FOR NOTHING.
NEIRO...

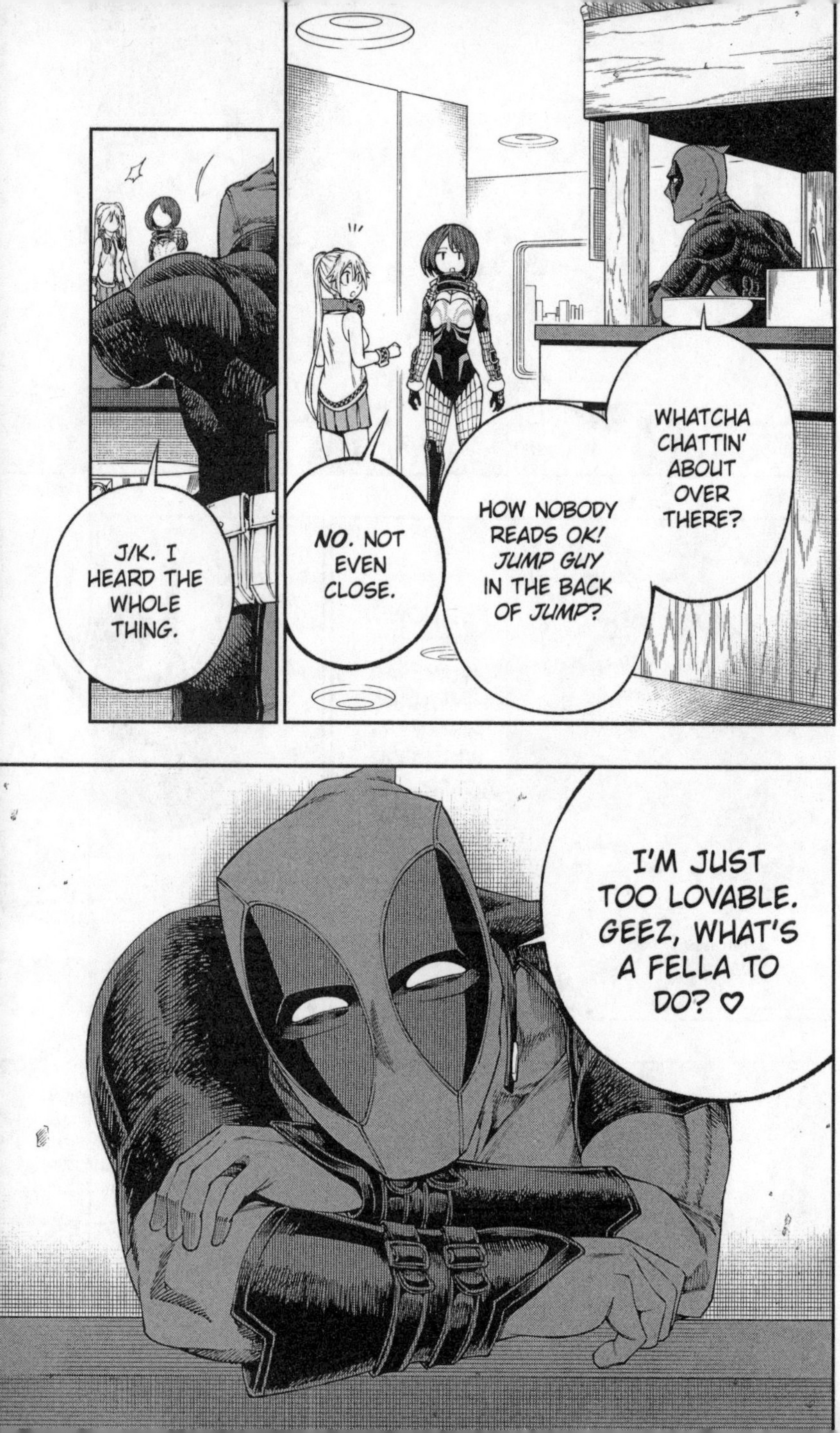
WHATCHA CHATTIN' ABOUT OVER THERE?
HOW NOBODY READS OK! JUMP GUY IN THE BACK OF JUMP?
NO. NOT EVEN CLOSE.
J/K. I HEARD THE WHOLE THING.
I'M JUST TOO LOVABLE. GEEZ, WHAT'S A FELLA TO DO? ♡

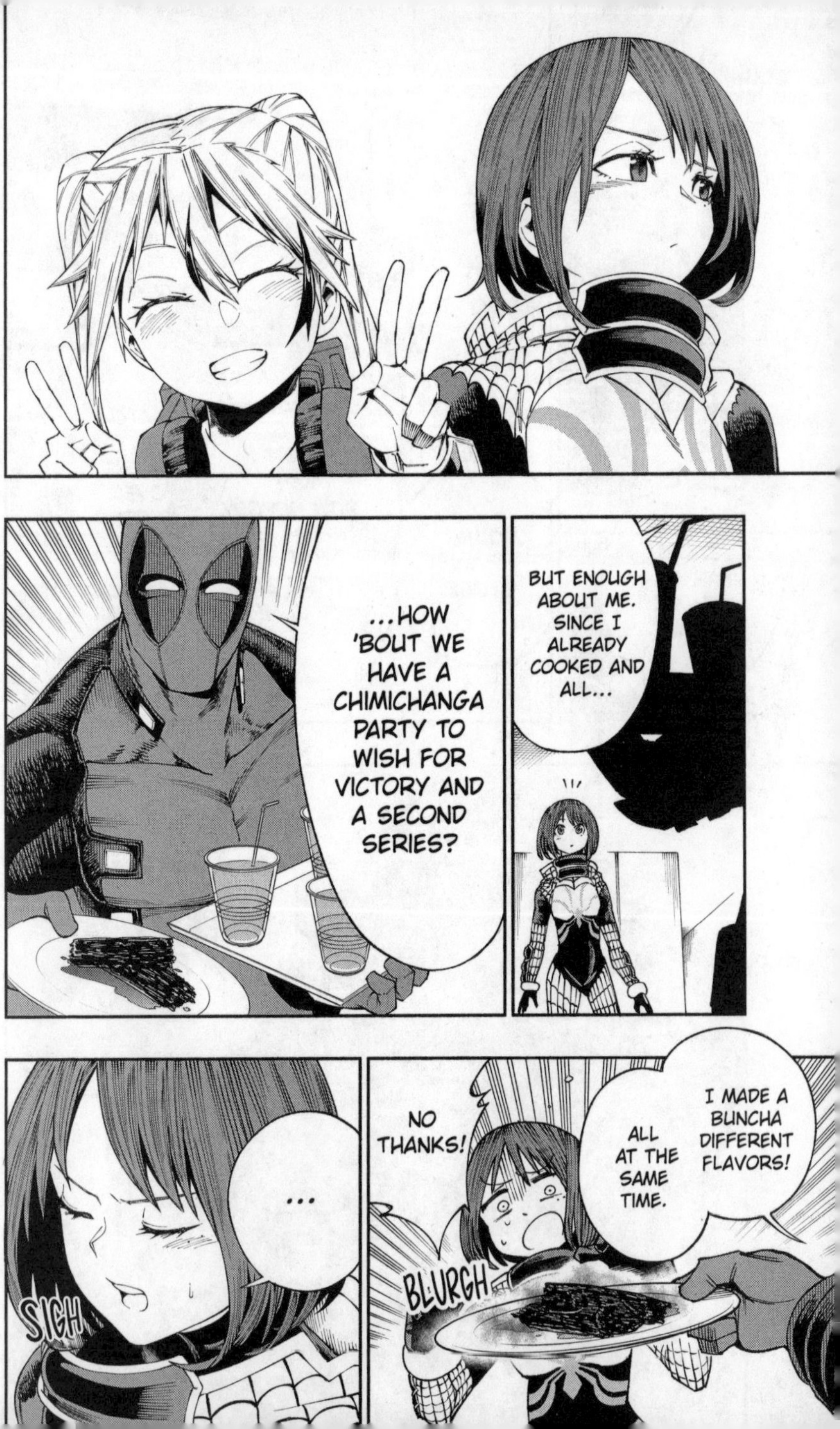
BUT ENOUGH ABOUT ME. SINCE I ALREADY COOKED AND ALL...
...HOW 'BOUT WE HAVE A CHIMICHANGA PARTY TO WISH FOR VICTORY AND A SECOND SERIES?
I MADE A BUNCHA DIFFERENT FLAVORS!
ALL AT THE SAME TIME.
NO THANKS!
BLURGH
...
SIGH

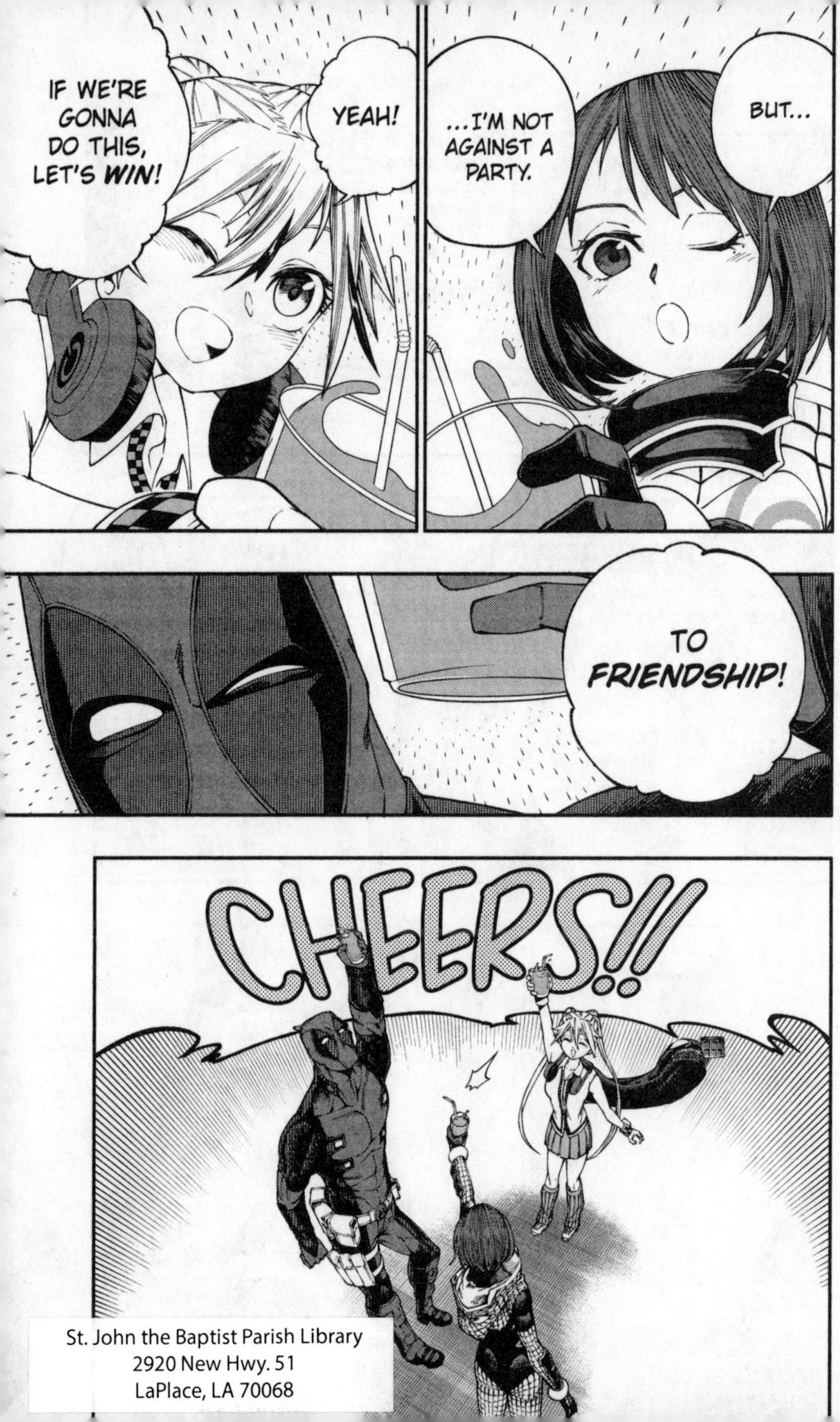
BUT...
...I'M NOT AGAINST A PARTY.
YEAH!
IF WE'RE GONNA DO THIS, LET'S ***WIN***!
TO ***FRIENDSHIP!***
CHEERS!!

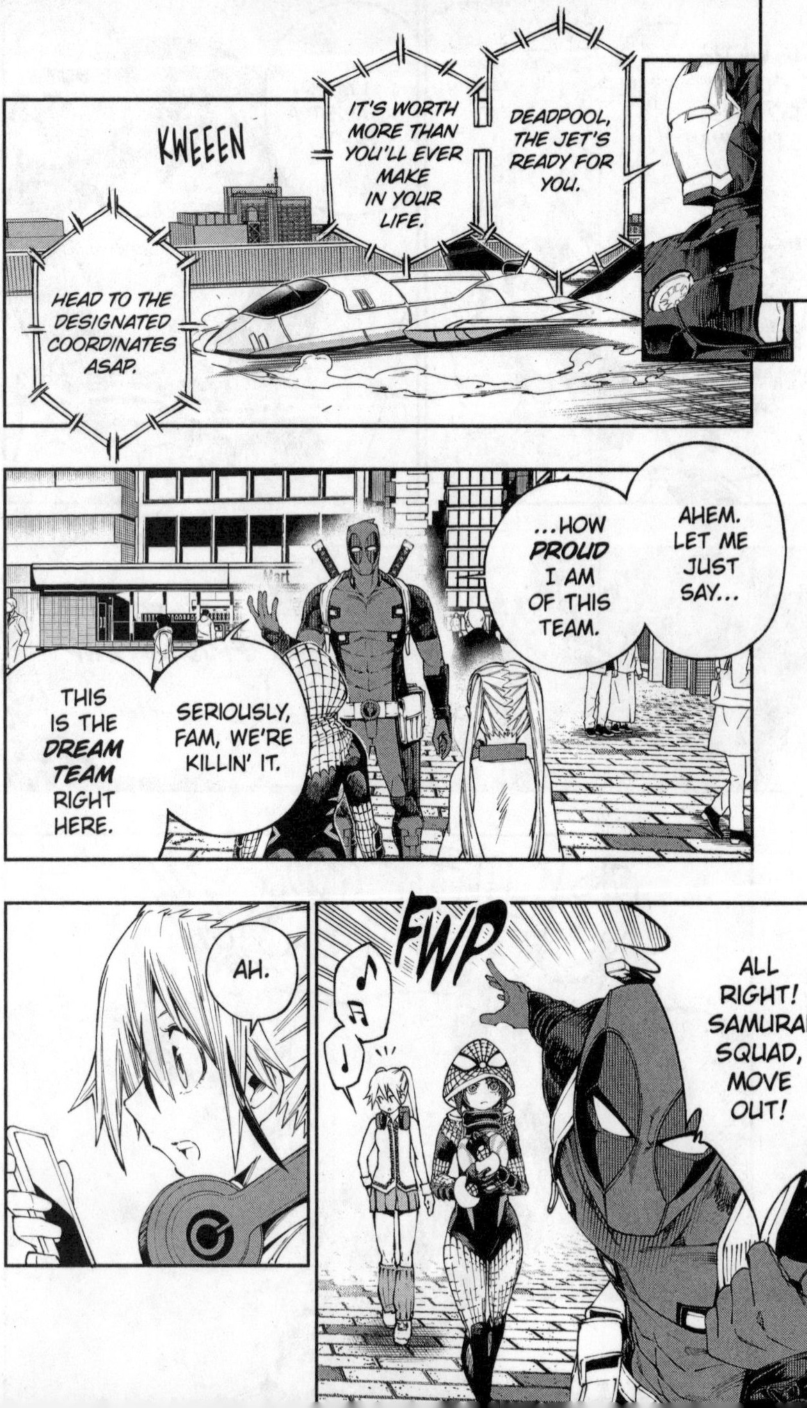
DEADPOOL, THE JET'S READY FOR YOU.
IT'S WORTH MORE THAN YOU'LL EVER MAKE IN YOUR LIFE.
KWEEEN
HEAD TO THE DESIGNATED COORDINATES ASAP.
AHEM. LET ME JUST SAY...
...HOW PROUD I AM OF THIS TEAM.
SERIOUSLY, FAM, WE'RE KILLIN' IT.
THIS IS THE DREAM TEAM RIGHT HERE.
FWP
ALL RIGHT! SAMURAI SQUAD, MOVE OUT!
AH.

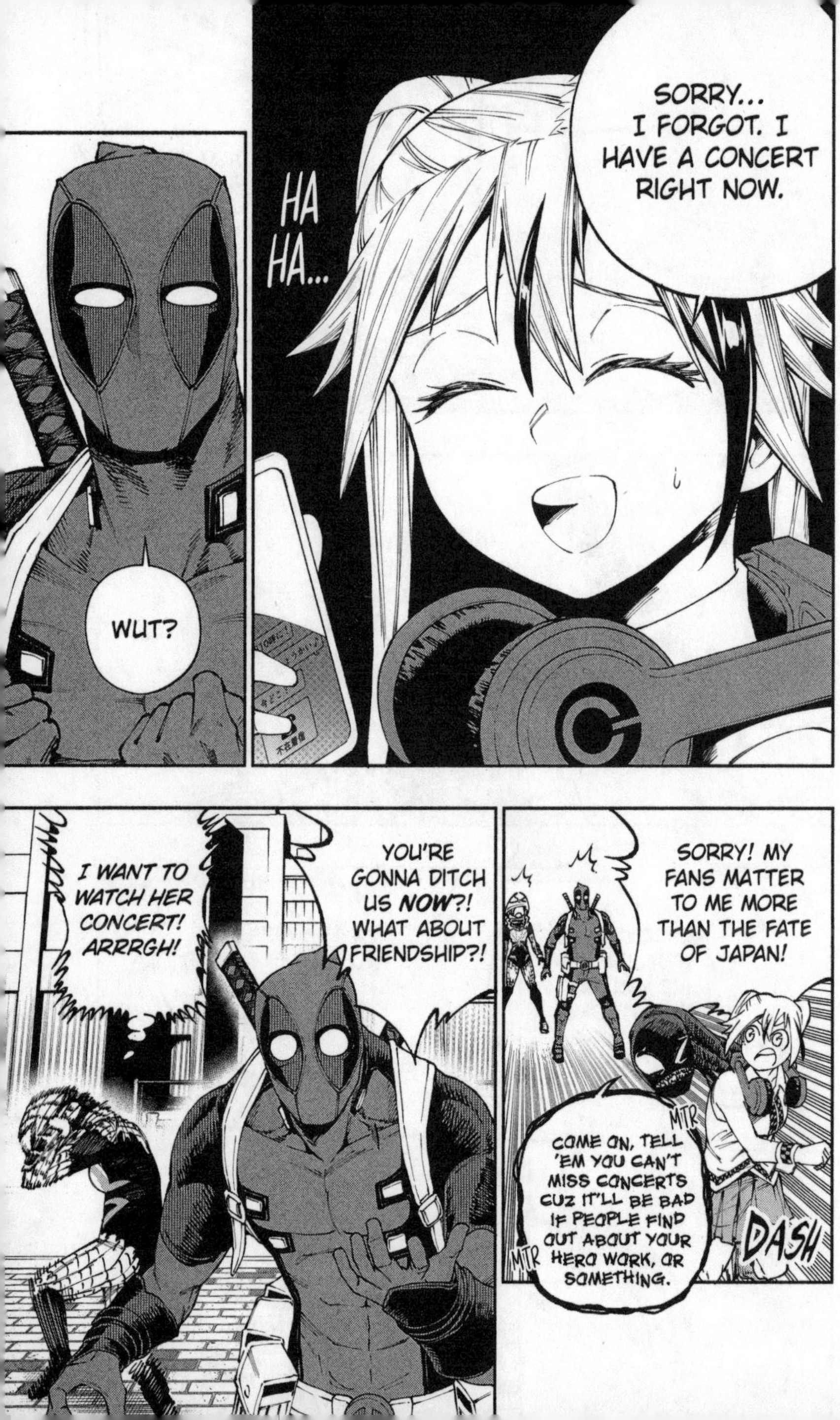
SORRY... I FORGOT. I HAVE A CONCERT RIGHT NOW.
HA HA...
WUT?
SORRY! MY FANS MATTER TO ME MORE THAN THE FATE OF JAPAN!
MTR
COME ON, TELL 'EM YOU CAN'T MISS CONCERTS CUZ IT'LL BE BAD IF PEOPLE FIND OUT ABOUT YOUR HERO WORK, OR SOMETHING.
MTR
DASH
YOU'RE GONNA DITCH US ***NOW***?! WHAT ABOUT FRIENDSHIP?!
I WANT TO WATCH HER CONCERT! ARRRGH!

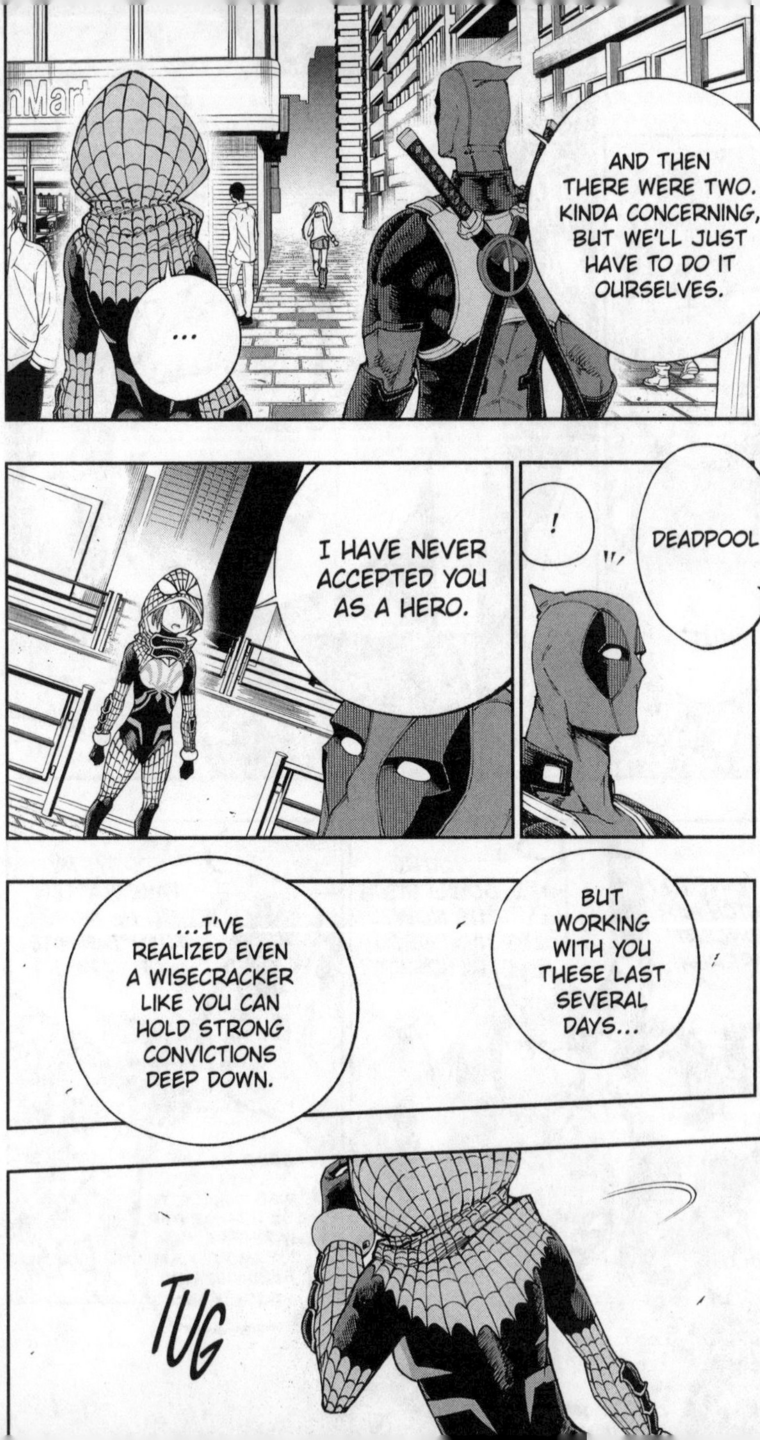
AND THEN THERE WERE TWO. KINDA CONCERNING, BUT WE'LL JUST HAVE TO DO IT OURSELVES.
...
DEADPOOL.
!
I HAVE NEVER ACCEPTED YOU AS A HERO.
BUT WORKING WITH YOU THESE LAST SEVERAL DAYS...
...I'VE REALIZED EVEN A WISECRACKER LIKE YOU CAN HOLD STRONG CONVICTIONS DEEP DOWN.
TUG

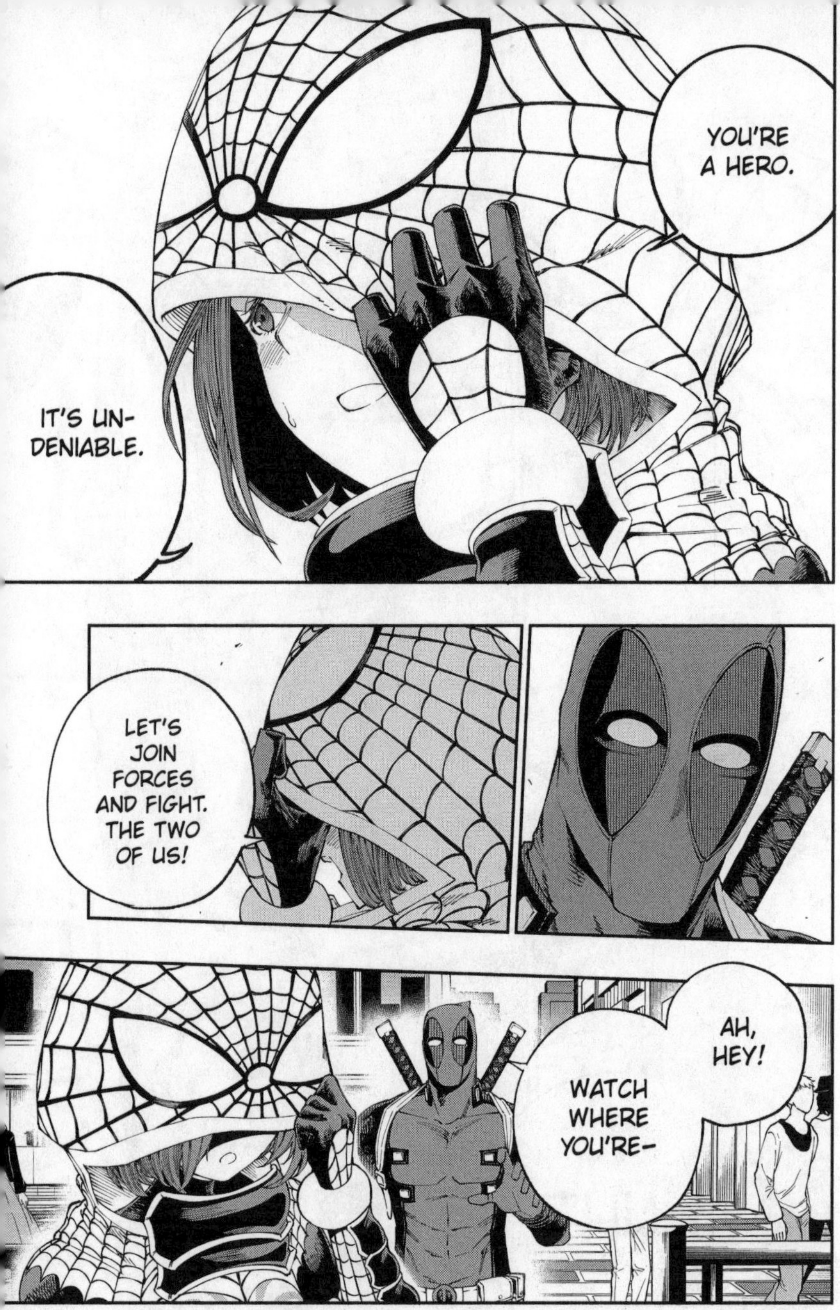
YOU'RE A HERO.
IT'S UN-DENIABLE.
LET'S JOIN FORCES AND FIGHT. THE TWO OF US!
AH, HEY!
WATCH WHERE YOU'RE-

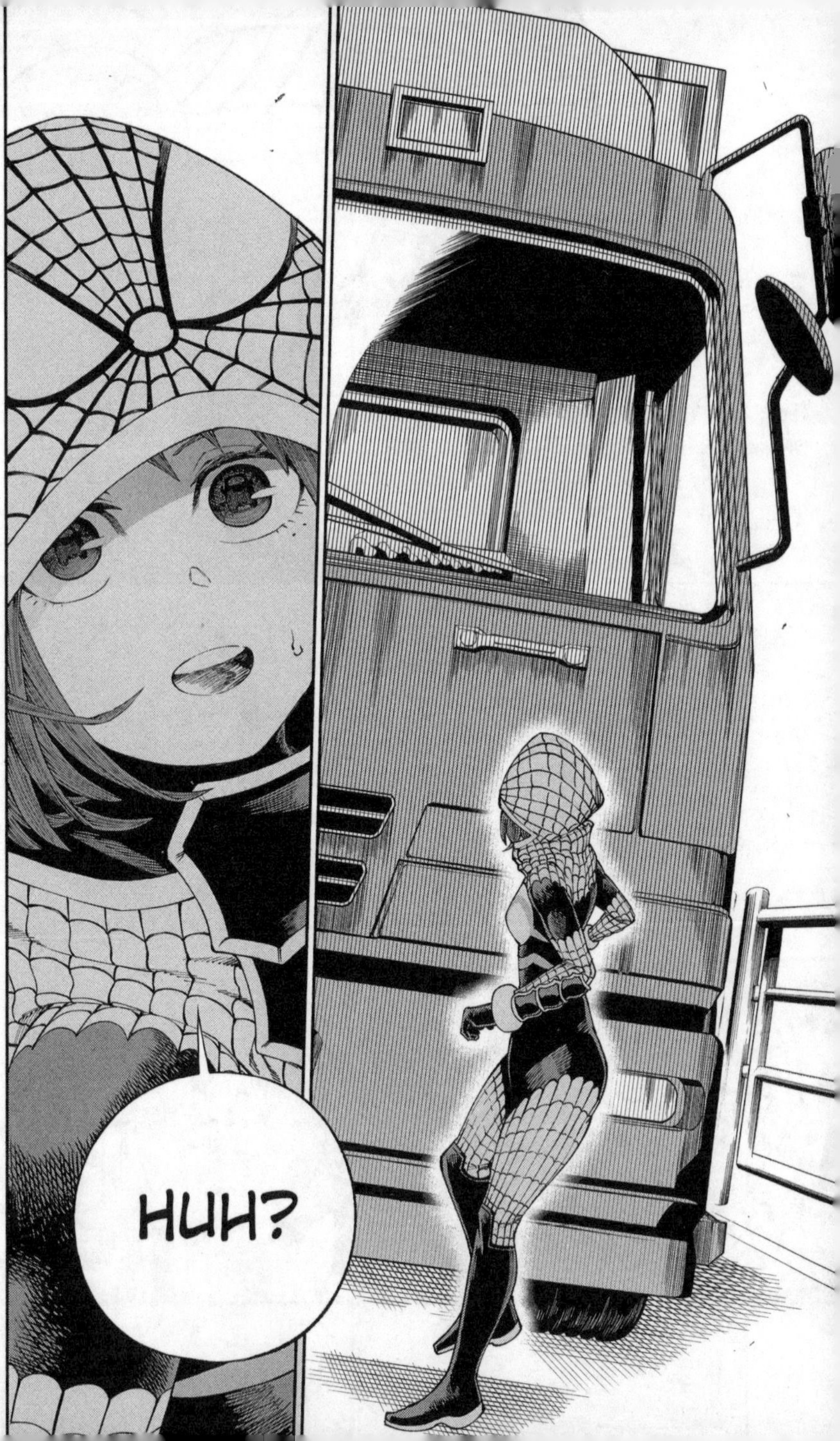
HUH?

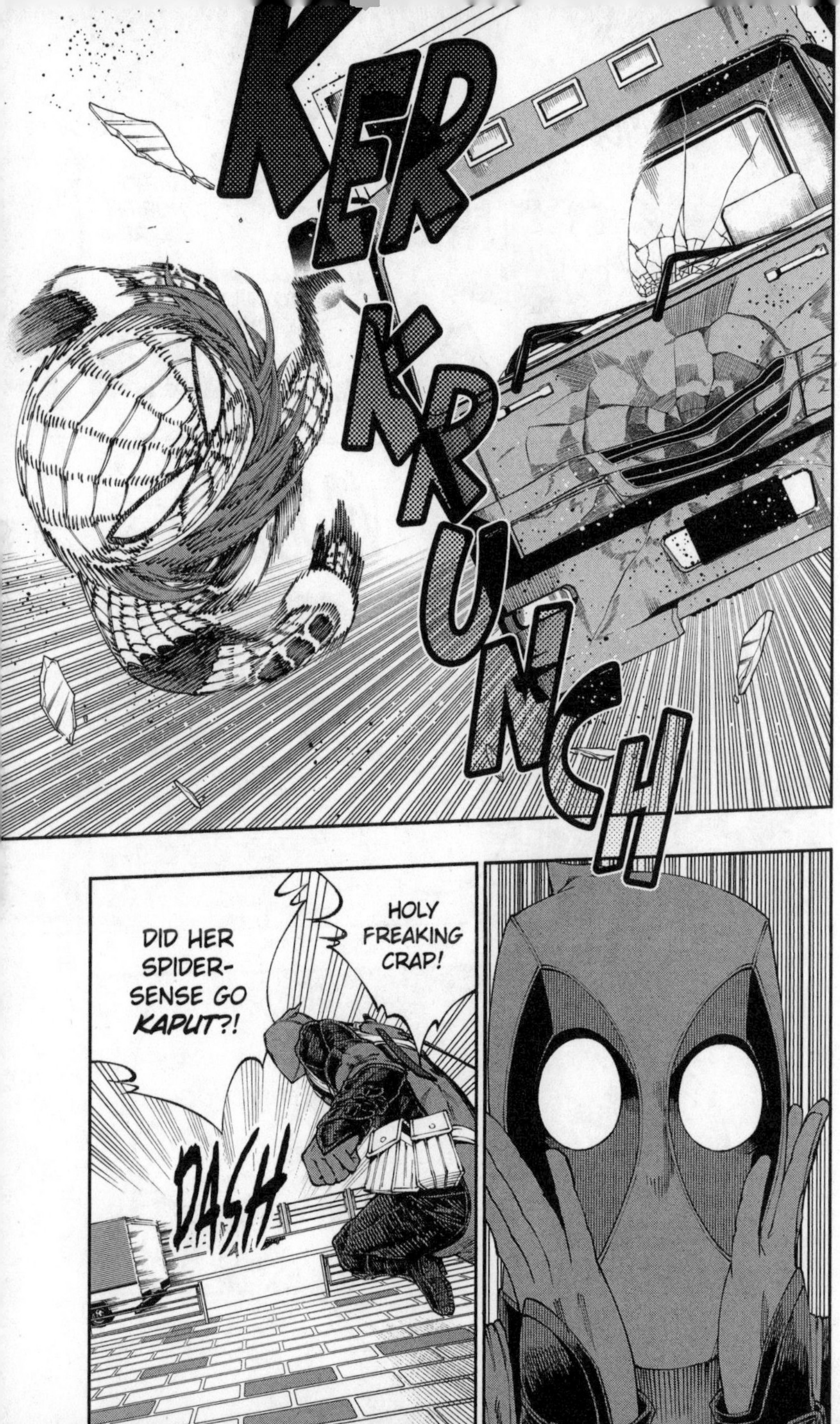
KERKRUNCH
HOLY FREAKING CRAP!
DID HER SPIDER-SENSE GO *KAPUT*?!
DASH

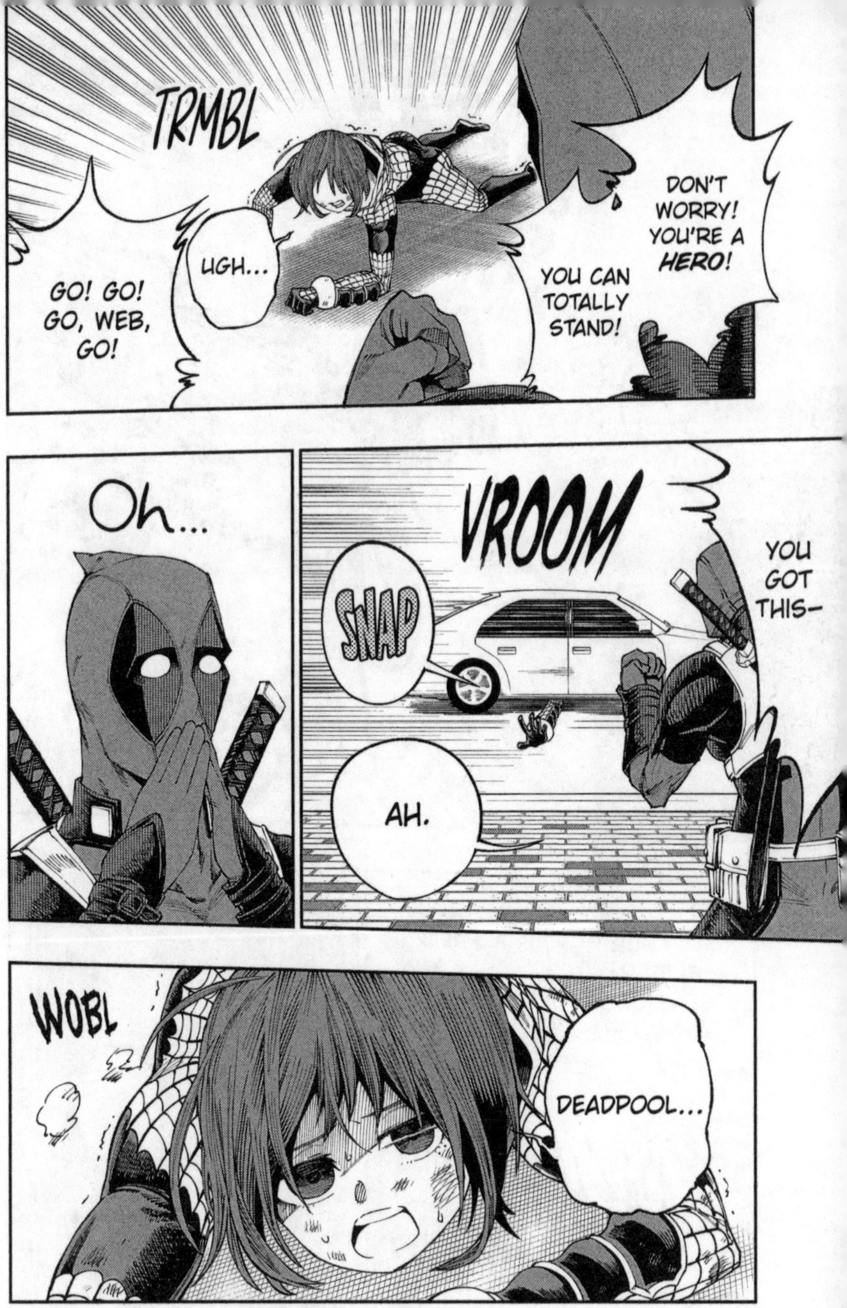
DON'T WORRY! YOU'RE A HERO!
TRMBL
YOU CAN TOTALLY STAND!
UGH...
GO! GO! GO, WEB, GO!
YOU GOT THIS—
VROOM
SNAP
AH.
Oh...
DEADPOOL...
WOBL

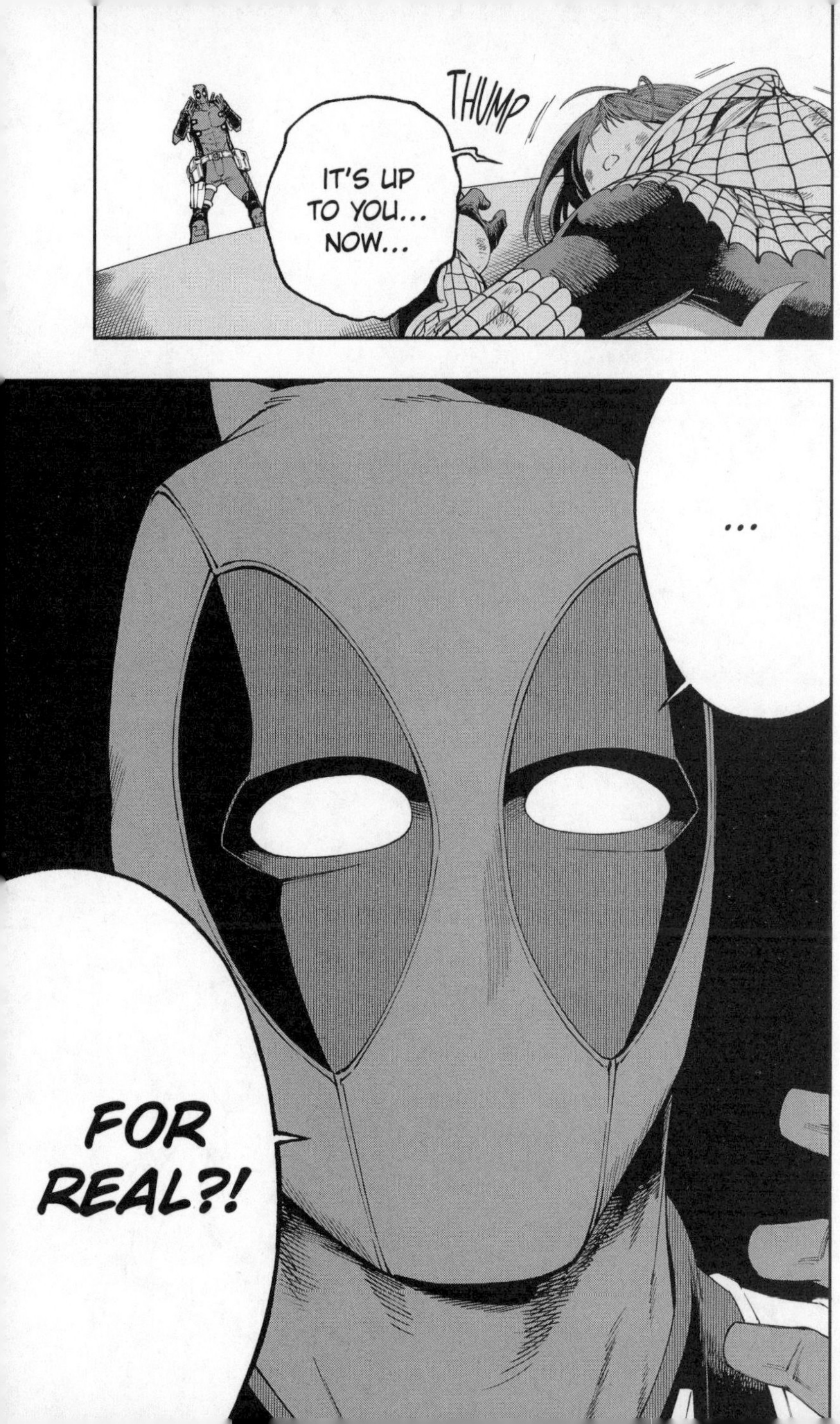
THUMP
IT'S UP TO YOU... NOW...
...
FOR REAL?!

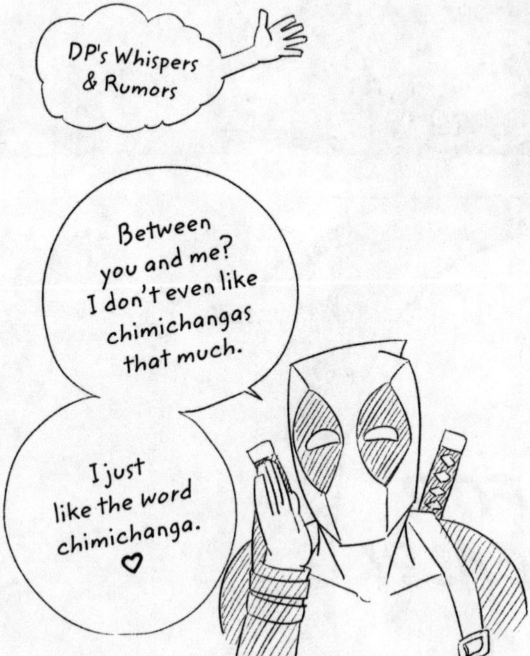
DP's Whispers & Rumors
Between you and me? I don't even like chimichangas that much.
I just like the word chimichanga. ♡

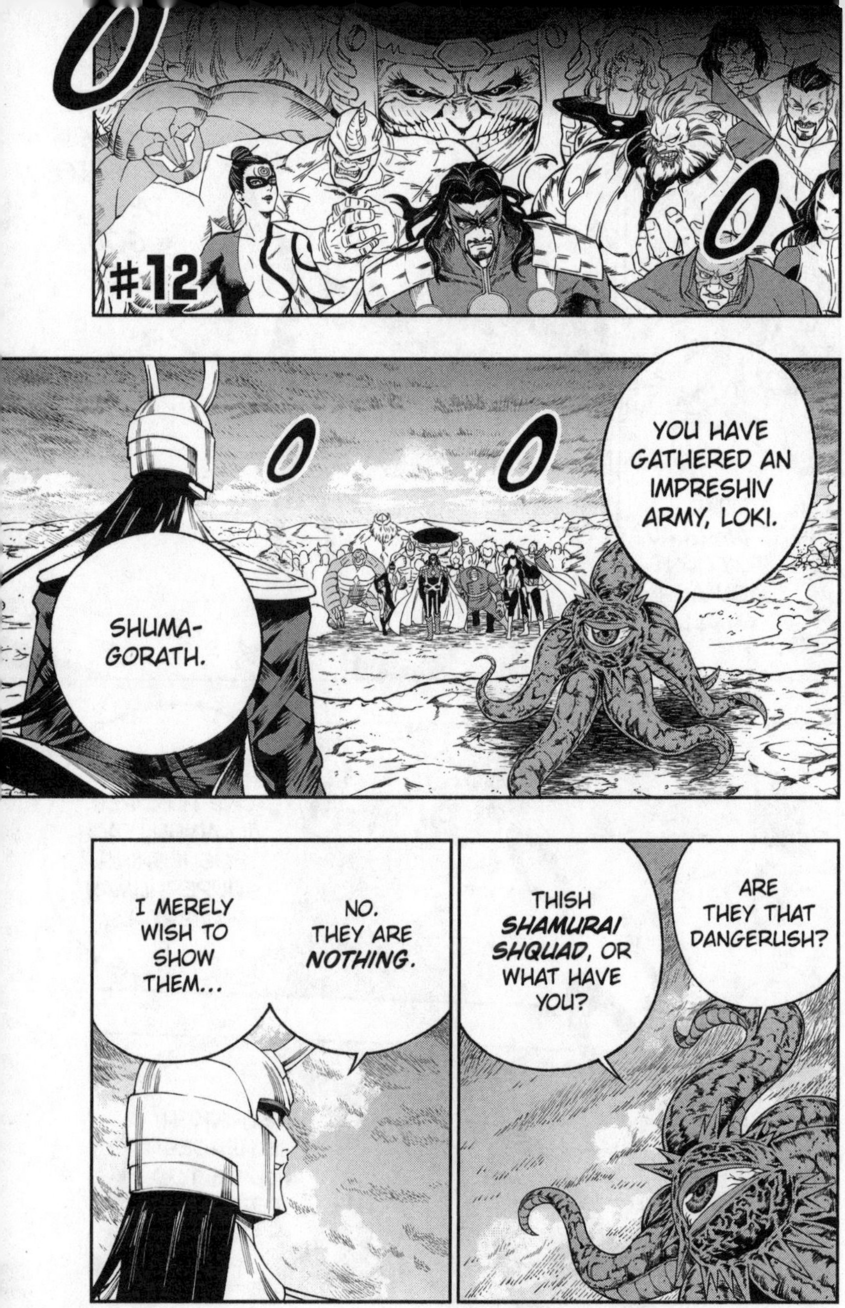

#12
YOU HAVE GATHERED AN IMPRESHIV ARMY, LOKI.
SHUMA-GORATH.
ARE THEY THAT DANGERUSH?
THISH *SHAMURAI SHQUAD*, OR WHAT HAVE YOU?
NO. THEY ARE *NOTHING*.
I MERELY WISH TO SHOW THEM...

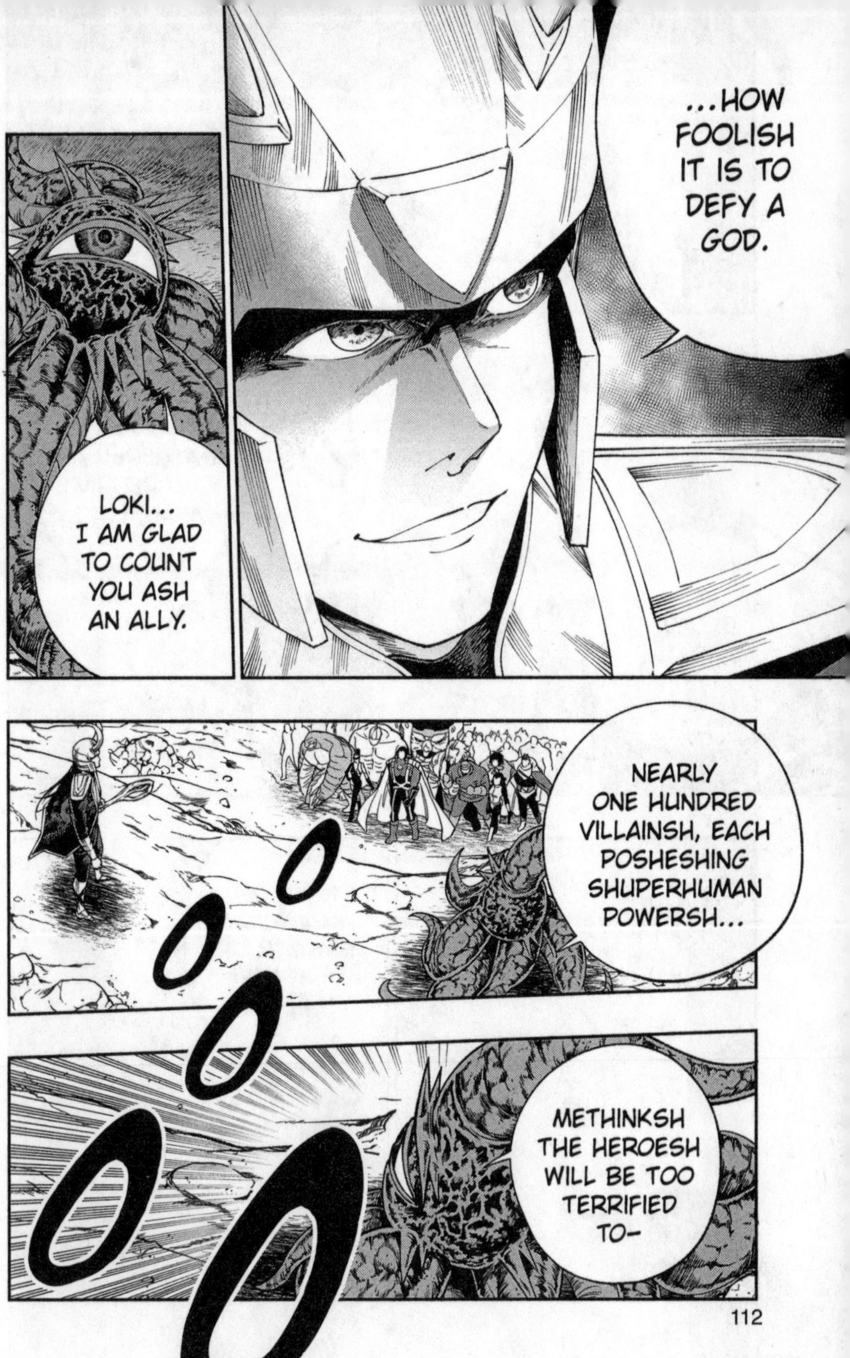
...HOW FOOLISH IT IS TO DEFY A GOD.
LOKI... I AM GLAD TO COUNT YOU ASH AN ALLY.
NEARLY ONE HUNDRED VILLAINSH, EACH POSHESHING SHUPERHUMAN POWERSH...
METHINKSH THE HEROESH WILL BE TOO TERRIFIED TO-

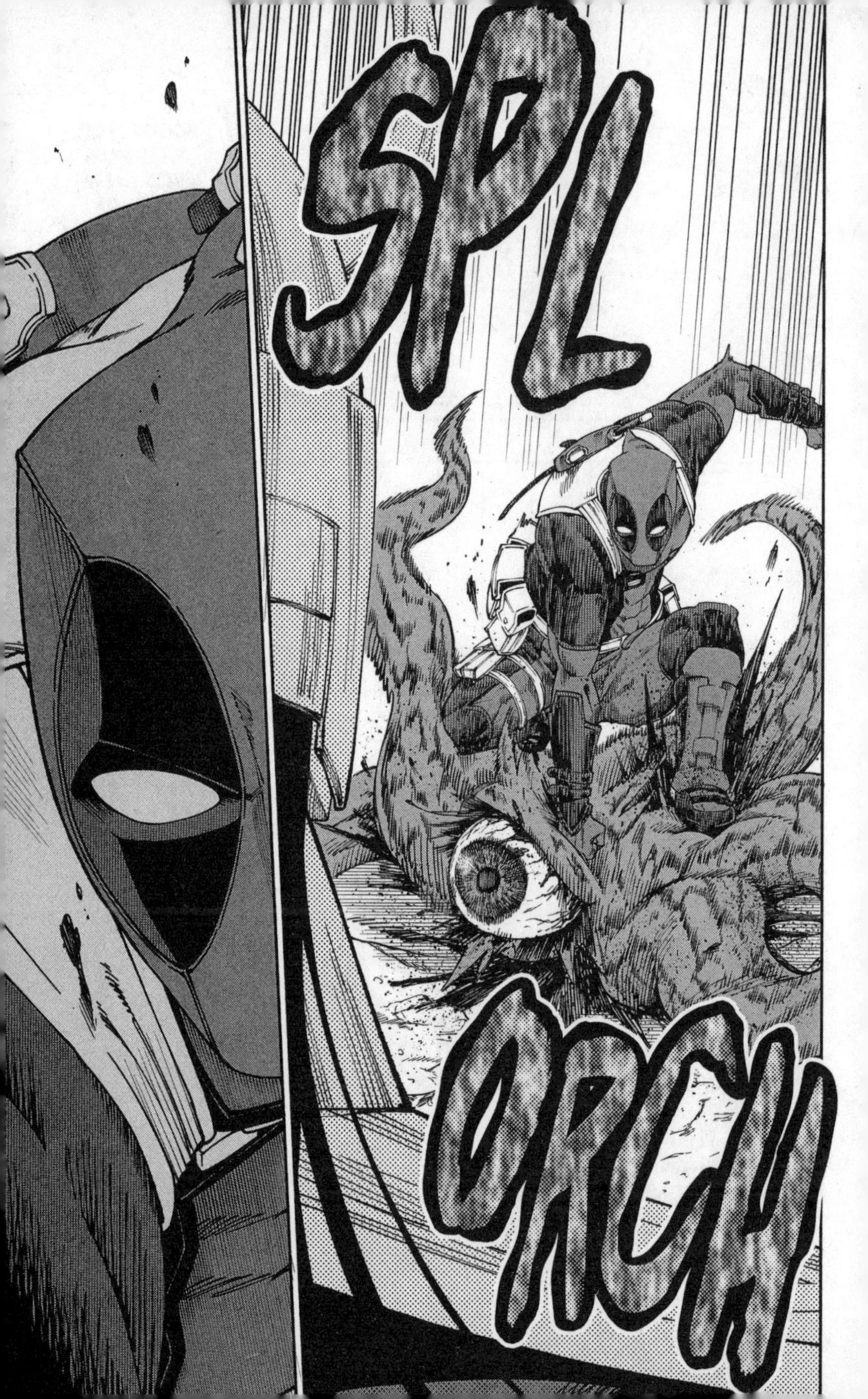
SPL
ORCH

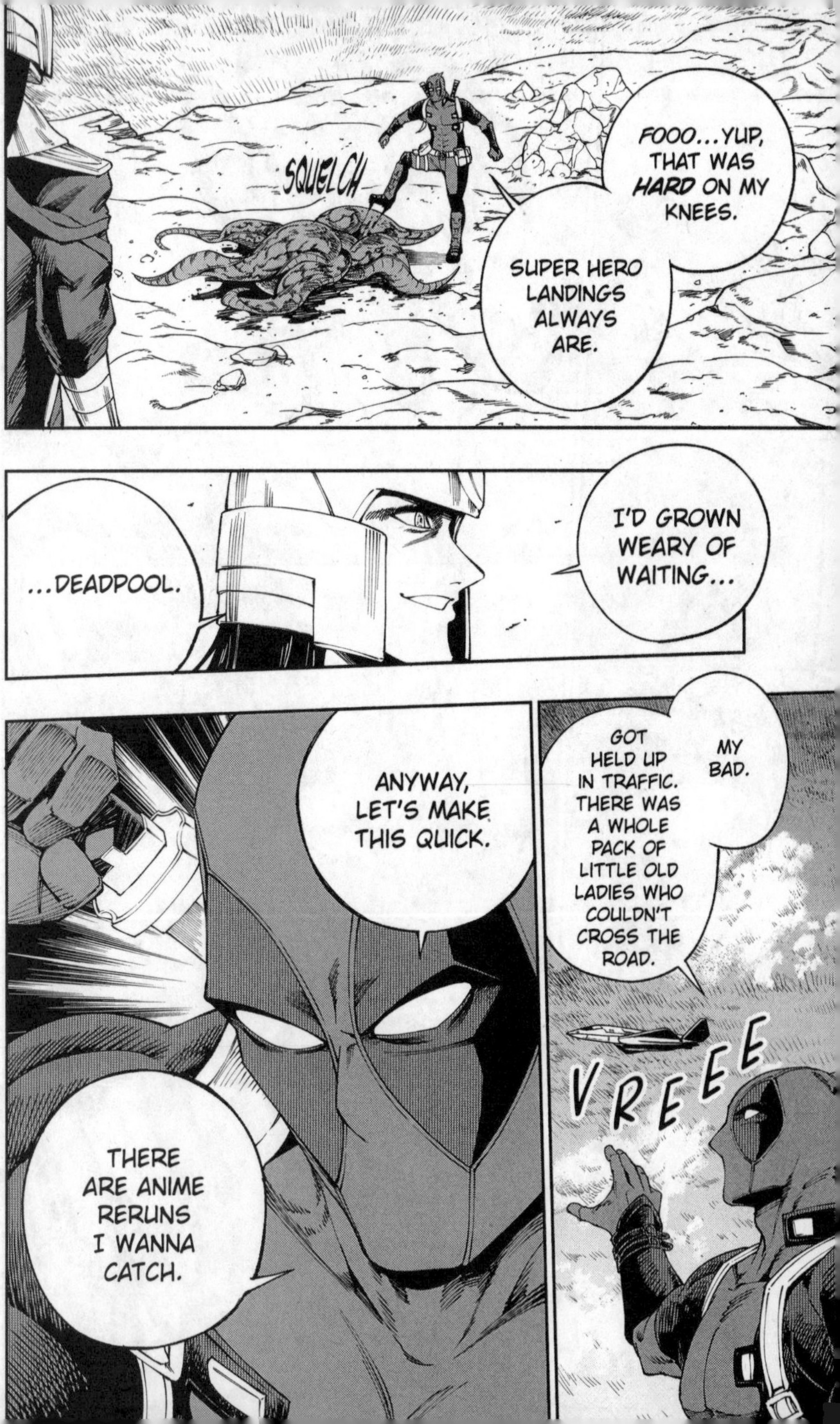
FOOO...YUP, THAT WAS HARD ON MY KNEES.
SQUELCH
SUPER HERO LANDINGS ALWAYS ARE.
I'D GROWN WEARY OF WAITING...
...DEADPOOL.
MY BAD.
GOT HELD UP IN TRAFFIC. THERE WAS A WHOLE PACK OF LITTLE OLD LADIES WHO COULDN'T CROSS THE ROAD.
VREEE
ANYWAY, LET'S MAKE THIS QUICK.
THERE ARE ANIME RERUNS I WANNA CATCH.

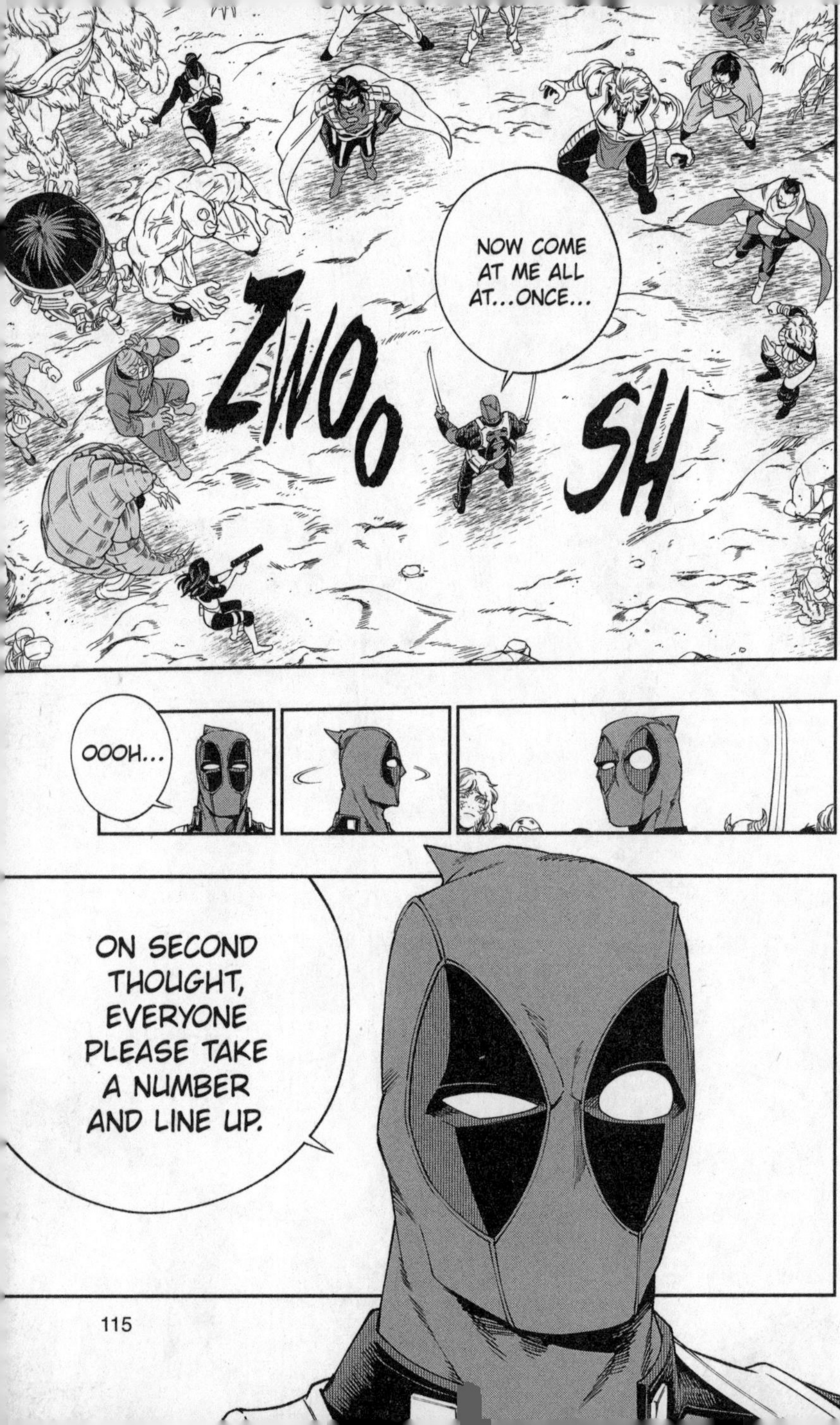
NOW COME AT ME ALL AT...ONCE...
ZWOOSH
OOOH...
ON SECOND THOUGHT, EVERYONE PLEASE TAKE A NUMBER AND LINE UP.

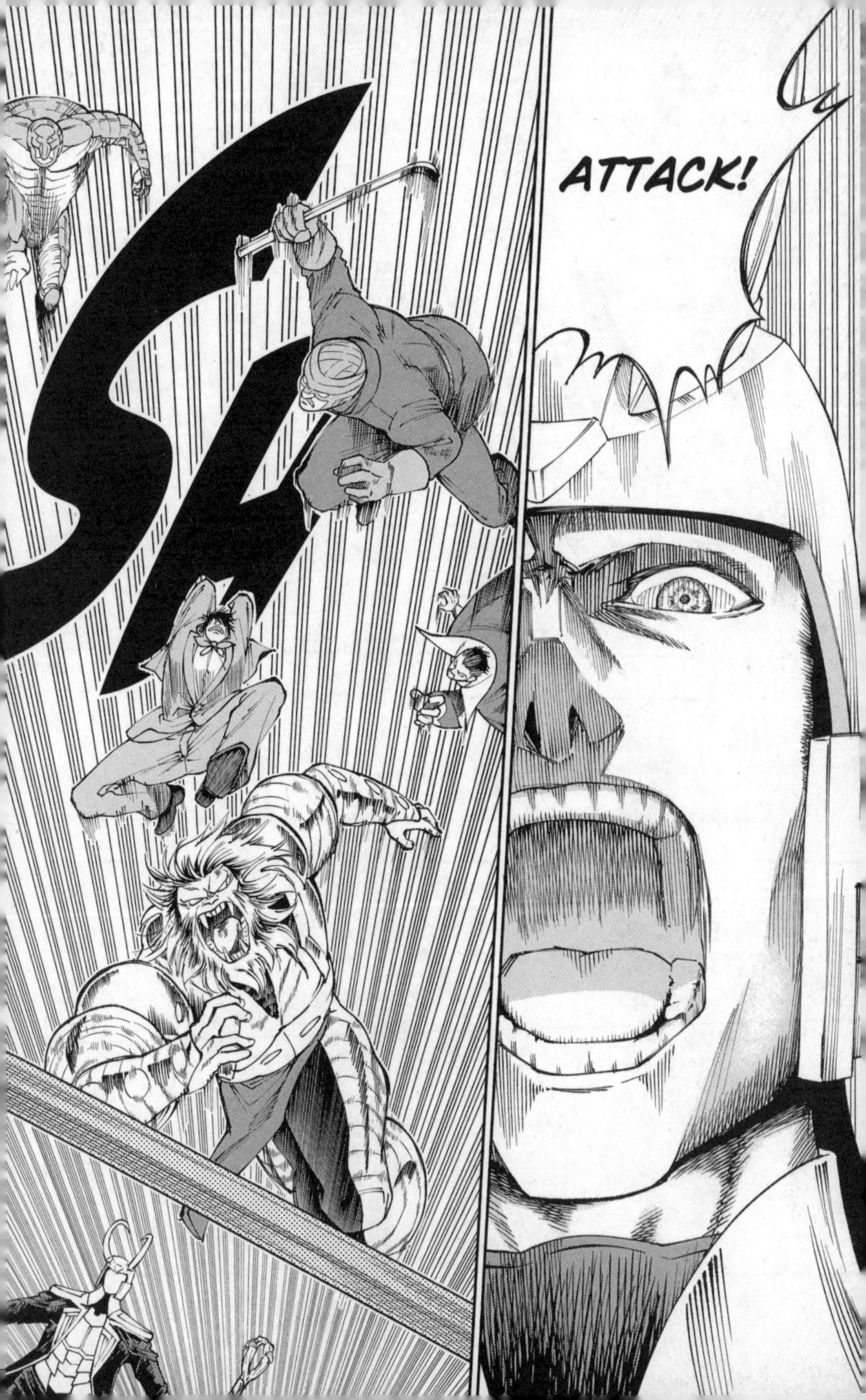
ATTACK!

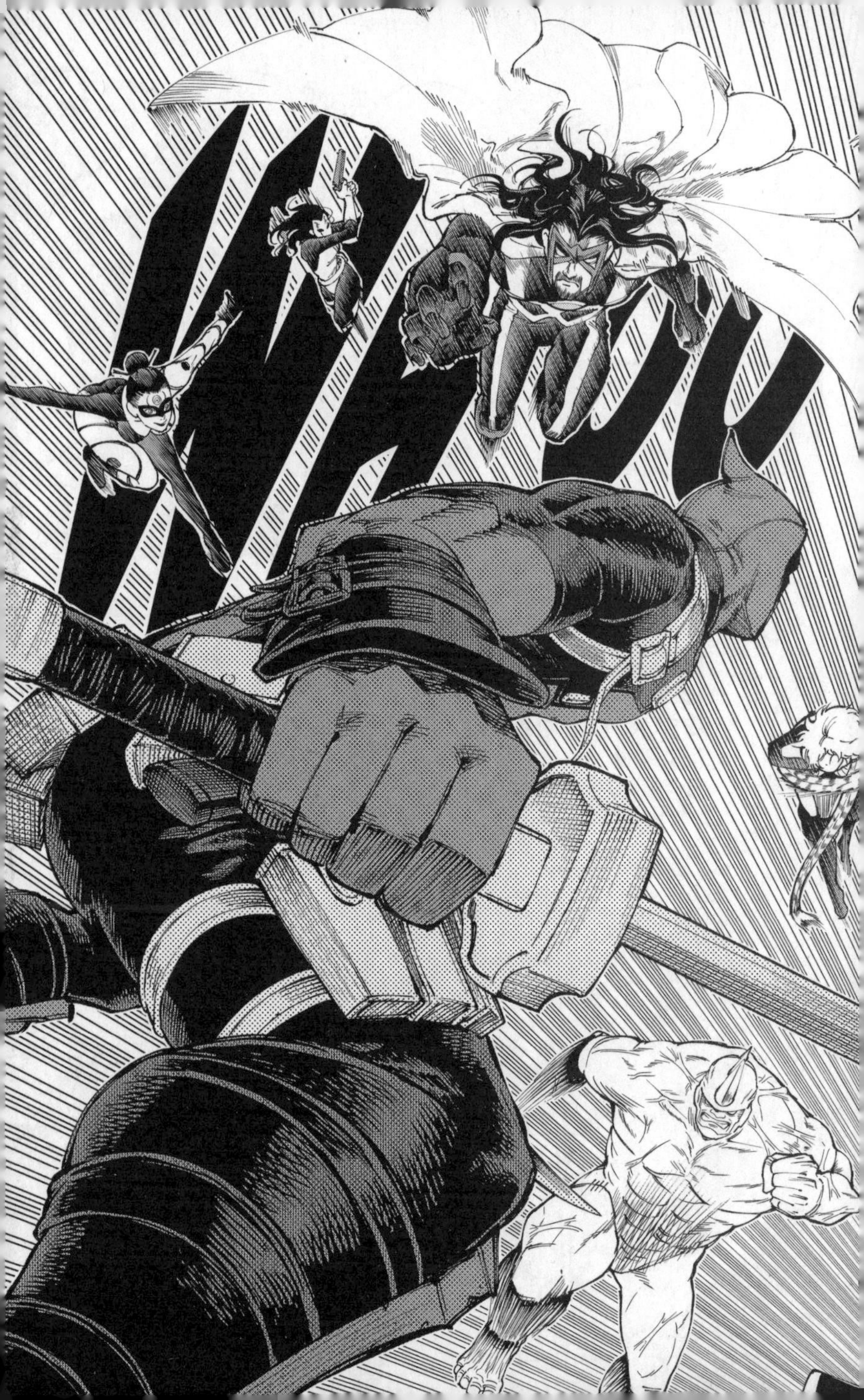

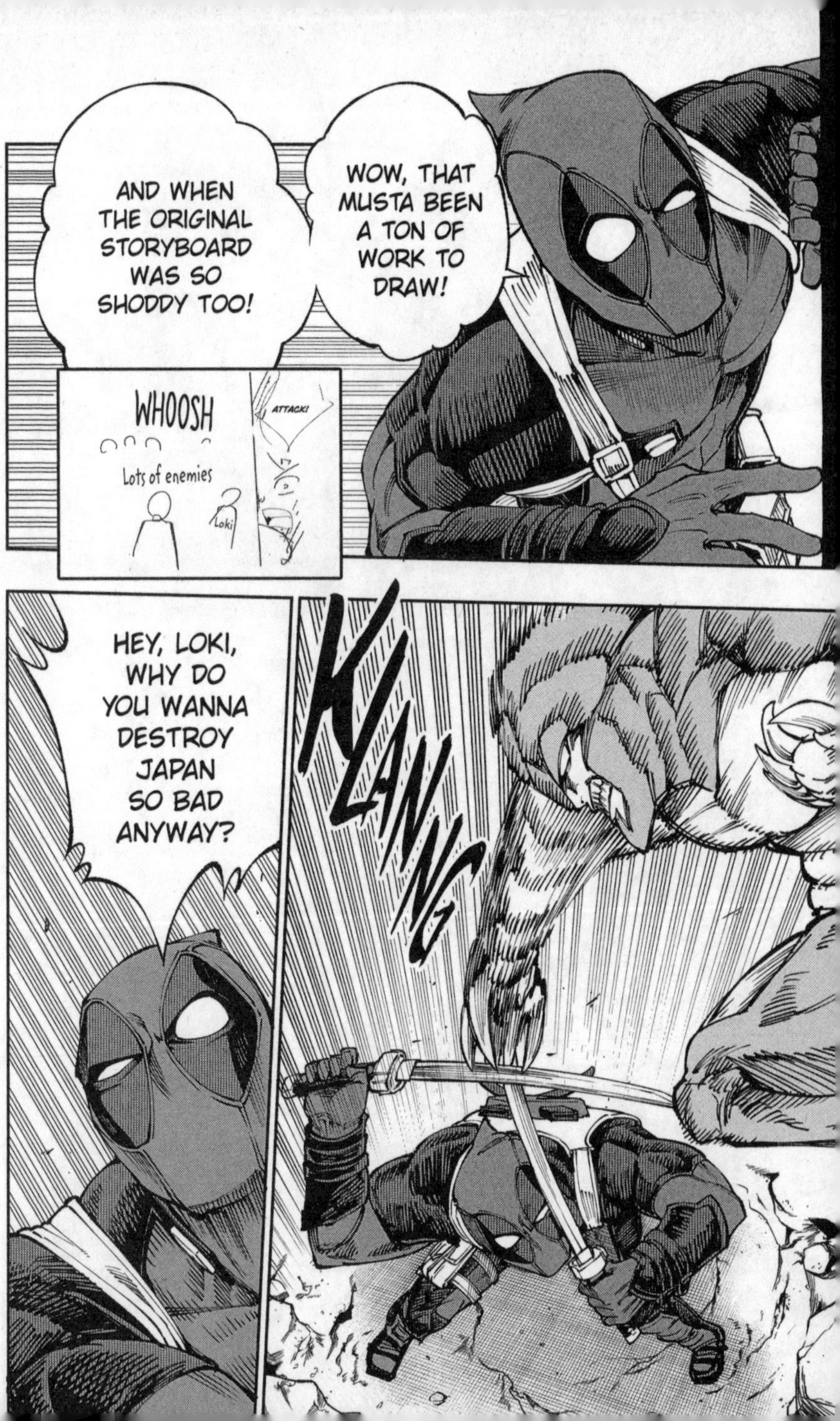
WOW, THAT MUSTA BEEN A TON OF WORK TO DRAW!
AND WHEN THE ORIGINAL STORYBOARD WAS SO SHODDY TOO!
ATTACK!
WHOOSH
Lots of enemies
Loki
KLANNG
HEY, LOKI, WHY DO YOU WANNA DESTROY JAPAN SO BAD ANYWAY?

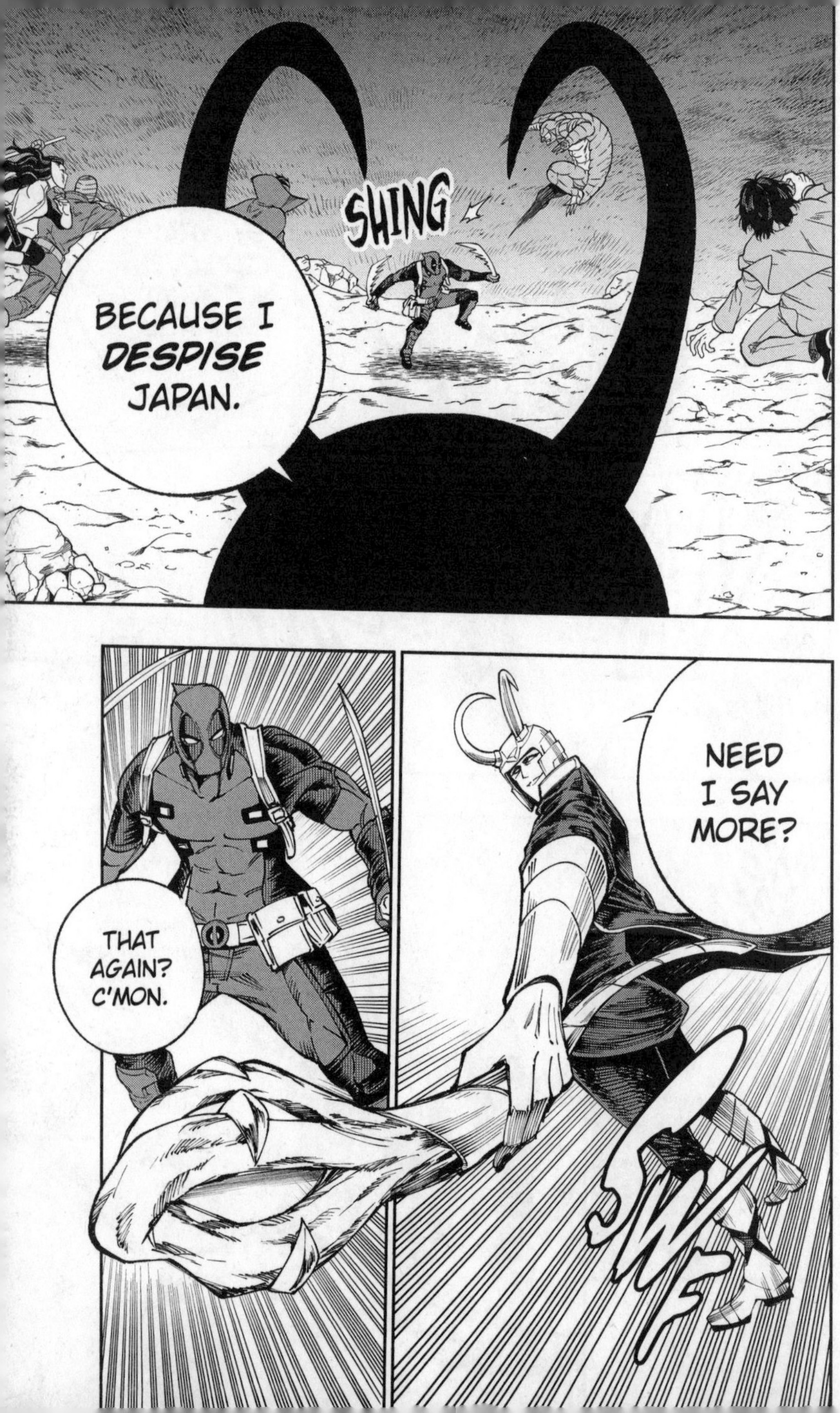
SHING
BECAUSE I DESPISE JAPAN.
NEED I SAY MORE?
THAT AGAIN? C'MON.

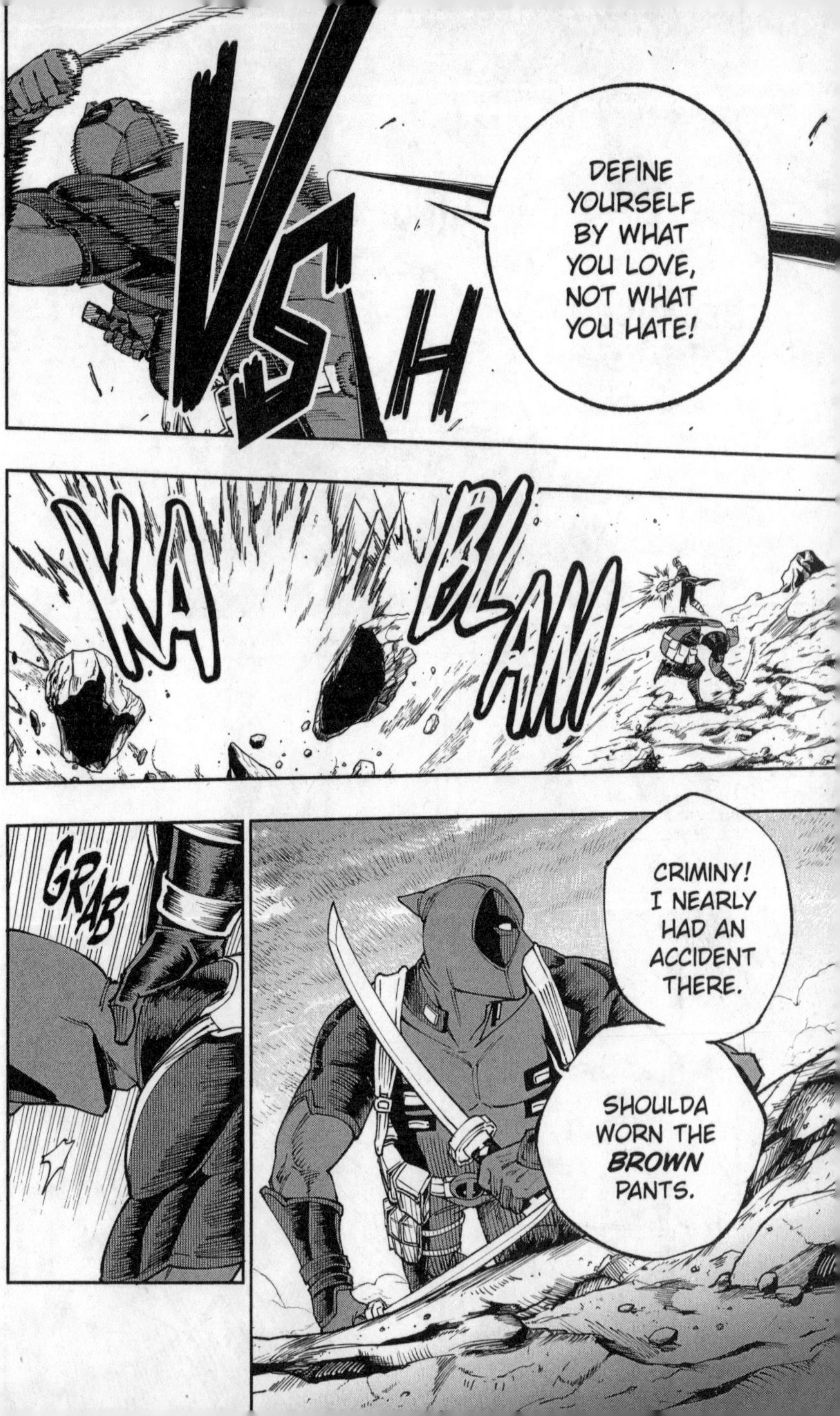
VSH
DEFINE YOURSELF BY WHAT YOU LOVE, NOT WHAT YOU HATE!
KA
BLAM
CRIMINY! I NEARLY HAD AN ACCIDENT THERE.
SHOULDA WORN THE *BROWN* PANTS.
GRAB

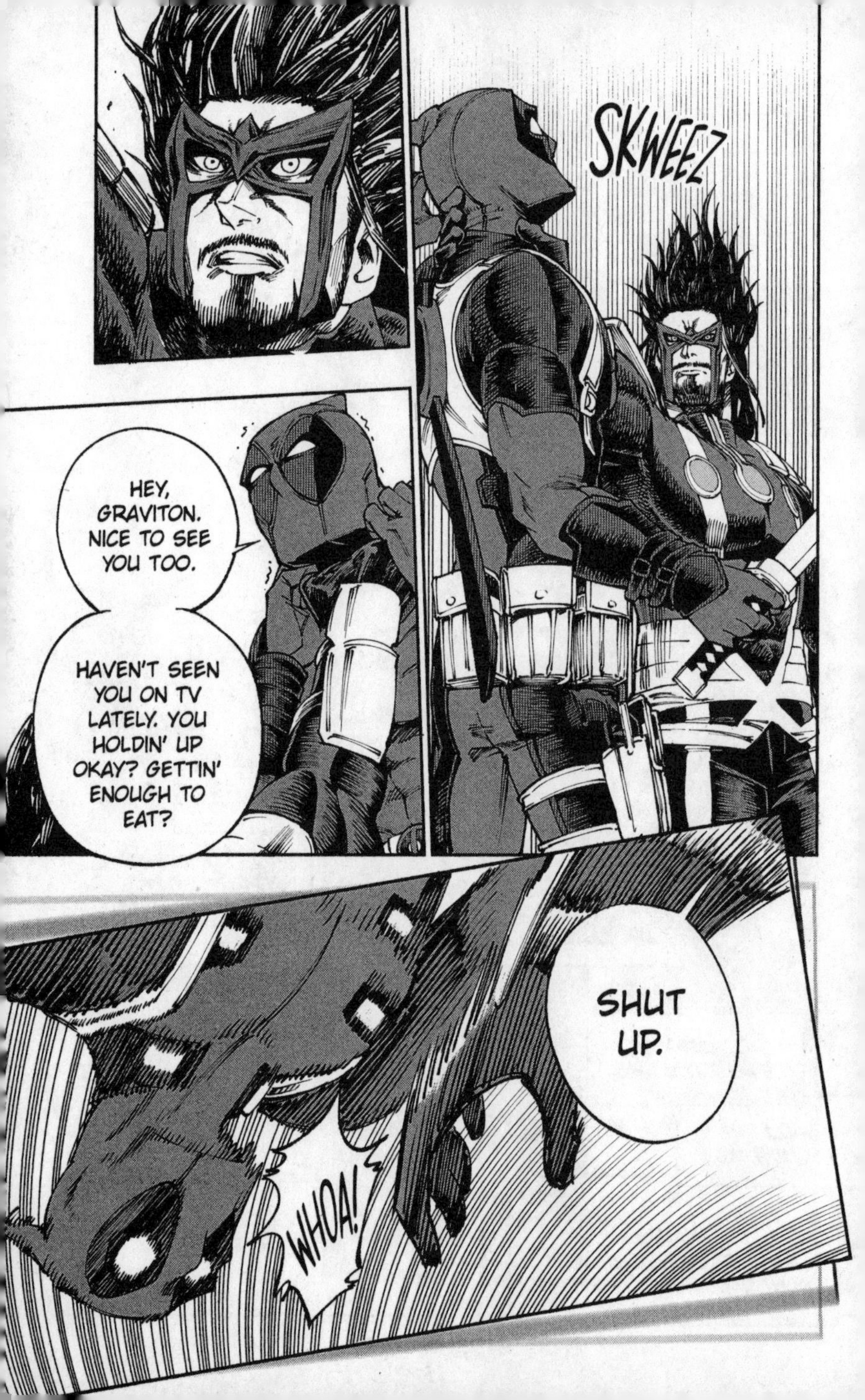
SKWEEZ
HEY, GRAVITON. NICE TO SEE YOU TOO.
HAVEN'T SEEN YOU ON TV LATELY. YOU HOLDIN' UP OKAY? GETTIN' ENOUGH TO EAT?
SHUT UP.
WHOA!

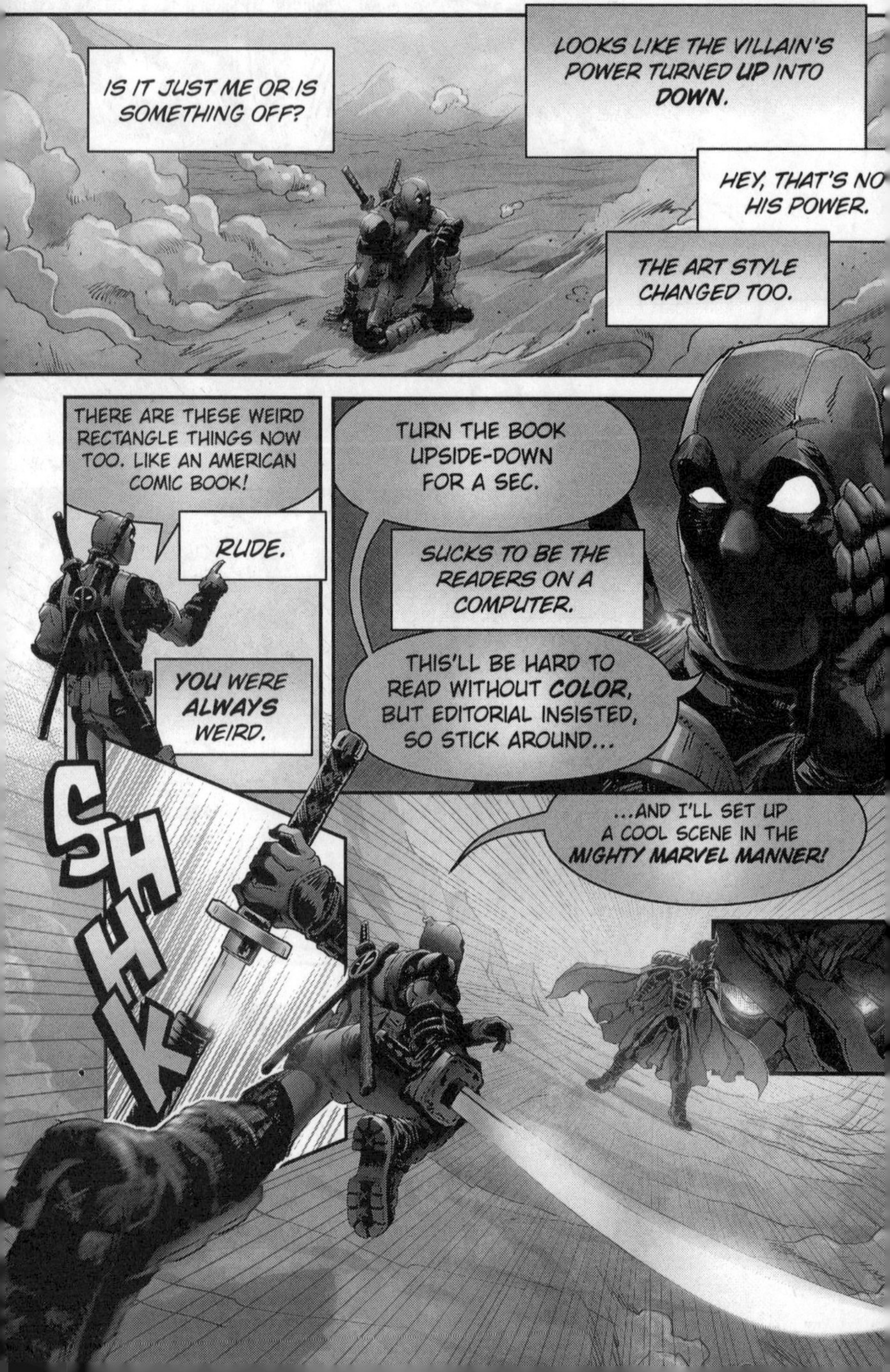
LOOKS LIKE THE VILLAIN'S POWER TURNED **UP** INTO **DOWN**.
HEY, THAT'S NO HIS POWER.
THE ART STYLE CHANGED TOO.
IS IT JUST ME OR IS SOMETHING OFF?
TURN THE BOOK UPSIDE-DOWN FOR A SEC.
SUCKS TO BE THE READERS ON A COMPUTER.
THIS'LL BE HARD TO READ WITHOUT **COLOR**, BUT EDITORIAL INSISTED, SO STICK AROUND...
THERE ARE THESE WEIRD RECTANGLE THINGS NOW TOO. LIKE AN AMERICAN COMIC BOOK!
RUDE.
YOU WERE **ALWAYS** WEIRD.
...AND I'LL SET UP A COOL SCENE IN THE **MIGHTY MARVEL MANNER!**
SHHK

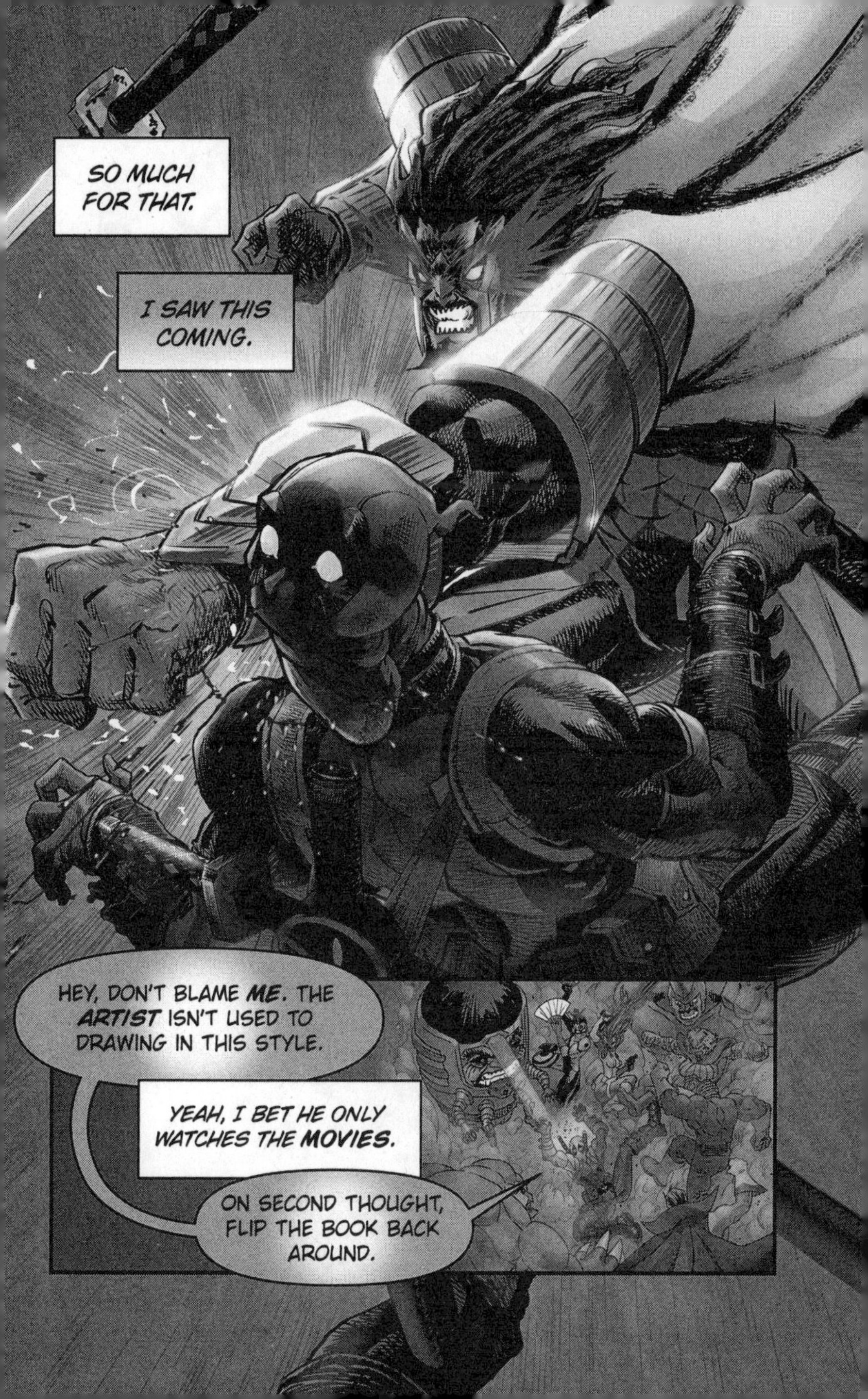
SO MUCH FOR THAT.
I SAW THIS COMING.
HEY, DON'T BLAME **ME**. THE **ARTIST** ISN'T USED TO DRAWING IN THIS STYLE.
YEAH, I BET HE ONLY WATCHES THE **MOVIES**.
ON SECOND THOUGHT, FLIP THE BOOK BACK AROUND.

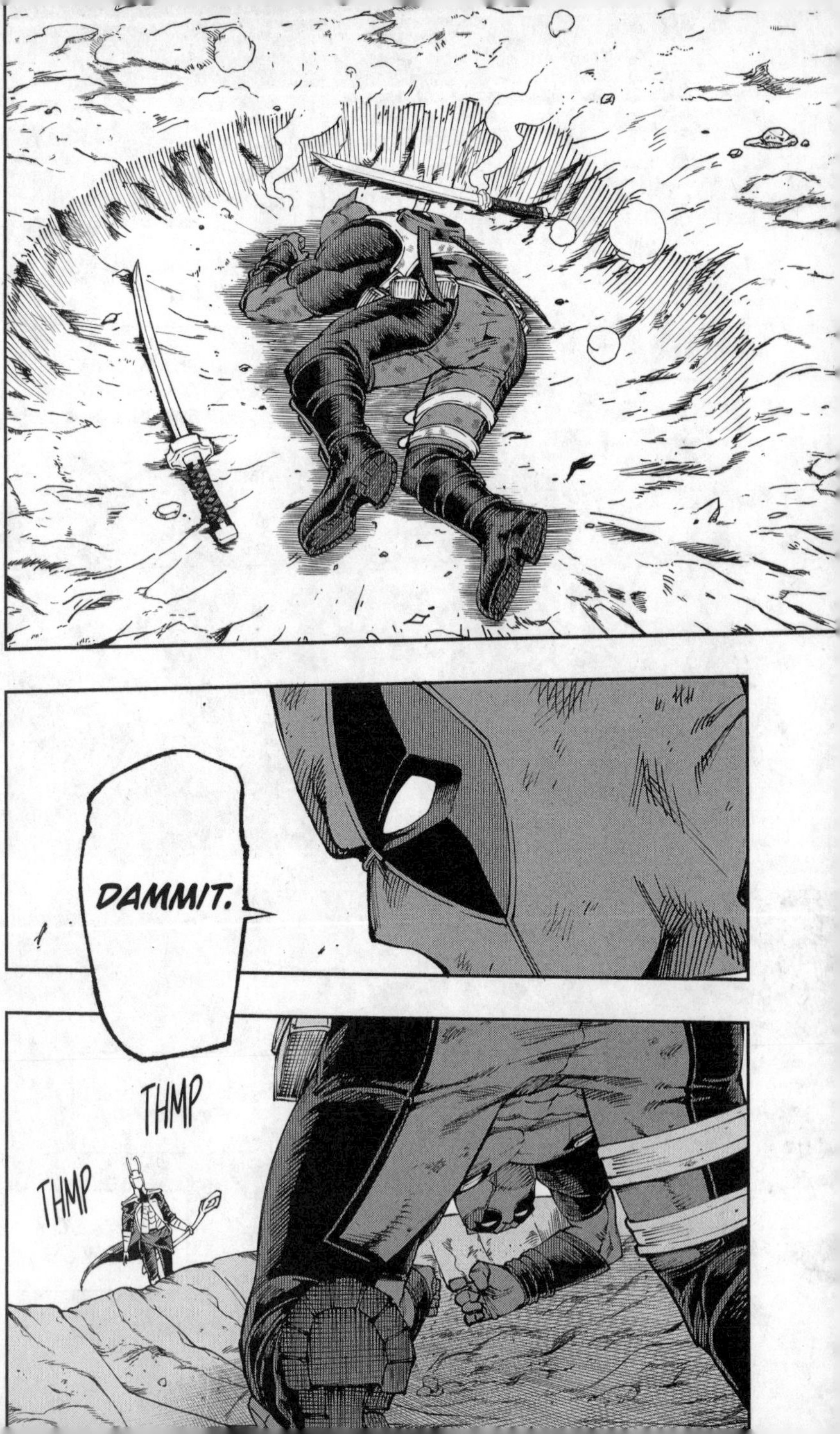
DAMMIT.
THMP
THMP

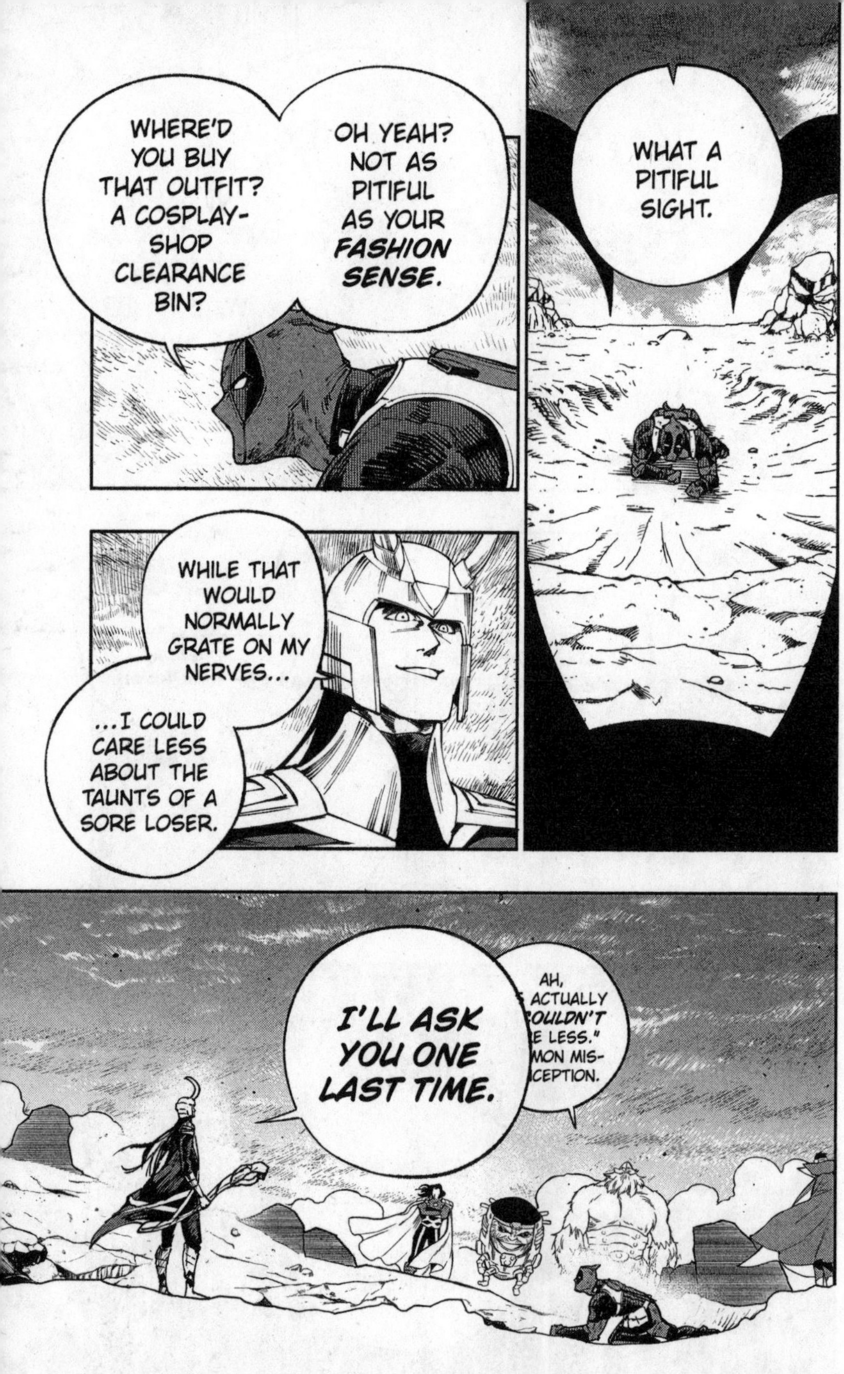
WHAT A PITIFUL SIGHT.
OH YEAH? NOT AS PITIFUL AS YOUR FASHION SENSE.
WHERE'D YOU BUY THAT OUTFIT? A COSPLAY-SHOP CLEARANCE BIN?
WHILE THAT WOULD NORMALLY GRATE ON MY NERVES...
...I COULD CARE LESS ABOUT THE TAUNTS OF A SORE LOSER.
AH, ACTUALLY OULDN'T E LESS." MON MIS- CEPTION.
I'LL ASK YOU ONE LAST TIME.

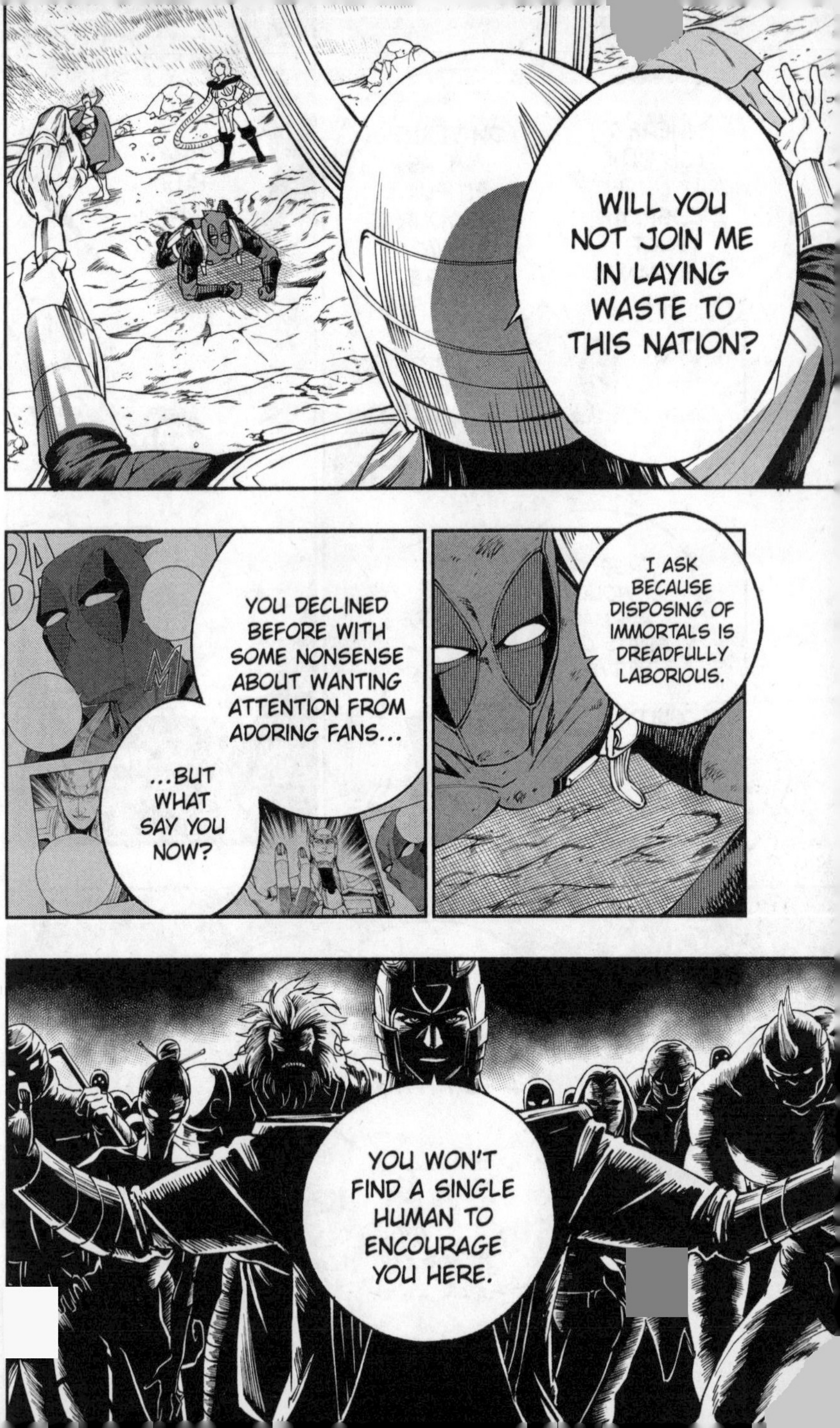
WILL YOU NOT JOIN ME IN LAYING WASTE TO THIS NATION?
I ASK BECAUSE DISPOSING OF IMMORTALS IS DREADFULLY LABORIOUS.
YOU DECLINED BEFORE WITH SOME NONSENSE ABOUT WANTING ATTENTION FROM ADORING FANS...
...BUT WHAT SAY YOU NOW?
YOU WON'T FIND A SINGLE HUMAN TO ENCOURAGE YOU HERE.

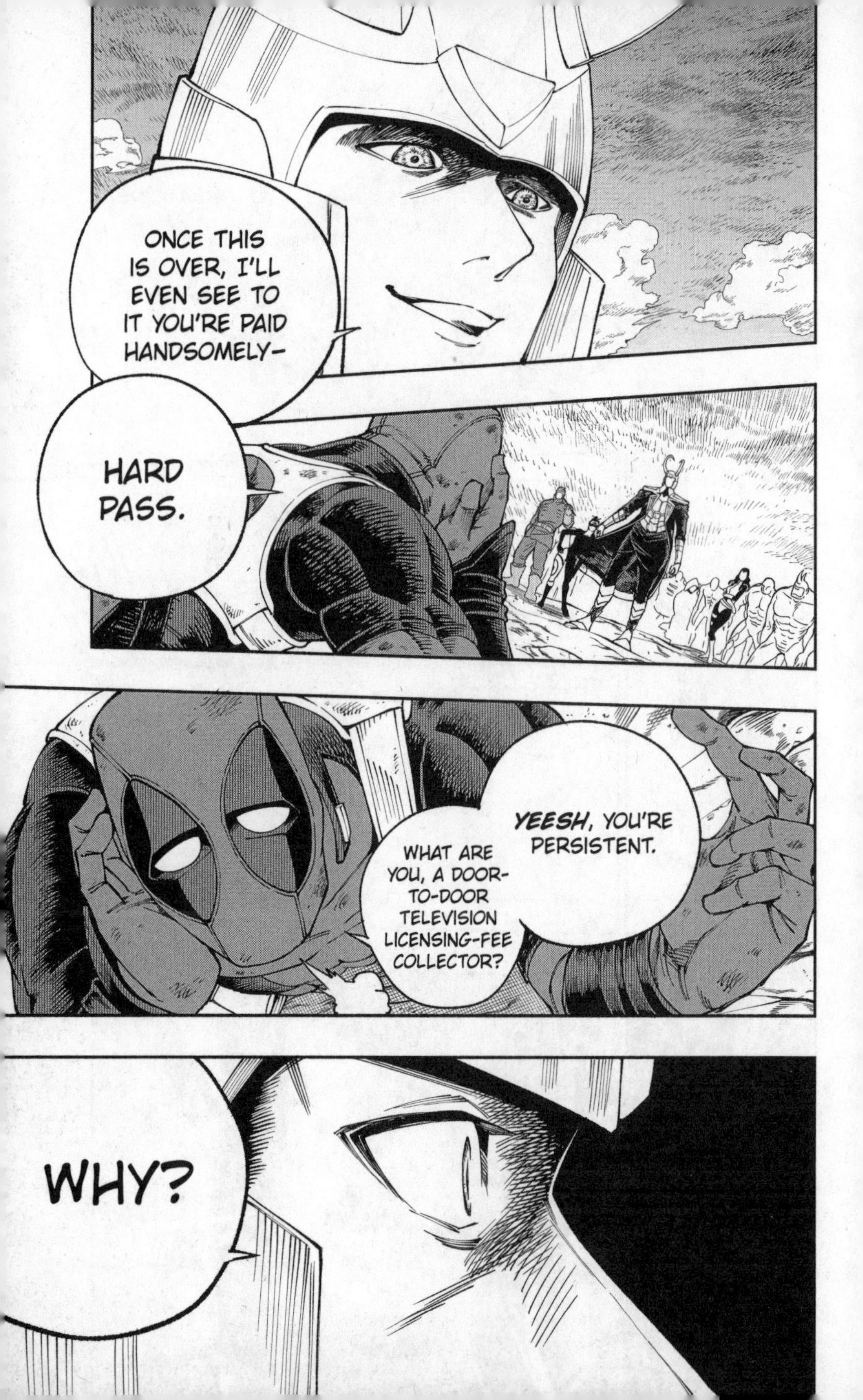
ONCE THIS IS OVER, I'LL EVEN SEE TO IT YOU'RE PAID HANDSOMELY-
HARD PASS.
YEESH, YOU'RE PERSISTENT.
WHAT ARE YOU, A DOOR-TO-DOOR TELEVISION LICENSING-FEE COLLECTOR?
WHY?

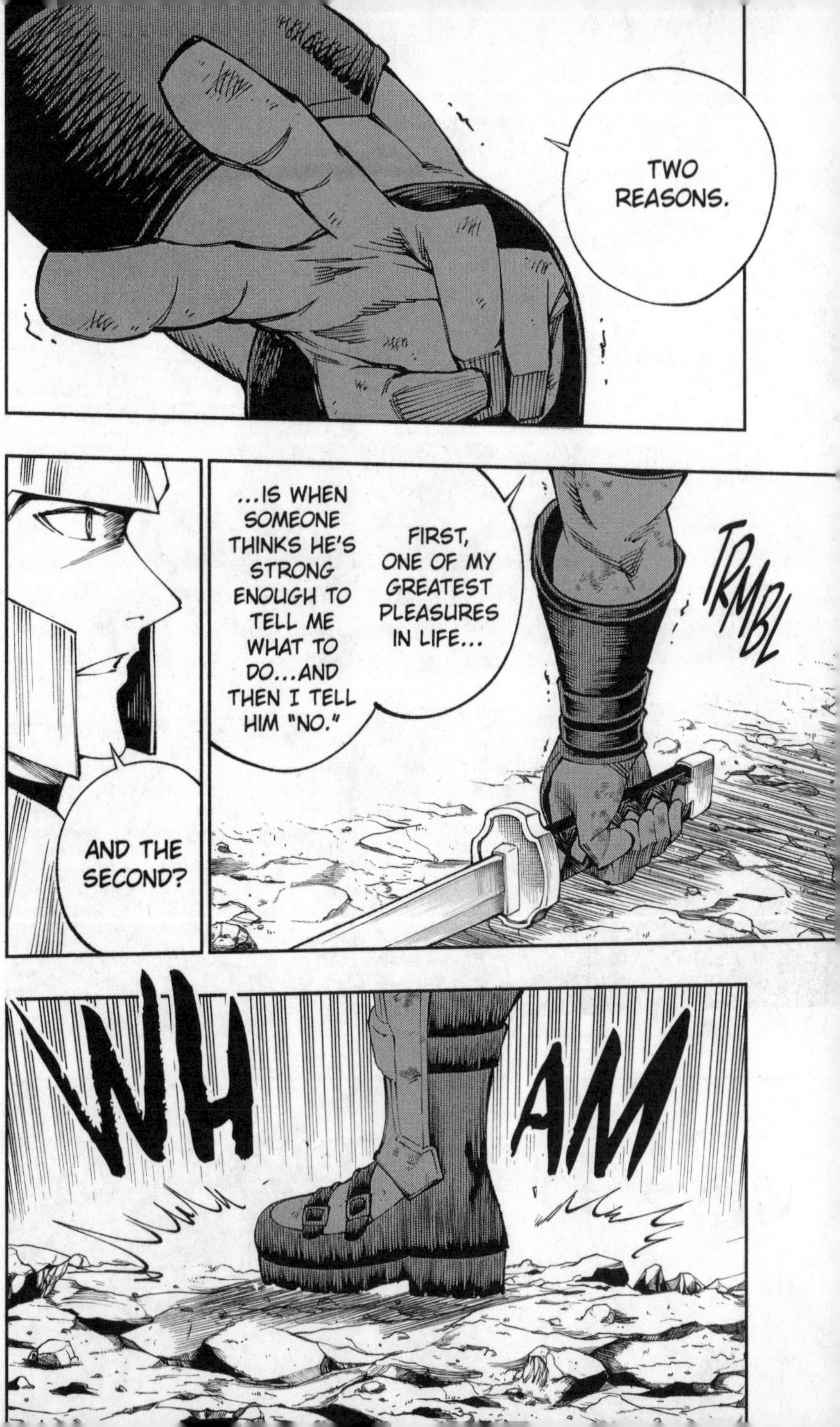
TWO REASONS.
TRMBL
FIRST, ONE OF MY GREATEST PLEASURES IN LIFE...
...IS WHEN SOMEONE THINKS HE'S STRONG ENOUGH TO TELL ME WHAT TO DO...AND THEN I TELL HIM "NO."
AND THE SECOND?
WHAM

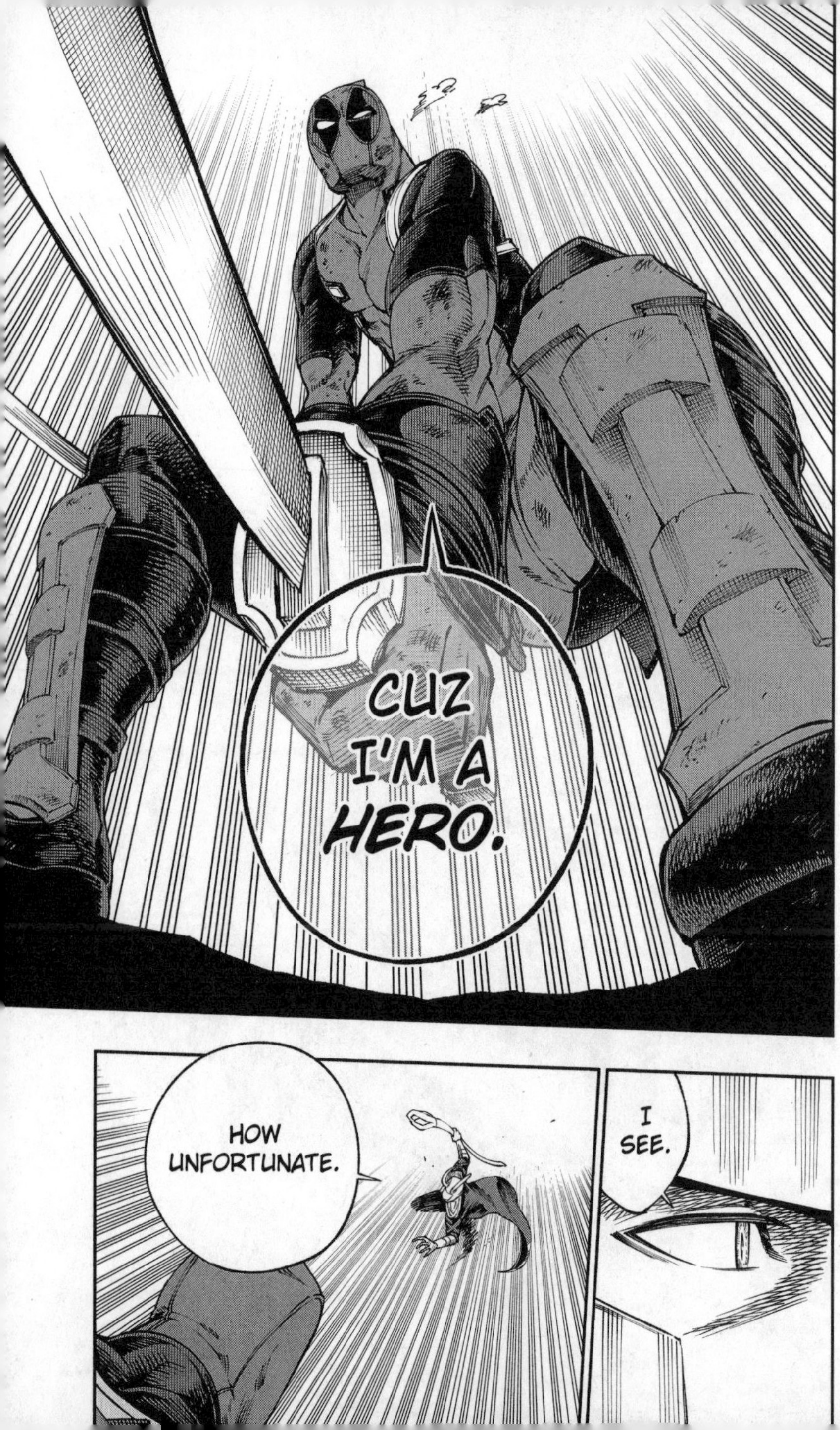
CUZ I'M A HERO.
I SEE.
HOW UNFORTUNATE.

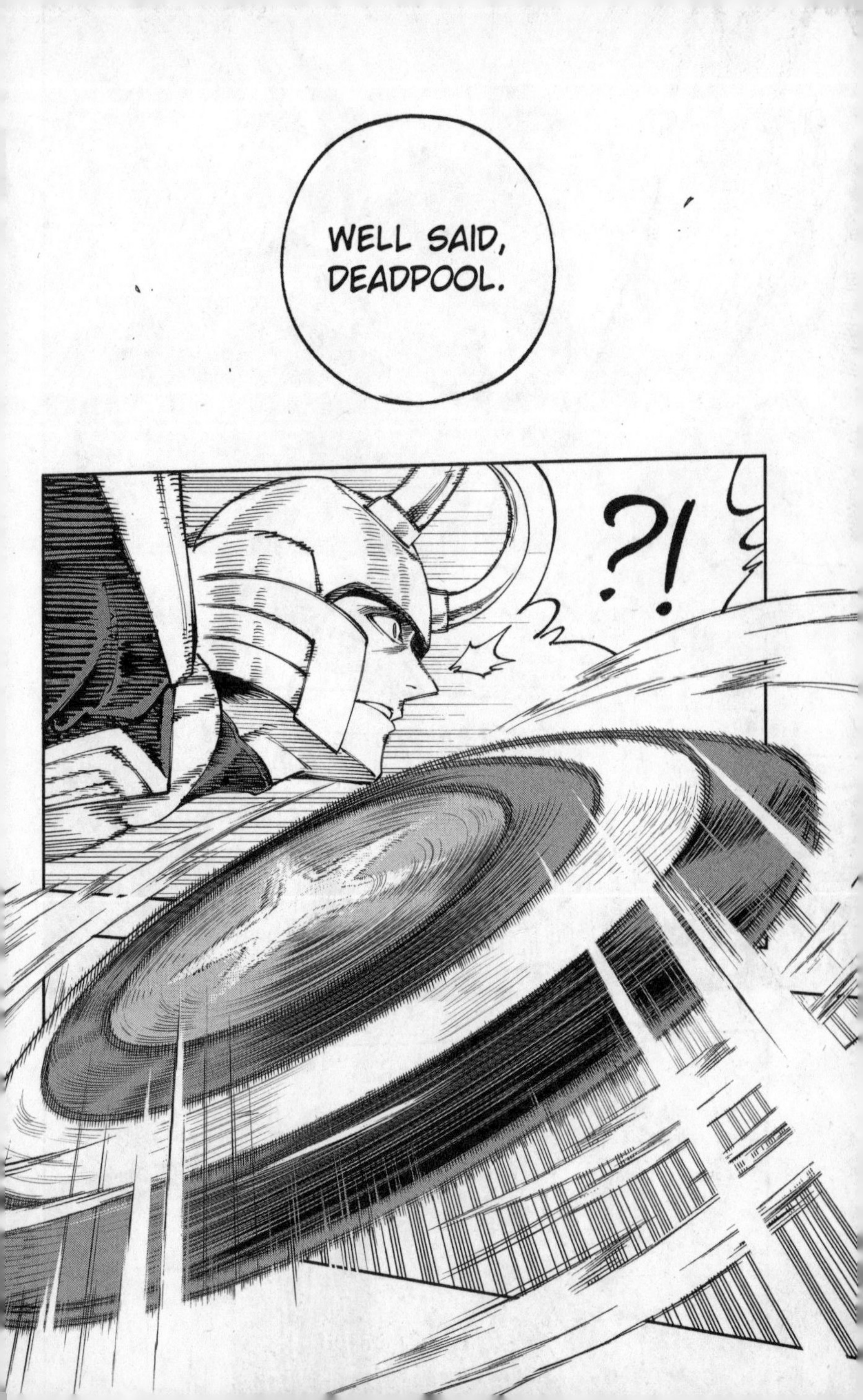
WELL SAID, DEADPOOL.
?!

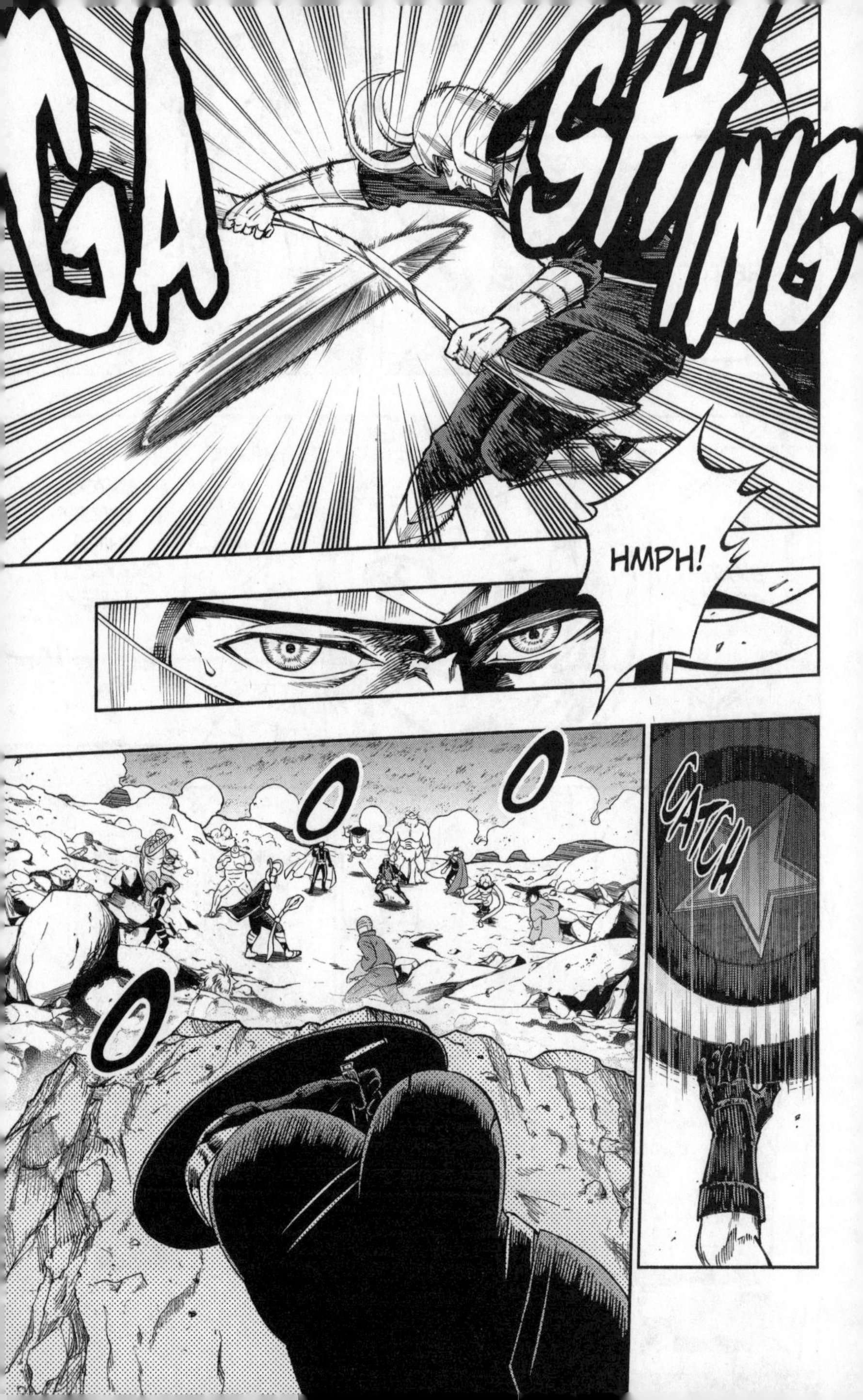
GA
GSHING
HMPH!
CATCH

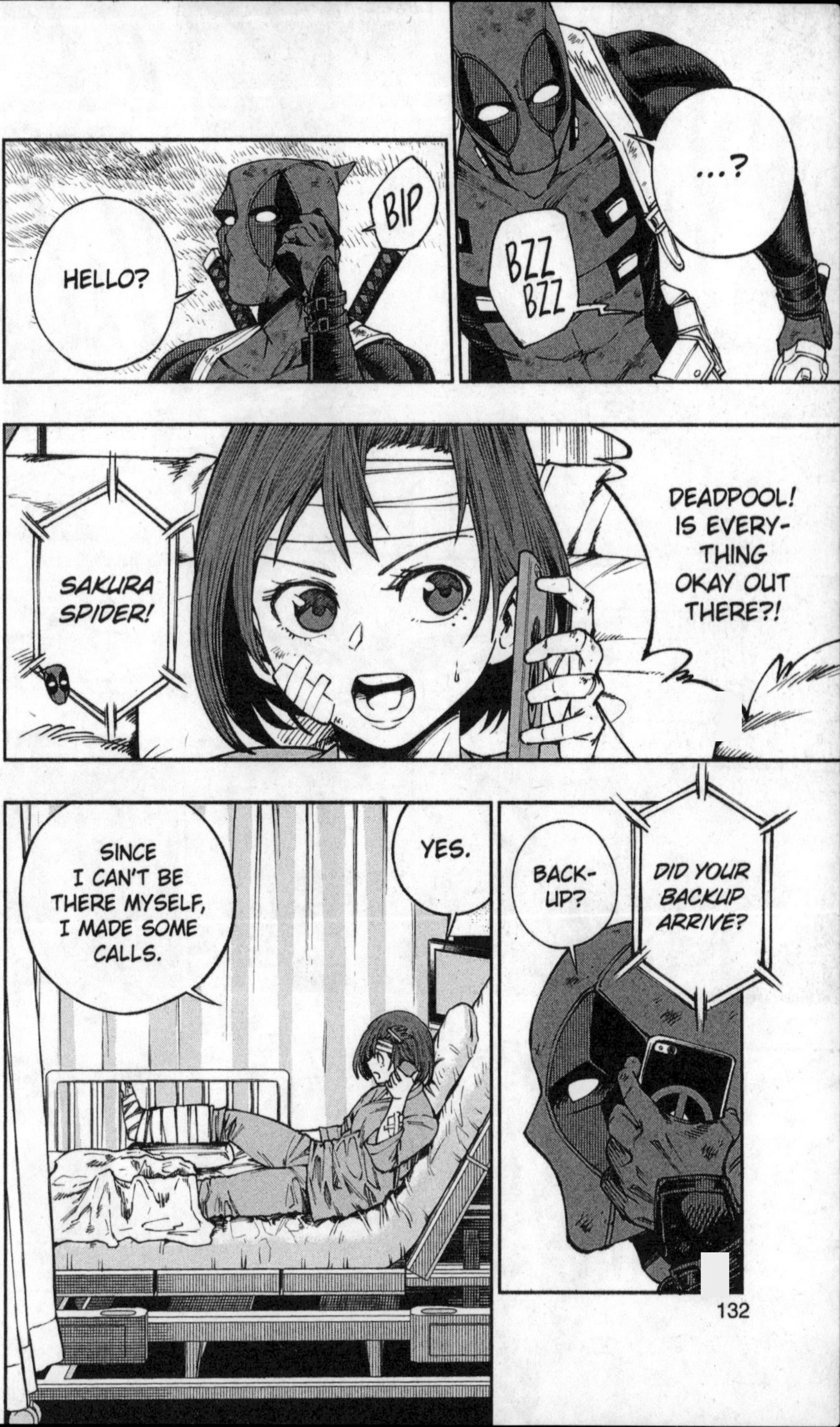
...?
BZZ BZZ
BIP
HELLO?
DEADPOOL! IS EVERY-THING OKAY OUT THERE?!
SAKURA SPIDER!
DID YOUR BACKUP ARRIVE?
BACK-UP?
YES.
SINCE I CAN'T BE THERE MYSELF, I MADE SOME CALLS.

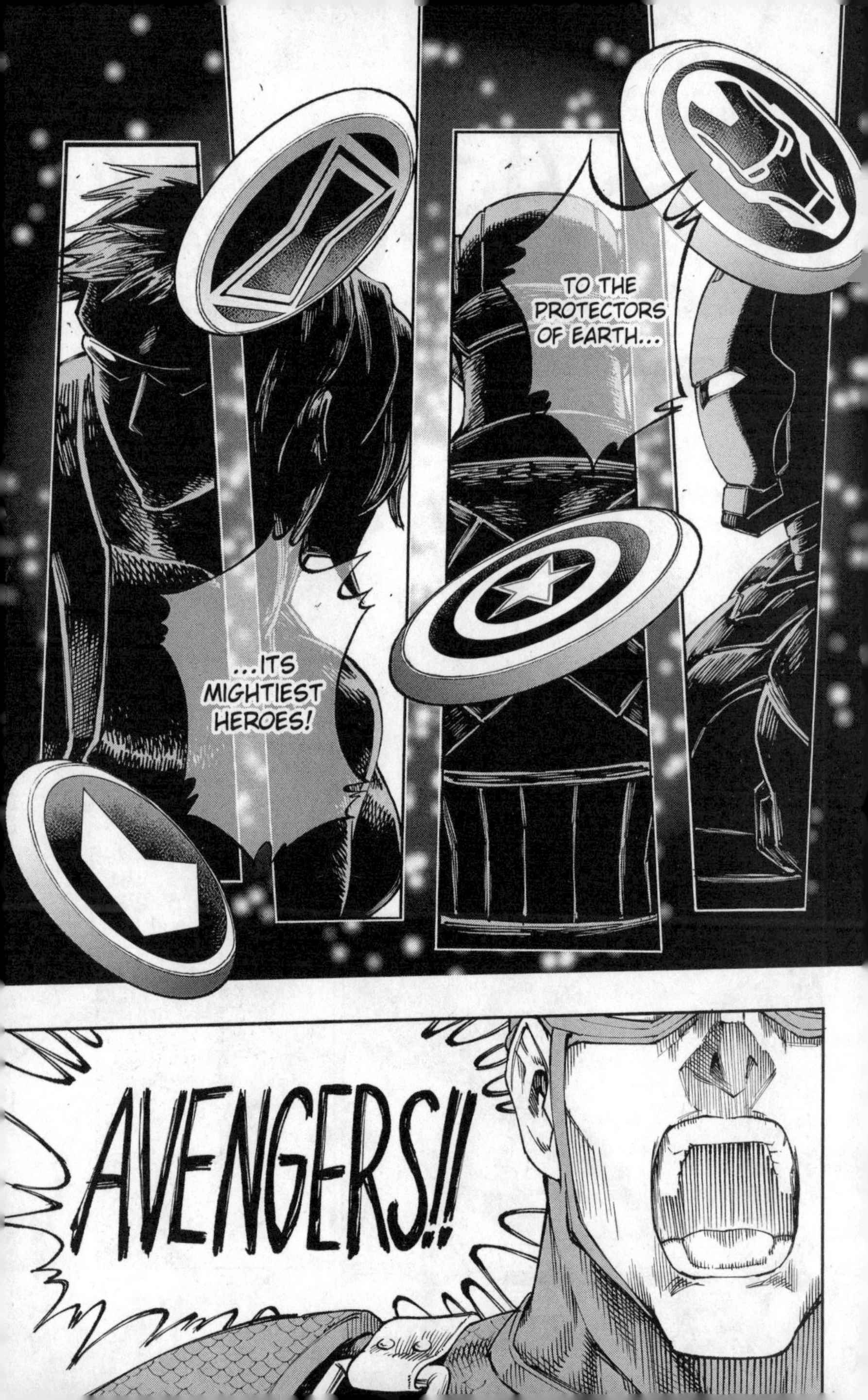
TO THE PROTECTORS OF EARTH...
...ITS MIGHTIEST HEROES!
AVENGERS!!

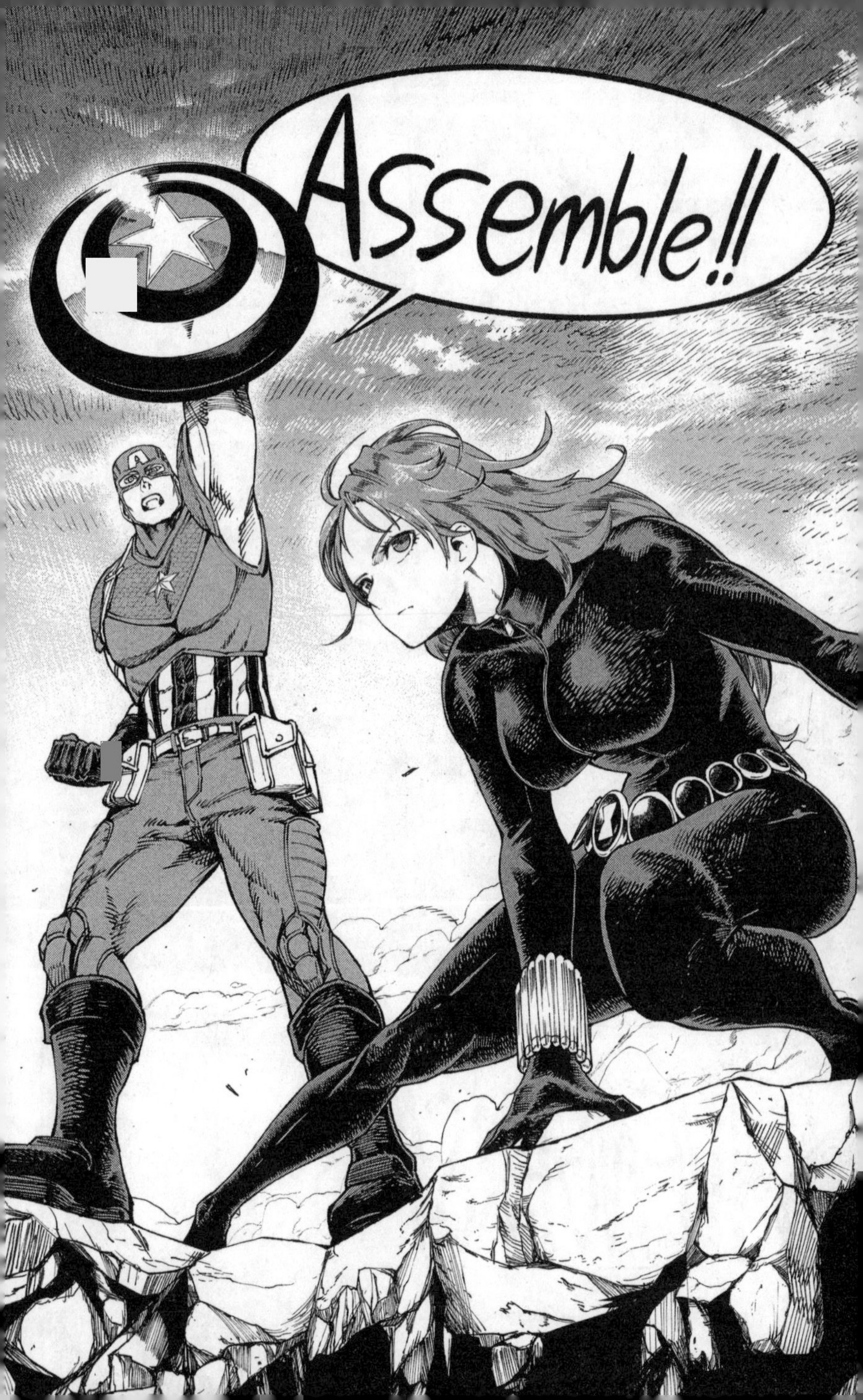
Assemble!!

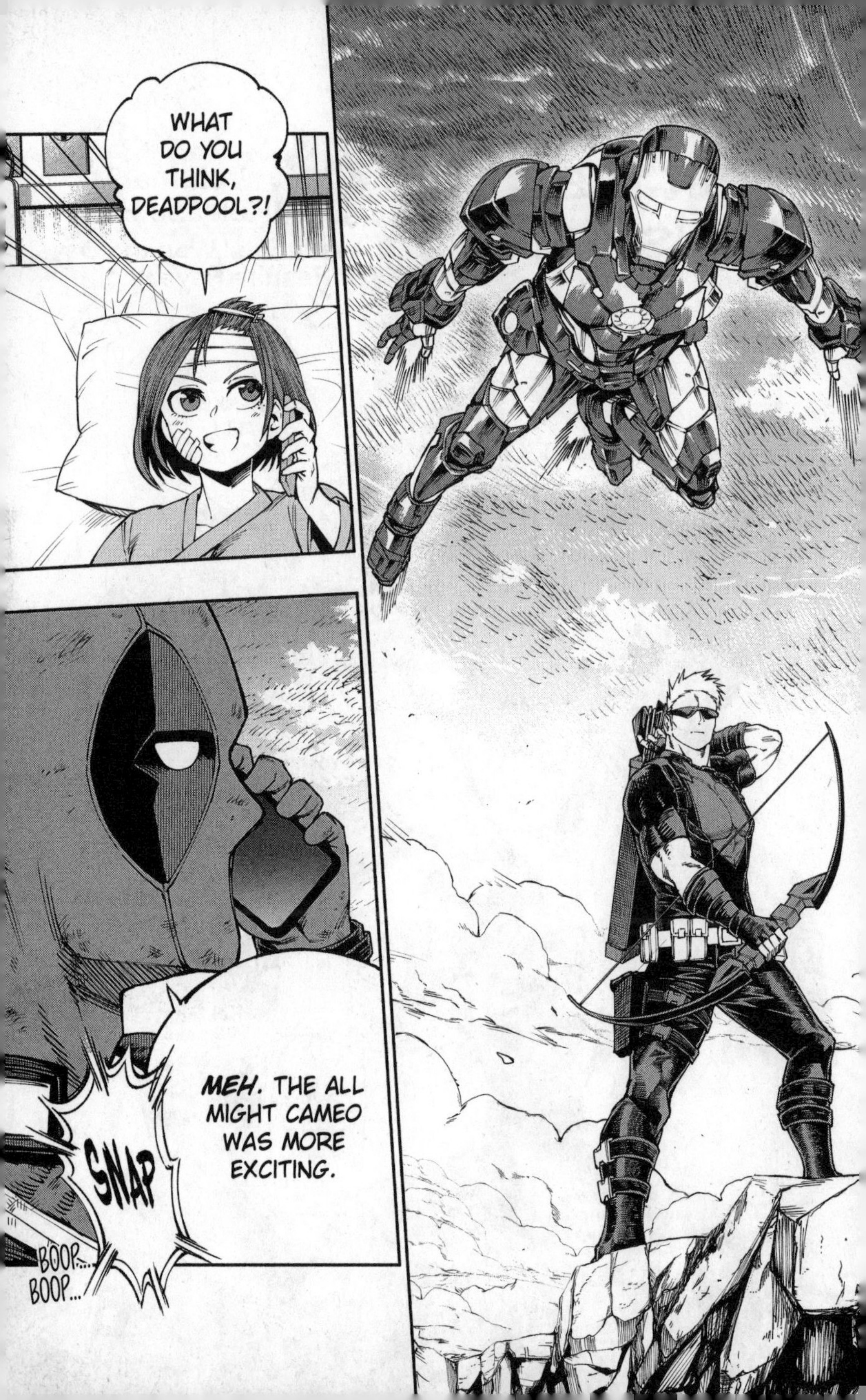
WHAT DO YOU THINK, DEADPOOL?!
SNAP
MEH. THE ALL MIGHT CAMEO WAS MORE EXCITING.
BOOP... BOOP...

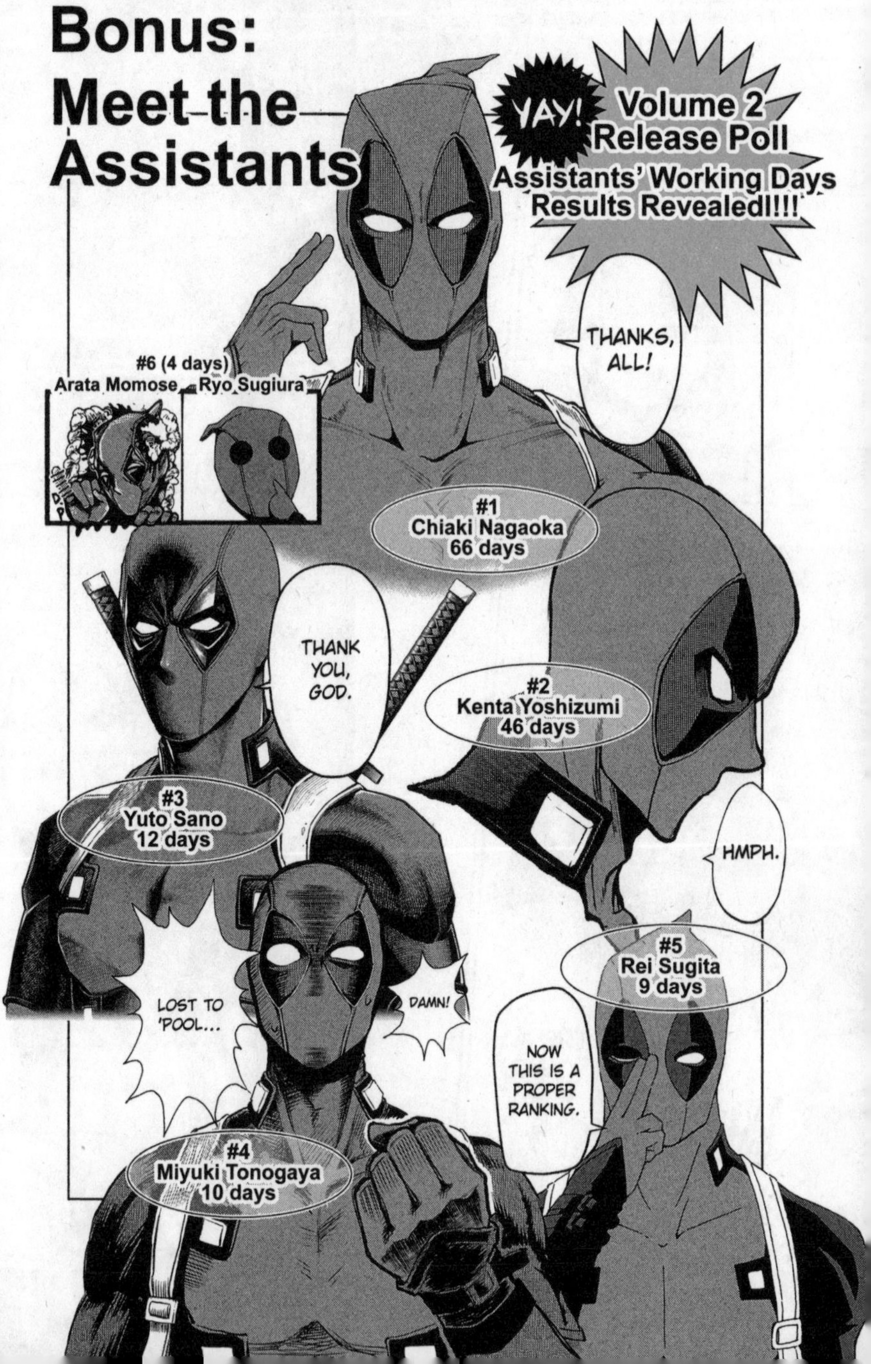
Bonus: Meet the Assistants
YAY! Volume 2 Release Poll
Assistants' Working Days Results Revealed!!!!
THANKS, ALL!
#1 Chiaki Nagaoka 66 days
#6 (4 days)
Arata Momose
Ryo Sugiura
HMPH.
#2 Kenta Yoshizumi 46 days
THANK YOU, GOD.
#3 Yuto Sano 12 days
#5 Rei Sugita 9 days
NOW THIS IS A PROPER RANKING.
DAMN!
LOST TO 'POOL...
#4 Miyuki Tonogaya 10 days

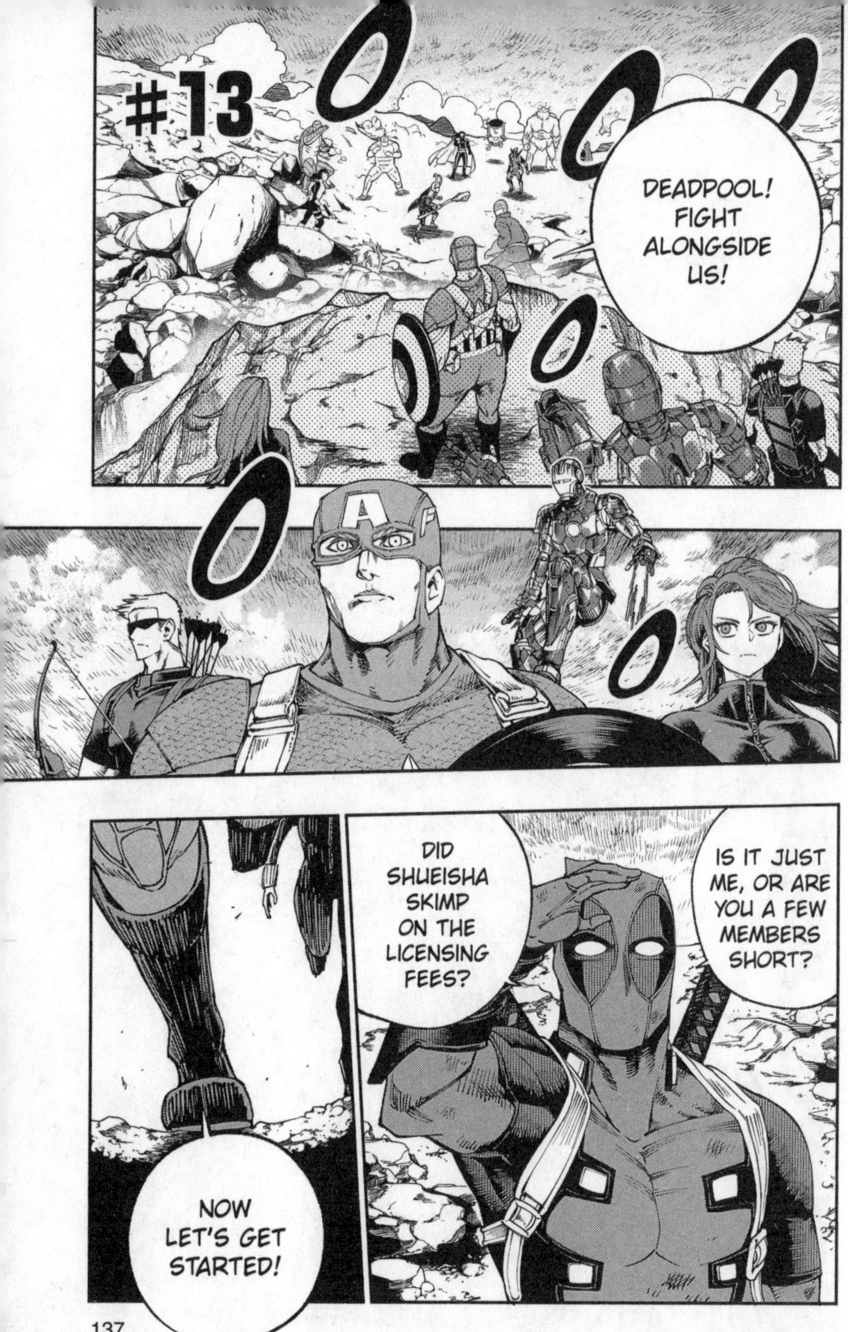
#13
DEADPOOL! FIGHT ALONGSIDE US!
IS IT JUST ME, OR ARE YOU A FEW MEMBERS SHORT?
DID SHUEISHA SKIMP ON THE LICENSING FEES?
NOW LET'S GET STARTED!

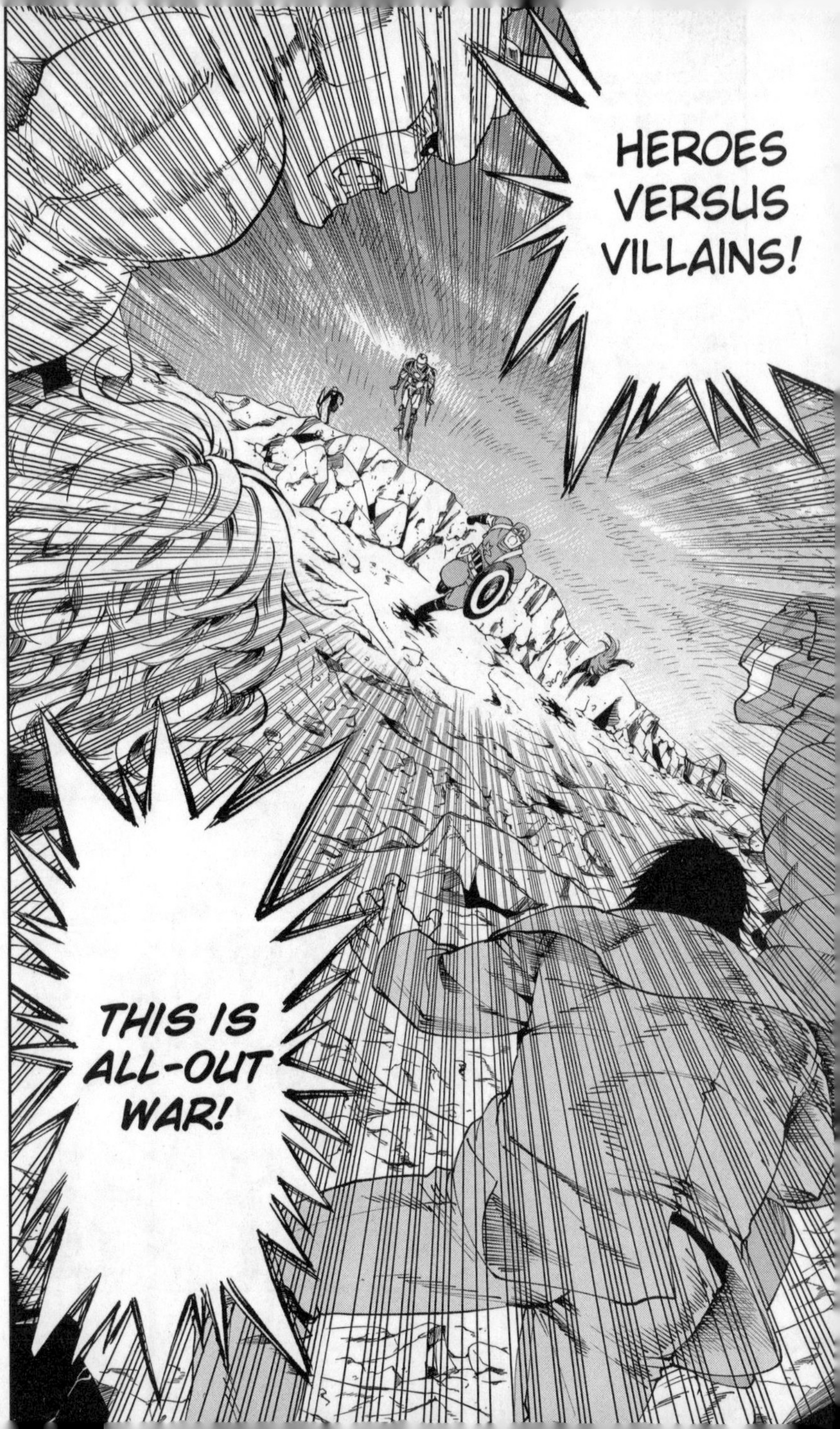
HEROES VERSUS VILLAINS!
THIS IS ALL-OUT WAR!

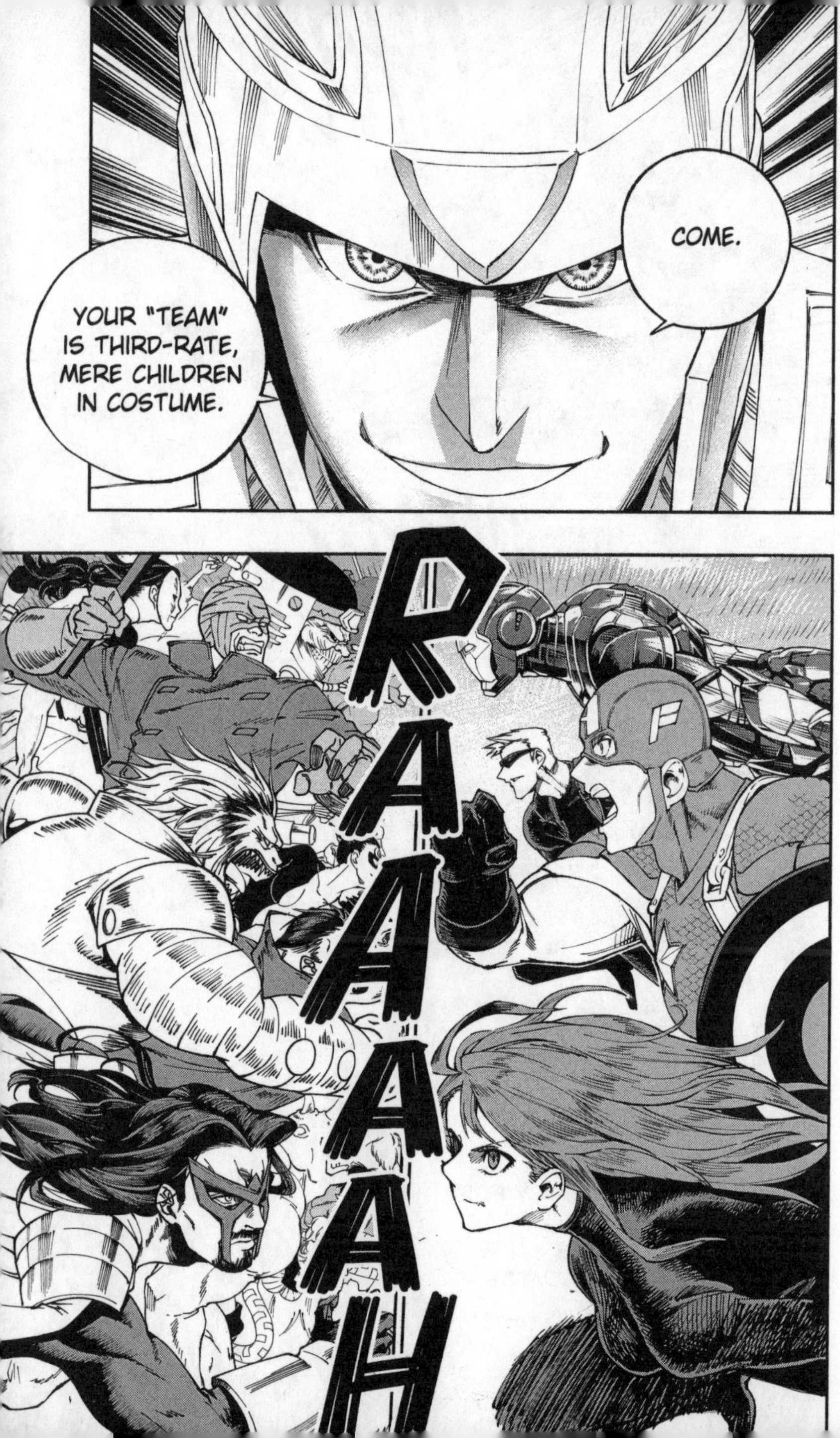
COME.
YOUR "TEAM" IS THIRD-RATE, MERE CHILDREN IN COSTUME.
RAAAAH

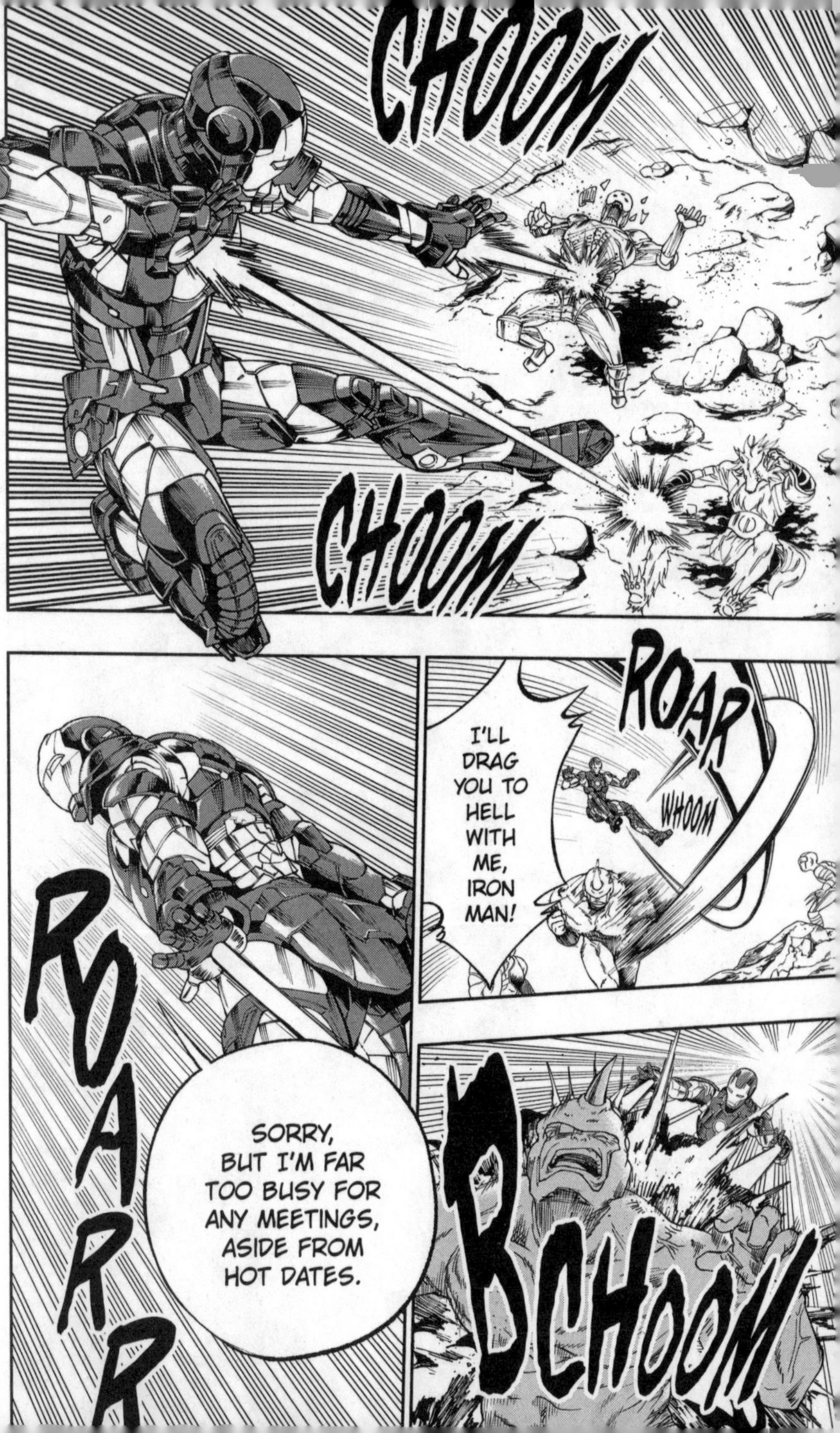
CHOOM
CHOOM
ROAR
I'LL DRAG YOU TO HELL WITH ME, IRON MAN!
WHOOM
BCHOOM
ROARR
SORRY, BUT I'M FAR TOO BUSY FOR ANY MEETINGS, ASIDE FROM HOT DATES.

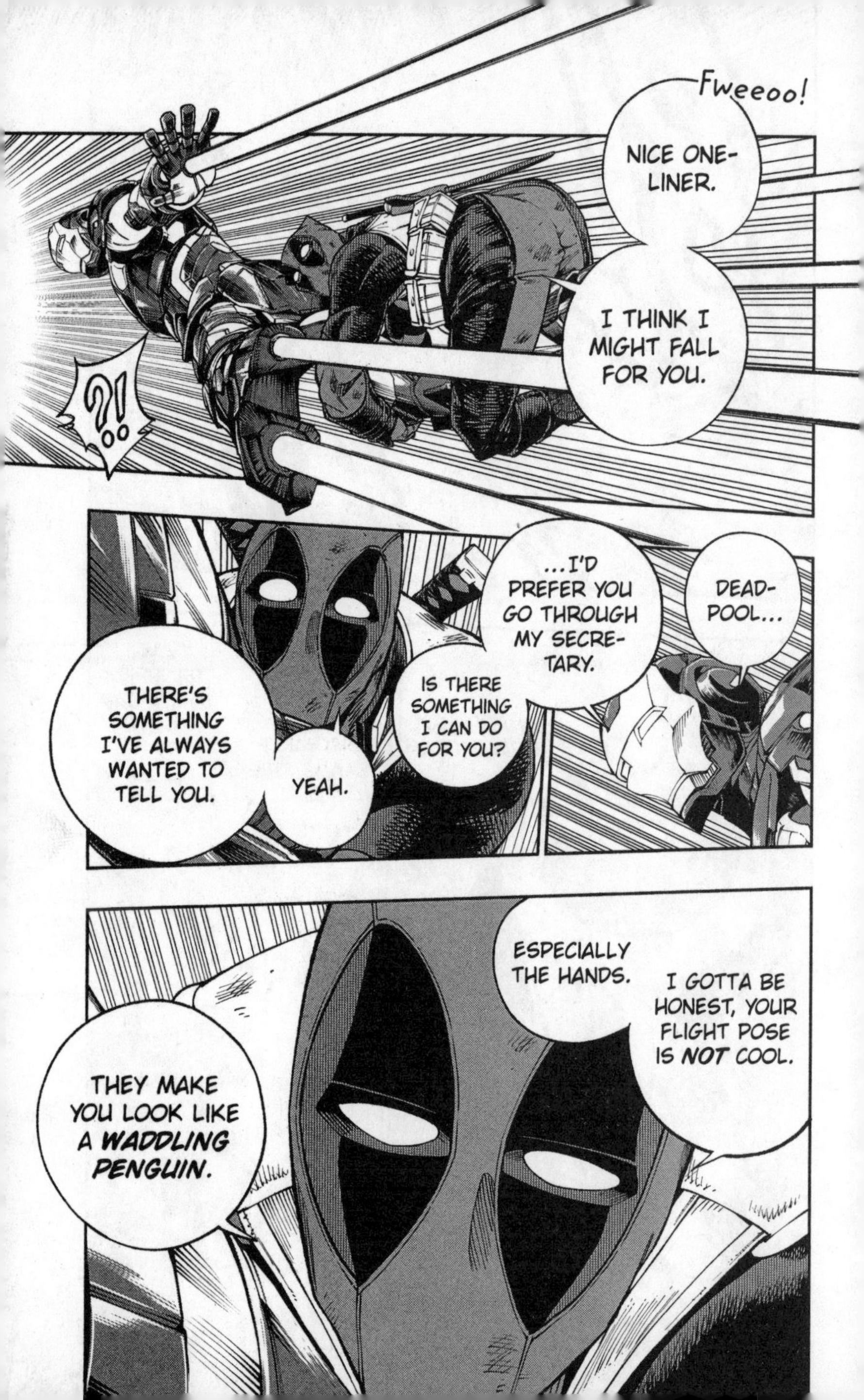
Fweeoo!
NICE ONE-LINER.
I THINK I MIGHT FALL FOR YOU.
?!
DEAD-POOL...
...I'D PREFER YOU GO THROUGH MY SECRETARY.
IS THERE SOMETHING I CAN DO FOR YOU?
YEAH.
THERE'S SOMETHING I'VE ALWAYS WANTED TO TELL YOU.
I GOTTA BE HONEST, YOUR FLIGHT POSE IS ***NOT*** COOL.
ESPECIALLY THE HANDS.
THEY MAKE YOU LOOK LIKE A ***WADDLING PENGUIN***.

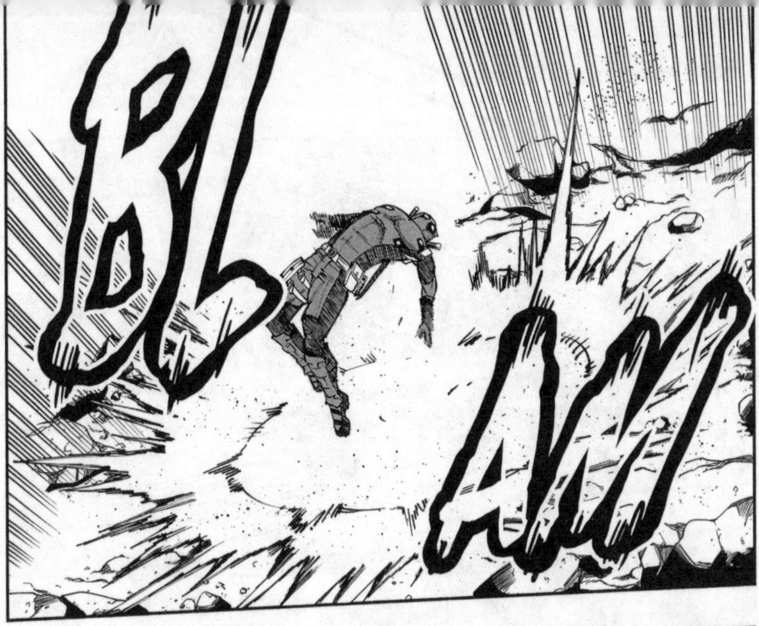
BLAM

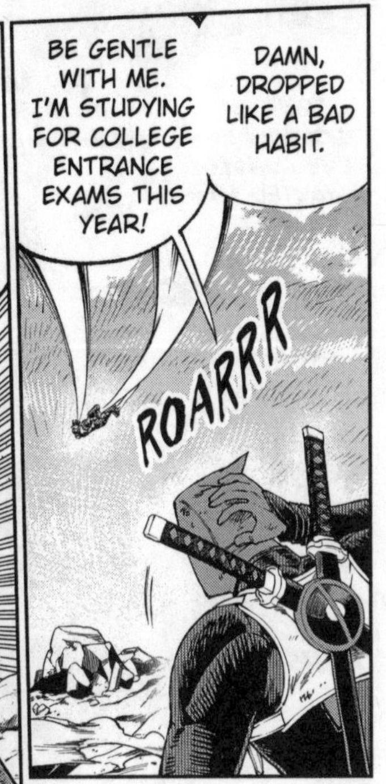
DAMN, DROPPED LIKE A BAD HABIT.
BE GENTLE WITH ME. I'M STUDYING FOR COLLEGE ENTRANCE EXAMS THIS YEAR!
ROARRR

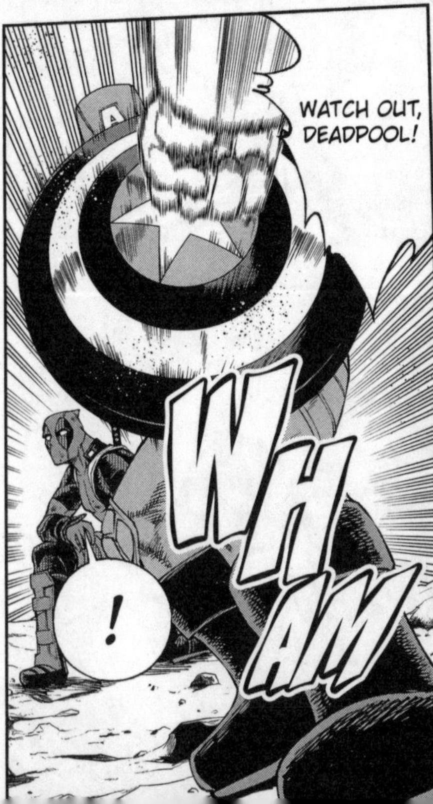
WATCH OUT, DEADPOOL!
WHAM
!

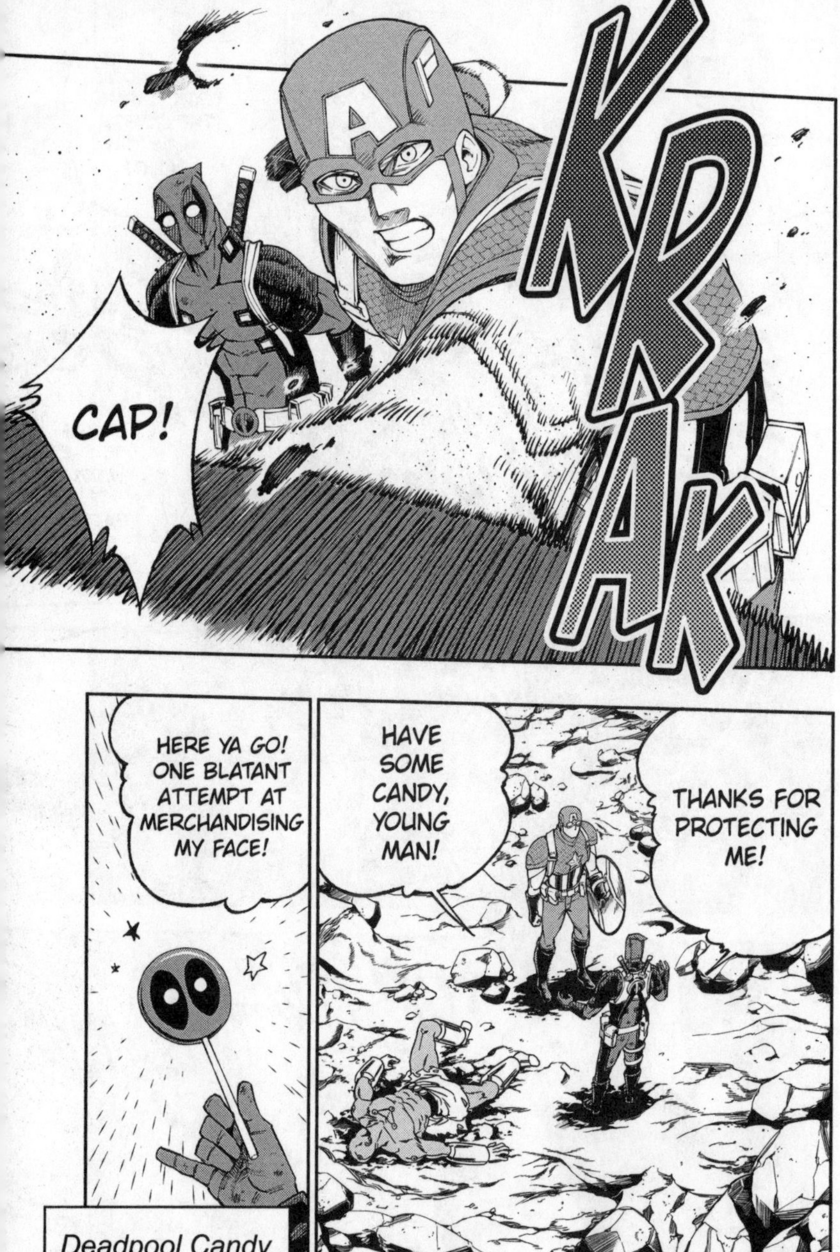
CAP!
KRAK
THANKS FOR PROTECTING ME!
HAVE SOME CANDY, YOUNG MAN!
HERE YA GO! ONE BLATANT ATTEMPT AT MERCHANDISING MY FACE!
Deadpool Candy 680 yen (plus tax)

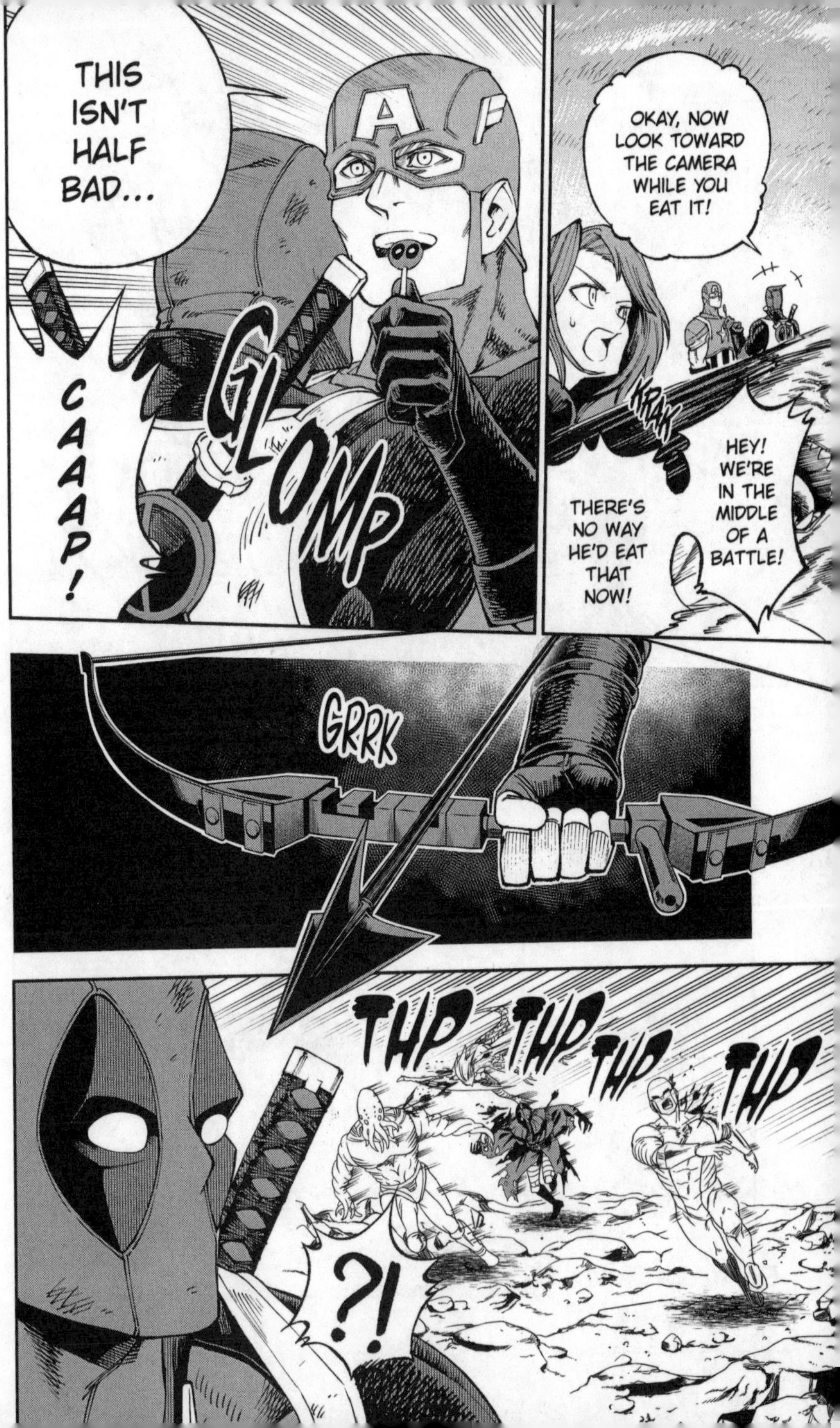
OKAY, NOW LOOK TOWARD THE CAMERA WHILE YOU EAT IT!
KRAK
HEY! WE'RE IN THE MIDDLE OF A BATTLE!
THERE'S NO WAY HE'D EAT THAT NOW!
THIS ISN'T HALF BAD...
GLOMP
CAAAAP!
GRRK
THP THP THP THP
?!

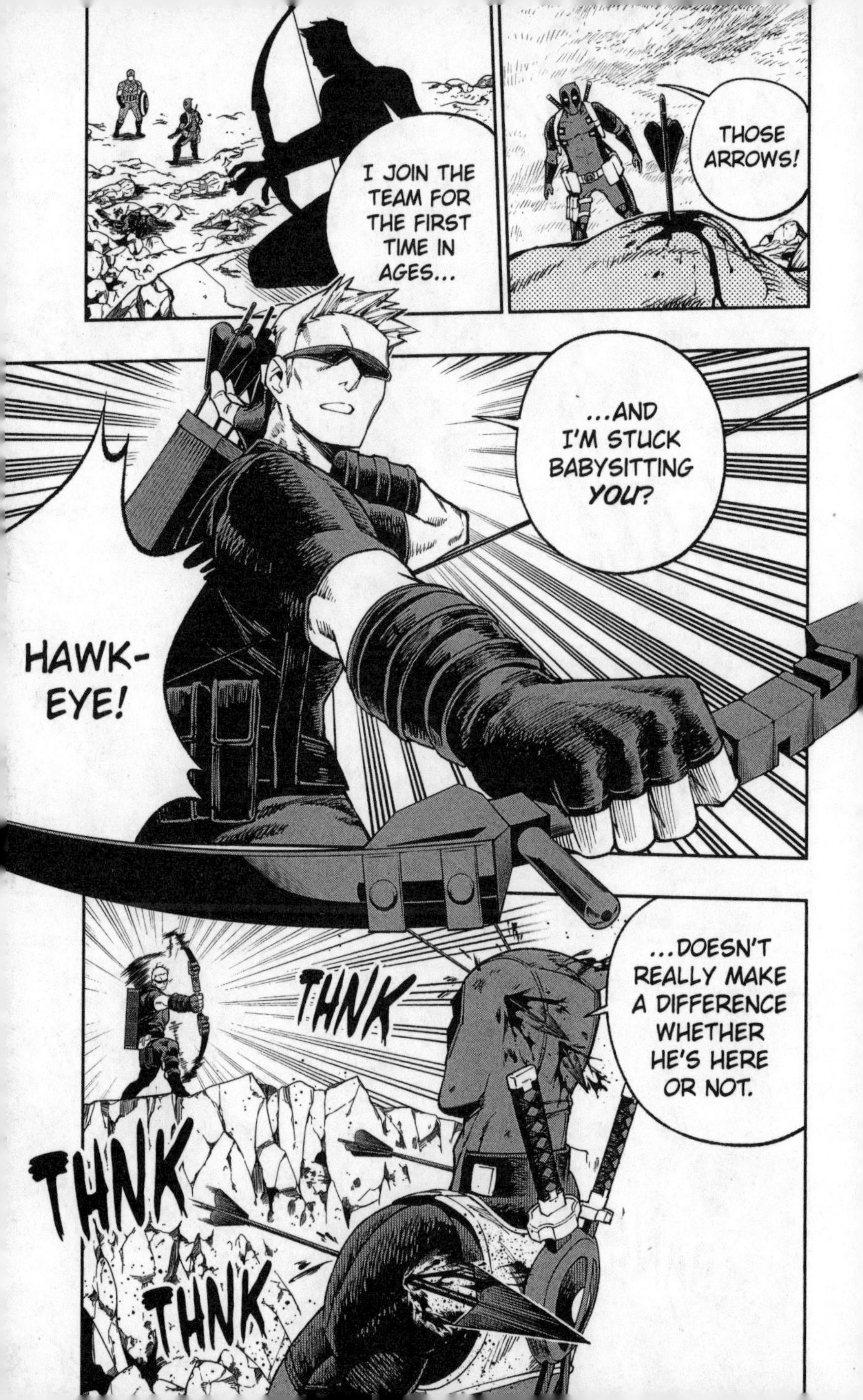
THOSE ARROWS!
I JOIN THE TEAM FOR THE FIRST TIME IN AGES...
...AND I'M STUCK BABYSITTING *YOU*?
HAWK-EYE!
...DOESN'T REALLY MAKE A DIFFERENCE WHETHER HE'S HERE OR NOT.
THNK
THNK
THNK

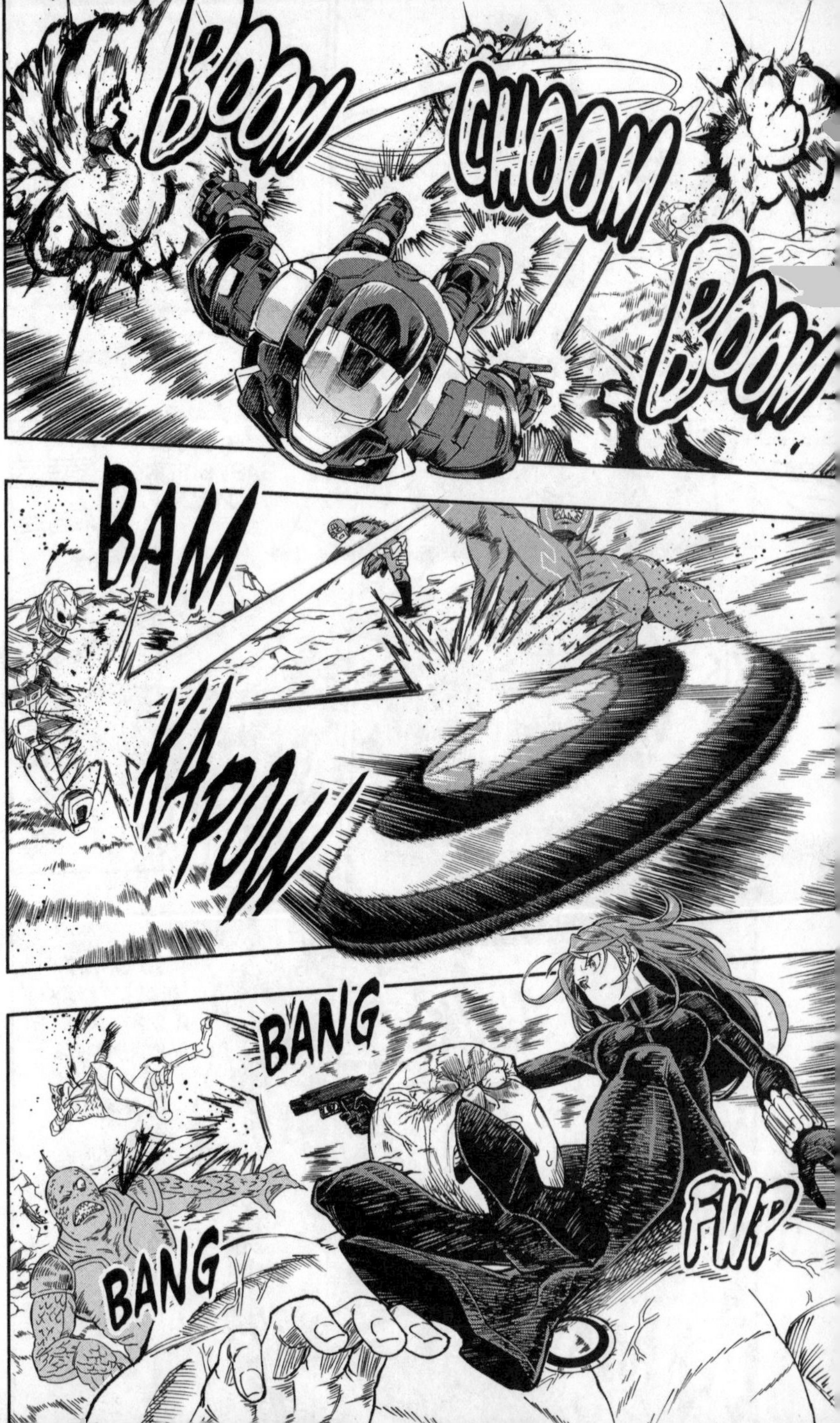
BOOM
CHOOM
BOOM
BAM
KAPOW
FWIP
BANG
BANG

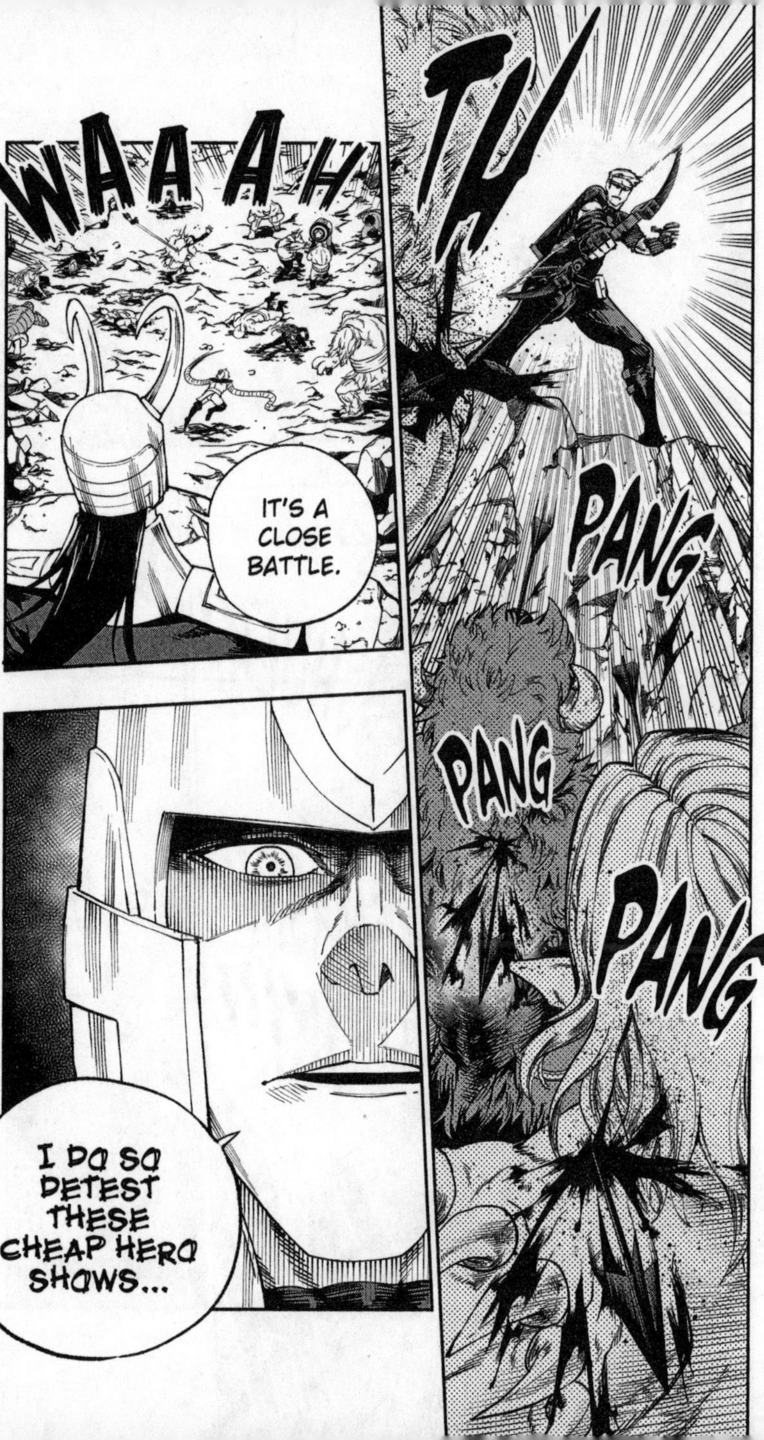

TH
PANG
PANG
PANG
WAAAAH
IT'S A CLOSE BATTLE.
I DO SO DETEST THESE CHEAP HERO SHOWS...

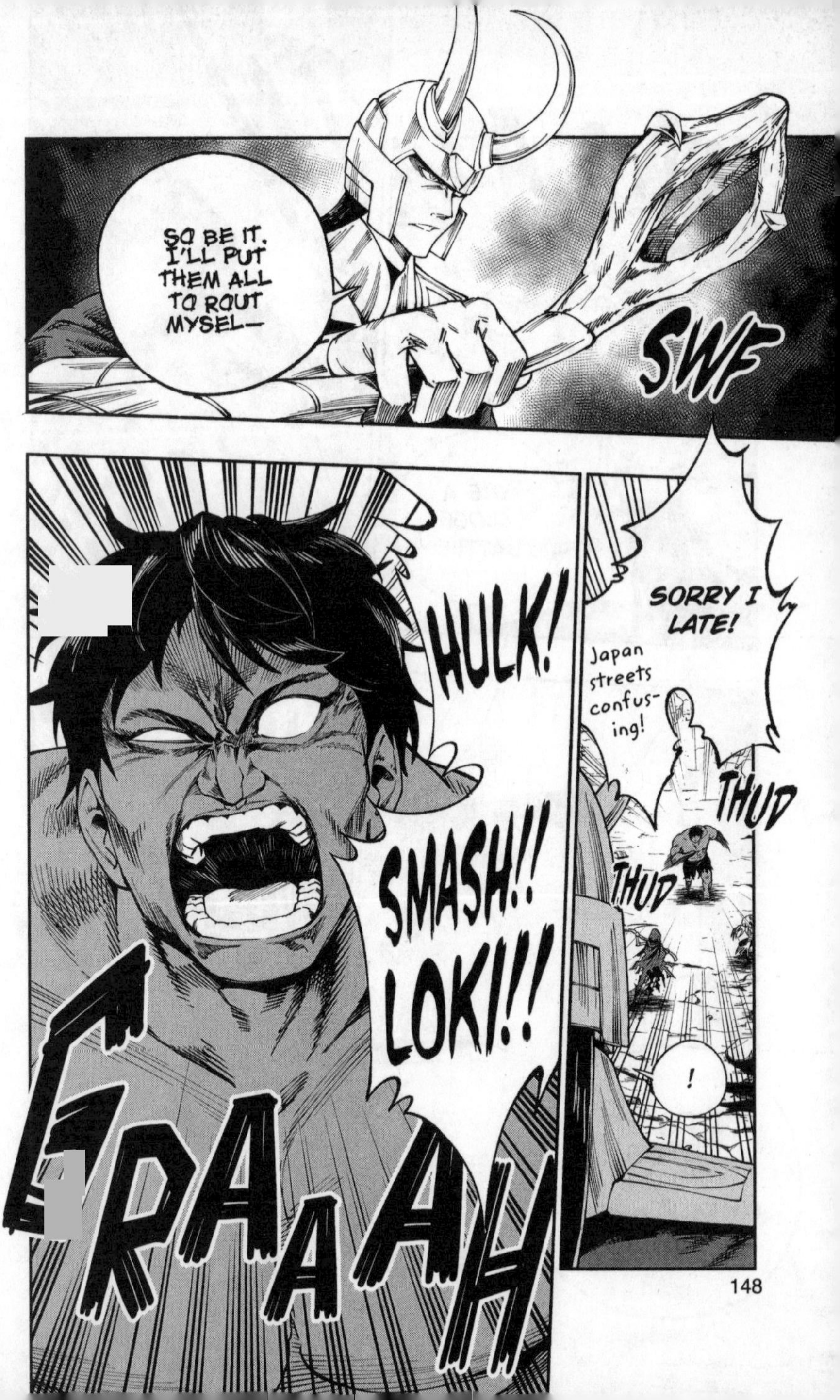
SO BE IT. I'LL PUT THEM ALL TO ROUT MYSEL—
SWF
SORRY I LATE!
Japan streets confus-ing!
THUD
THUD
!
HULK!
SMASH!! LOKI!!
RAAAH

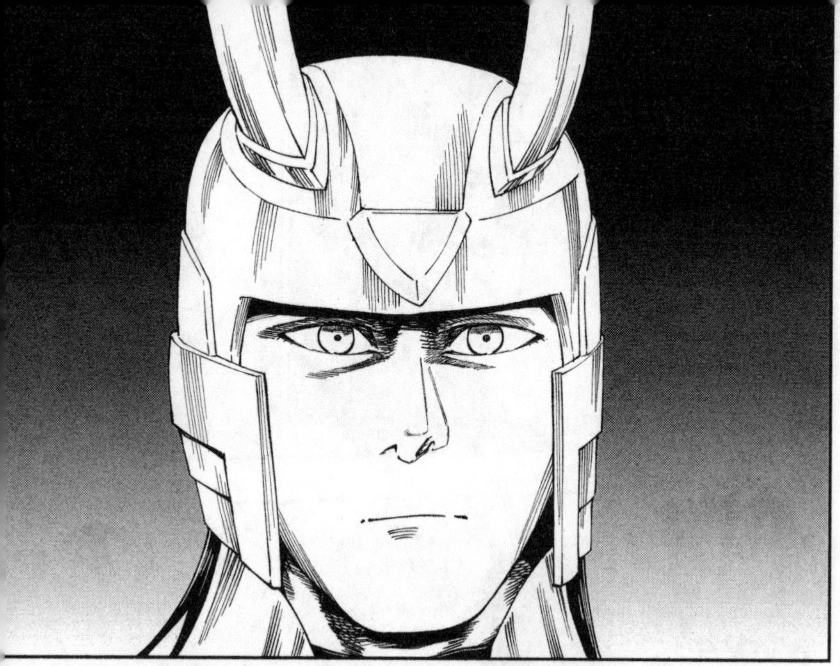

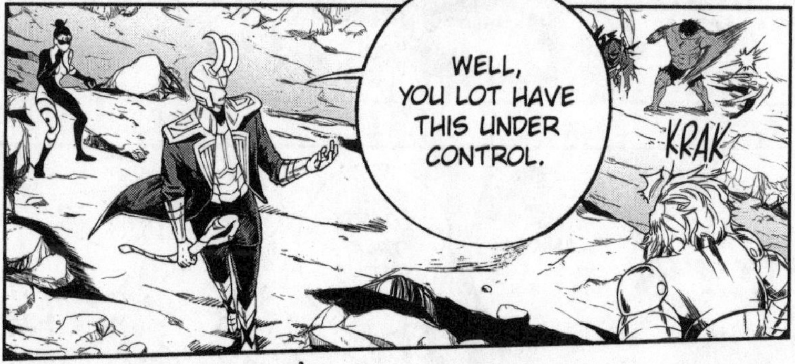
KRAK
WELL, YOU LOT HAVE THIS UNDER CONTROL.

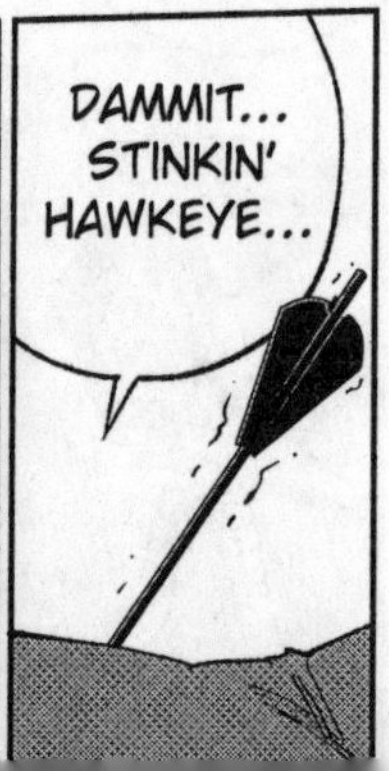
DAMMIT... STINKIN' HAWKEYE...

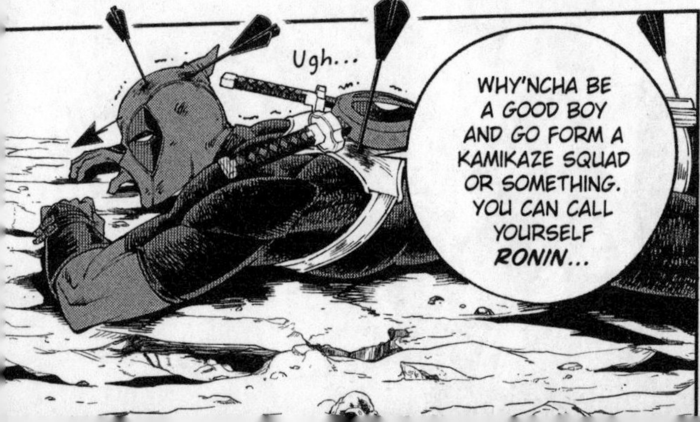
WHY'NCHA BE A GOOD BOY AND GO FORM A KAMIKAZE SQUAD OR SOMETHING. YOU CAN CALL YOURSELF *RONIN*...
Ugh...

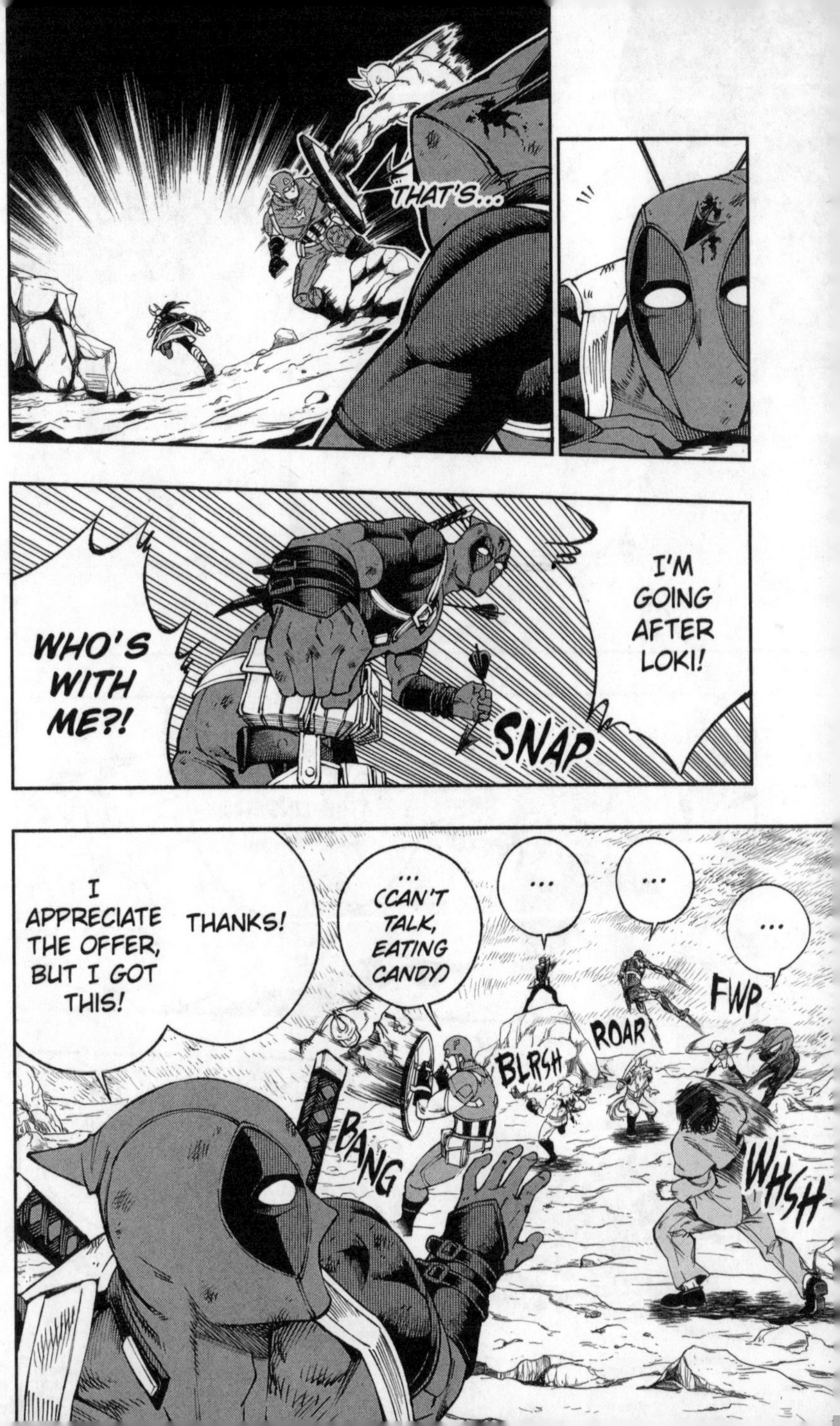
THAT'S...
I'M GOING AFTER LOKI!
SNAP
WHO'S WITH ME?!
...
...
...
FWP
... (CAN'T TALK, EATING CANDY)
ROAR
WHSH
BLRSH
I APPRECIATE THE OFFER, BUT I GOT THIS! THANKS!
BANG

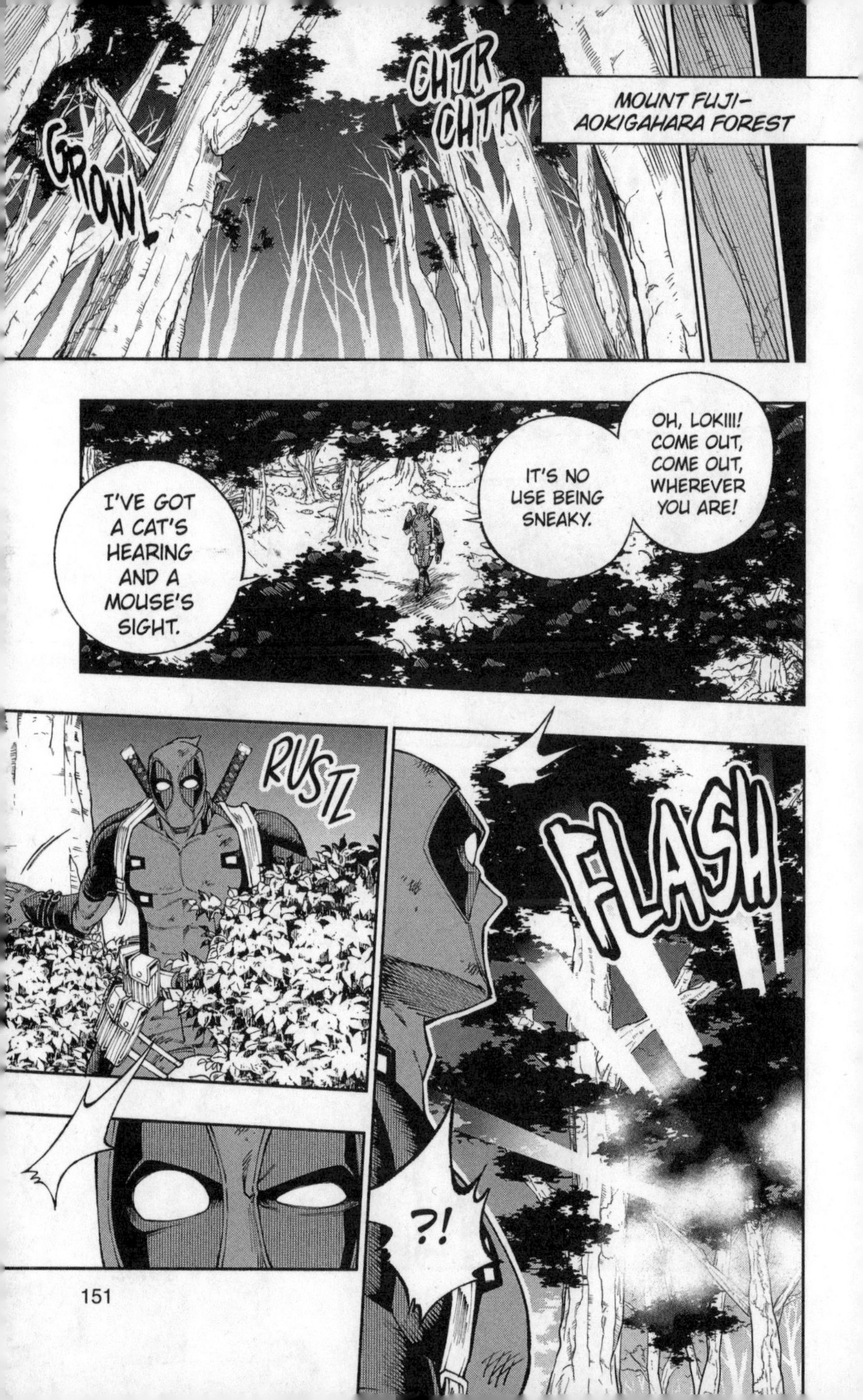
MOUNT FUJI-
AOKIGAHARA FOREST
CHTR CHTR
GROWL
OH, LOKIII! COME OUT, COME OUT, WHEREVER YOU ARE!
IT'S NO USE BEING SNEAKY.
I'VE GOT A CAT'S HEARING AND A MOUSE'S SIGHT.
FLASH
?!
RUSTL

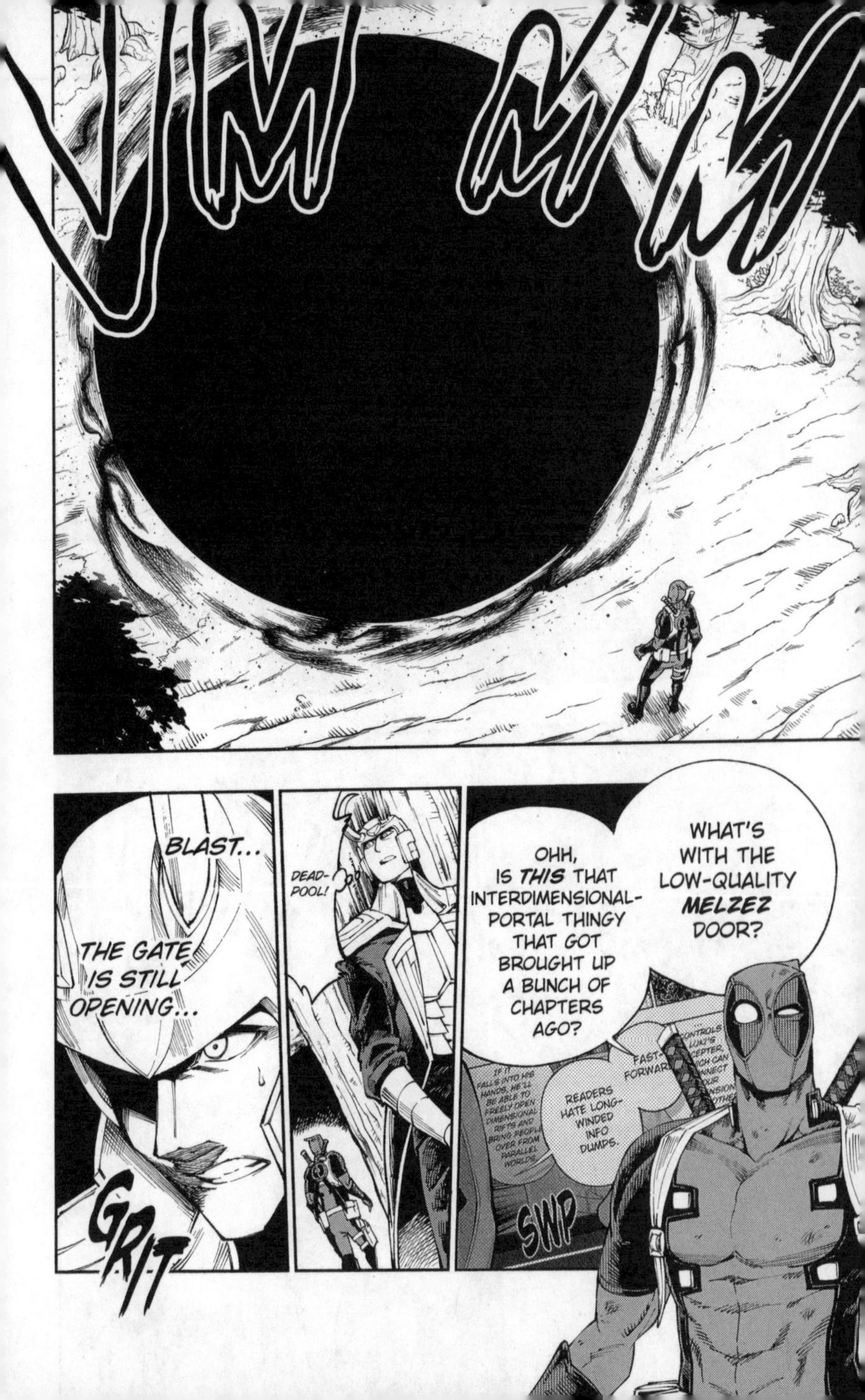
WHAT'S WITH THE LOW-QUALITY MELZEZ DOOR?
OHH, IS THIS THAT INTERDIMENSIONAL-PORTAL THINGY THAT GOT BROUGHT UP A BUNCH OF CHAPTERS AGO?
FAST-FORWARD
READERS HATE LONG-WINDED INFO DUMPS.
IF IT FALLS INTO HIS HANDS, HE'LL BE ABLE TO FREELY OPEN DIMENSIONAL RIFTS AND BRING PEOPLE OVER FROM PARALLEL WORLDS.
SWP
DEAD-POOL!
BLAST...
THE GATE IS STILL OPENING...
GRIT

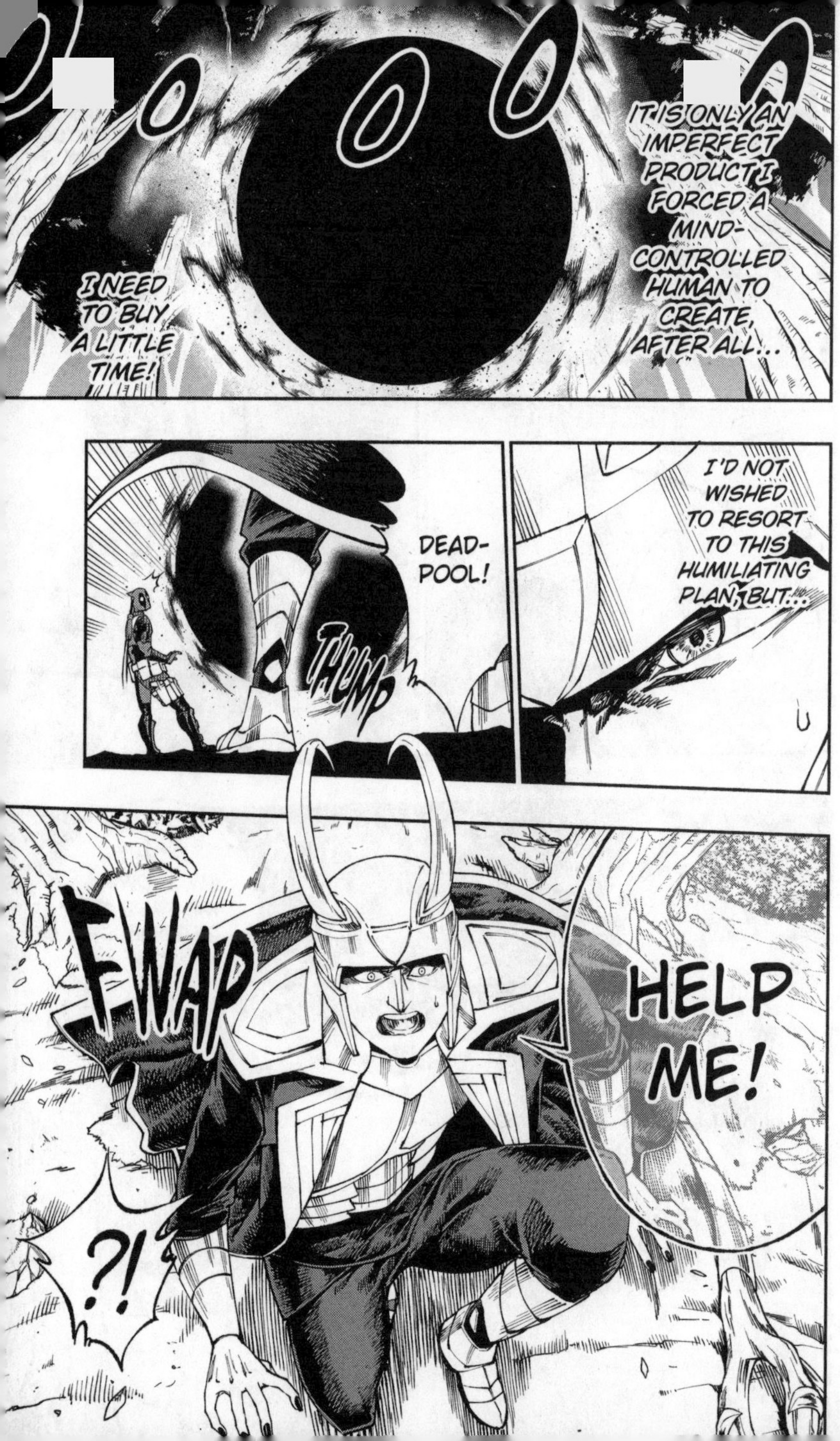
IT IS ONLY AN IMPERFECT PRODUCT I FORCED A MIND-CONTROLLED HUMAN TO CREATE, AFTER ALL...
I NEED TO BUY A LITTLE TIME!
I'D NOT WISHED TO RESORT TO THIS HUMILIATING PLAN, BUT...
DEAD-POOL!
THUMP
HELP ME!
FWAP
?!

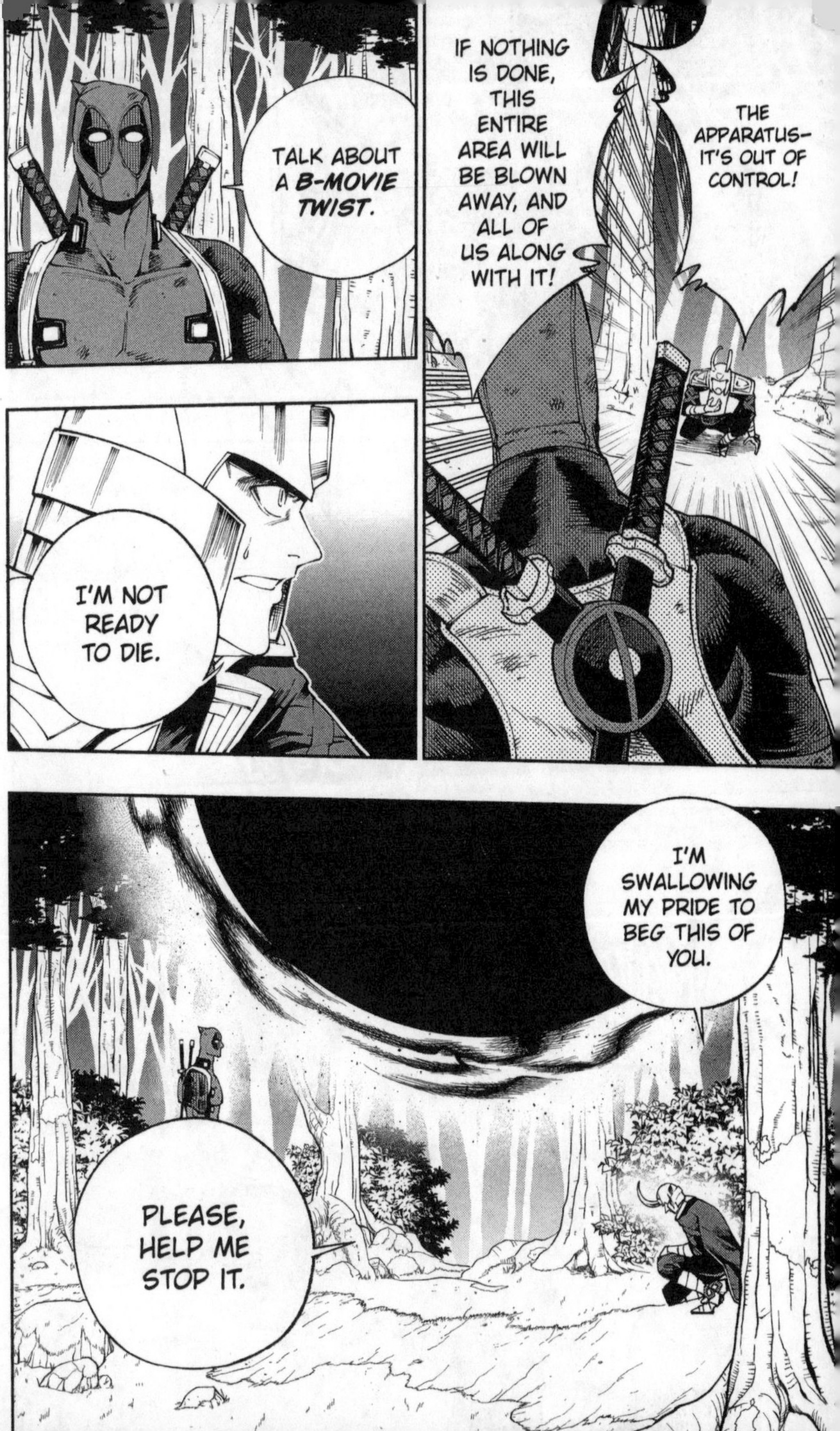
THE APPARATUS- IT'S OUT OF CONTROL!
IF NOTHING IS DONE, THIS ENTIRE AREA WILL BE BLOWN AWAY, AND ALL OF US ALONG WITH IT!
TALK ABOUT A *B-MOVIE TWIST*.
I'M NOT READY TO DIE.
I'M SWALLOWING MY PRIDE TO BEG THIS OF YOU.
PLEASE, HELP ME STOP IT.

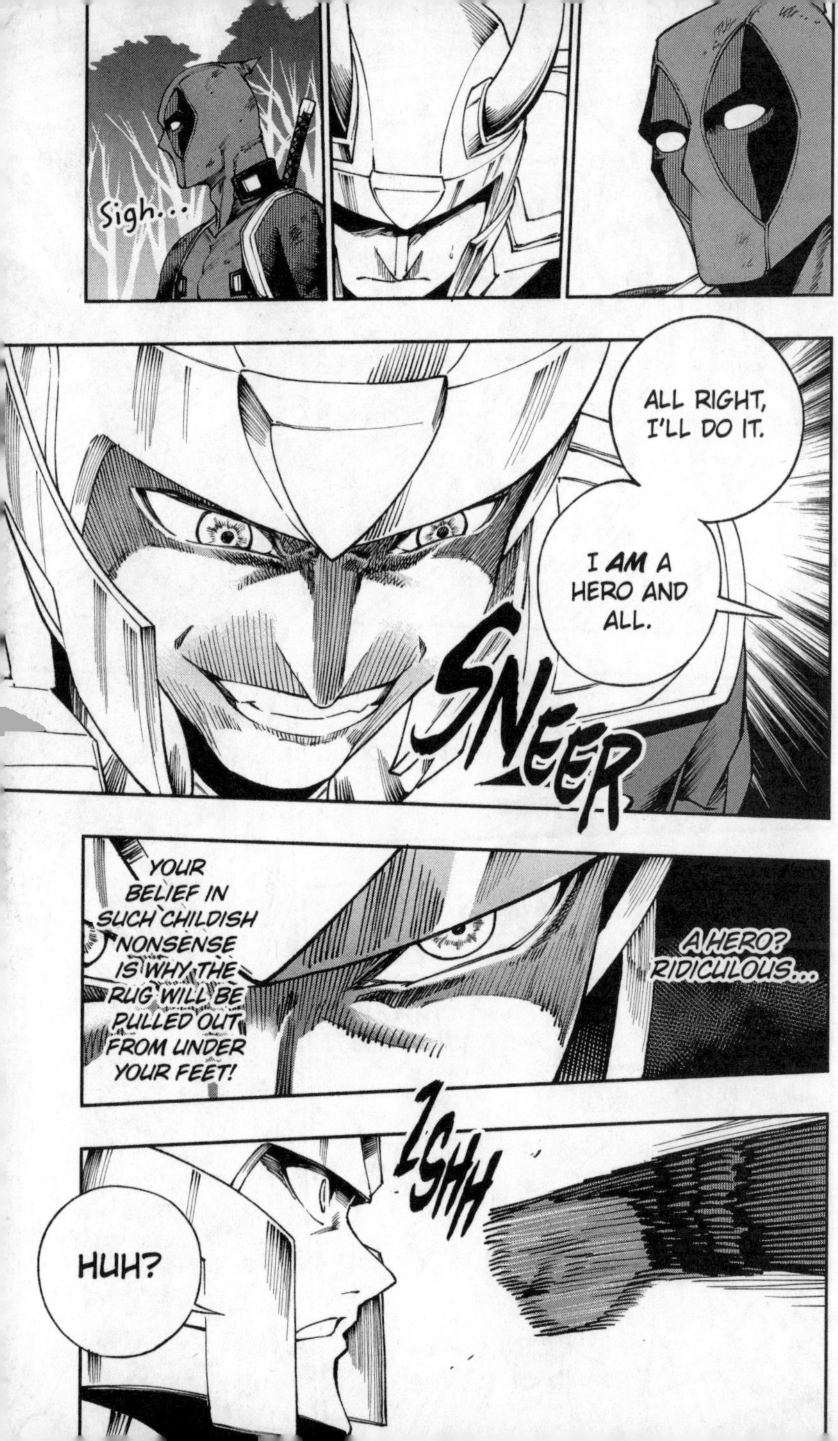
Sigh...
ALL RIGHT, I'LL DO IT.
I *AM* A HERO AND ALL.
SNEER
A HERO? RIDICULOUS...
YOUR BELIEF IN SUCH CHILDISH NONSENSE IS WHY THE RUG WILL BE PULLED OUT FROM UNDER YOUR FEET!
ZSHH
HUH?

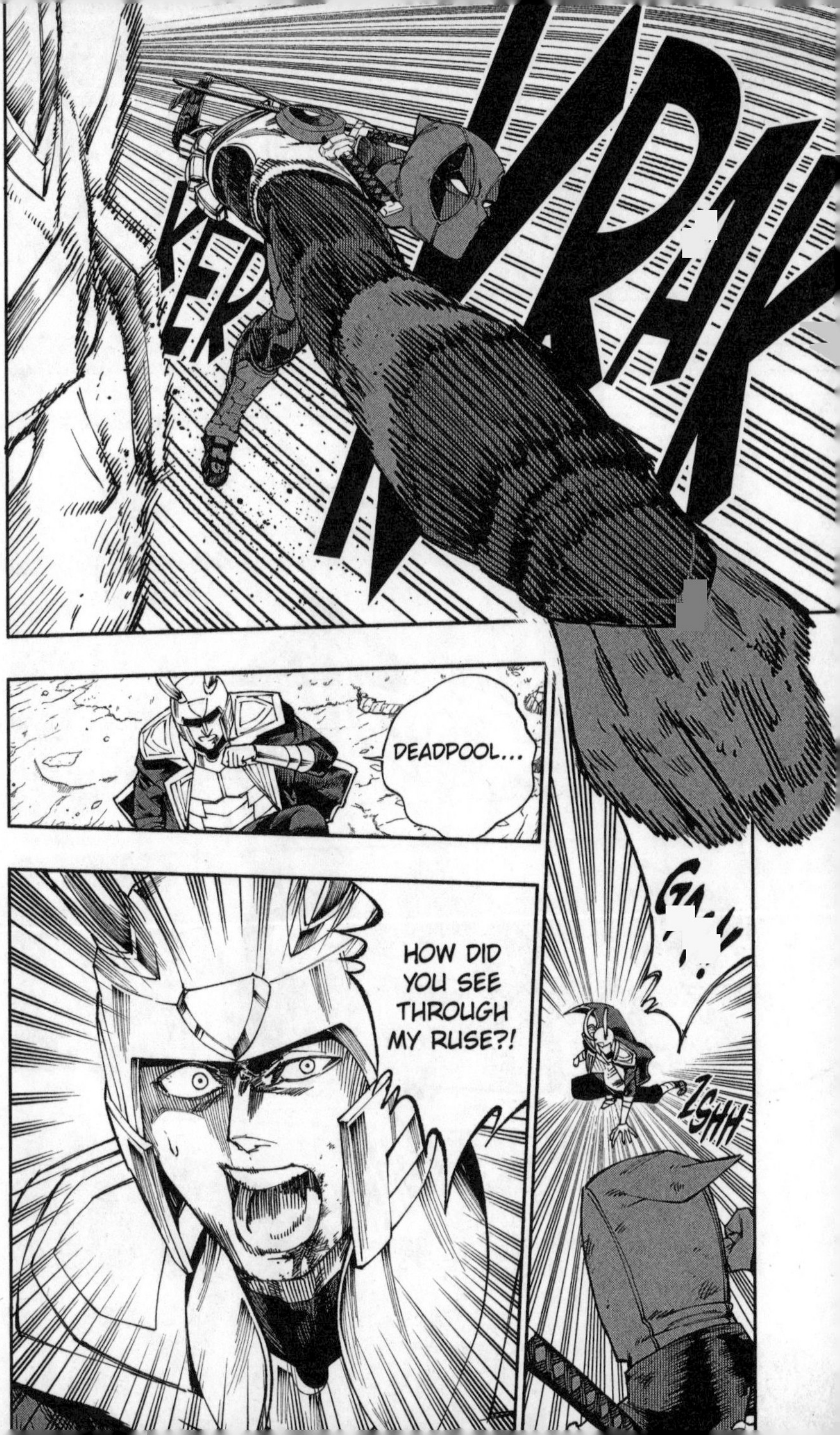
KER
ZSHH
DEADPOOL...
HOW DID YOU SEE THROUGH MY RUSE?!

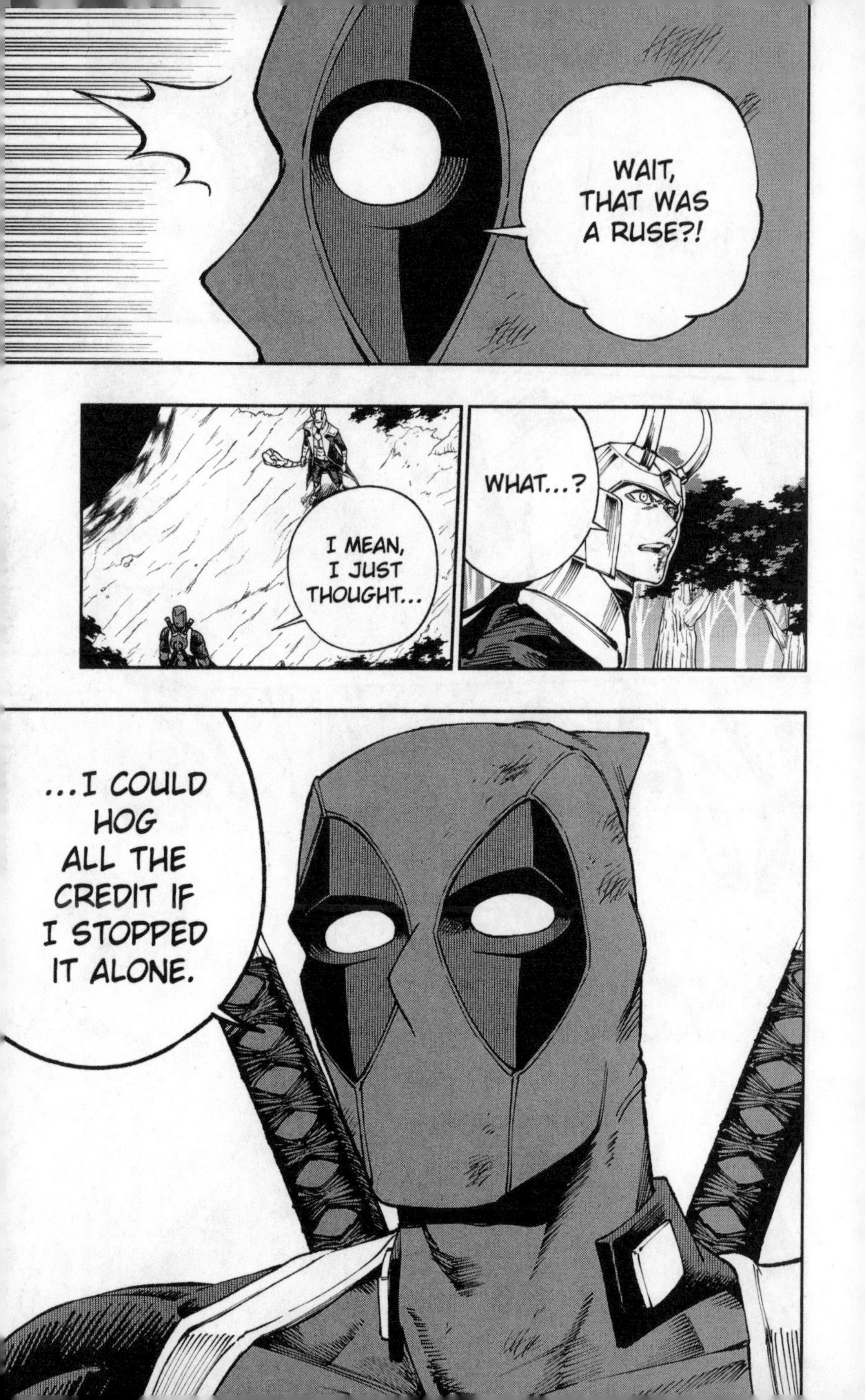
WAIT, THAT WAS A RUSE?!
WHAT...?
I MEAN, I JUST THOUGHT...
...I COULD HOG ALL THE CREDIT IF I STOPPED IT ALONE.

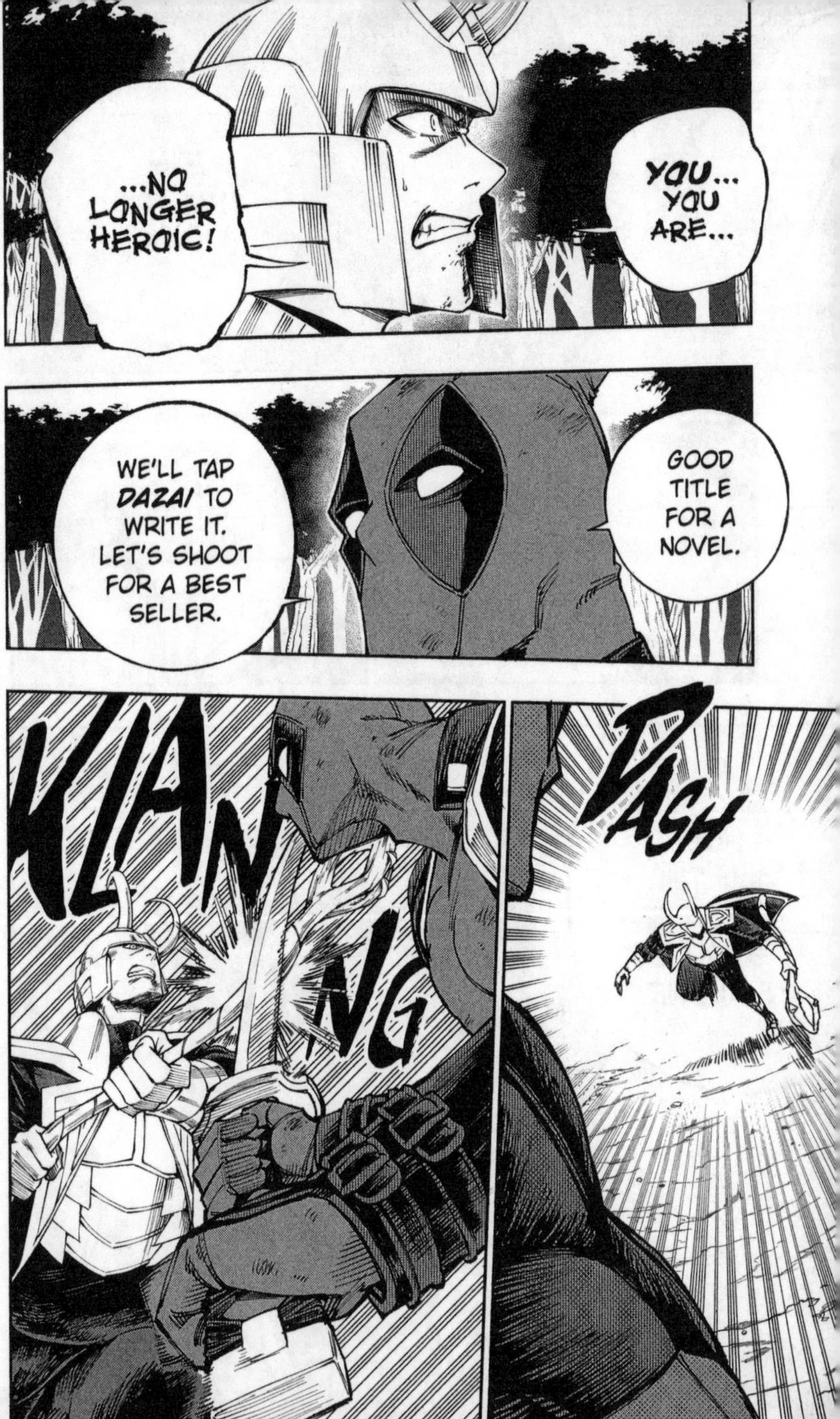
YOU... YOU ARE...
...NO LONGER HEROIC!
GOOD TITLE FOR A NOVEL.
WE'LL TAP *DAZAI* TO WRITE IT. LET'S SHOOT FOR A BEST SELLER.
DASH
KLANNG

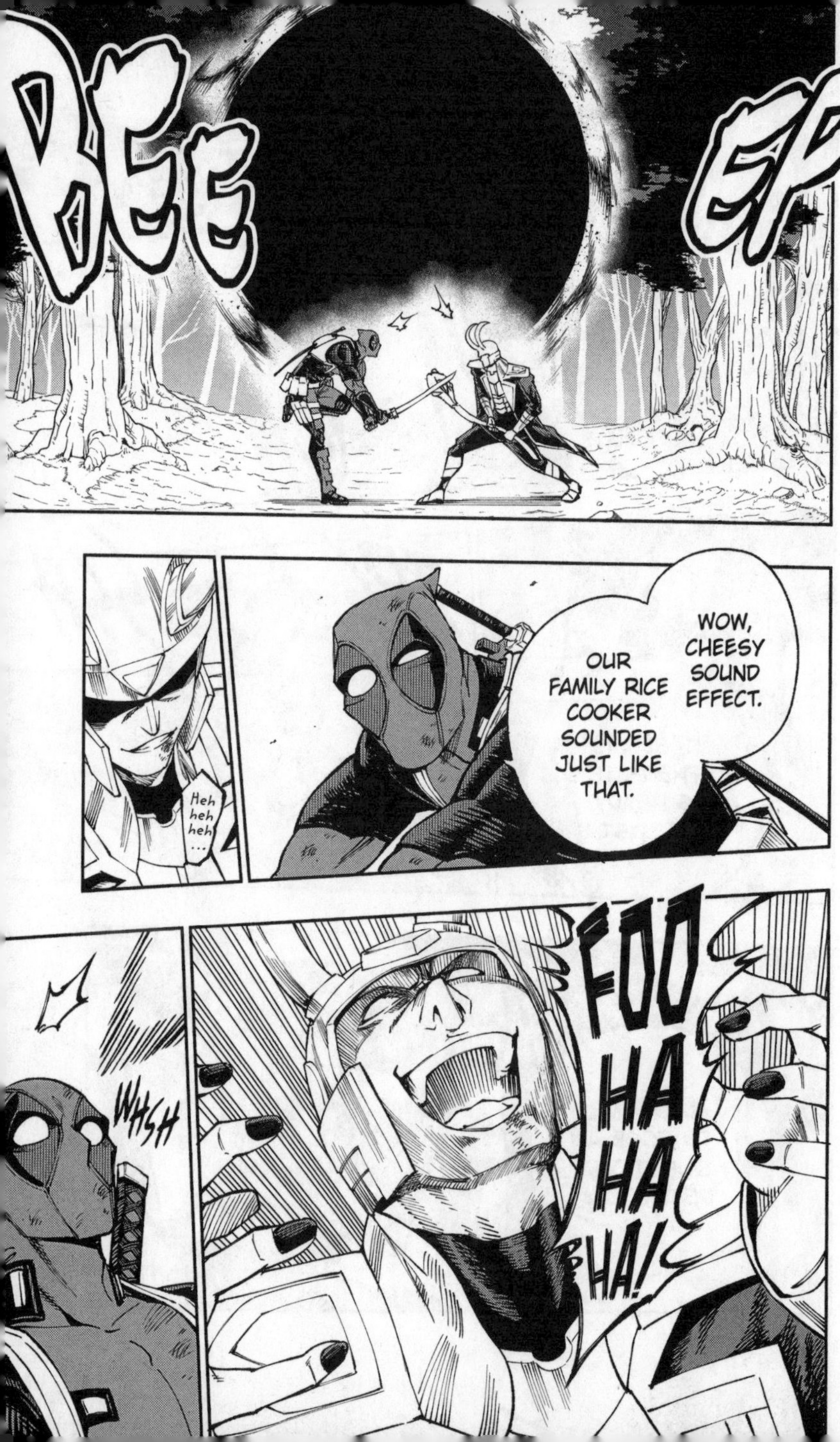
BEEEP
WOW, CHEESY SOUND EFFECT.
OUR FAMILY RICE COOKER SOUNDED JUST LIKE THAT.
Heh heh heh...
FOO HA HA HA HA!
WHSH

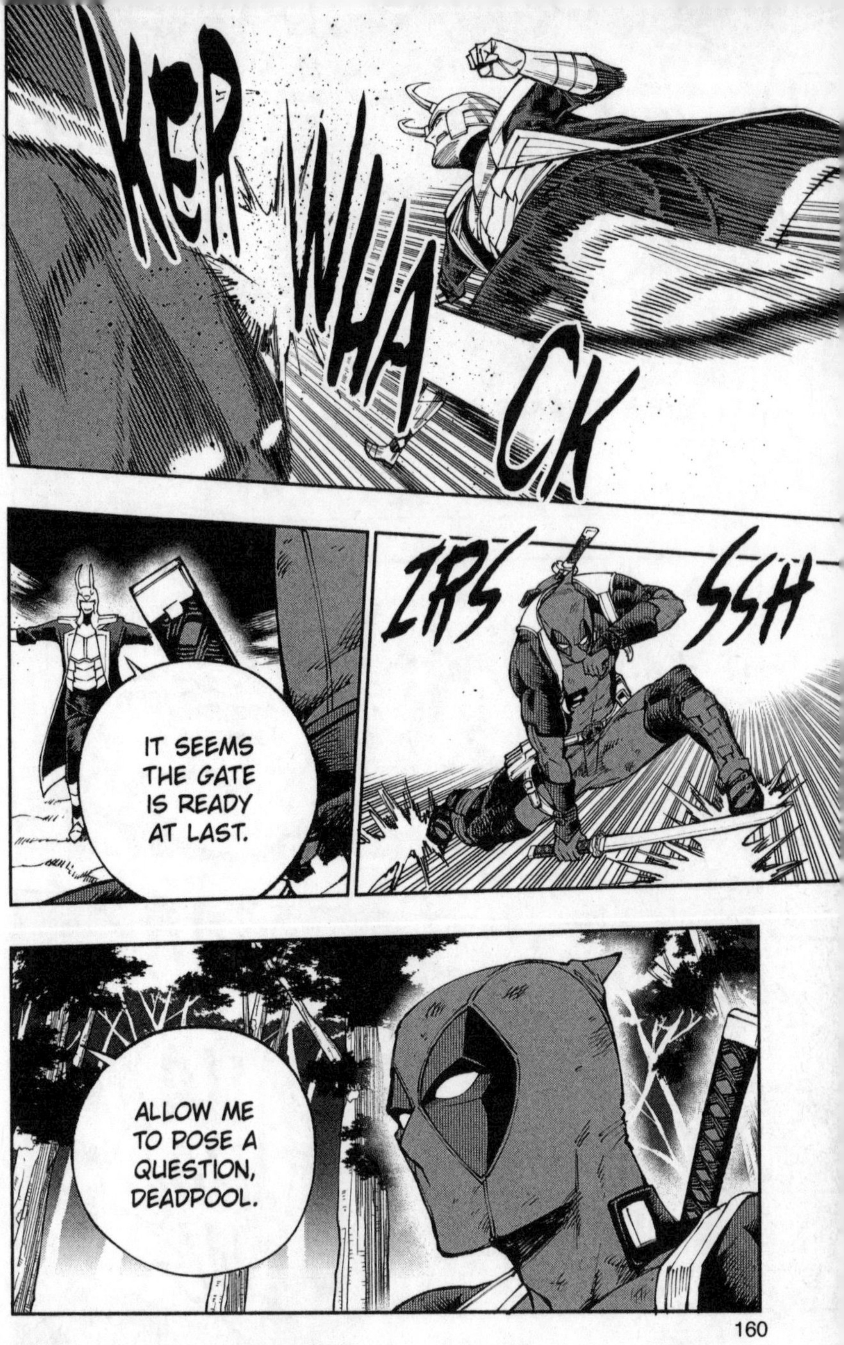
KERWHACK
ZRSSSH
IT SEEMS THE GATE IS READY AT LAST.
ALLOW ME TO POSE A QUESTION, DEADPOOL.

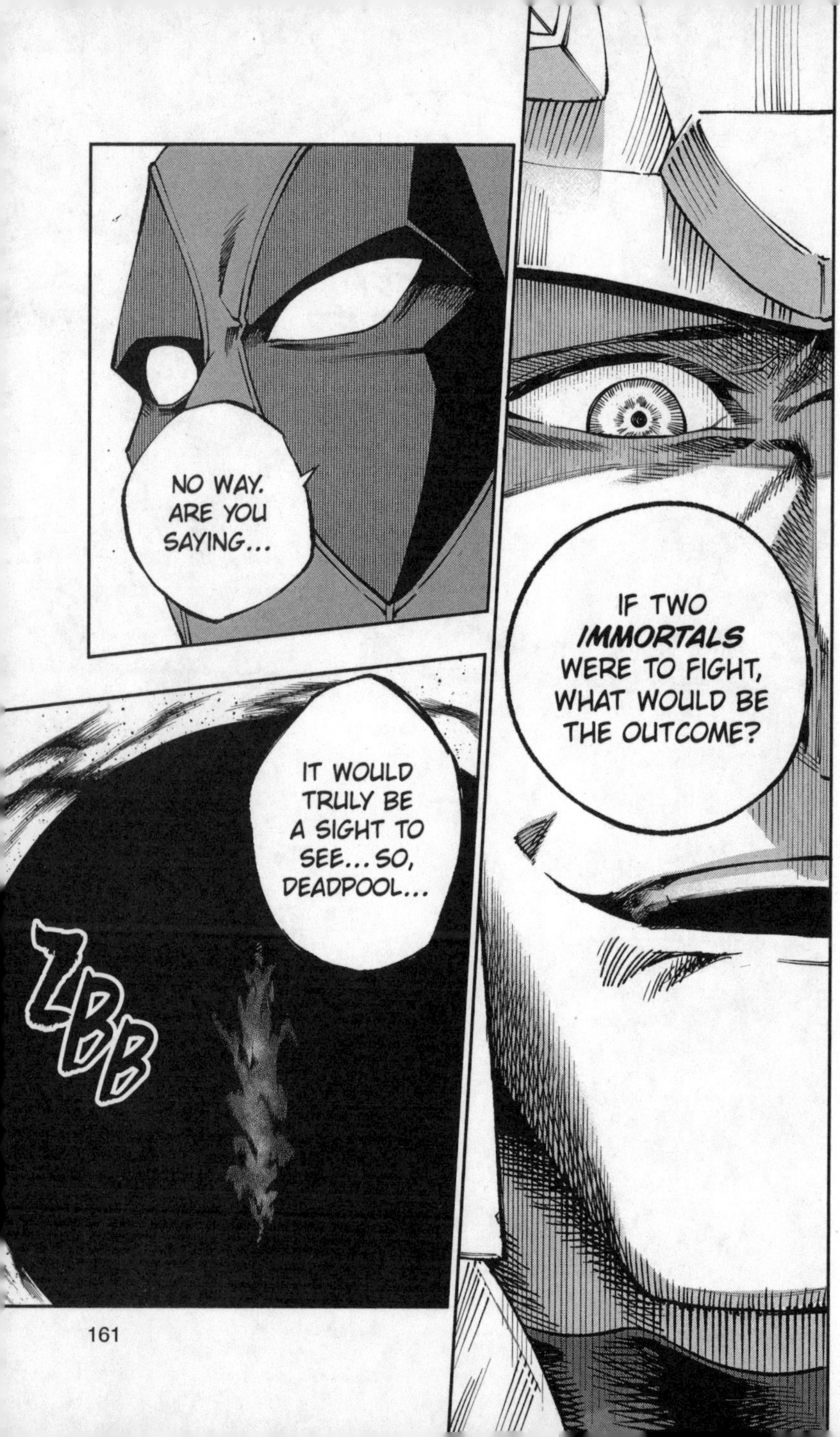
IF TWO *IMMORTALS* WERE TO FIGHT, WHAT WOULD BE THE OUTCOME?
NO WAY. ARE YOU SAYING...
IT WOULD TRULY BE A SIGHT TO SEE... SO, DEADPOOL...
ZBB

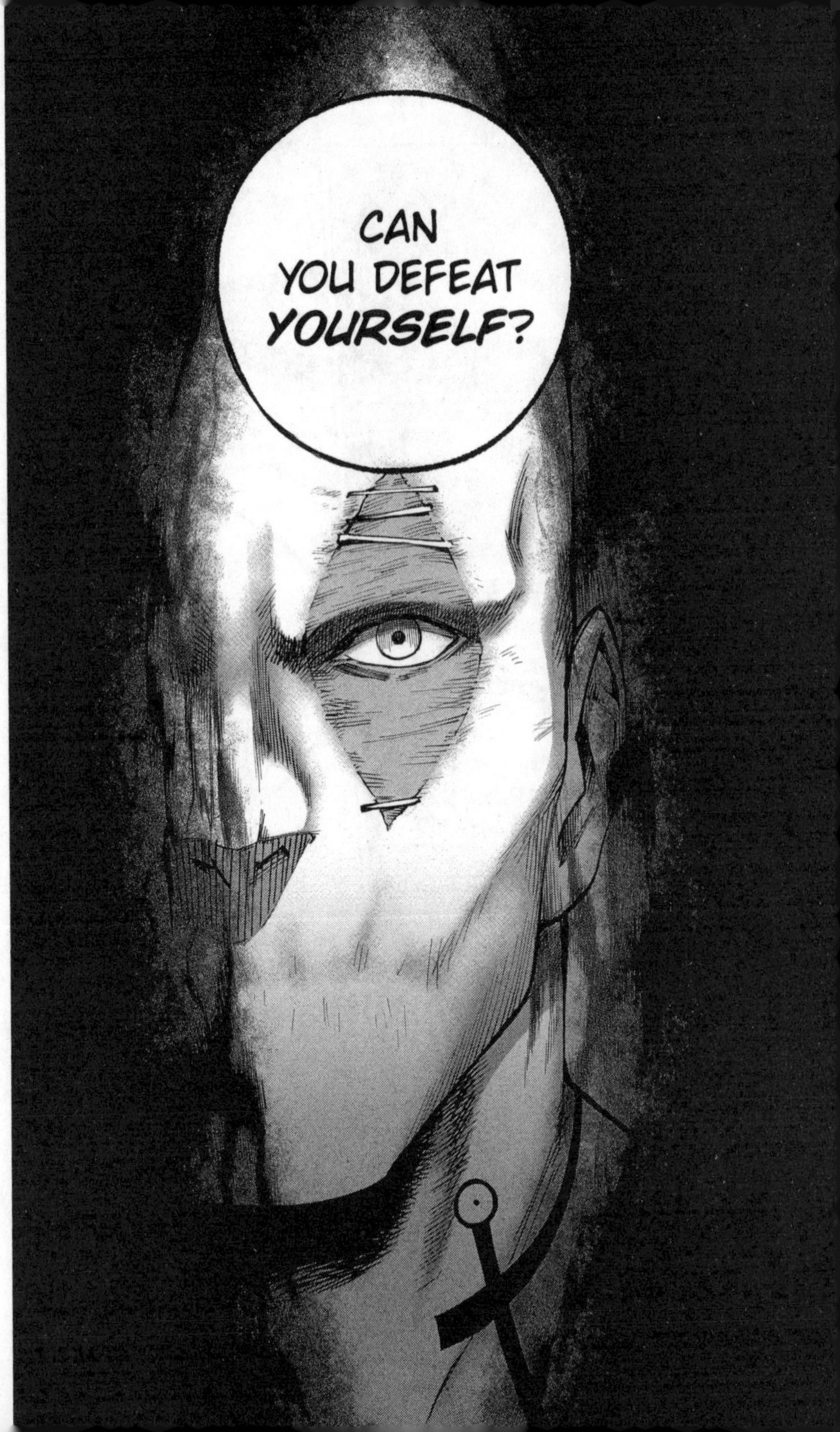
CAN YOU DEFEAT YOURSELF?

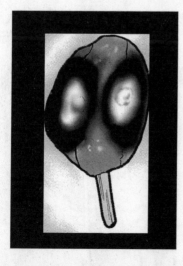

The popsicle
is...so-so.
Pretty much
like Wolverine.

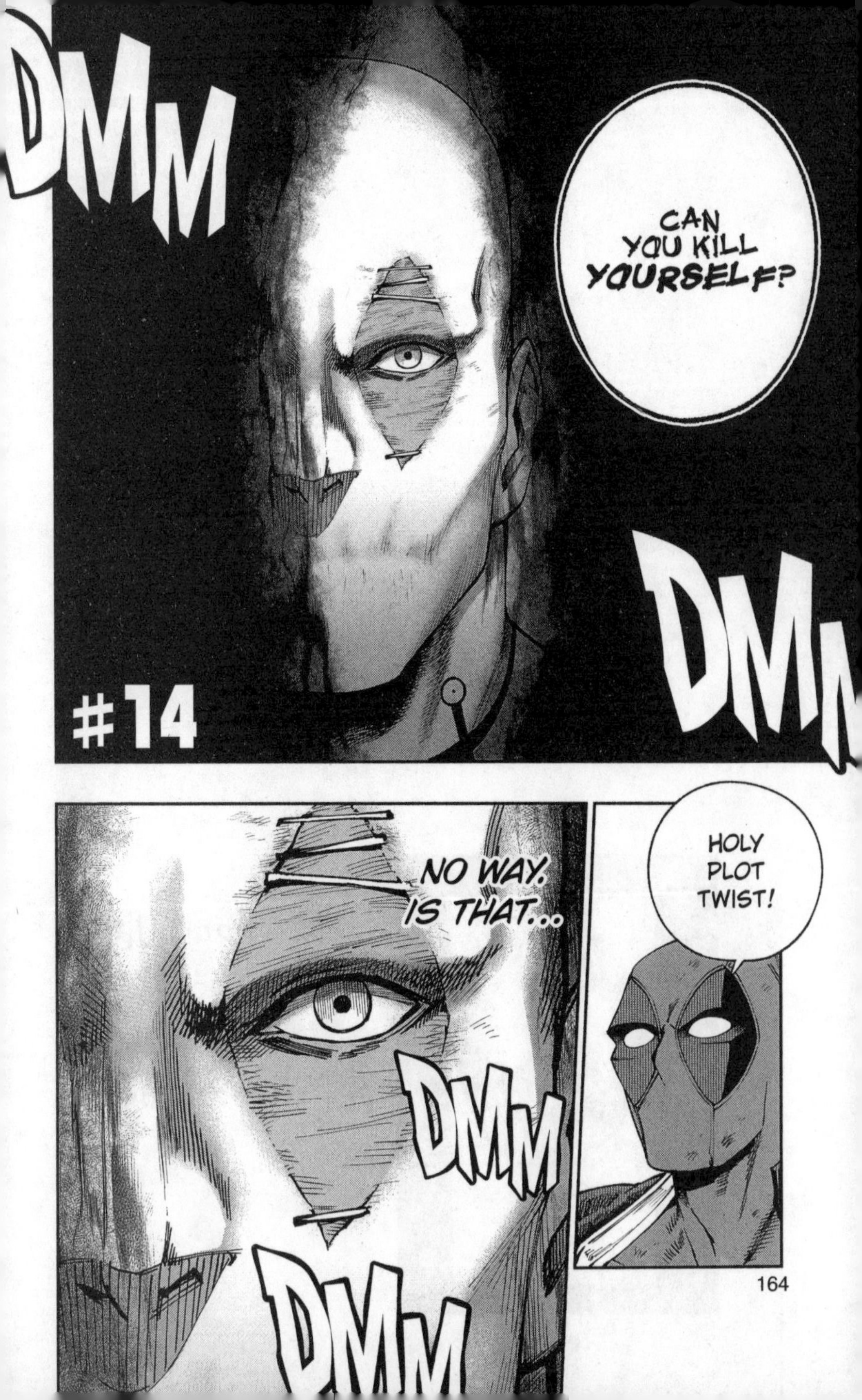
CAN YOU KILL YOURSELF?
DMM
DM
#14
HOLY PLOT TWIST!
NO WAY. IS THAT...
DMM
DMM

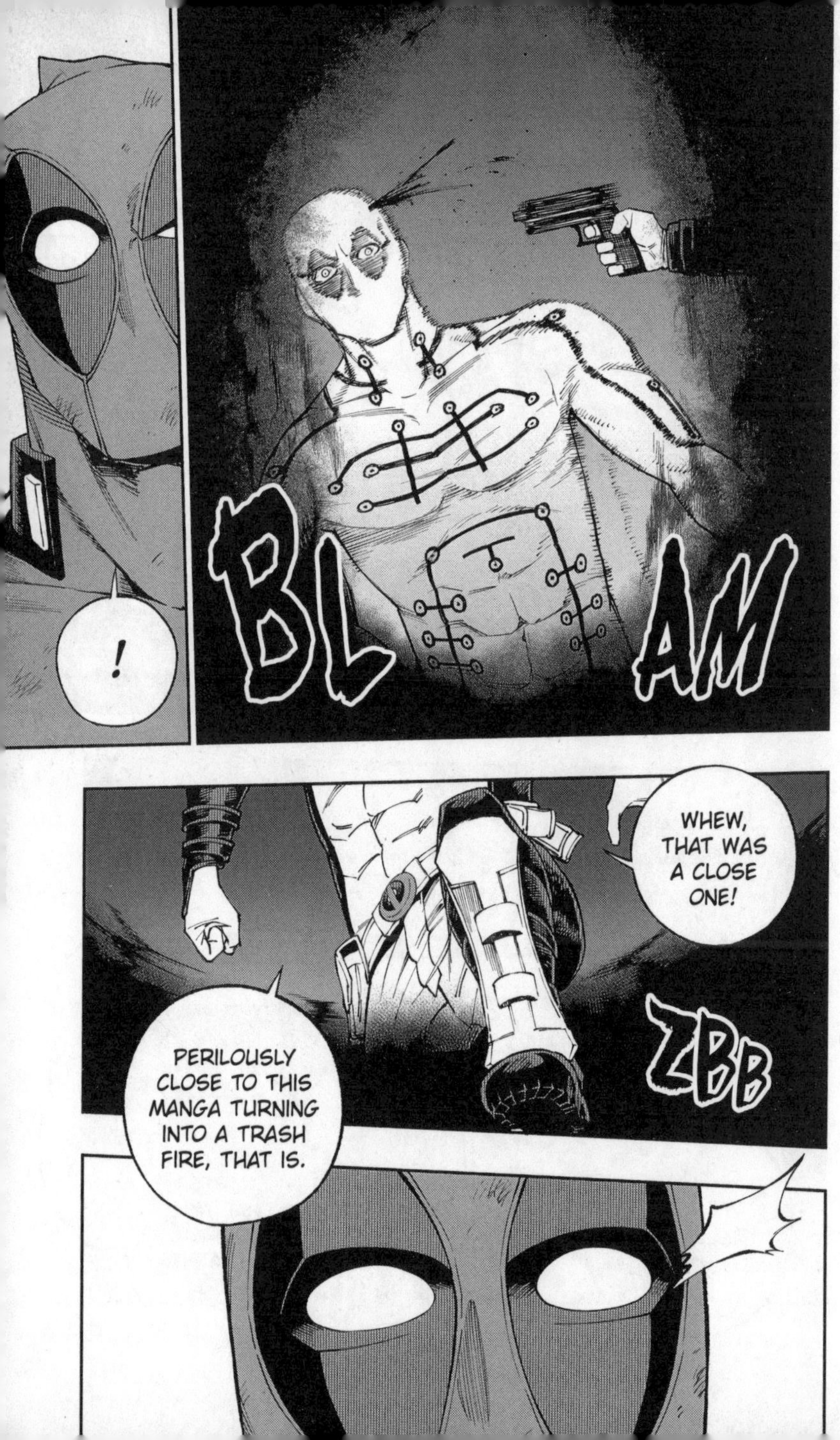
BLAM
!
WHEW, THAT WAS A CLOSE ONE!
ZBB
PERILOUSLY CLOSE TO THIS MANGA TURNING INTO A TRASH FIRE, THAT IS.

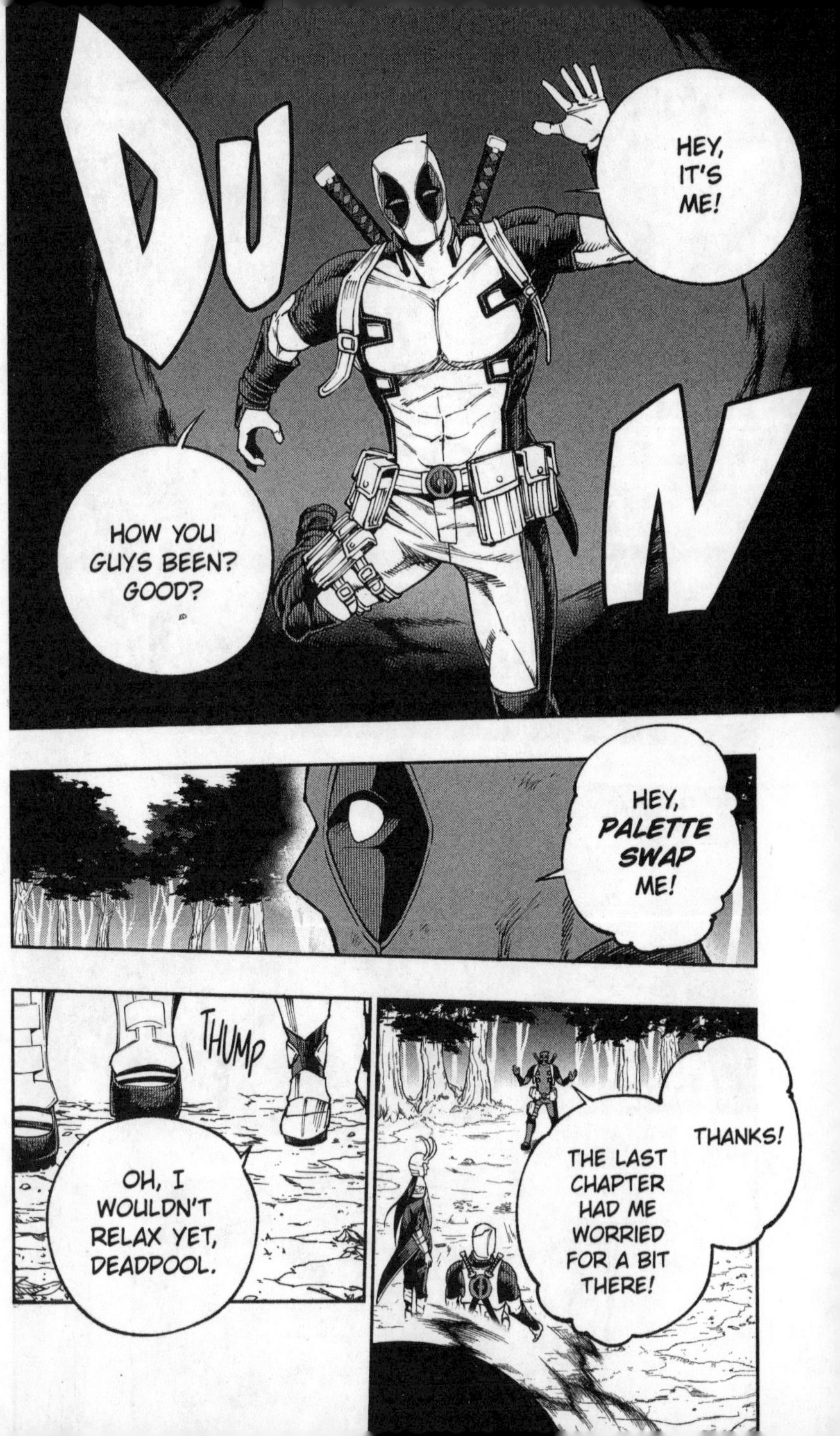
DUN
HEY, IT'S ME!
HOW YOU GUYS BEEN? GOOD?
HEY, PALETTE SWAP ME!
THANKS!
THE LAST CHAPTER HAD ME WORRIED FOR A BIT THERE!
THUMP
OH, I WOULDN'T RELAX YET, DEADPOOL.

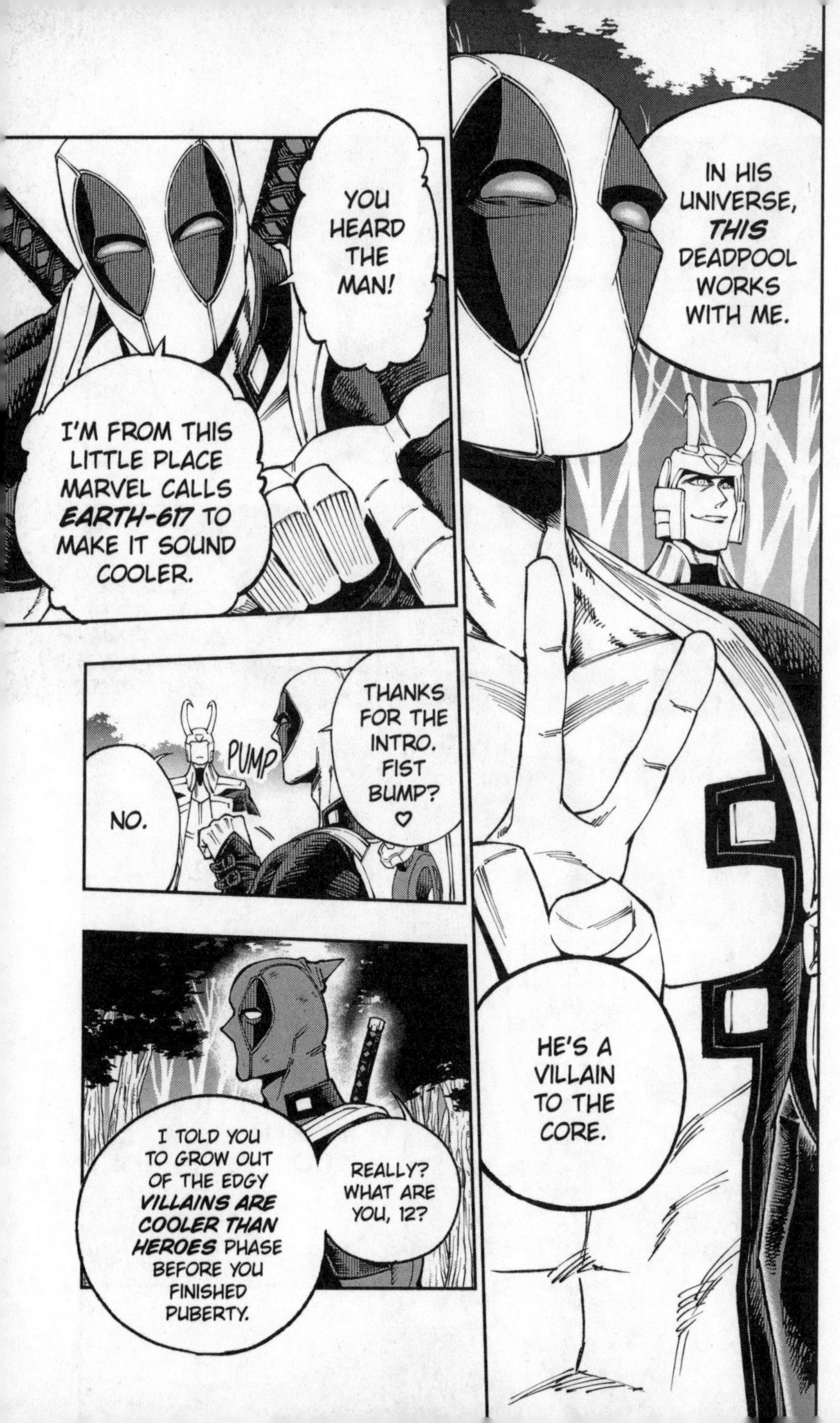
IN HIS UNIVERSE, *THIS* DEADPOOL WORKS WITH ME.
HE'S A VILLAIN TO THE CORE.
YOU HEARD THE MAN!
I'M FROM THIS LITTLE PLACE MARVEL CALLS *EARTH-617* TO MAKE IT SOUND COOLER.
THANKS FOR THE INTRO. FIST BUMP? ♡
PUMP
NO.
REALLY? WHAT ARE YOU, 12?
I TOLD YOU TO GROW OUT OF THE EDGY *VILLAINS ARE COOLER THAN HEROES* PHASE BEFORE YOU FINISHED PUBERTY.

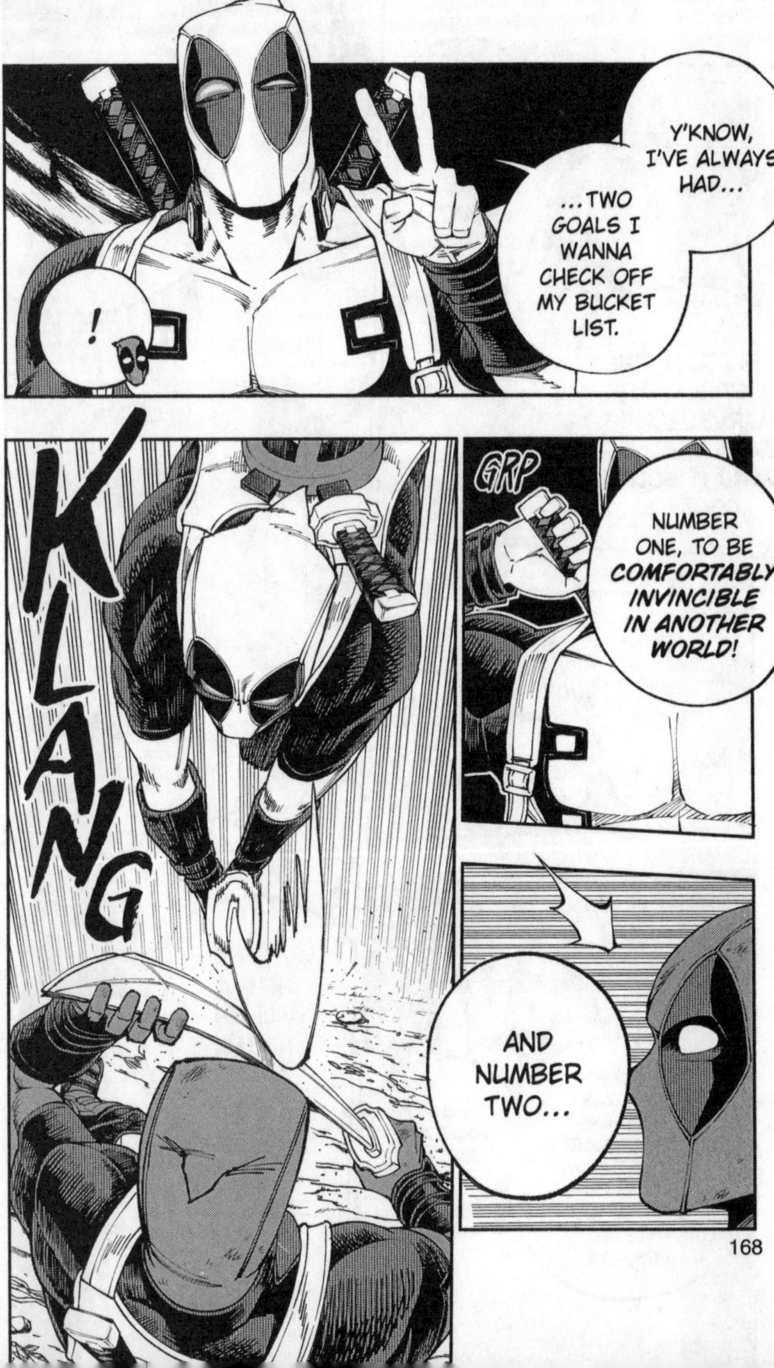
Y'KNOW, I'VE ALWAYS HAD...
...TWO GOALS I WANNA CHECK OFF MY BUCKET LIST.
!
GRP
NUMBER ONE, TO BE **COMFORTABLY INVINCIBLE IN ANOTHER WORLD!**
AND NUMBER TWO...
KLANG

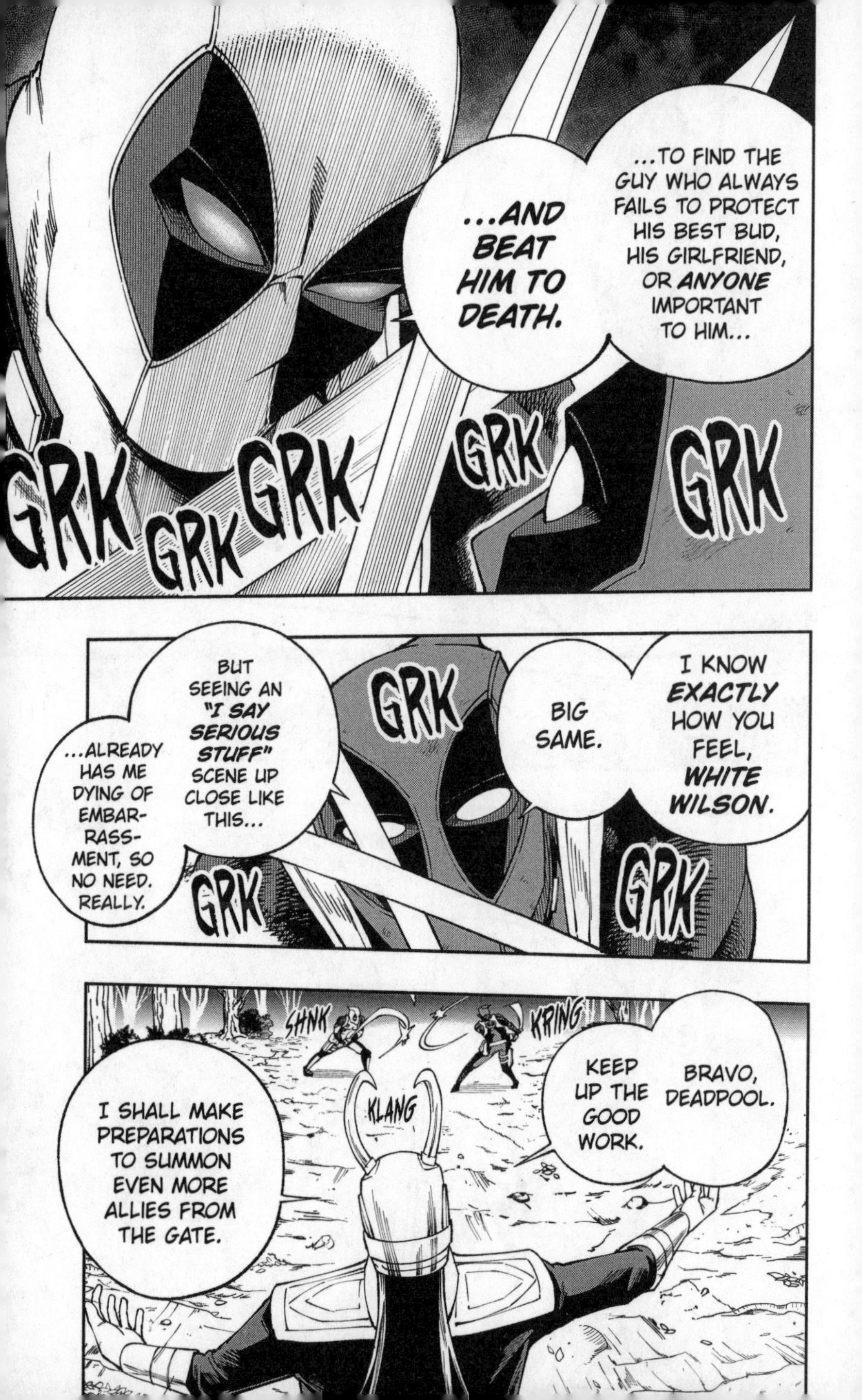
...TO FIND THE GUY WHO ALWAYS FAILS TO PROTECT HIS BEST BUD, HIS GIRLFRIEND, OR ANYONE IMPORTANT TO HIM...
...AND BEAT HIM TO DEATH.
GRK
GRK
GRK
GRK
GRK
I KNOW EXACTLY HOW YOU FEEL, WHITE WILSON.
BIG SAME.
GRK
BUT SEEING AN "I SAY SERIOUS STUFF" SCENE UP CLOSE LIKE THIS...
...ALREADY HAS ME DYING OF EMBAR-RASS-MENT, SO NO NEED. REALLY.
GRK
GRK
KRING
SHNK
BRAVO, DEADPOOL.
KEEP UP THE GOOD WORK.
KLANG
I SHALL MAKE PREPARATIONS TO SUMMON EVEN MORE ALLIES FROM THE GATE.

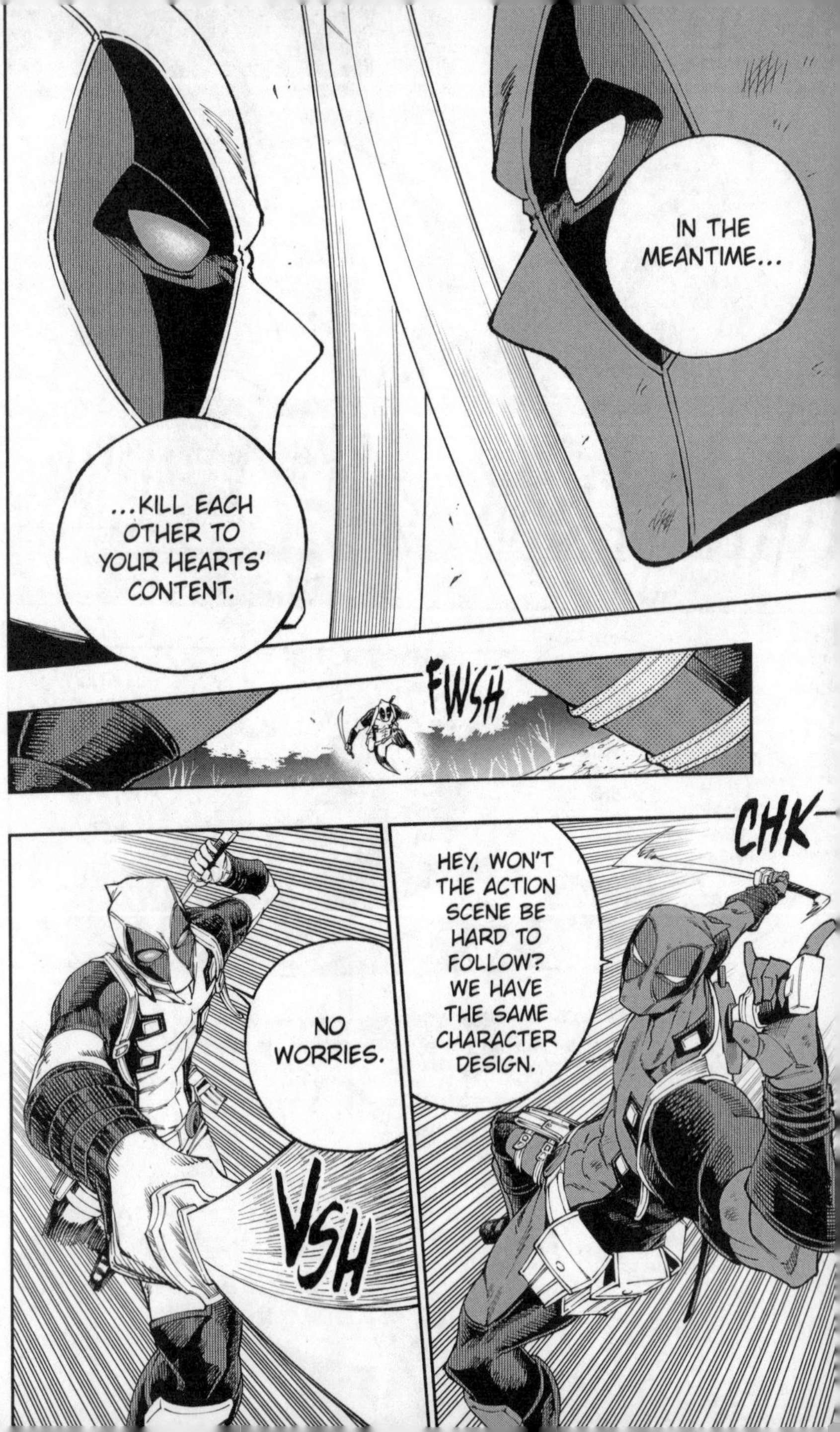
IN THE MEANTIME...
...KILL EACH OTHER TO YOUR HEARTS' CONTENT.
FWSH
CHK
HEY, WON'T THE ACTION SCENE BE HARD TO FOLLOW? WE HAVE THE SAME CHARACTER DESIGN.
NO WORRIES.
VSH

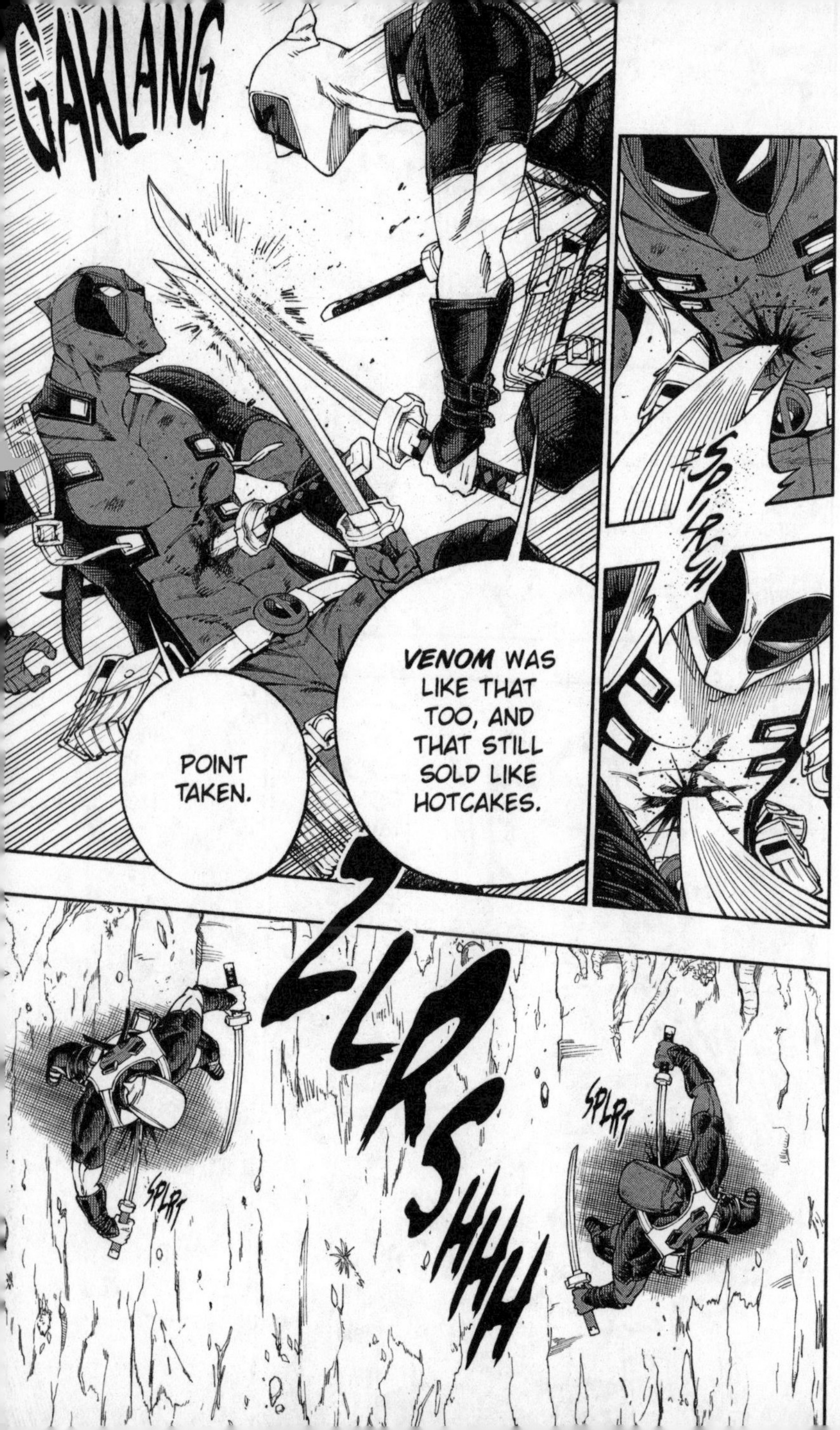
SPLRCH
GAKLANG
VENOM WAS LIKE THAT TOO, AND THAT STILL SOLD LIKE HOTCAKES.
POINT TAKEN.
ZLRSHHH
SPLRT
SPLRT

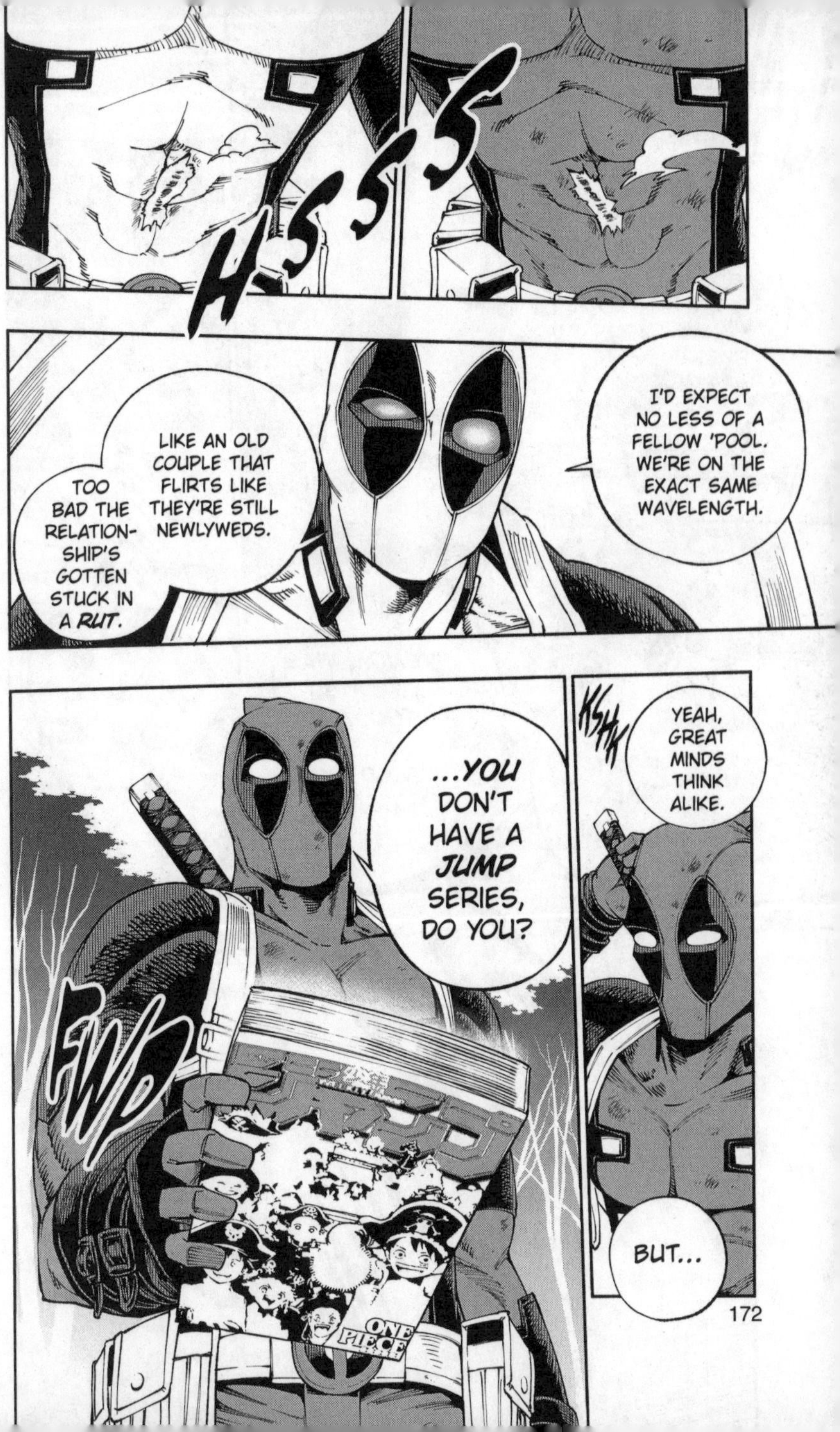
HSSSS
I'D EXPECT NO LESS OF A FELLOW 'POOL. WE'RE ON THE EXACT SAME WAVELENGTH.
LIKE AN OLD COUPLE THAT FLIRTS LIKE THEY'RE STILL NEWLYWEDS.
TOO BAD THE RELATION-SHIP'S GOTTEN STUCK IN A *RUT*.
KSHK
YEAH, GREAT MINDS THINK ALIKE.
BUT...
...*YOU* DON'T HAVE A *JUMP* SERIES, DO YOU?
FWP
ONE PIECE

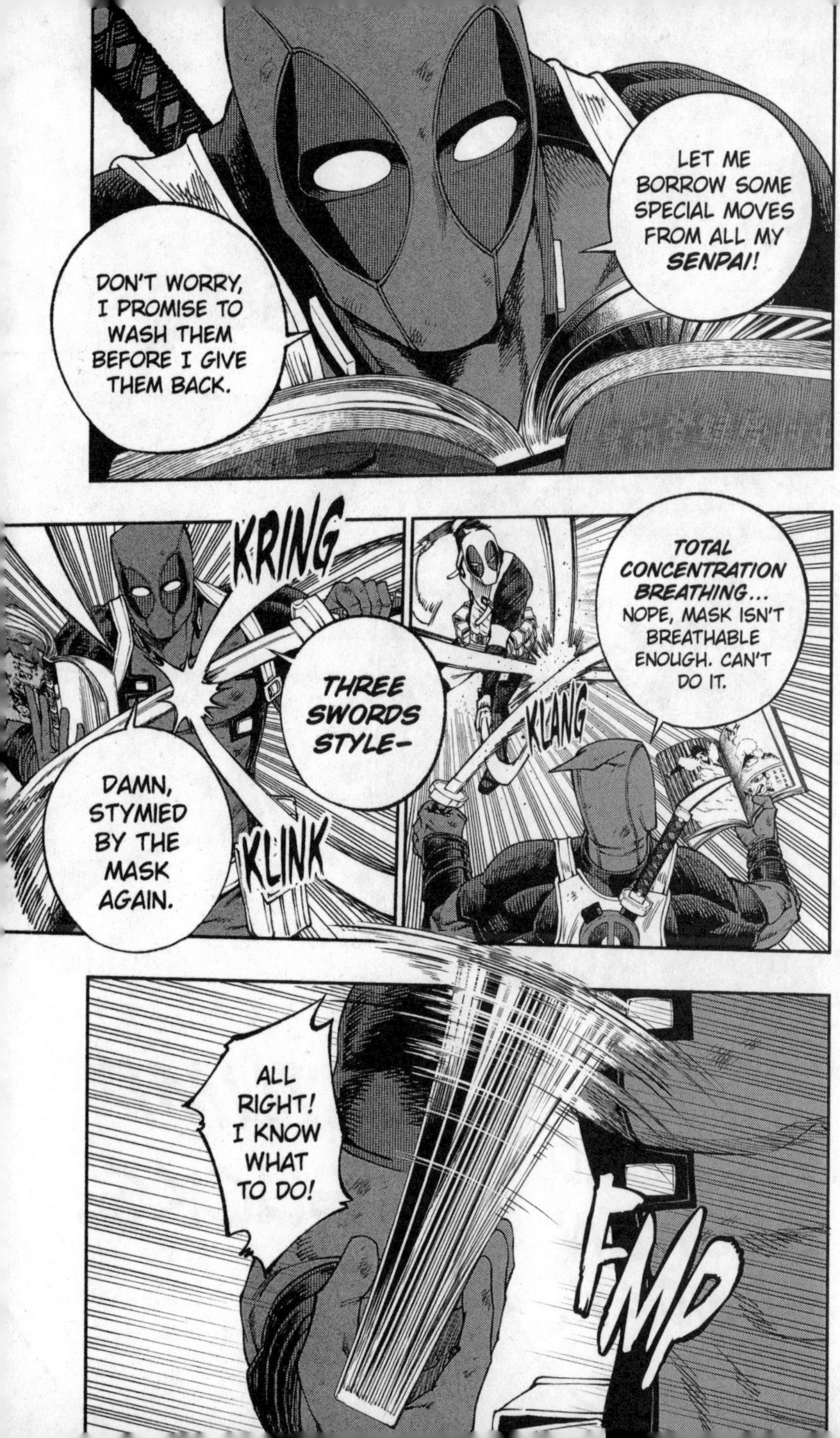
LET ME BORROW SOME SPECIAL MOVES FROM ALL MY *SENPAI!*
DON'T WORRY, I PROMISE TO WASH THEM BEFORE I GIVE THEM BACK.
TOTAL CONCENTRATION BREATHING... NOPE, MASK ISN'T BREATHABLE ENOUGH. CAN'T DO IT.
KLANG
KRING
THREE SWORDS STYLE-
KLINK
DAMN, STYMIED BY THE MASK AGAIN.
ALL RIGHT! I KNOW WHAT TO DO!
FMP

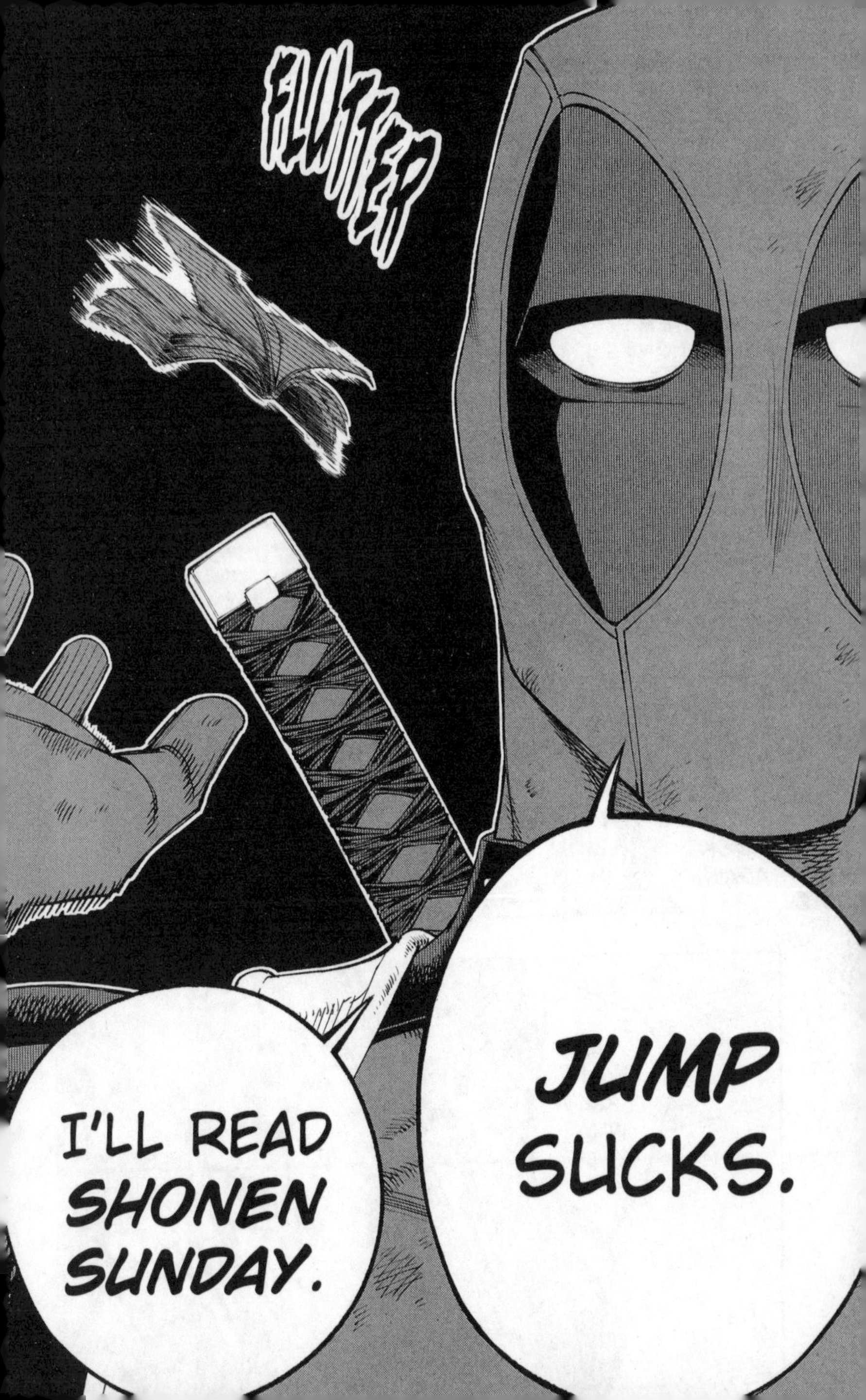
FLUTTER
JUMP SUCKS.
I'LL READ SHONEN SUNDAY.

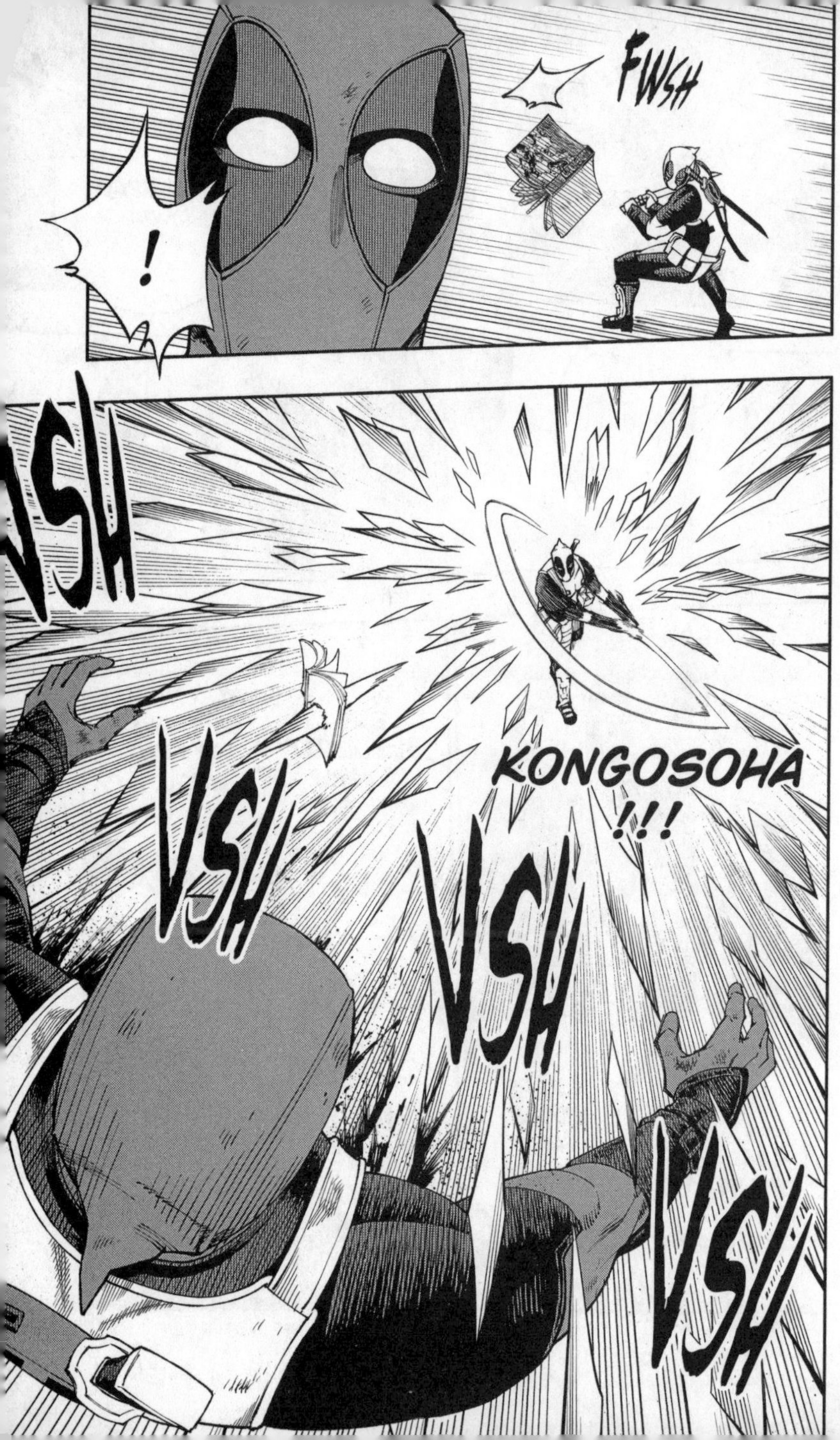
FWSH
!
KONGOSOHA!!!
VSH
VSH
VSH
VSH

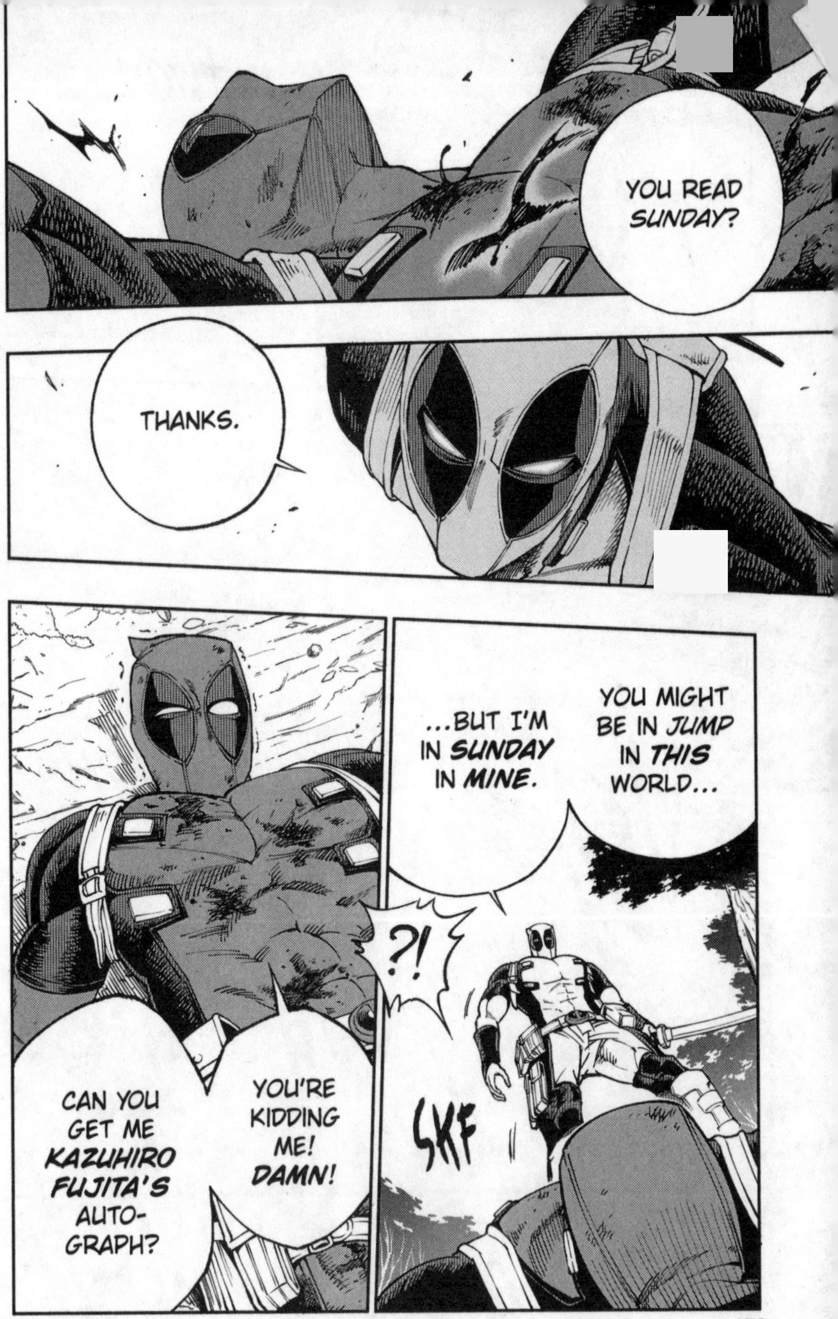
YOU READ SUNDAY?
THANKS.
YOU MIGHT BE IN JUMP IN THIS WORLD...
...BUT I'M IN SUNDAY IN MINE.
?!
SKF
YOU'RE KIDDING ME! DAMN!
CAN YOU GET ME KAZUHIRO FUJITA'S AUTO-GRAPH?

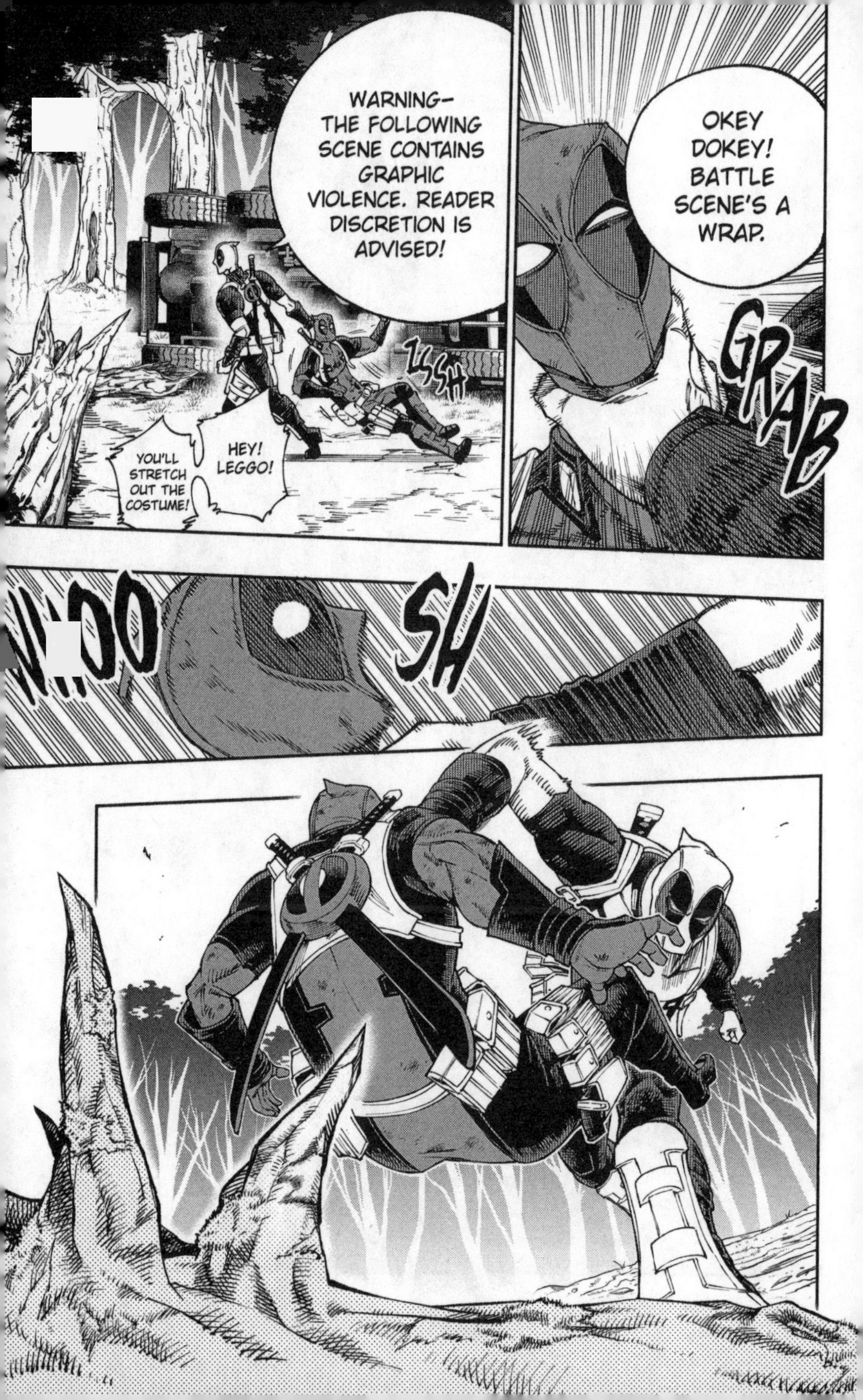
OKEY DOKEY! BATTLE SCENE'S A WRAP.
GRAB
WARNING– THE FOLLOWING SCENE CONTAINS GRAPHIC VIOLENCE. READER DISCRETION IS ADVISED!
HEY! LEGGO!
YOU'LL STRETCH OUT THE COSTUME!

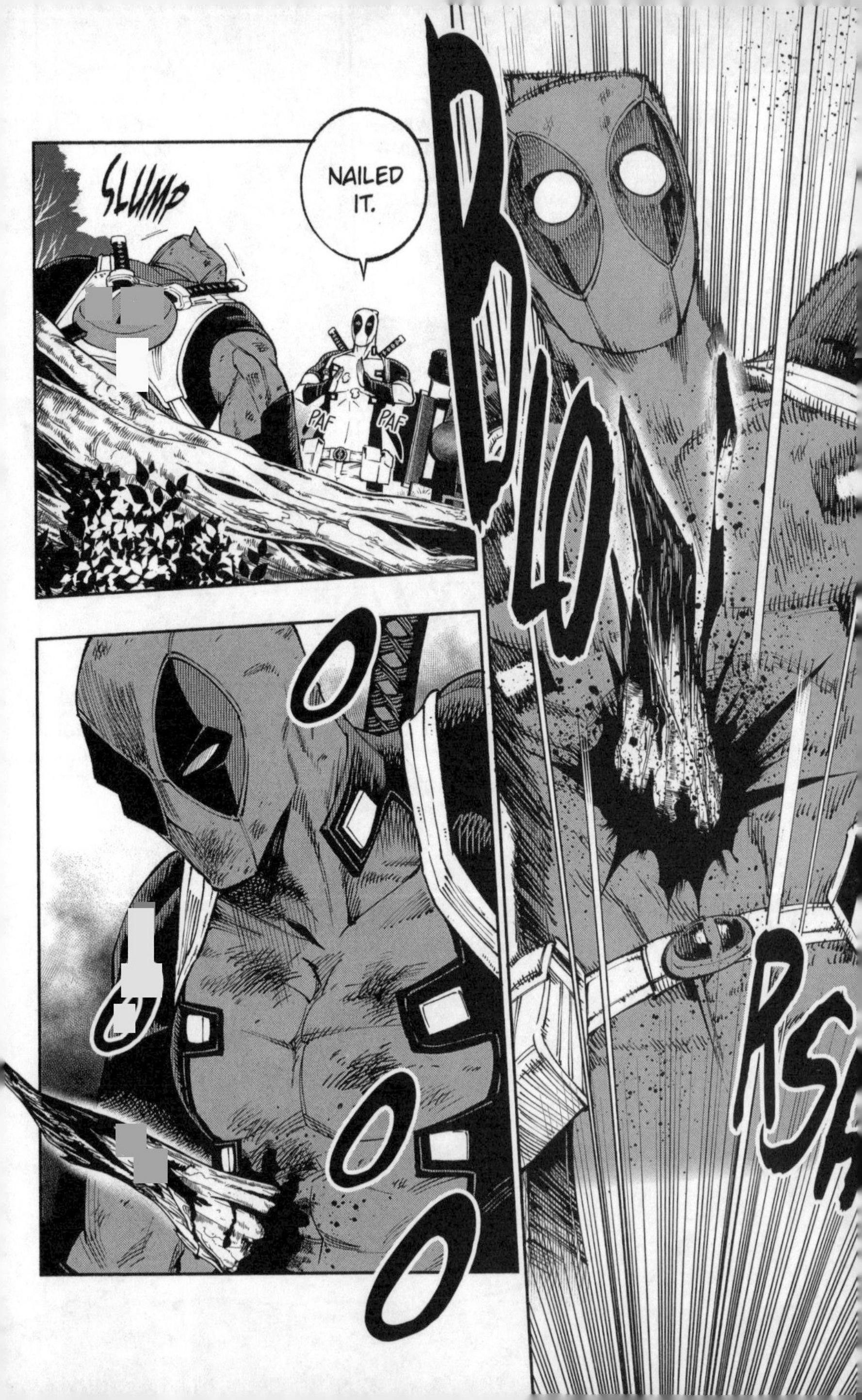
NAILED IT.
PAF
PAF
SLUMP

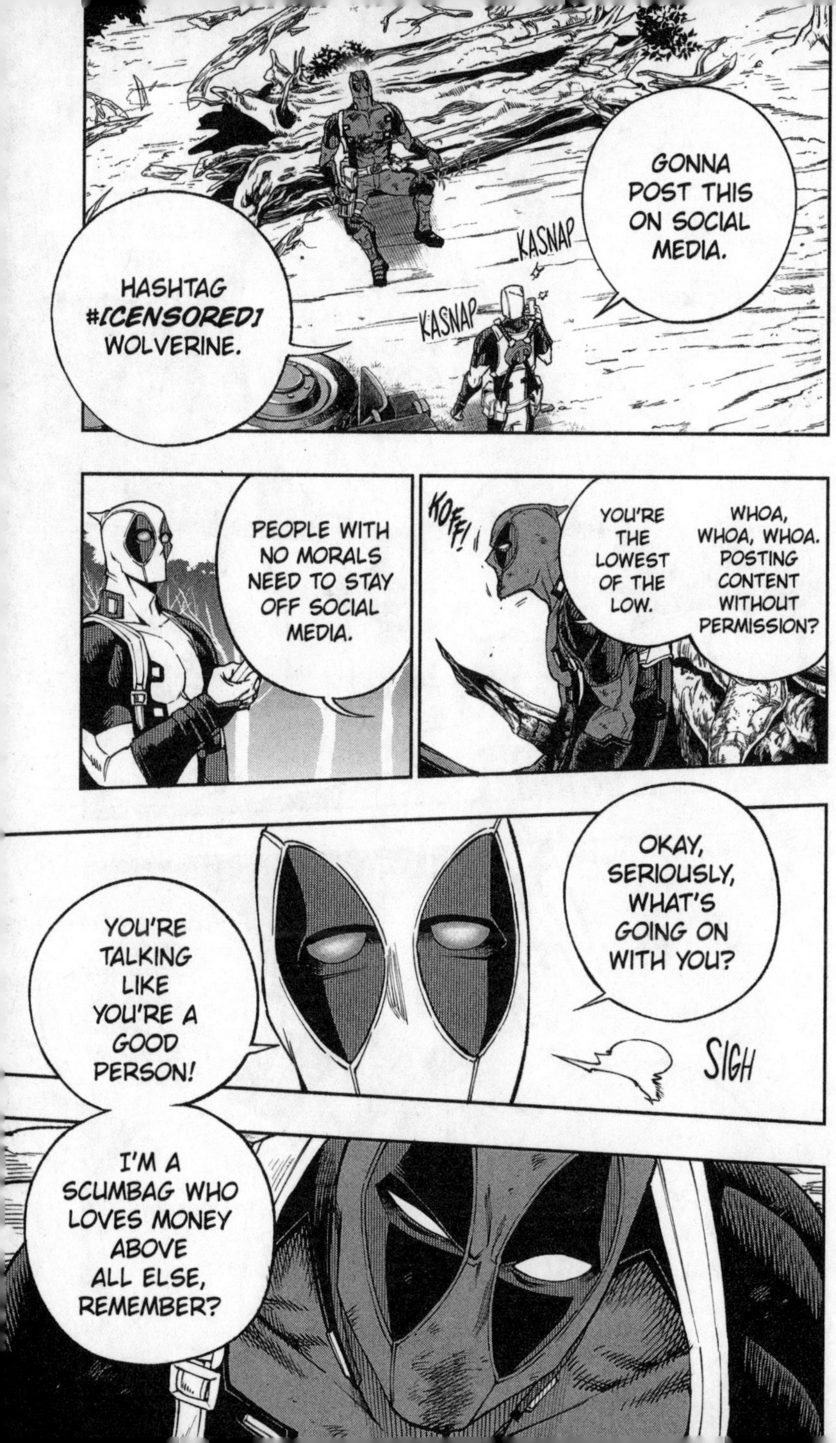
GONNA POST THIS ON SOCIAL MEDIA.
KASNAP
KASNAP
HASHTAG #[CENSORED] WOLVERINE.
KOFF!
WHOA, WHOA, WHOA. POSTING CONTENT WITHOUT PERMISSION?
YOU'RE THE LOWEST OF THE LOW.
PEOPLE WITH NO MORALS NEED TO STAY OFF SOCIAL MEDIA.
OKAY, SERIOUSLY, WHAT'S GOING ON WITH YOU?
SIGH
YOU'RE TALKING LIKE YOU'RE A GOOD PERSON!
I'M A SCUMBAG WHO LOVES MONEY ABOVE ALL ELSE, REMEMBER?

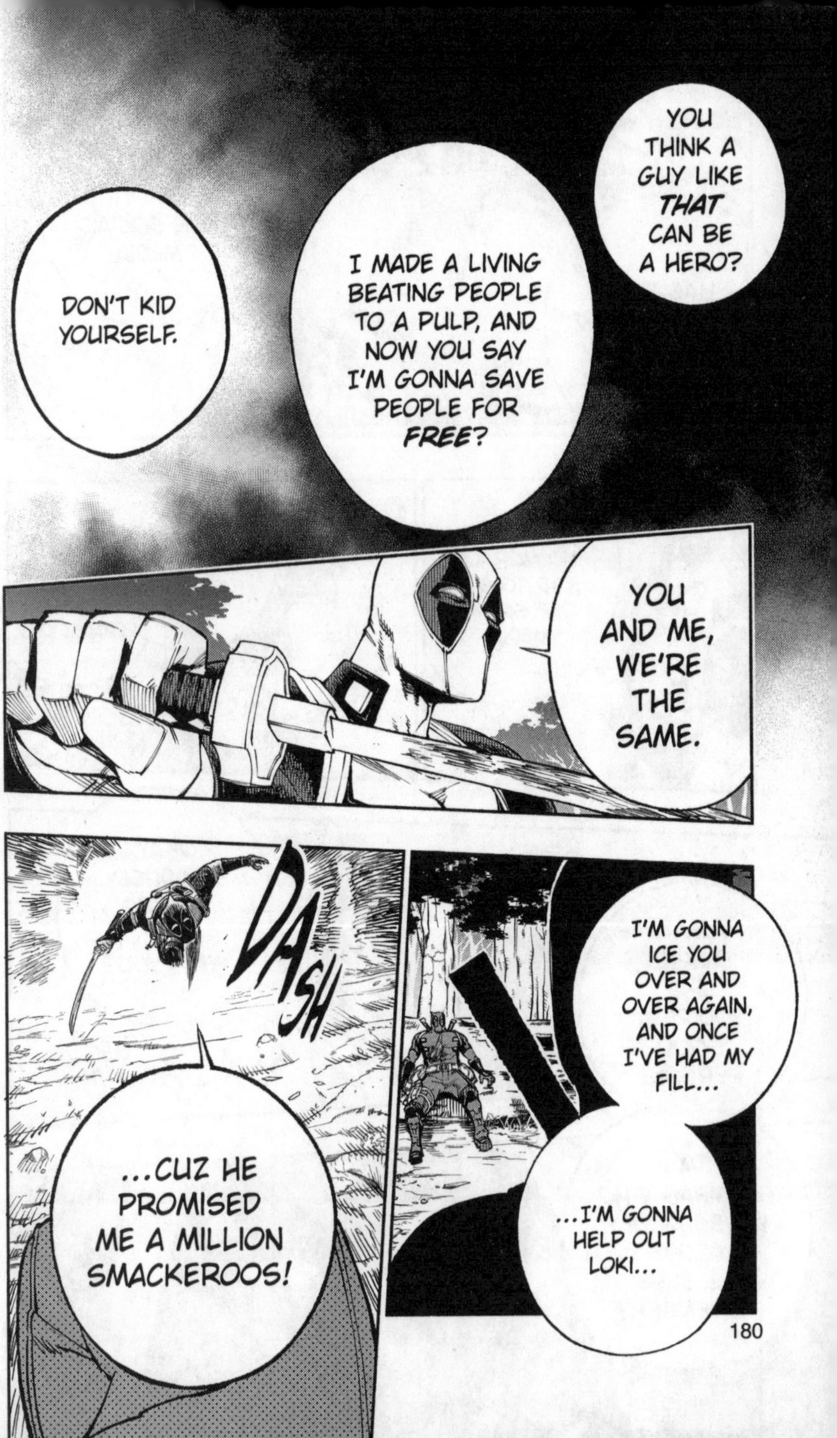
YOU THINK A GUY LIKE *THAT* CAN BE A HERO?
I MADE A LIVING BEATING PEOPLE TO A PULP, AND NOW YOU SAY I'M GONNA SAVE PEOPLE FOR *FREE*?
DON'T KID YOURSELF.
YOU AND ME, WE'RE THE SAME.
I'M GONNA ICE YOU OVER AND OVER AGAIN, AND ONCE I'VE HAD MY FILL...
...I'M GONNA HELP OUT LOKI...
DASH
...CUZ HE PROMISED ME A MILLION SMACKEROOS!

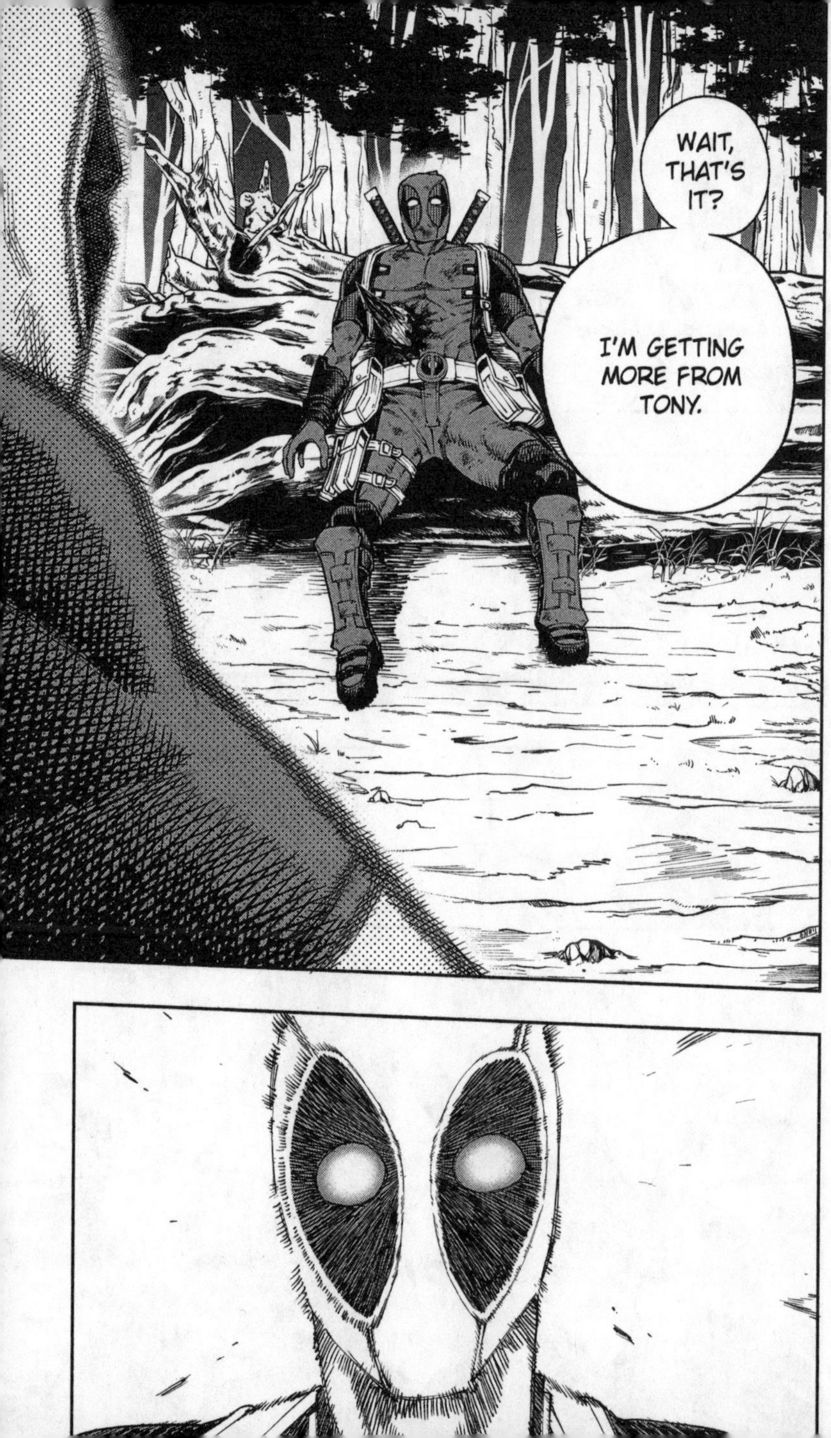
WAIT, THAT'S IT?
I'M GETTING MORE FROM TONY.

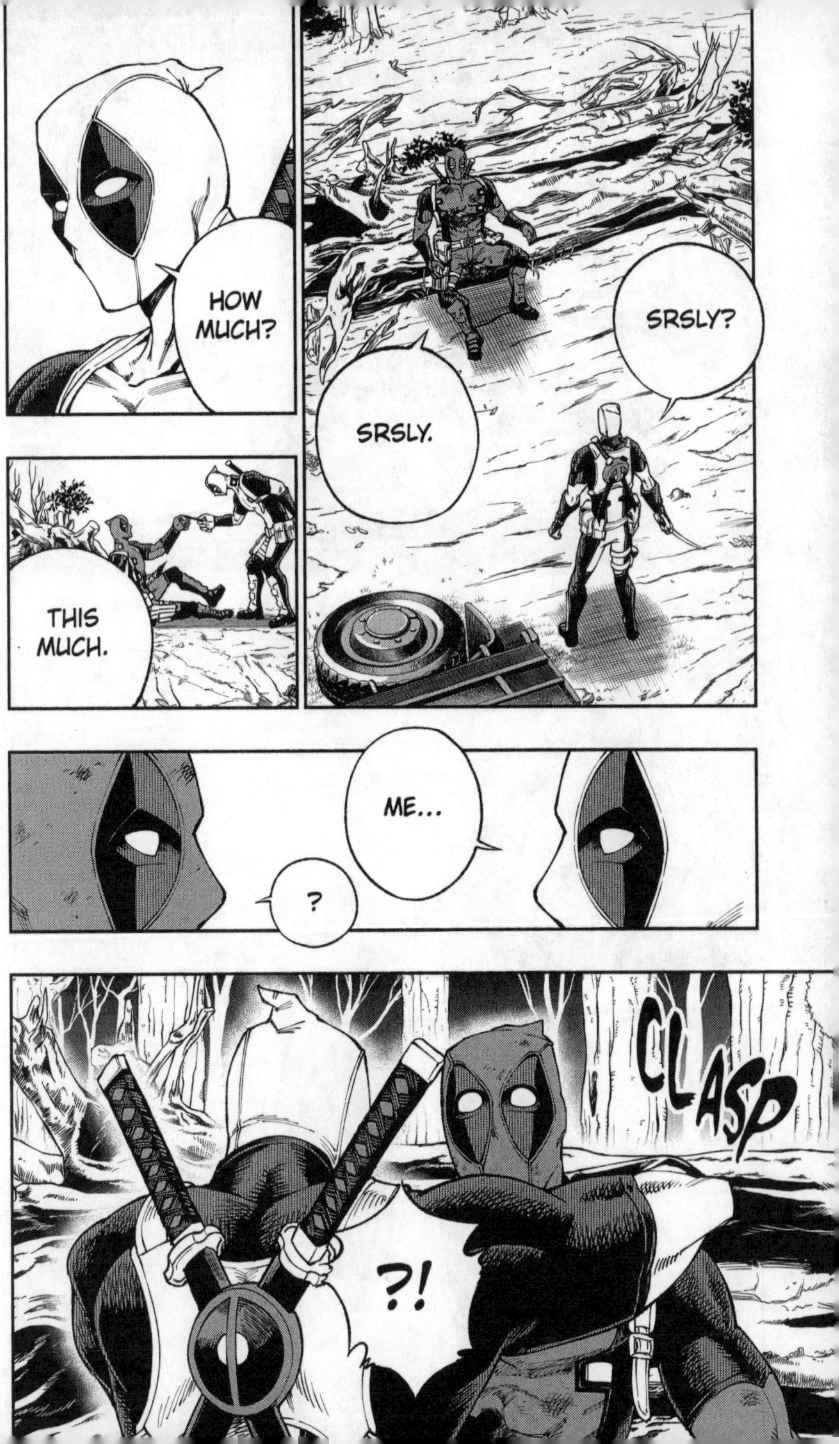
SRSLY?
SRSLY.
HOW MUCH?
THIS MUCH.
ME...
?
CLASP
?!

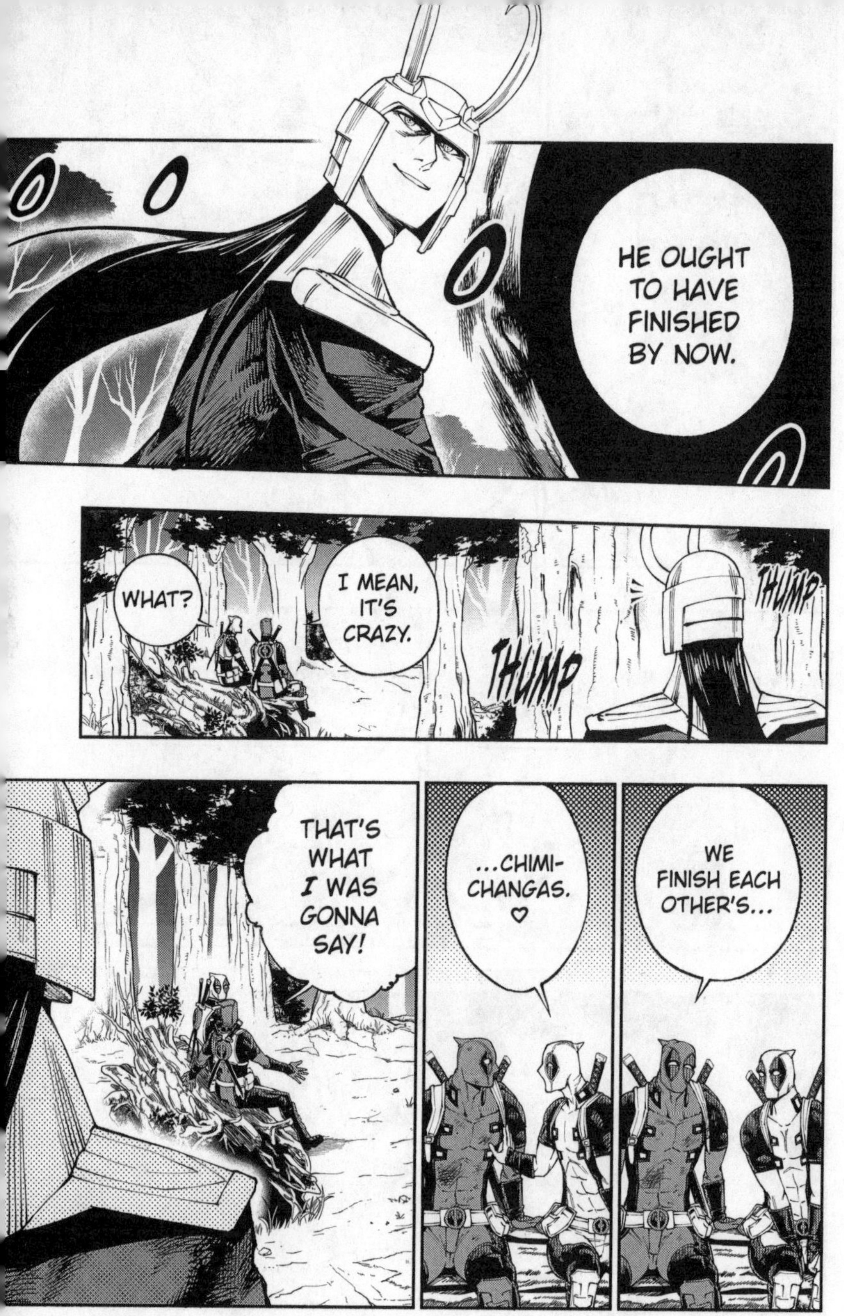
HE OUGHT TO HAVE FINISHED BY NOW.
THUMP
THUMP
I MEAN, IT'S CRAZY.
WHAT?
WE FINISH EACH OTHER'S...
...CHIMI-CHANGAS. ♡
THAT'S WHAT *I* WAS GONNA SAY!

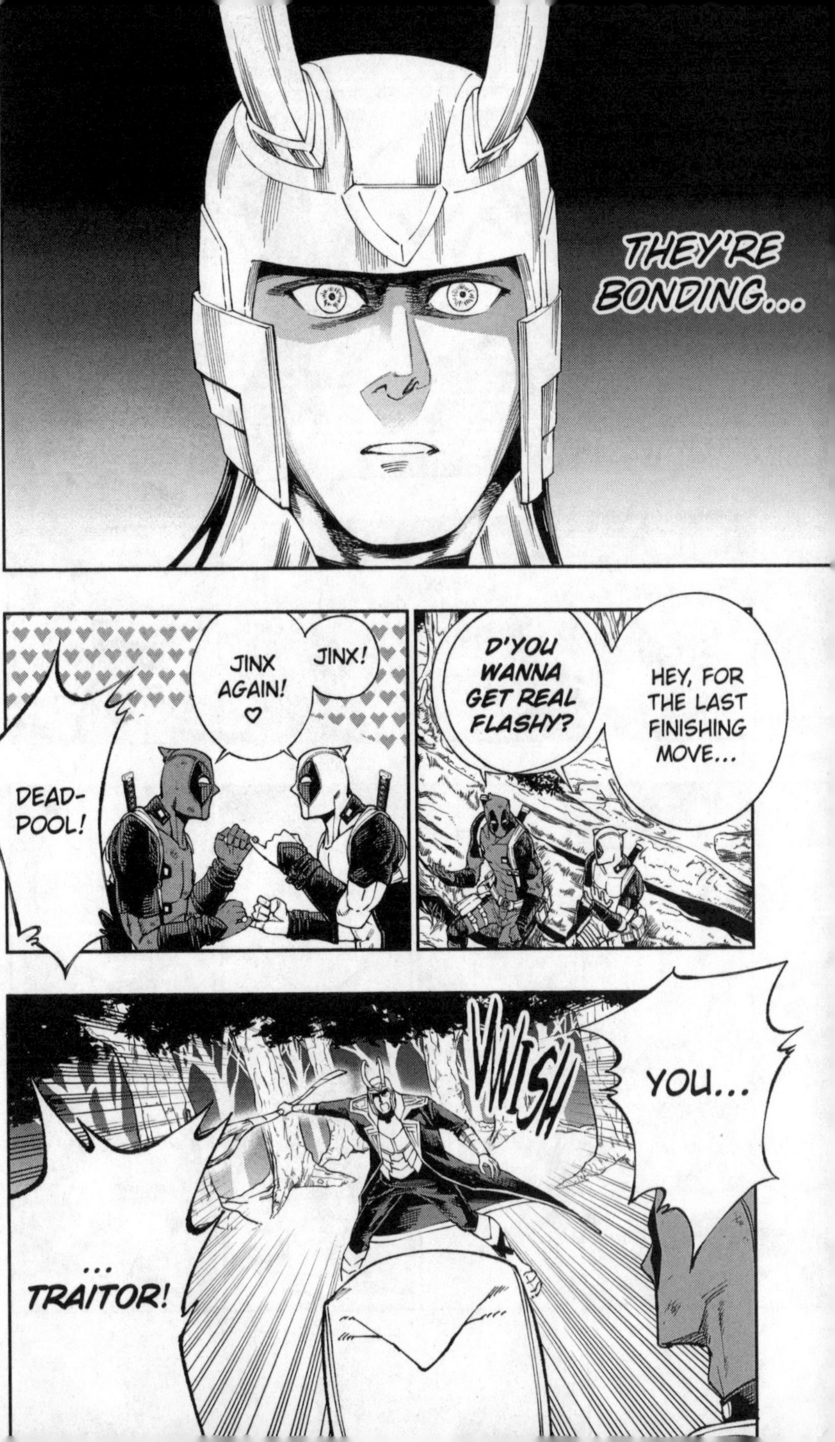
THEY'RE BONDING...
HEY, FOR THE LAST FINISHING MOVE...
D'YOU WANNA GET REAL FLASHY?
JINX!
JINX AGAIN! ♡
DEAD-POOL!
VWISH
YOU...
... TRAITOR!

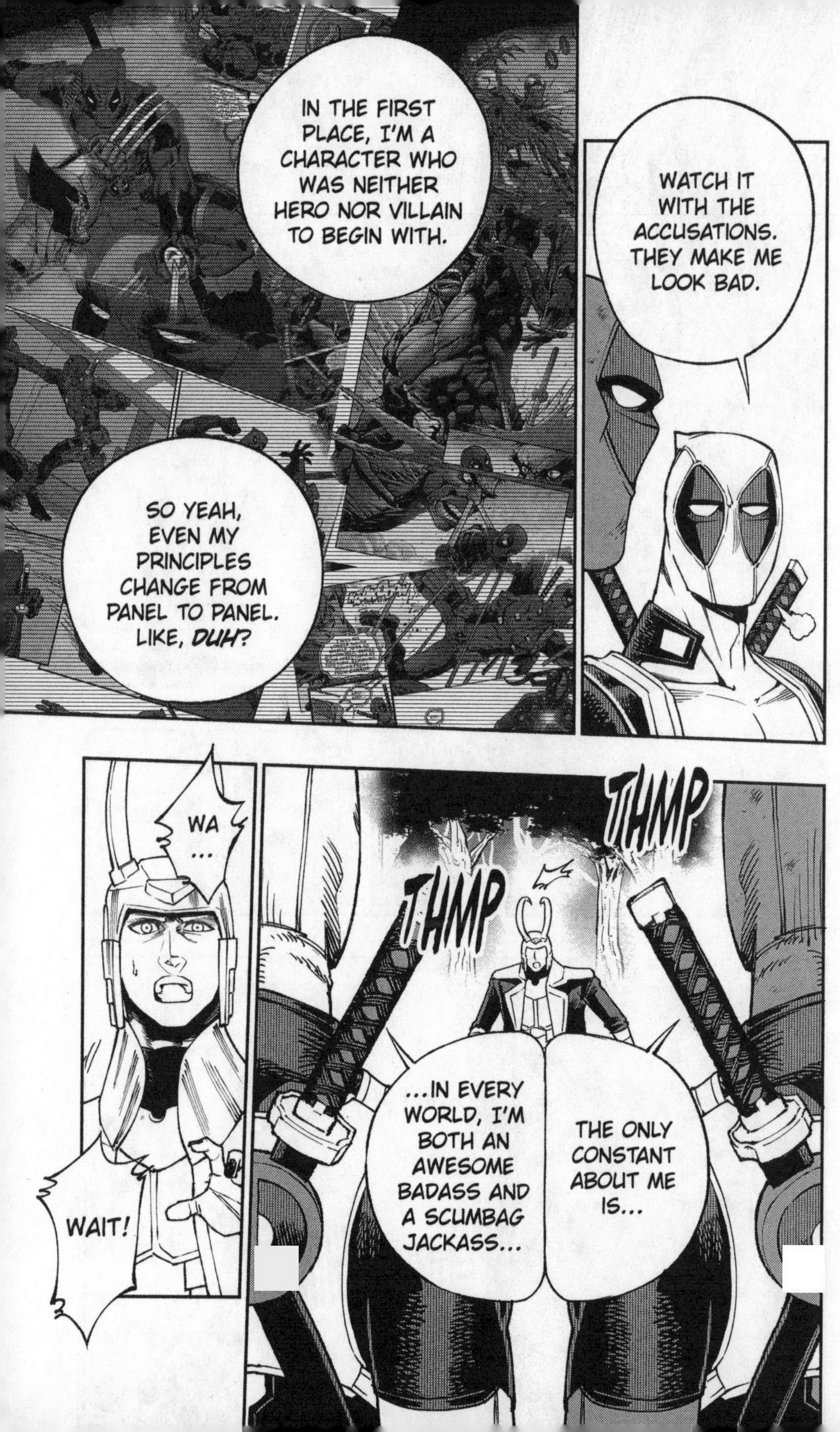
WATCH IT WITH THE ACCUSATIONS. THEY MAKE ME LOOK BAD.
IN THE FIRST PLACE, I'M A CHARACTER WHO WAS NEITHER HERO NOR VILLAIN TO BEGIN WITH.
SO YEAH, EVEN MY PRINCIPLES CHANGE FROM PANEL TO PANEL. LIKE, *DUH*?
THMP
THMP
THE ONLY CONSTANT ABOUT ME IS...
...IN EVERY WORLD, I'M BOTH AN AWESOME BADASS AND A SCUMBAG JACKASS...
WA ...
WAIT!

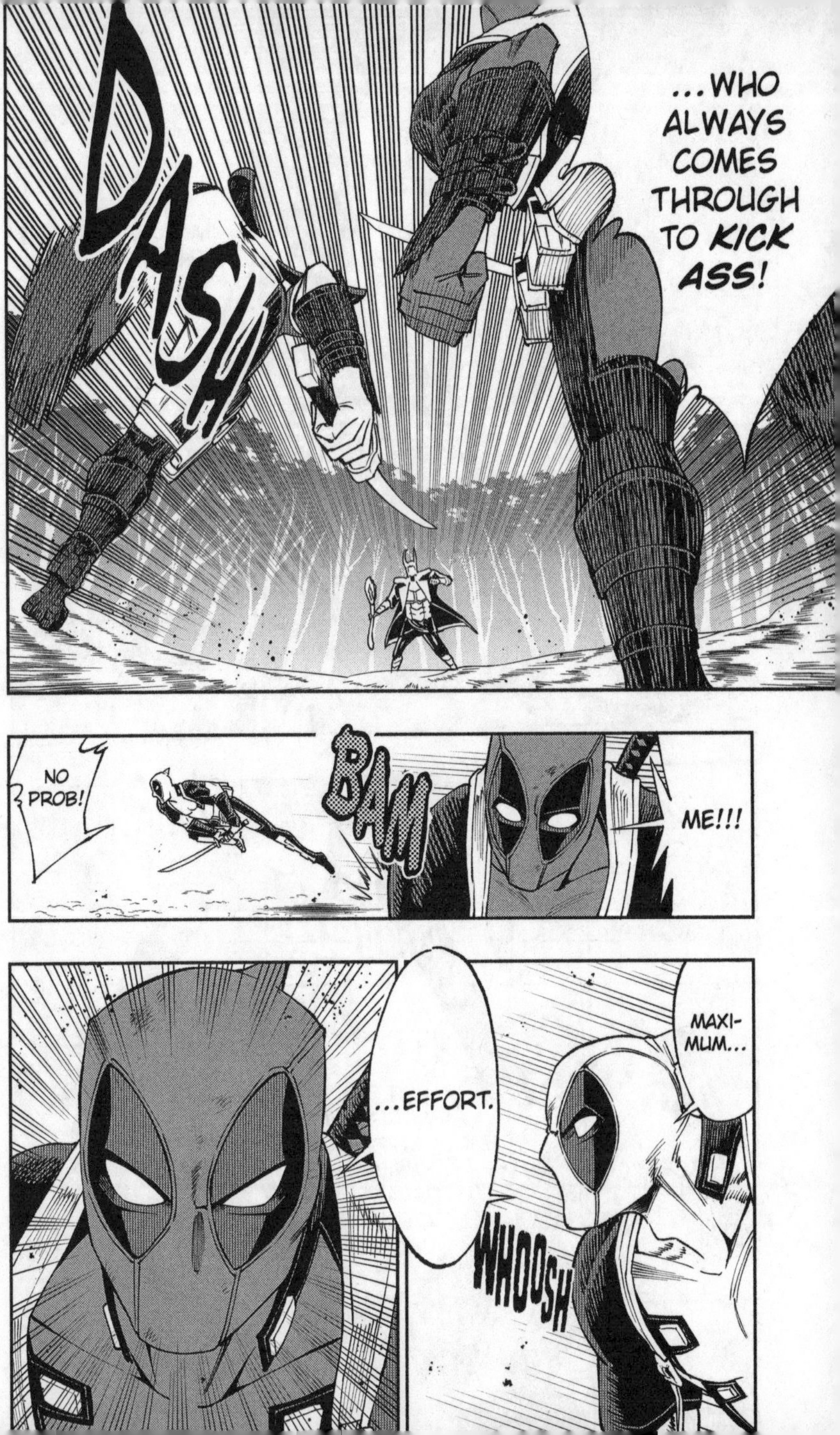
...WHO ALWAYS COMES THROUGH TO KICK ASS!
DASH
ME!!!
BAM
NO PROB!
MAXI-MUM...
WHOOSH
...EFFORT.

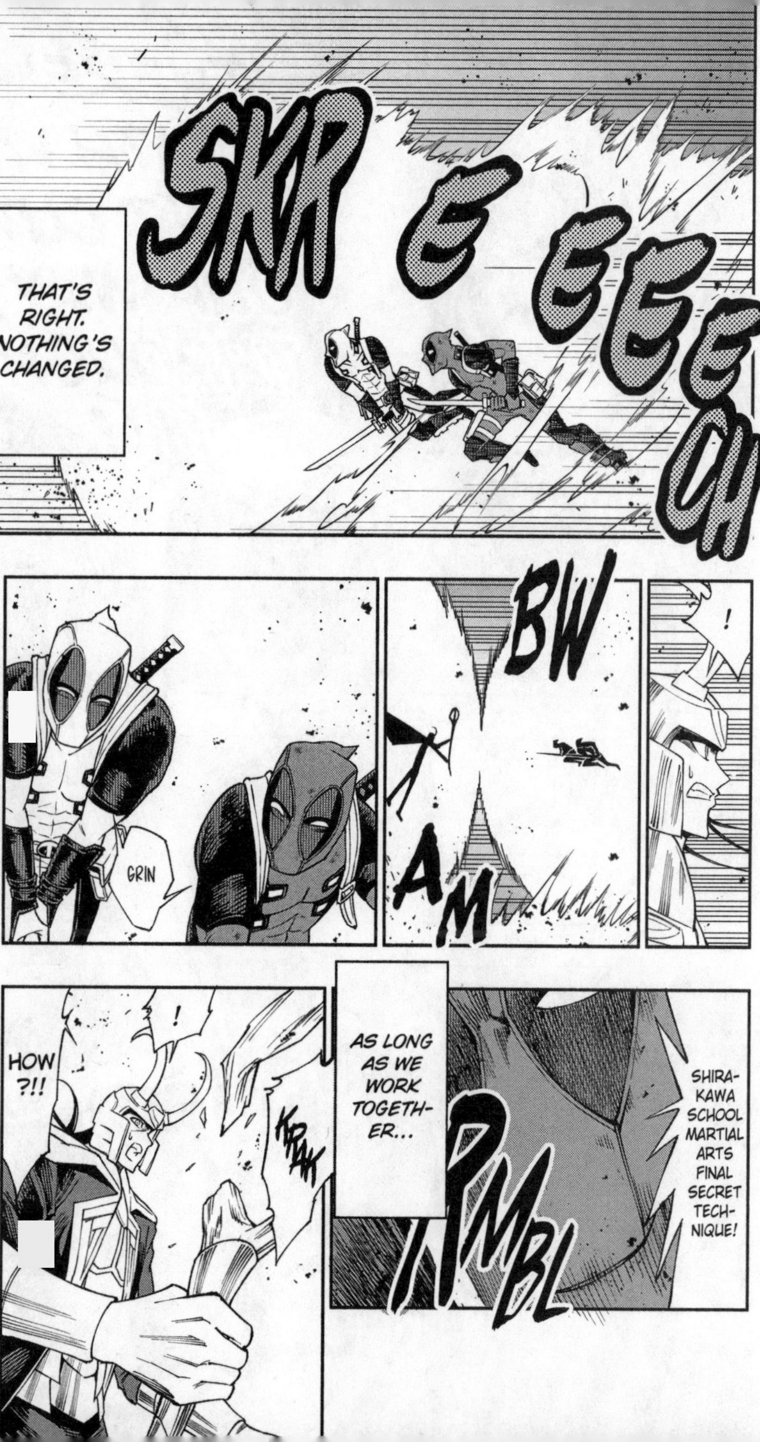
SKREEEEECH
THAT'S RIGHT. NOTHING'S CHANGED.
!
BWAM
GRIN
SHIRA-KAWA SCHOOL MARTIAL ARTS FINAL SECRET TECH-NIQUE!
AS LONG AS WE WORK TOGETH-ER...
!
HOW?!!
KRAK

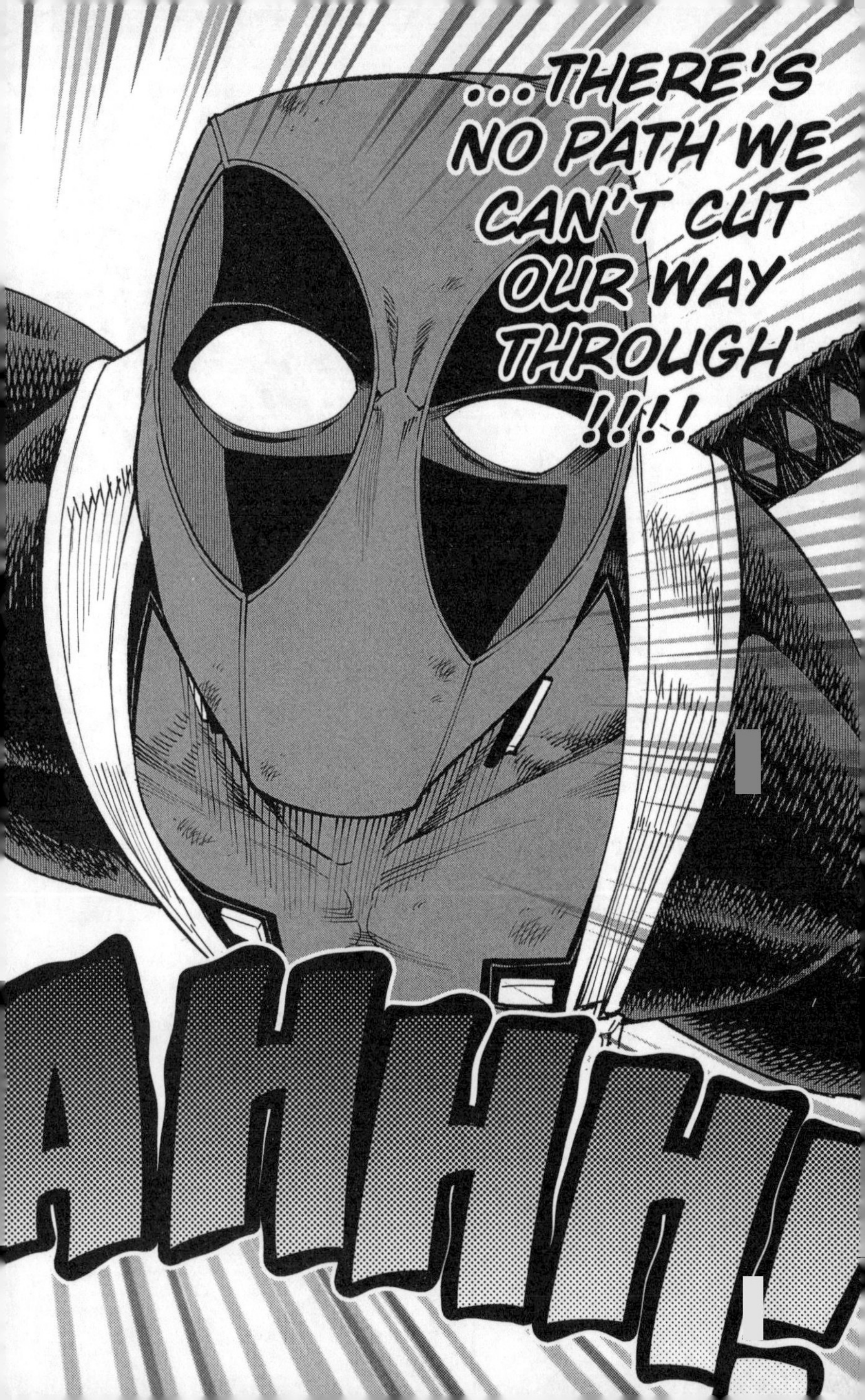
...THERE'S NO PATH WE CAN'T CUT OUR WAY THROUGH !!!!!
AHHHH!

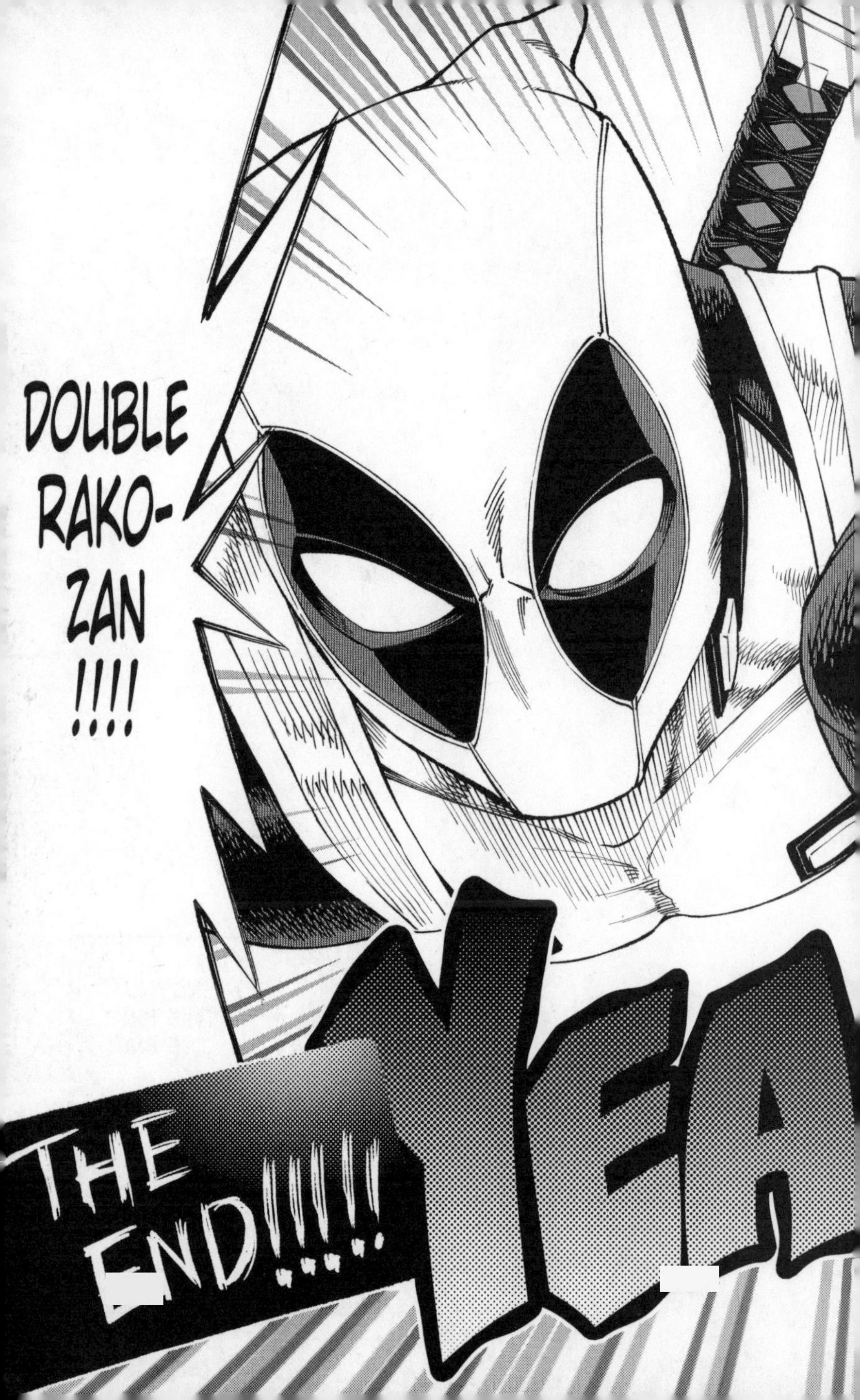
DOUBLE RAKO-ZAN !!!!
YEA
THE END!!!!!

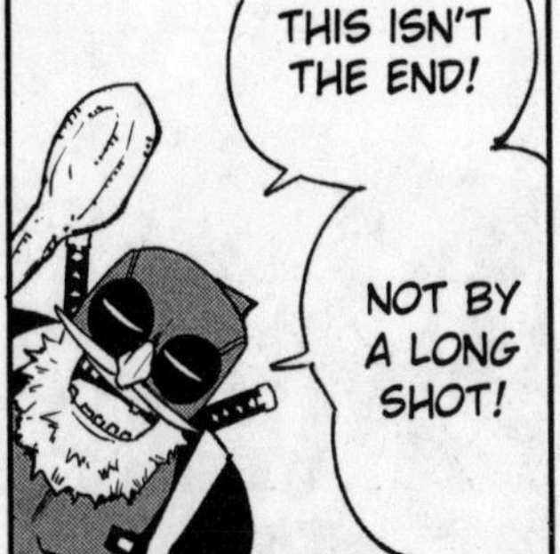
NO, NO, THIS ISN'T THE END!
NOT BY A LONG SHOT!

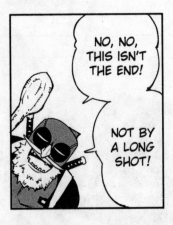

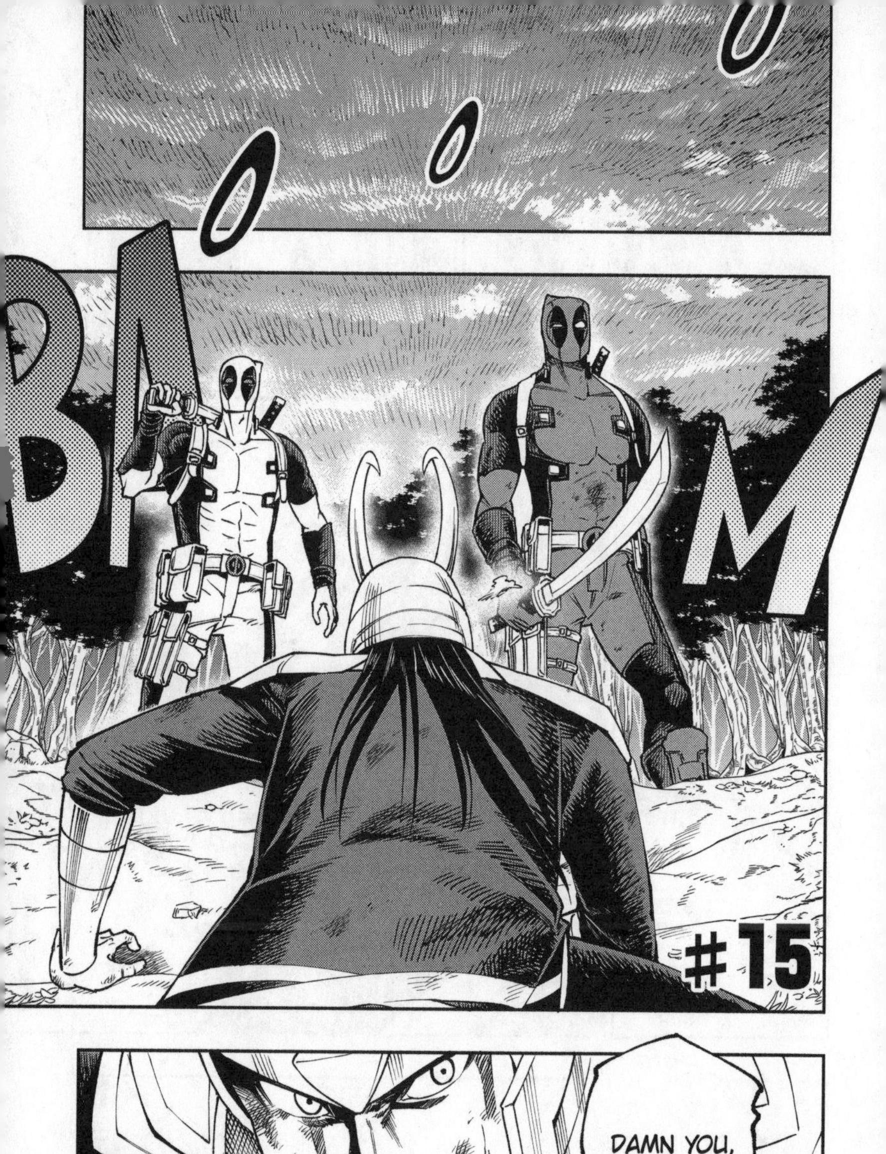

BAM
#15
DAMN YOU, DEADPOOL!

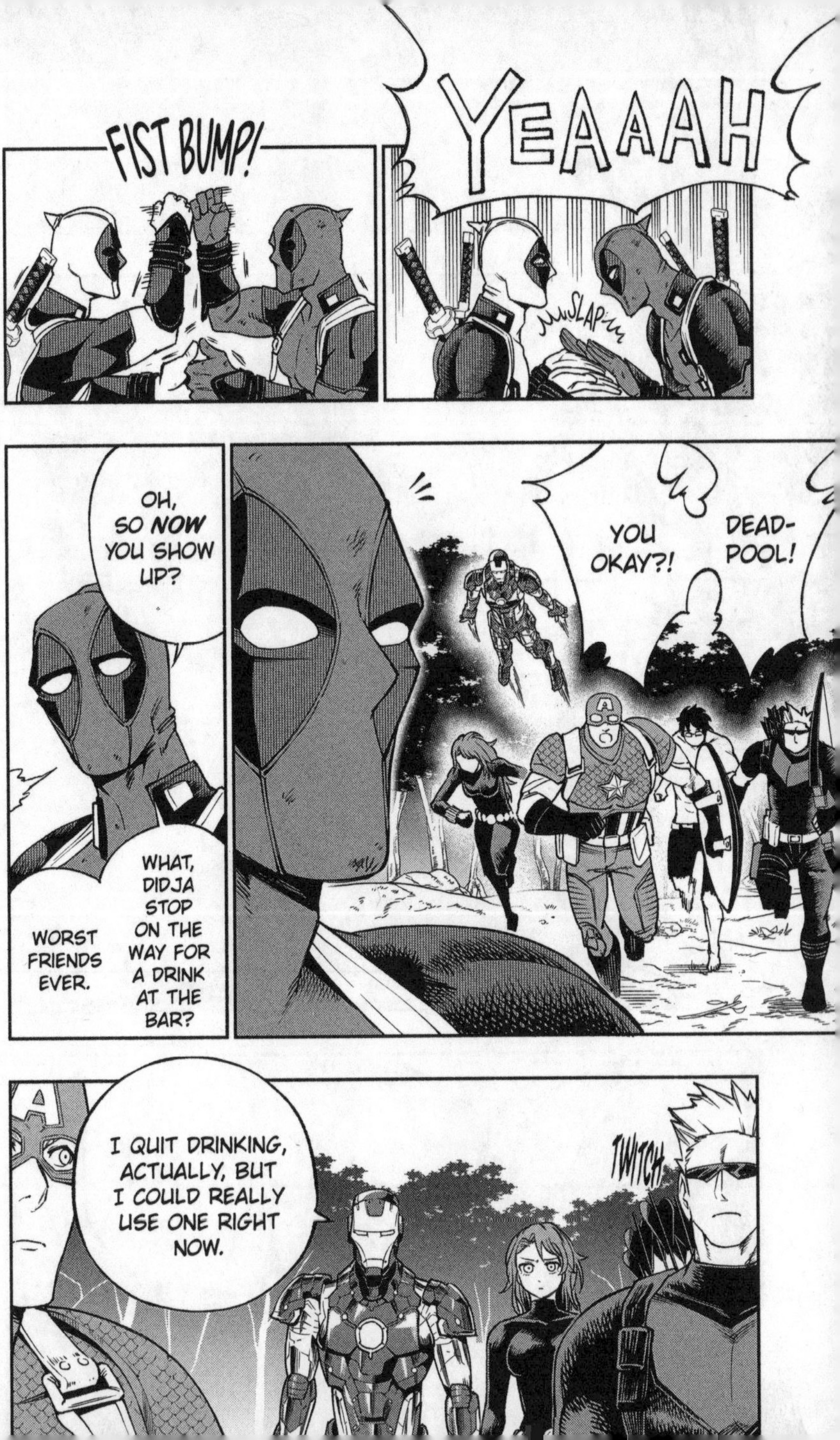
YEAAAH
SLAP
FIST BUMP!
DEAD-POOL!
YOU OKAY?!
OH, SO **NOW** YOU SHOW UP?
WHAT, DIDJA STOP ON THE WAY FOR A DRINK AT THE BAR?
WORST FRIENDS EVER.
I QUIT DRINKING, ACTUALLY, BUT I COULD REALLY USE ONE RIGHT NOW.
TWITCH

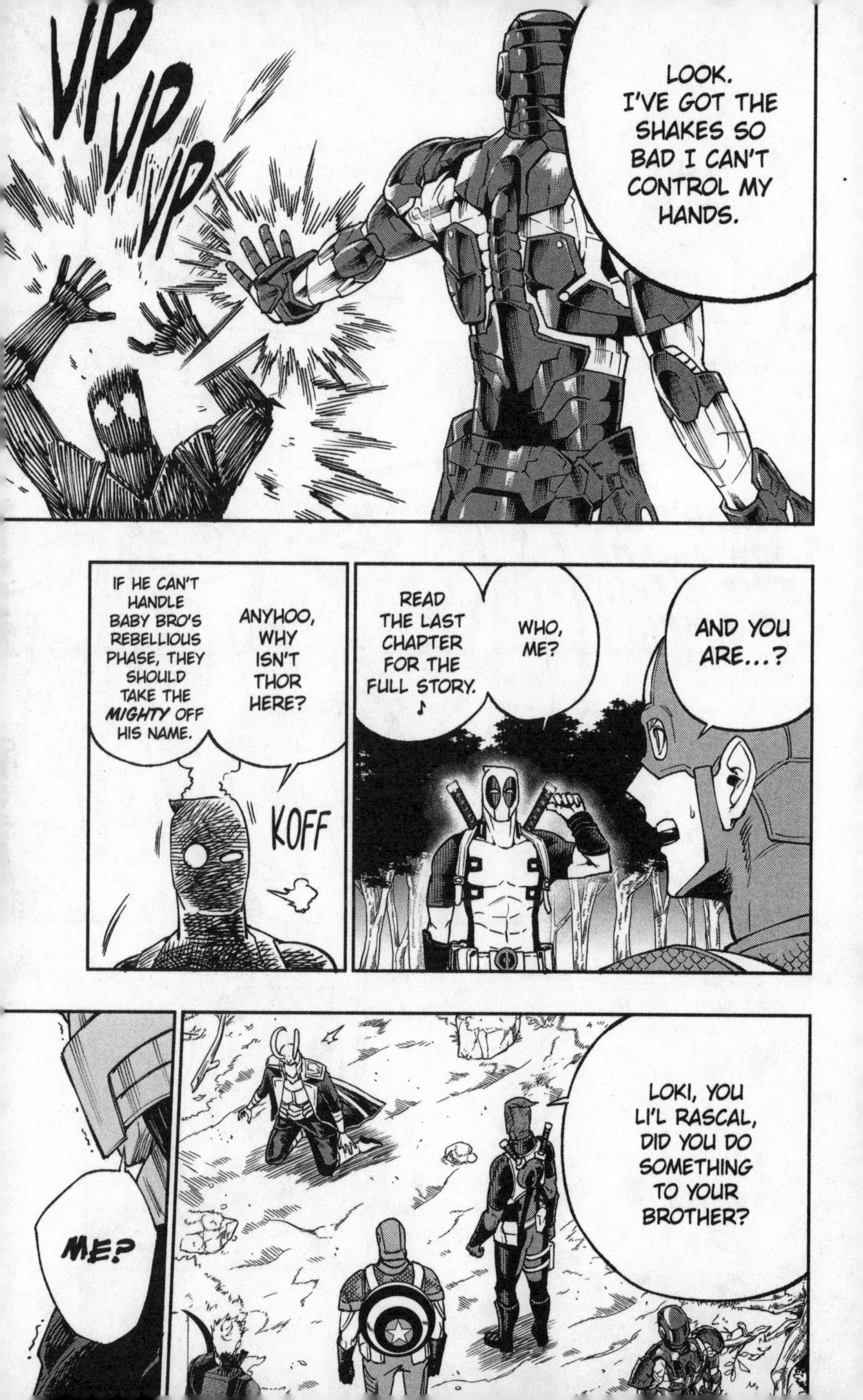
LOOK. I'VE GOT THE SHAKES SO BAD I CAN'T CONTROL MY HANDS.
VP VP VP
AND YOU ARE...?
WHO, ME?
READ THE LAST CHAPTER FOR THE FULL STORY. ♪
ANYHOO, WHY ISN'T THOR HERE?
IF HE CAN'T HANDLE BABY BRO'S REBELLIOUS PHASE, THEY SHOULD TAKE THE *MIGHTY* OFF HIS NAME.
KOFF
LOKI, YOU LI'L RASCAL, DID YOU DO SOMETHING TO YOUR BROTHER?
ME?

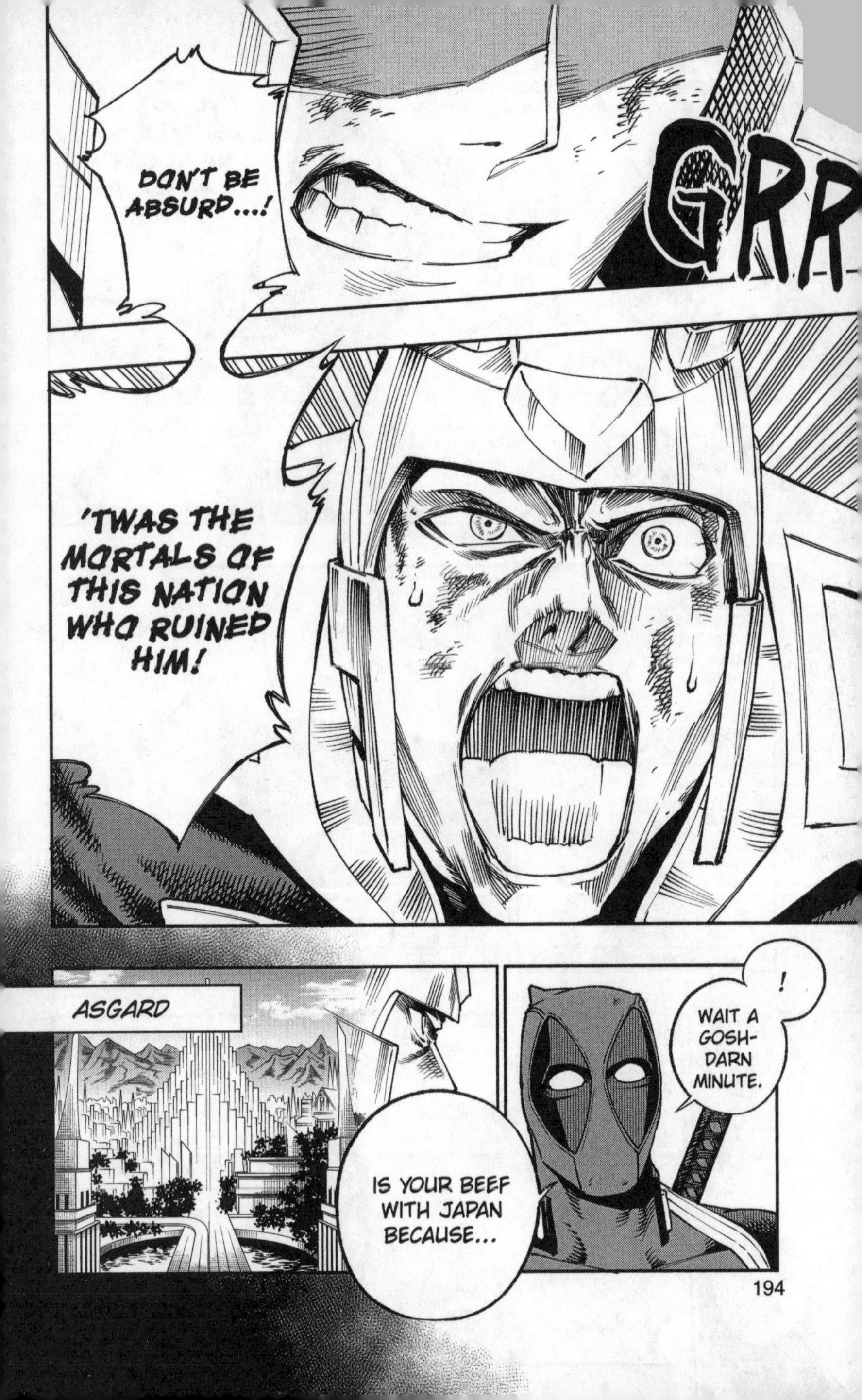
GRR
DON'T BE ABSURD...!
'TWAS THE MORTALS OF THIS NATION WHO RUINED HIM!
!
WAIT A GOSH-DARN MINUTE.
IS YOUR BEEF WITH JAPAN BECAUSE...
ASGARD

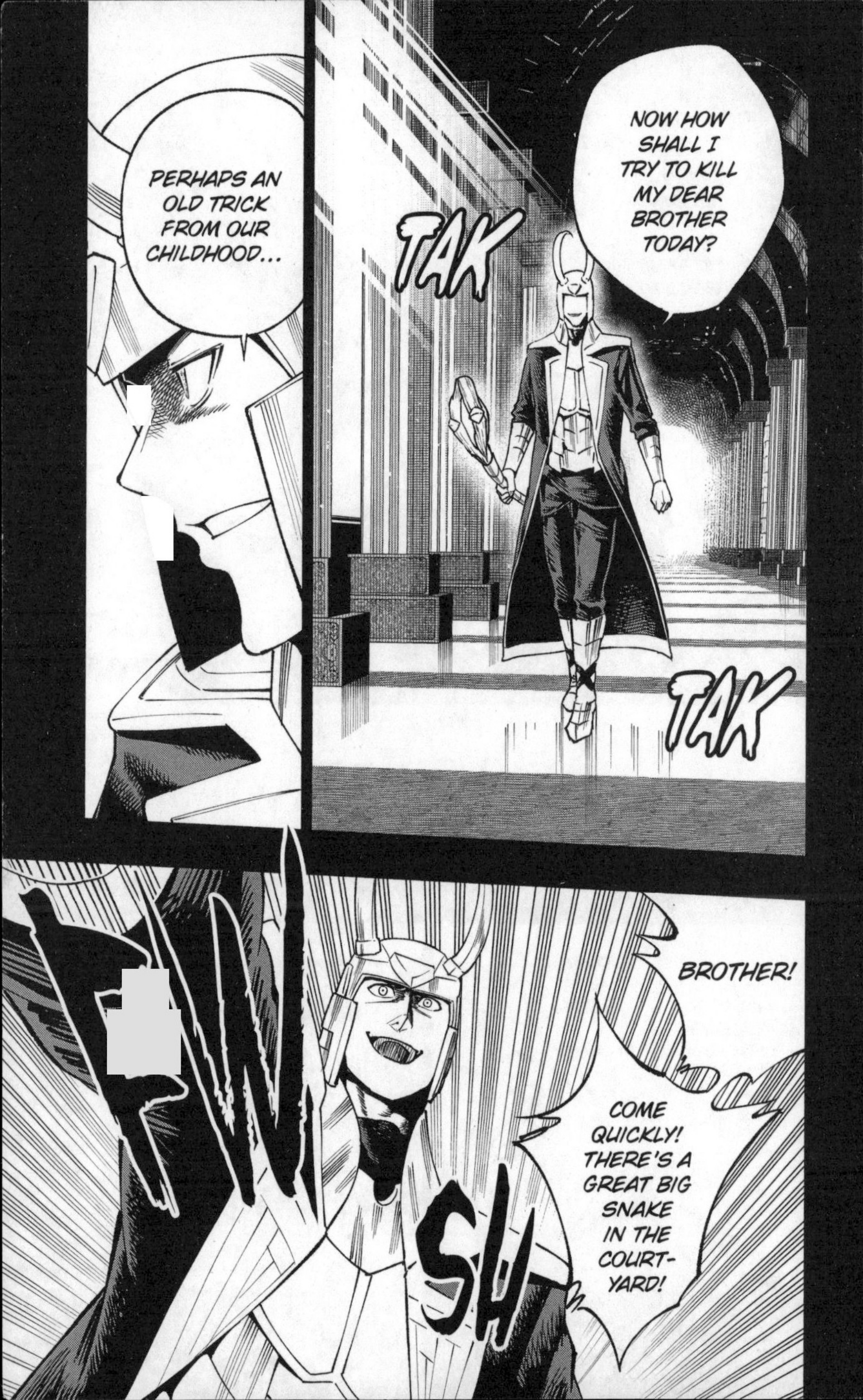
NOW HOW SHALL I TRY TO KILL MY DEAR BROTHER TODAY?
TAK
TAK
PERHAPS AN OLD TRICK FROM OUR CHILDHOOD...
BROTHER!
COME QUICKLY! THERE'S A GREAT BIG SNAKE IN THE COURT-YARD!
SH

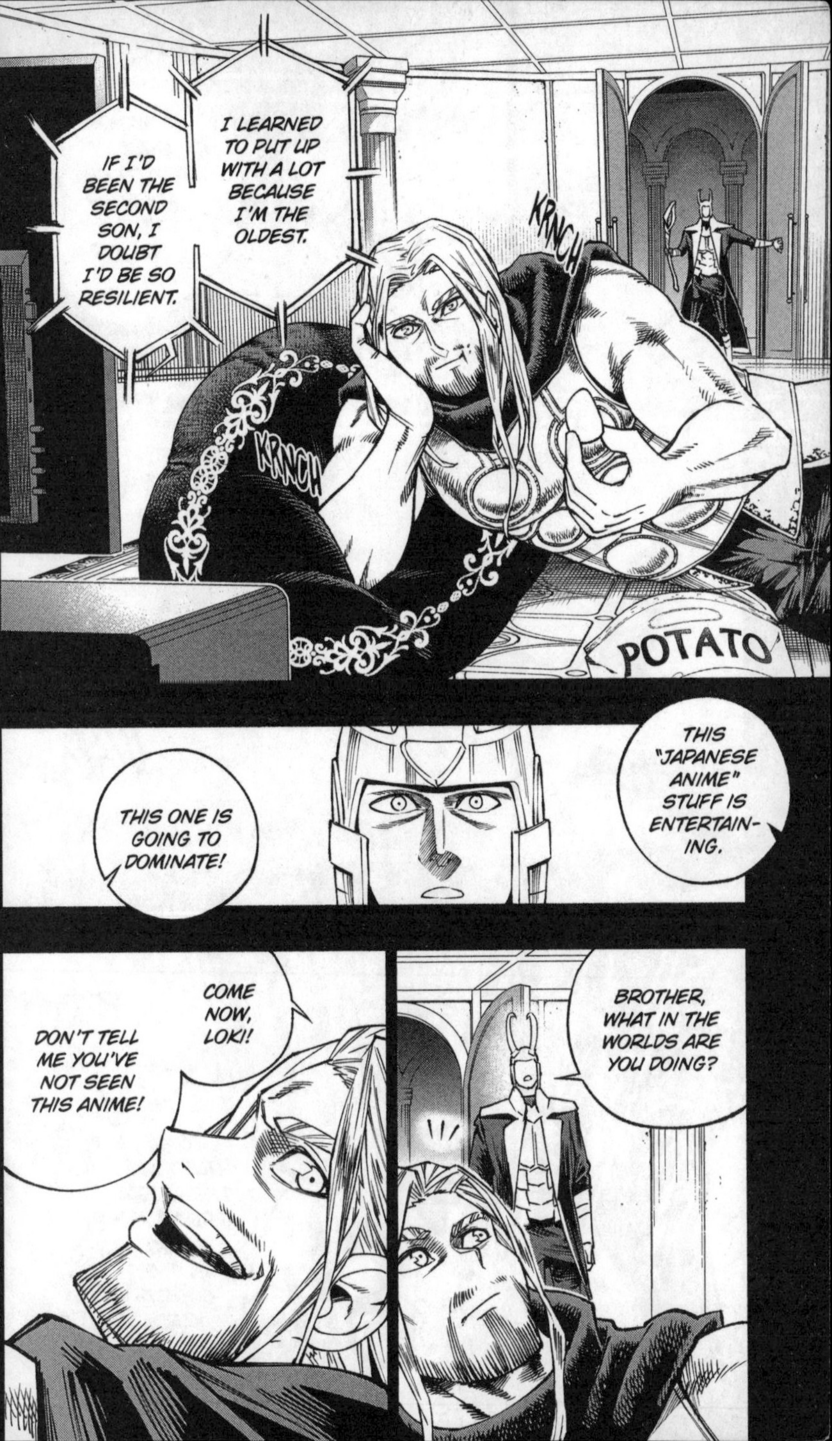
I LEARNED TO PUT UP WITH A LOT BECAUSE I'M THE OLDEST.
IF I'D BEEN THE SECOND SON, I DOUBT I'D BE SO RESILIENT.
KRNCH
KRNCH
POTATO
THIS "JAPANESE ANIME" STUFF IS ENTERTAINING.
THIS ONE IS GOING TO DOMINATE!
BROTHER, WHAT IN THE WORLDS ARE YOU DOING?
COME NOW, LOKI!
DON'T TELL ME YOU'VE NOT SEEN THIS ANIME!

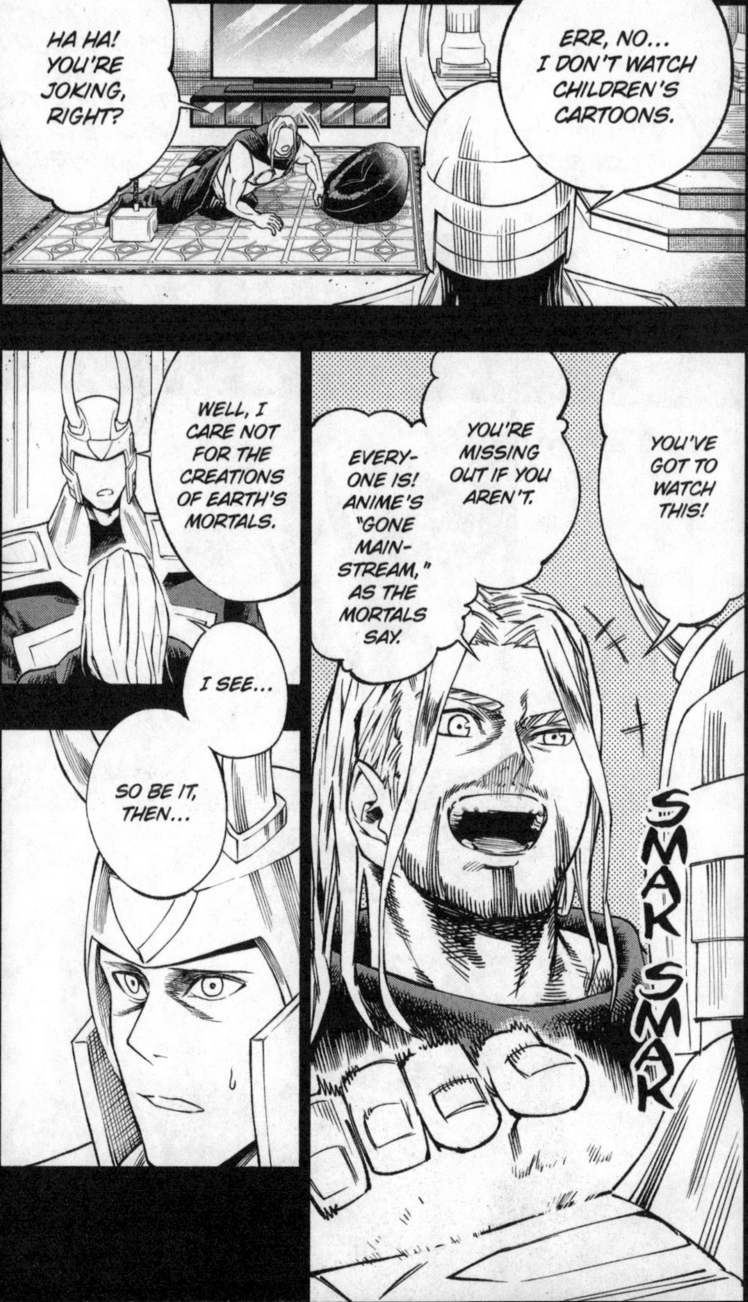

ERR, NO... I DON'T WATCH CHILDREN'S CARTOONS.
HA HA! YOU'RE JOKING, RIGHT?
YOU'VE GOT TO WATCH THIS!
YOU'RE MISSING OUT IF YOU AREN'T.
EVERYONE IS! ANIME'S "GONE MAINSTREAM," AS THE MORTALS SAY.
SMAK SMAK
WELL, I CARE NOT FOR THE CREATIONS OF EARTH'S MORTALS.
I SEE...
SO BE IT, THEN...

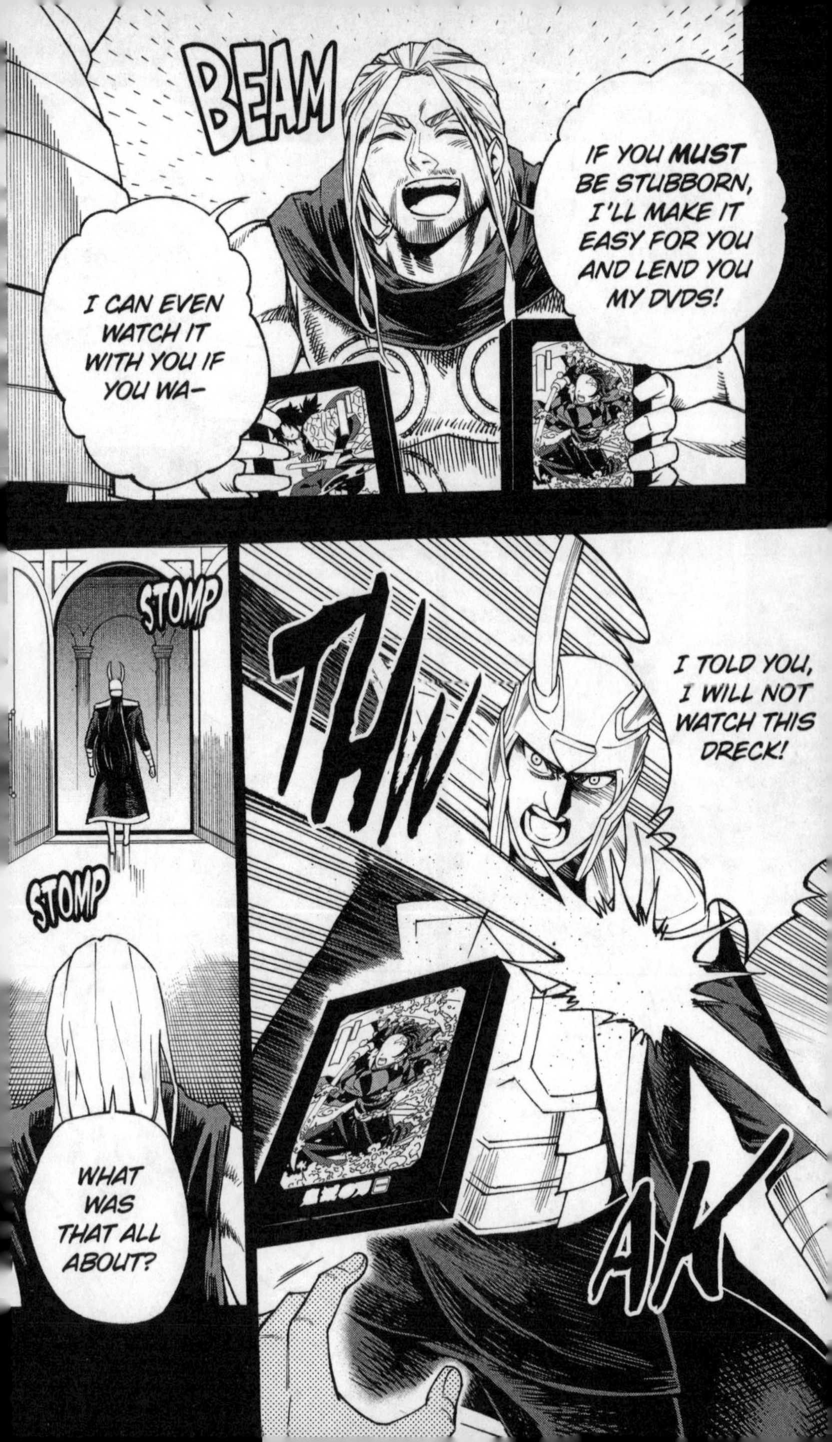
BEAM
IF YOU MUST BE STUBBORN, I'LL MAKE IT EASY FOR YOU AND LEND YOU MY DVDS!
I CAN EVEN WATCH IT WITH YOU IF YOU WA-
THW
I TOLD YOU, I WILL NOT WATCH THIS DRECK!
AK
STOMP
STOMP
WHAT WAS THAT ALL ABOUT?

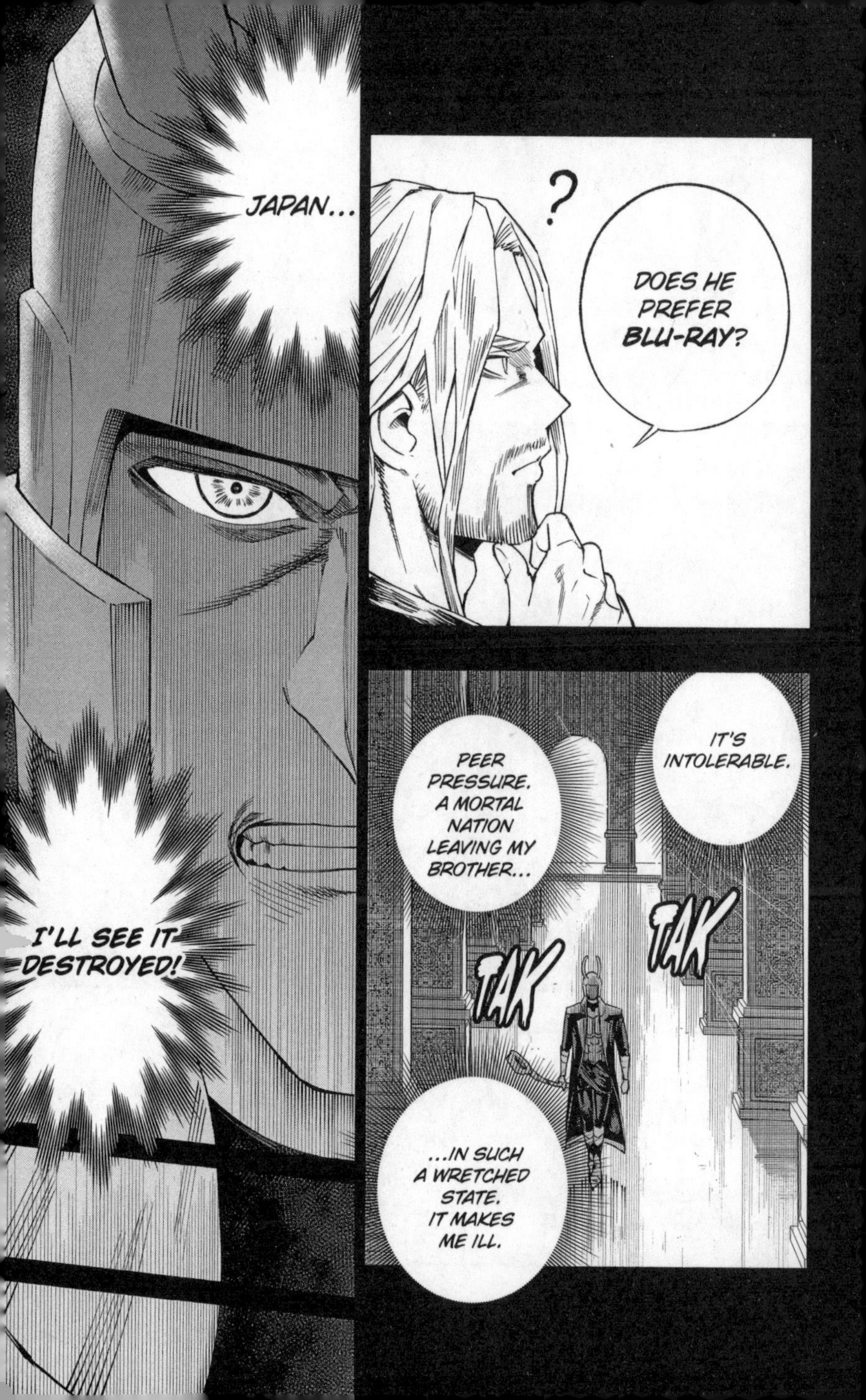
?
DOES HE PREFER BLU-RAY?
IT'S INTOLERABLE.
PEER PRESSURE. A MORTAL NATION LEAVING MY BROTHER...
TAK
TAK
...IN SUCH A WRETCHED STATE. IT MAKES ME ILL.
JAPAN...
I'LL SEE IT DESTROYED!

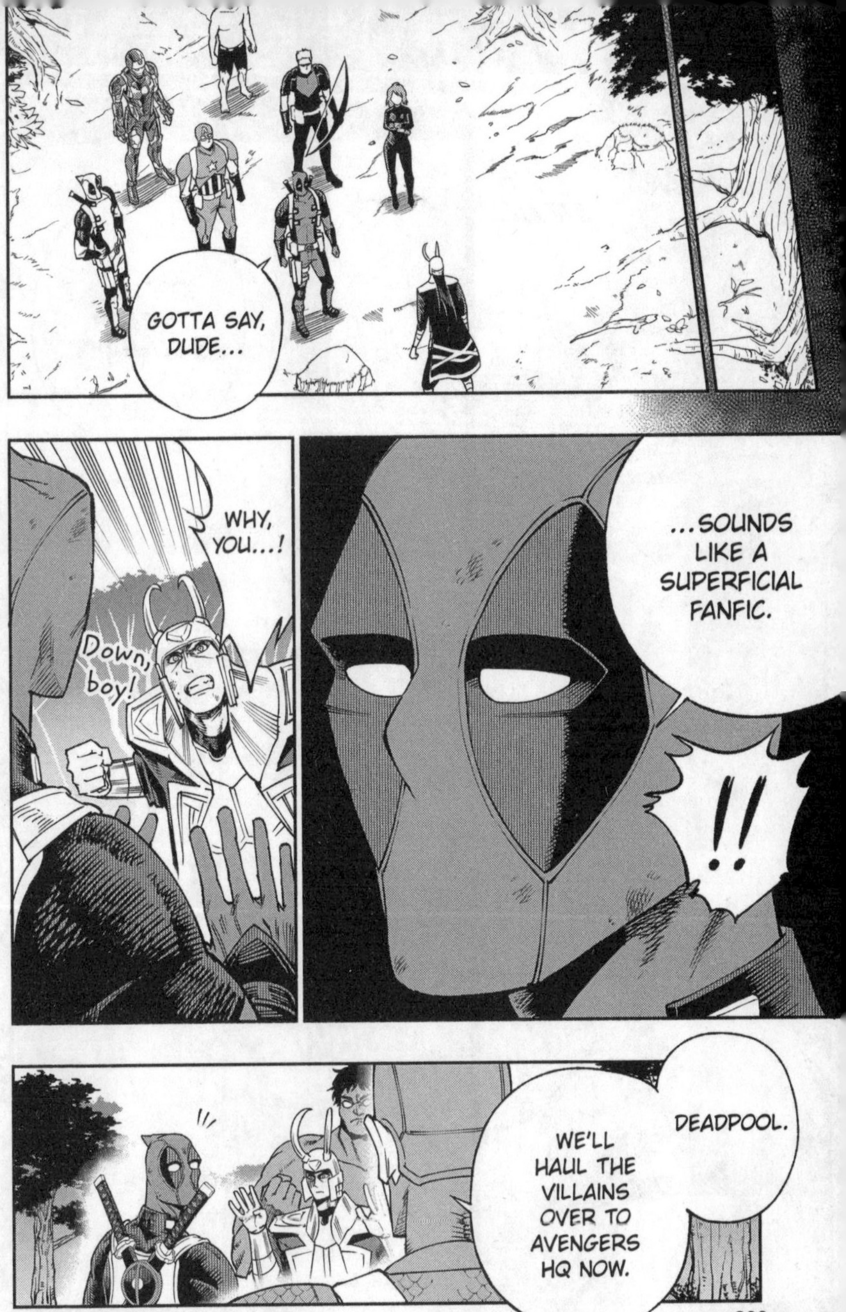
GOTTA SAY, DUDE...
...SOUNDS LIKE A SUPERFICIAL FANFIC.
!!
WHY, YOU...!
Down, boy!
DEADPOOL.
WE'LL HAUL THE VILLAINS OVER TO AVENGERS HQ NOW.

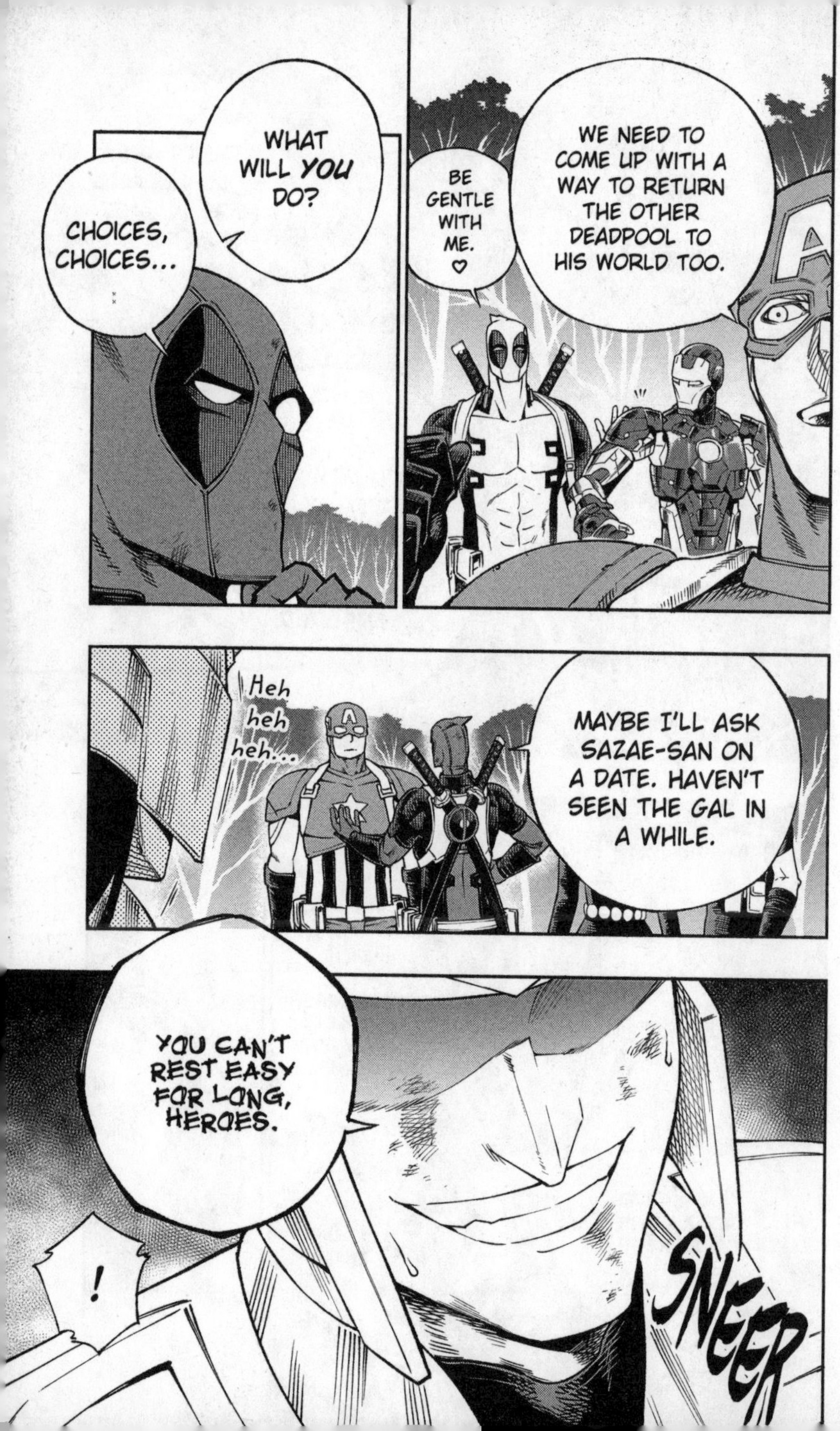
WE NEED TO COME UP WITH A WAY TO RETURN THE OTHER DEADPOOL TO HIS WORLD TOO.
BE GENTLE WITH ME. ♡
WHAT WILL *YOU* DO?
CHOICES, CHOICES...
MAYBE I'LL ASK SAZAE-SAN ON A DATE. HAVEN'T SEEN THE GAL IN A WHILE.
Heh heh heh...
YOU CAN'T REST EASY FOR LONG, HEROES.
SNEER
!

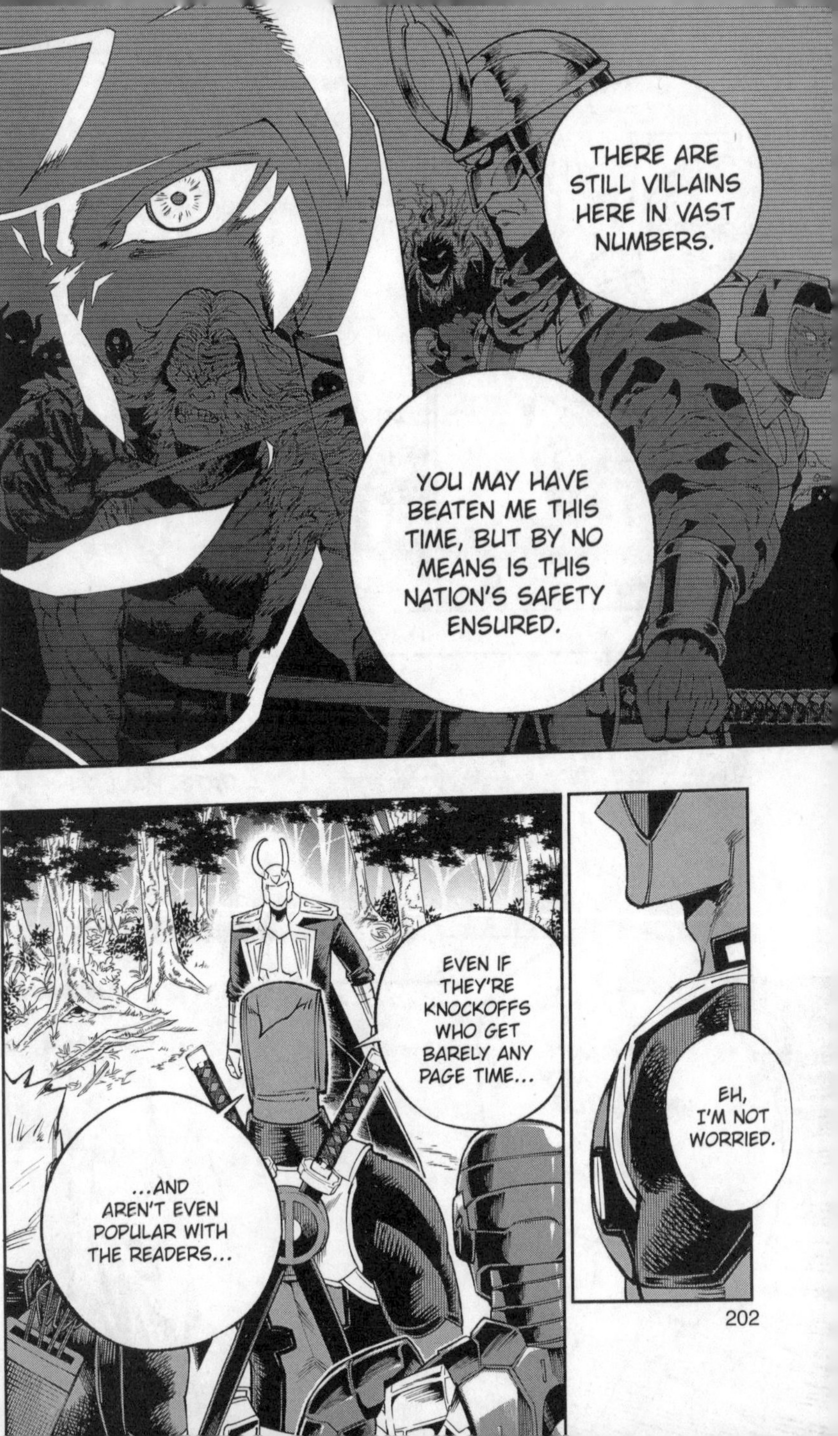
THERE ARE STILL VILLAINS HERE IN VAST NUMBERS.
YOU MAY HAVE BEATEN ME THIS TIME, BUT BY NO MEANS IS THIS NATION'S SAFETY ENSURED.
EH, I'M NOT WORRIED.
EVEN IF THEY'RE KNOCKOFFS WHO GET BARELY ANY PAGE TIME...
...AND AREN'T EVEN POPULAR WITH THE READERS...

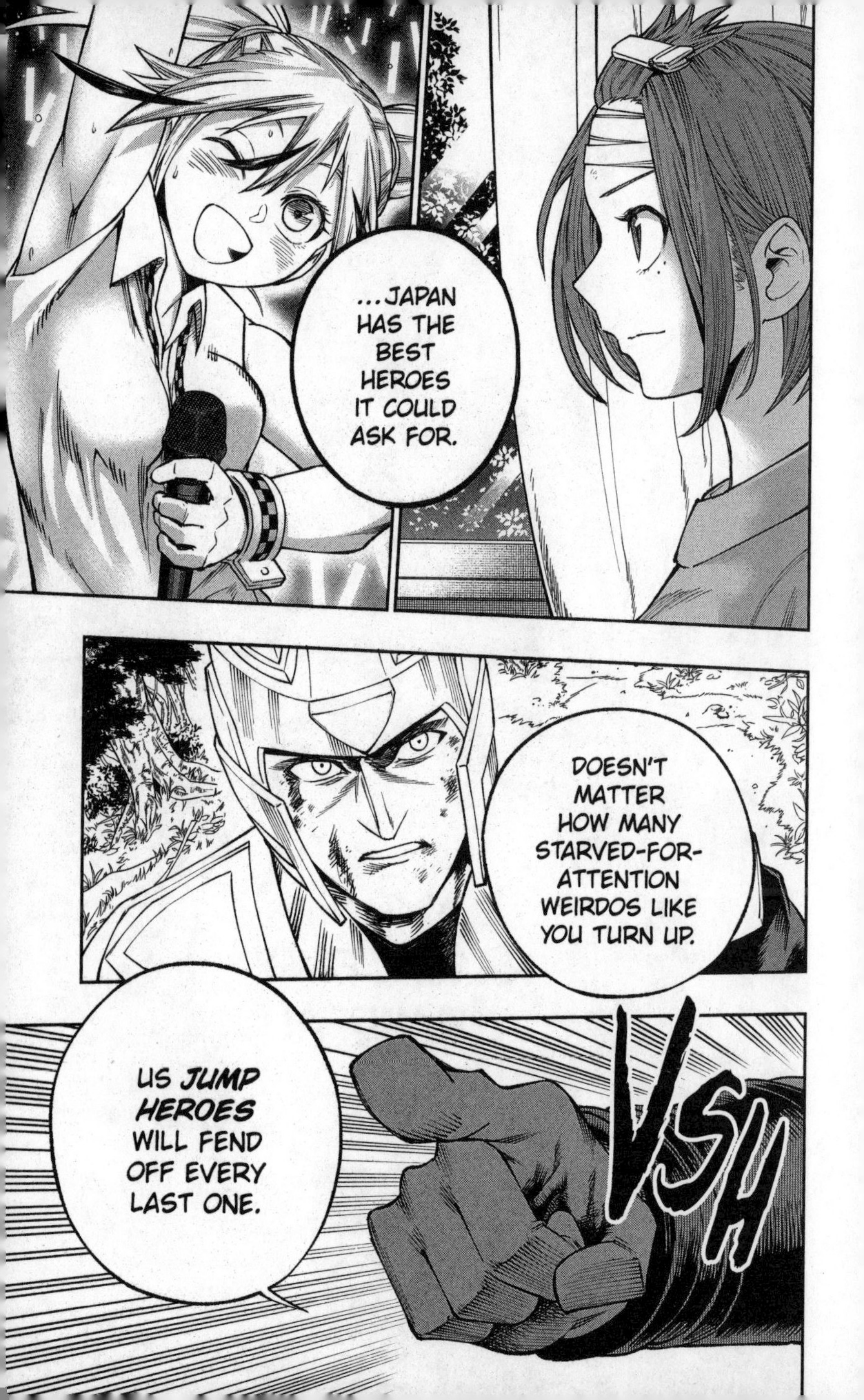
...JAPAN HAS THE BEST HEROES IT COULD ASK FOR.
DOESN'T MATTER HOW MANY STARVED-FOR-ATTENTION WEIRDOS LIKE YOU TURN UP.
VSH
US *JUMP HEROES* WILL FEND OFF EVERY LAST ONE.

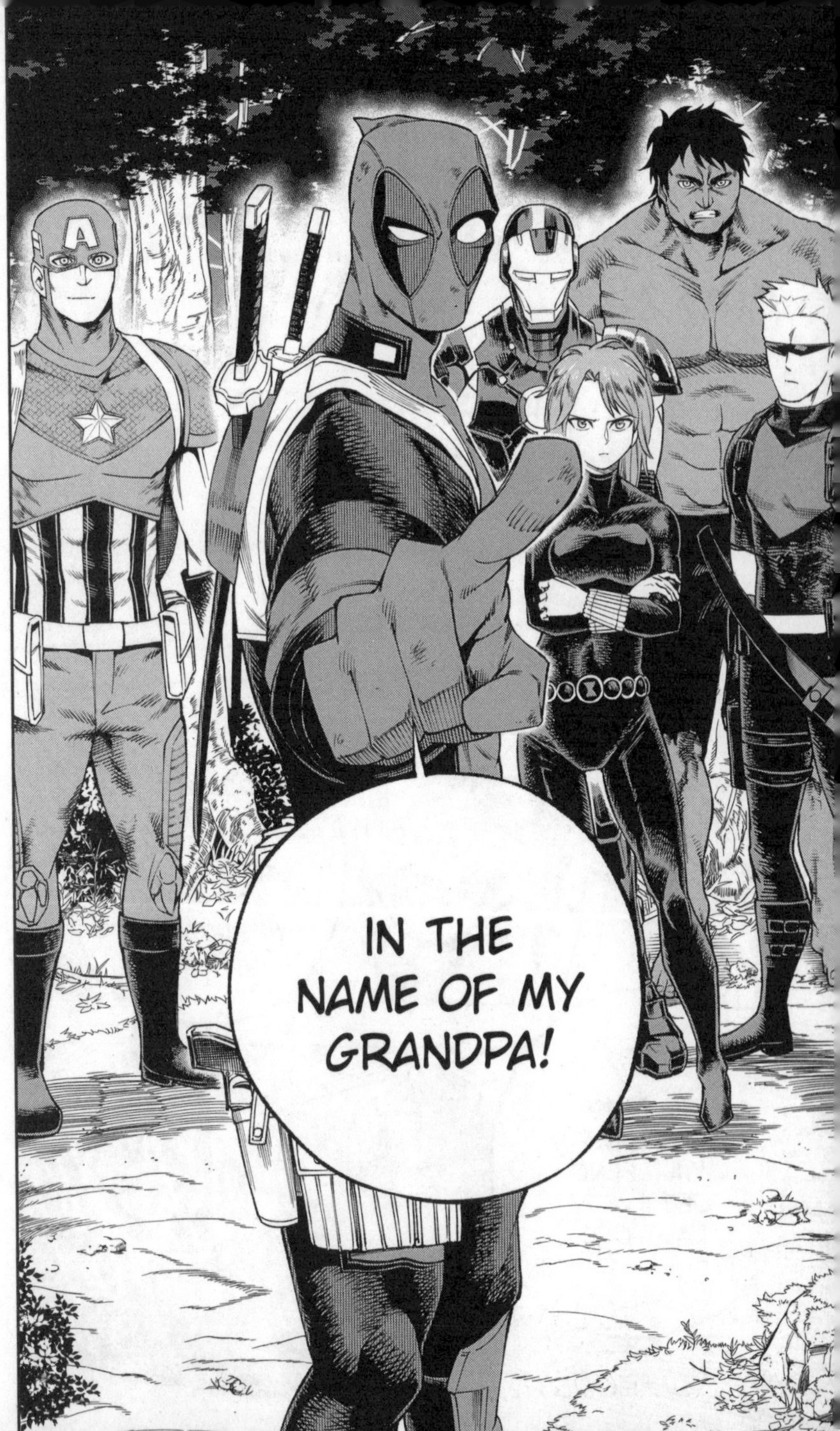
IN THE NAME OF MY GRANDPA!

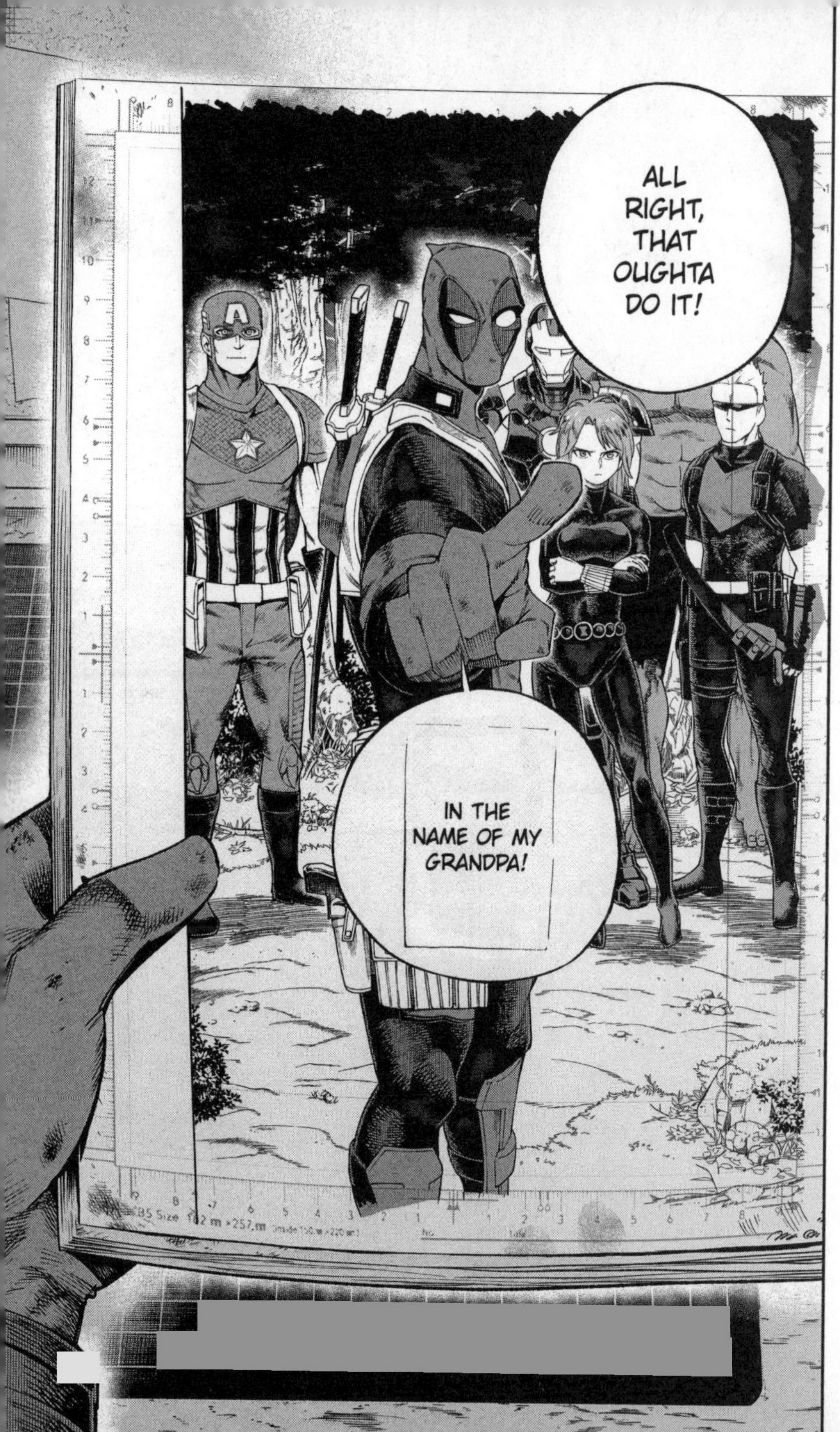
ALL RIGHT, THAT OUGHTA DO IT!
IN THE NAME OF MY GRANDPA!

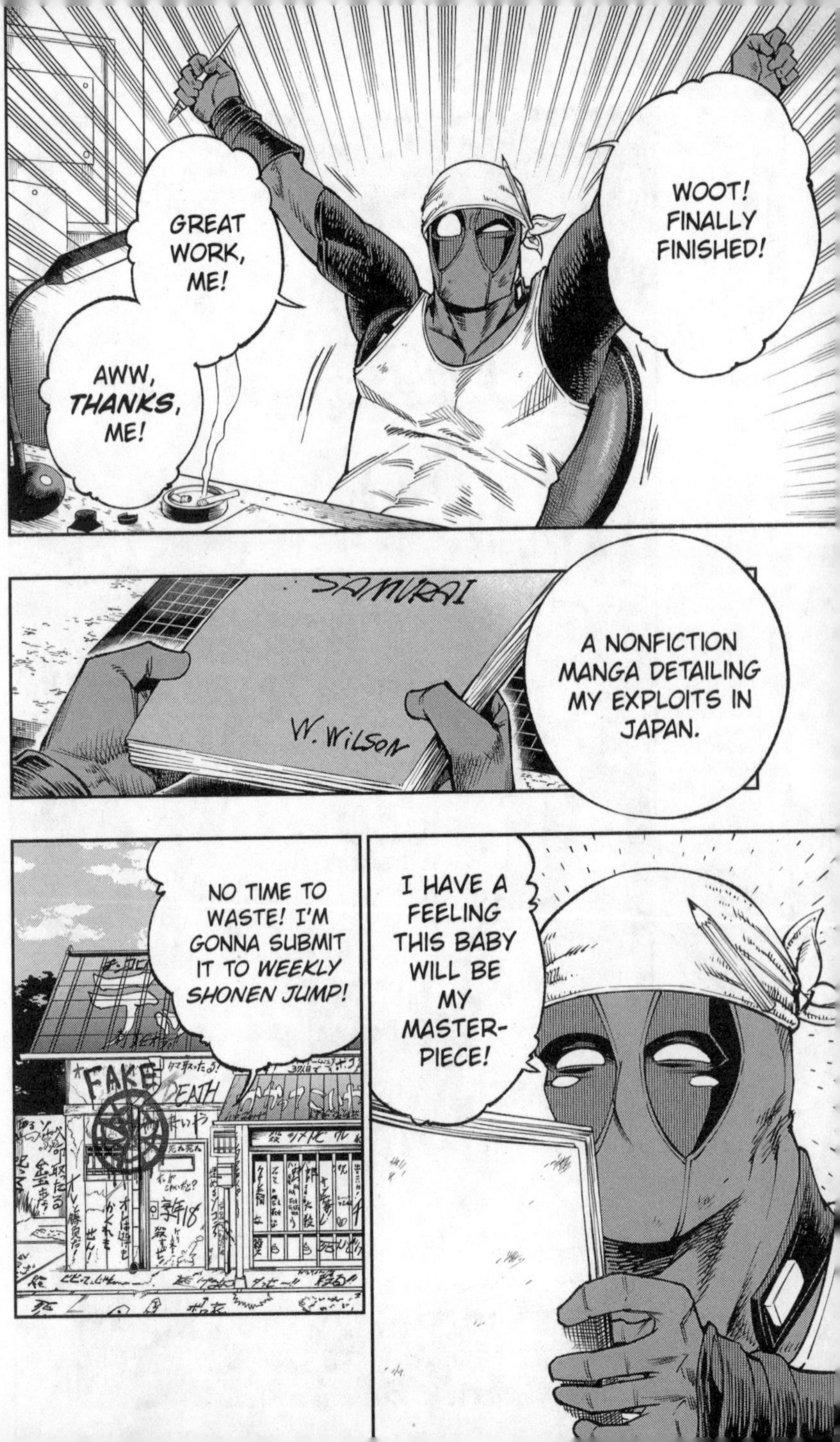
WOOT! FINALLY FINISHED!
GREAT WORK, ME!
AWW, *THANKS*, ME!
A NONFICTION MANGA DETAILING MY EXPLOITS IN JAPAN.
SAMURAI
W. Wilson
I HAVE A FEELING THIS BABY WILL BE MY MASTER-PIECE!
NO TIME TO WASTE! I'M GONNA SUBMIT IT TO *WEEKLY SHONEN JUMP!*
FAKE
DEATH

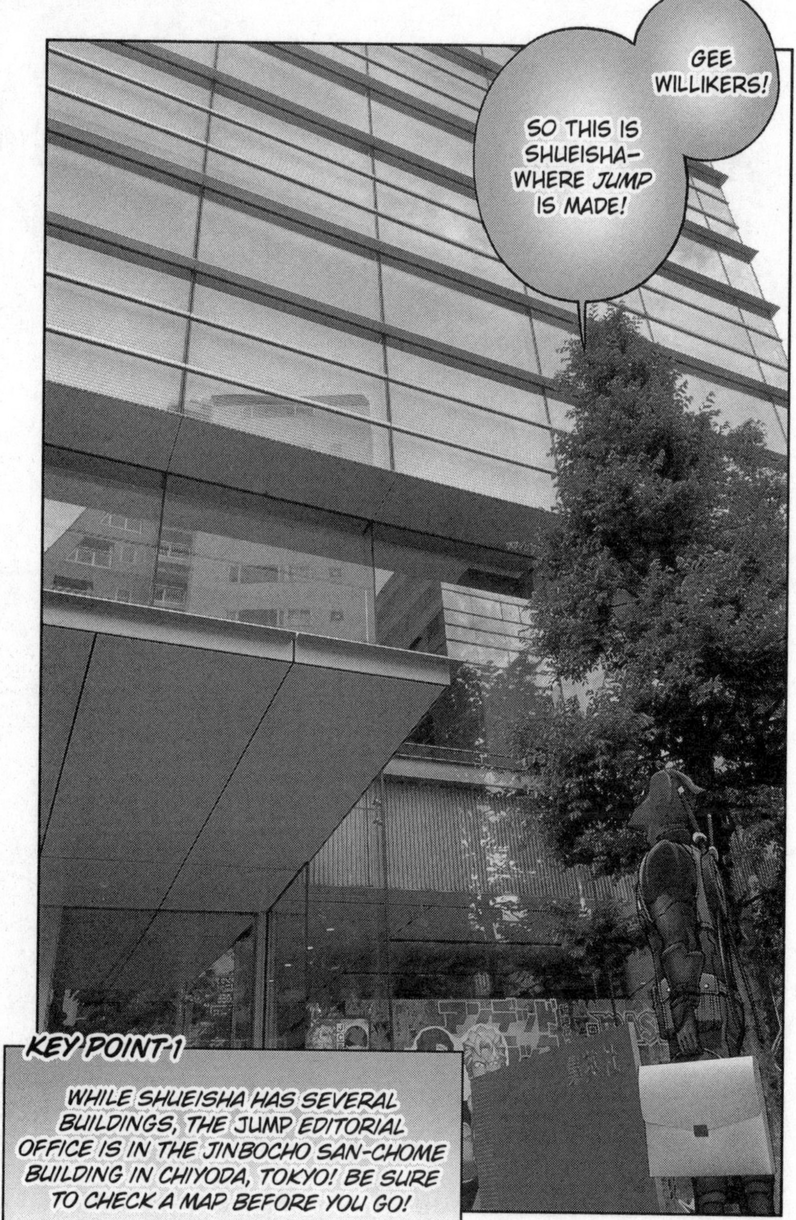
GEE WILLIKERS!
SO THIS IS SHUEISHA—WHERE *JUMP* IS MADE!
KEY POINT 1
WHILE SHUEISHA HAS SEVERAL BUILDINGS, THE JUMP EDITORIAL OFFICE IS IN THE JINBOCHO SAN-CHOME BUILDING IN CHIYODA, TOKYO! BE SURE TO CHECK A MAP BEFORE YOU GO!

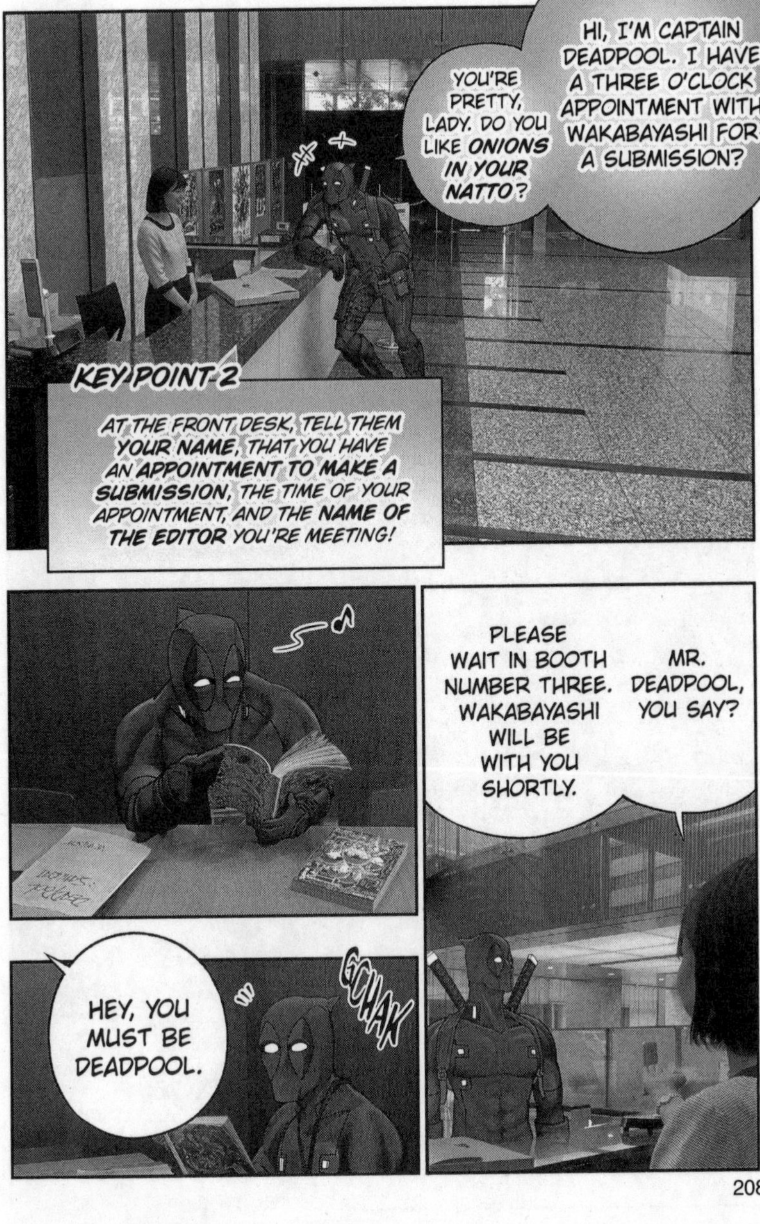
HI, I'M CAPTAIN DEADPOOL. I HAVE A THREE O'CLOCK APPOINTMENT WITH WAKABAYASHI FOR A SUBMISSION?
YOU'RE PRETTY, LADY. DO YOU LIKE ONIONS IN YOUR NATTO?
KEY POINT 2
AT THE FRONT DESK, TELL THEM YOUR NAME, THAT YOU HAVE AN APPOINTMENT TO MAKE A SUBMISSION, THE TIME OF YOUR APPOINTMENT, AND THE NAME OF THE EDITOR YOU'RE MEETING!
MR. DEADPOOL, YOU SAY?
PLEASE WAIT IN BOOTH NUMBER THREE. WAKABAYASHI WILL BE WITH YOU SHORTLY.
GCHAK
HEY, YOU MUST BE DEADPOOL.

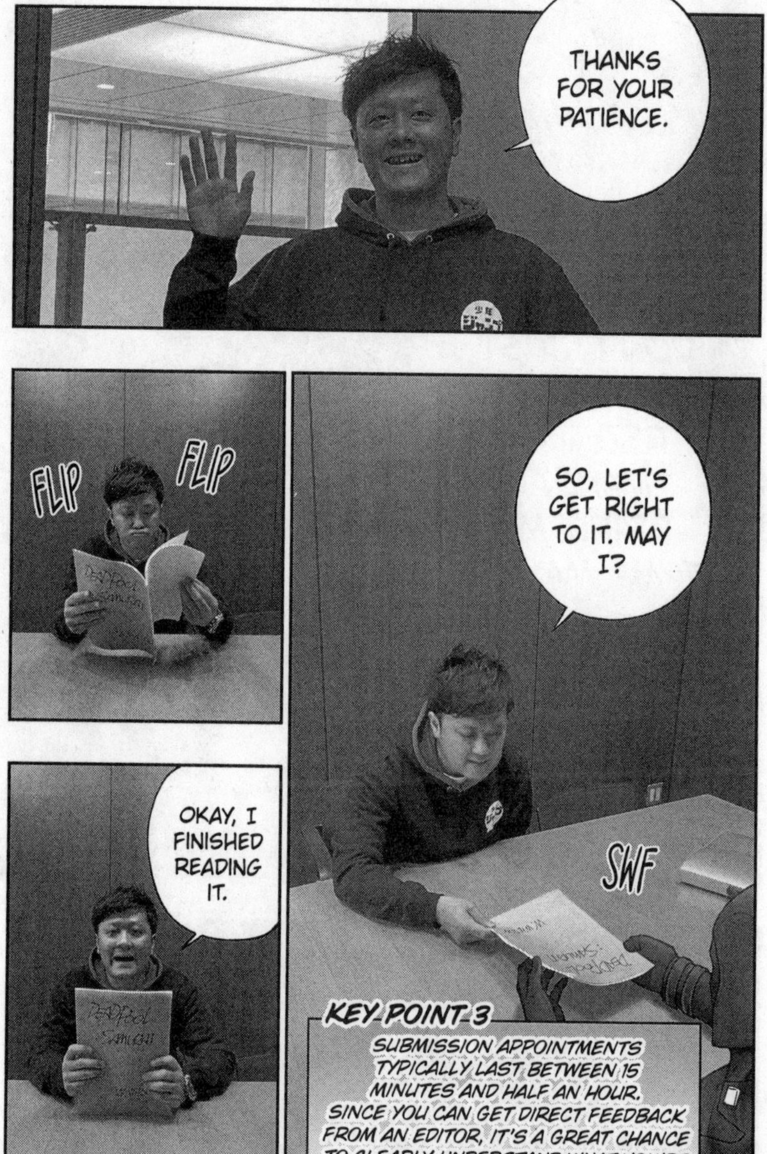
THANKS FOR YOUR PATIENCE.
SO, LET'S GET RIGHT TO IT. MAY I?
SWF
KEY POINT 3
SUBMISSION APPOINTMENTS TYPICALLY LAST BETWEEN 15 MINUTES AND HALF AN HOUR. SINCE YOU CAN GET DIRECT FEEDBACK FROM AN EDITOR, IT'S A GREAT CHANCE TO CLEARLY UNDERSTAND WHAT YOU'RE DOING WELL AND WHERE YOU HAVE ROOM TO IMPROVE!
FLIP
FLIP
OKAY, I FINISHED READING IT.

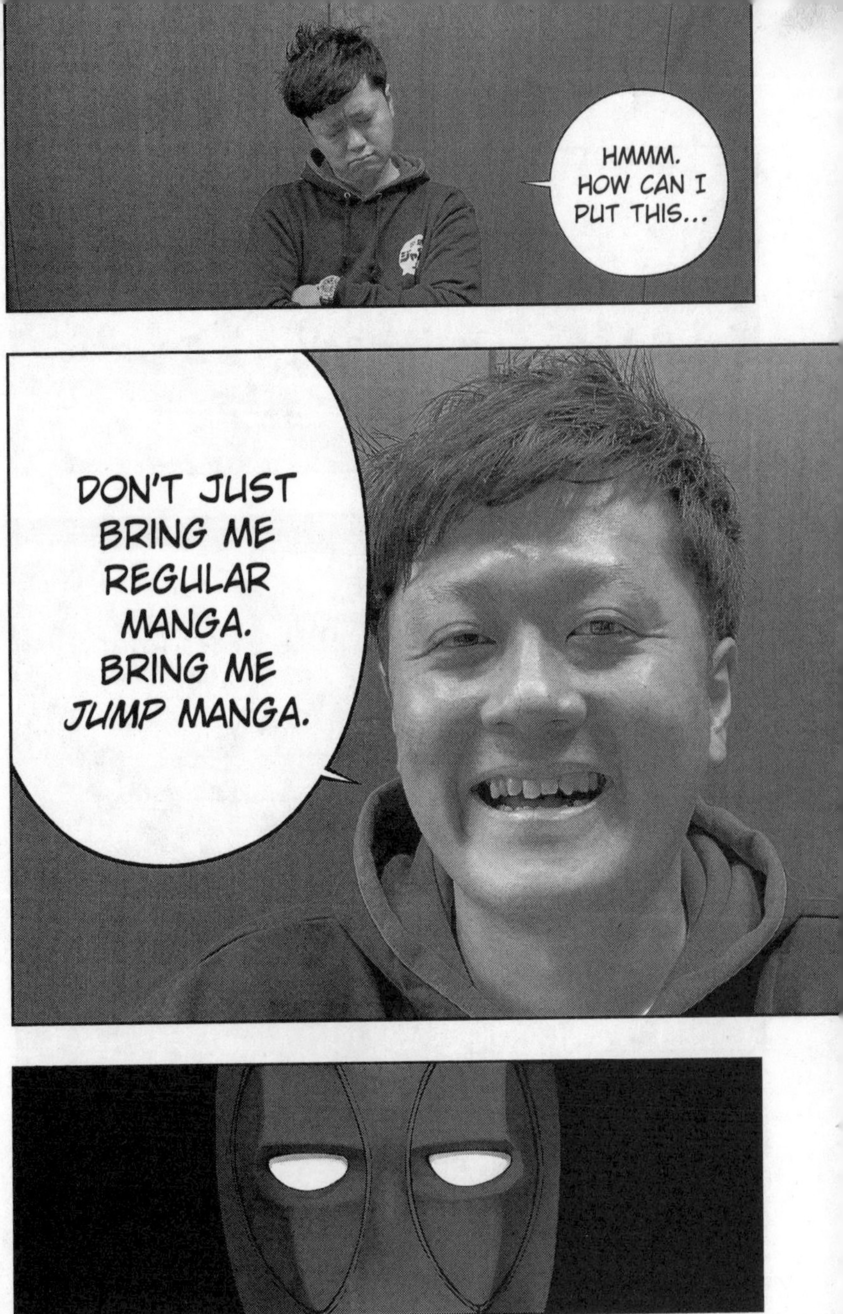
HMMM. HOW CAN I PUT THIS...
DON'T JUST BRING ME REGULAR MANGA. BRING ME JUMP MANGA.

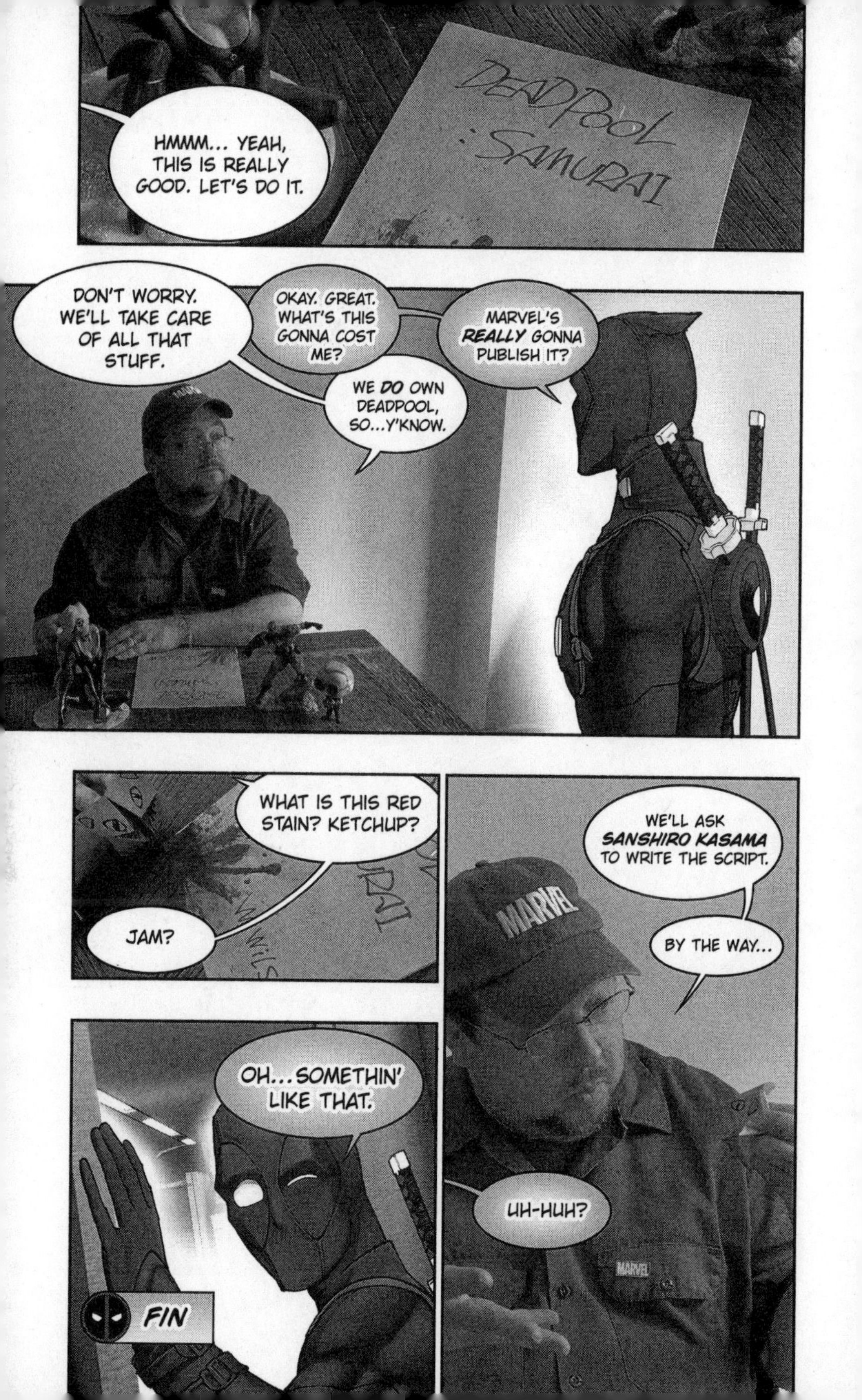
DEADPOOL : SAMURAI
HMMM... YEAH, THIS IS REALLY GOOD. LET'S DO IT.
MARVEL'S *REALLY* GONNA PUBLISH IT?
OKAY. GREAT. WHAT'S THIS GONNA COST ME?
DON'T WORRY. WE'LL TAKE CARE OF ALL THAT STUFF.
WE *DO* OWN DEADPOOL, SO...Y'KNOW.
WE'LL ASK ***SANSHIRO KASAMA*** TO WRITE THE SCRIPT.
MARVEL
BY THE WAY...
UH-HUH?
WHAT IS THIS RED STAIN? KETCHUP?
JAM?
OH...SOMETHIN' LIKE THAT.
FIN

DEADPOOL SAMURAI

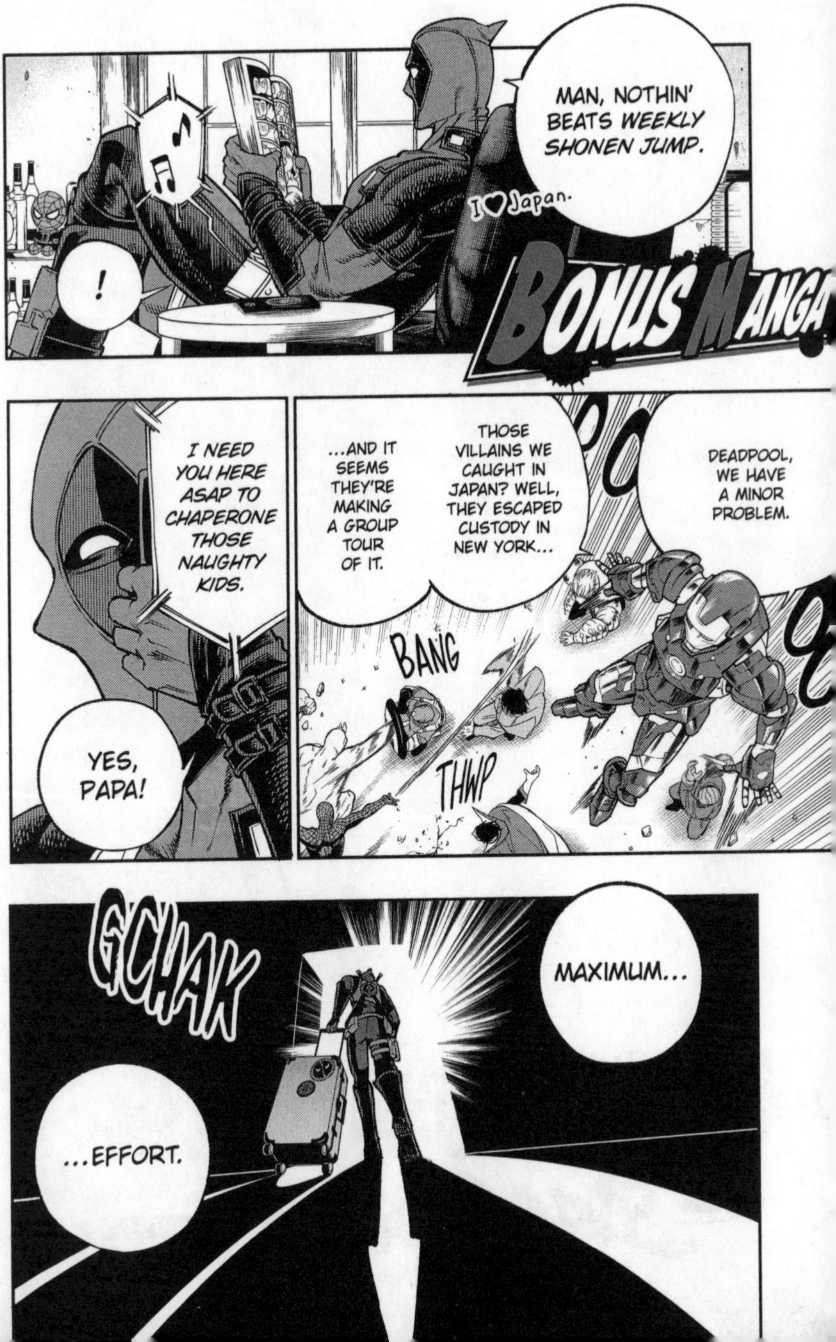
MAN, NOTHIN' BEATS WEEKLY SHONEN JUMP.
I ♥ Japan.
BONUS MANGA
!
DEADPOOL, WE HAVE A MINOR PROBLEM.
THOSE VILLAINS WE CAUGHT IN JAPAN? WELL, THEY ESCAPED CUSTODY IN NEW YORK...
...AND IT SEEMS THEY'RE MAKING A GROUP TOUR OF IT.
BANG
THWP
I NEED YOU HERE ASAP TO CHAPERONE THOSE NAUGHTY KIDS.
YES, PAPA!
GCHAK
MAXIMUM...
...EFFORT.

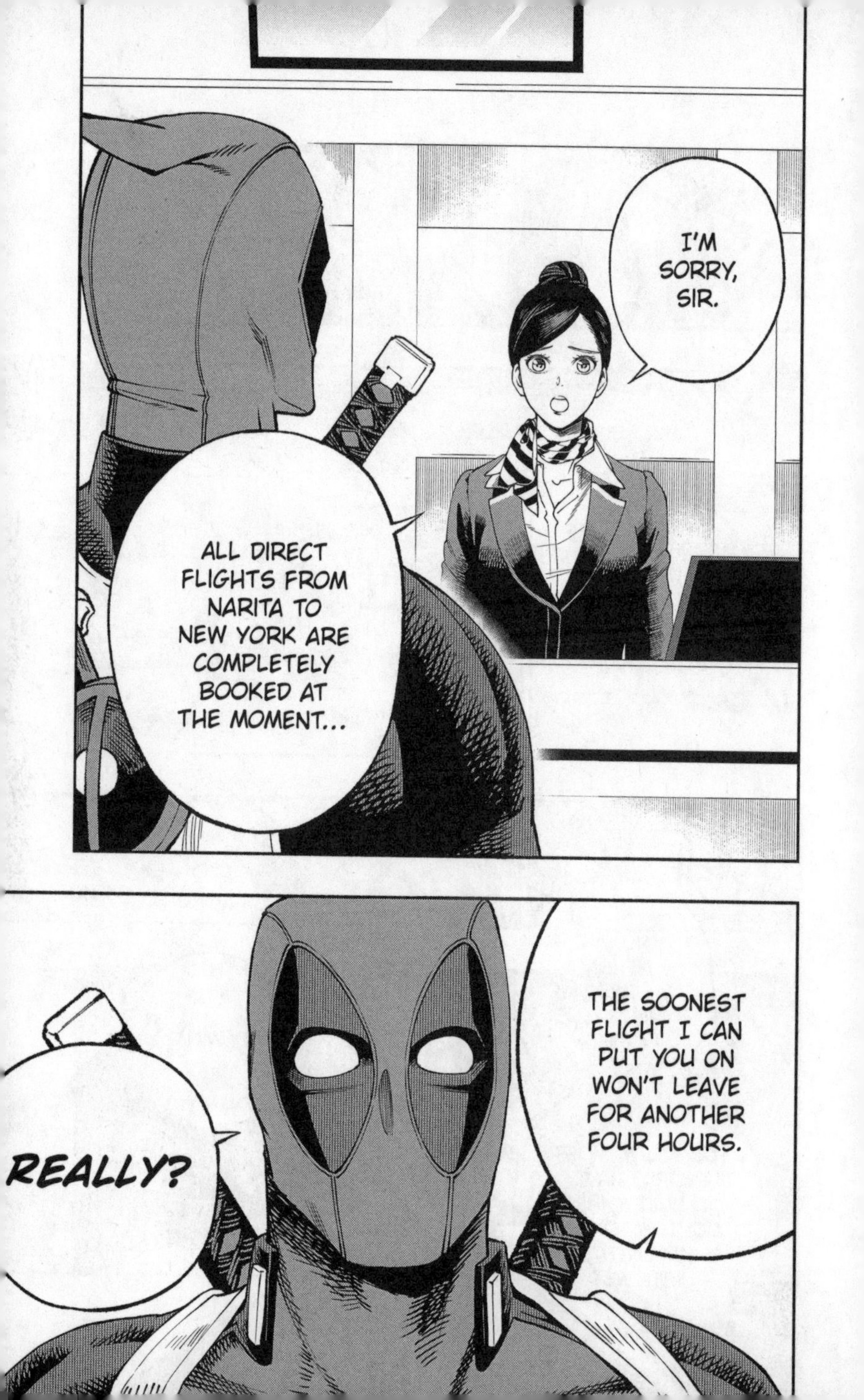
I'M SORRY, SIR.
ALL DIRECT FLIGHTS FROM NARITA TO NEW YORK ARE COMPLETELY BOOKED AT THE MOMENT...
THE SOONEST FLIGHT I CAN PUT YOU ON WON'T LEAVE FOR ANOTHER FOUR HOURS.
REALLY?

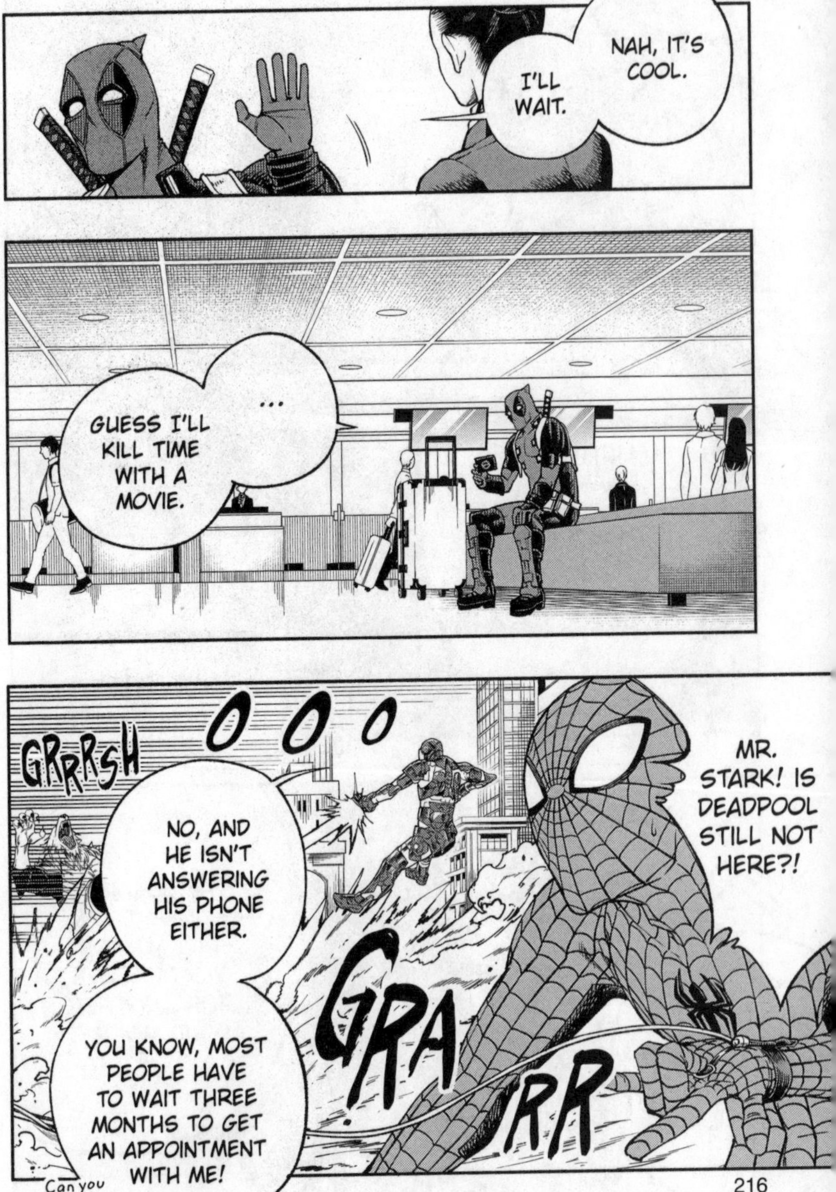
NAH, IT'S COOL.
I'LL WAIT.
...
GUESS I'LL KILL TIME WITH A MOVIE.
MR. STARK! IS DEADPOOL STILL NOT HERE?!
OOO
GRRRSH
NO, AND HE ISN'T ANSWERING HIS PHONE EITHER.
GRARR
YOU KNOW, MOST PEOPLE HAVE TO WAIT THREE MONTHS TO GET AN APPOINTMENT WITH ME!

Can you believe the gall of this guy?

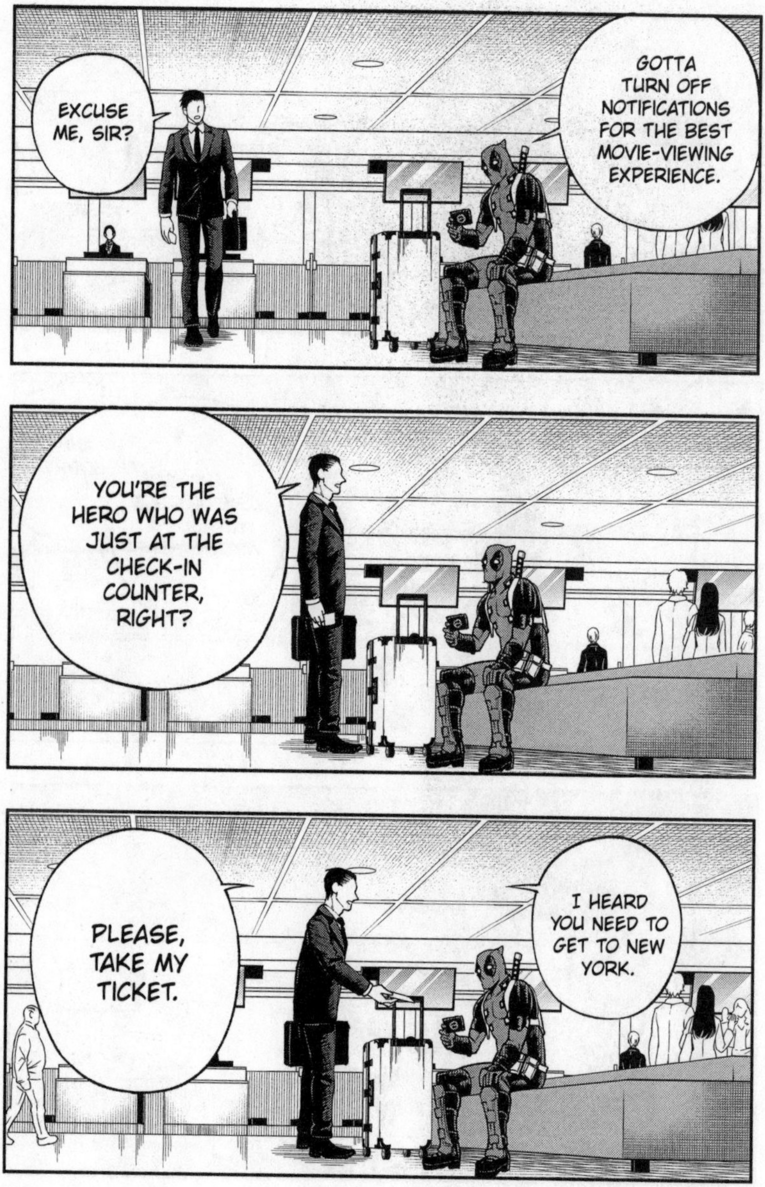
GOTTA TURN OFF NOTIFICATIONS FOR THE BEST MOVIE-VIEWING EXPERIENCE.
EXCUSE ME, SIR?
YOU'RE THE HERO WHO WAS JUST AT THE CHECK-IN COUNTER, RIGHT?
I HEARD YOU NEED TO GET TO NEW YORK.
PLEASE, TAKE MY TICKET.

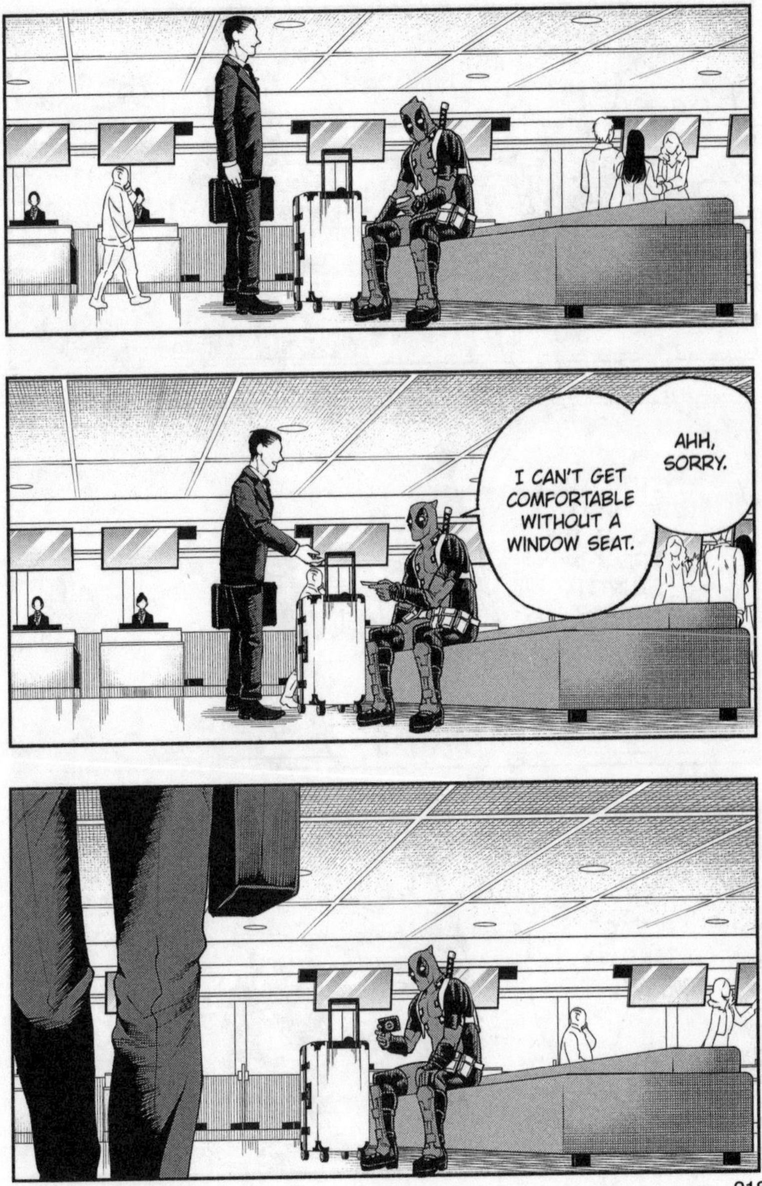
AHH, SORRY.
I CAN'T GET COMFORTABLE WITHOUT A WINDOW SEAT.

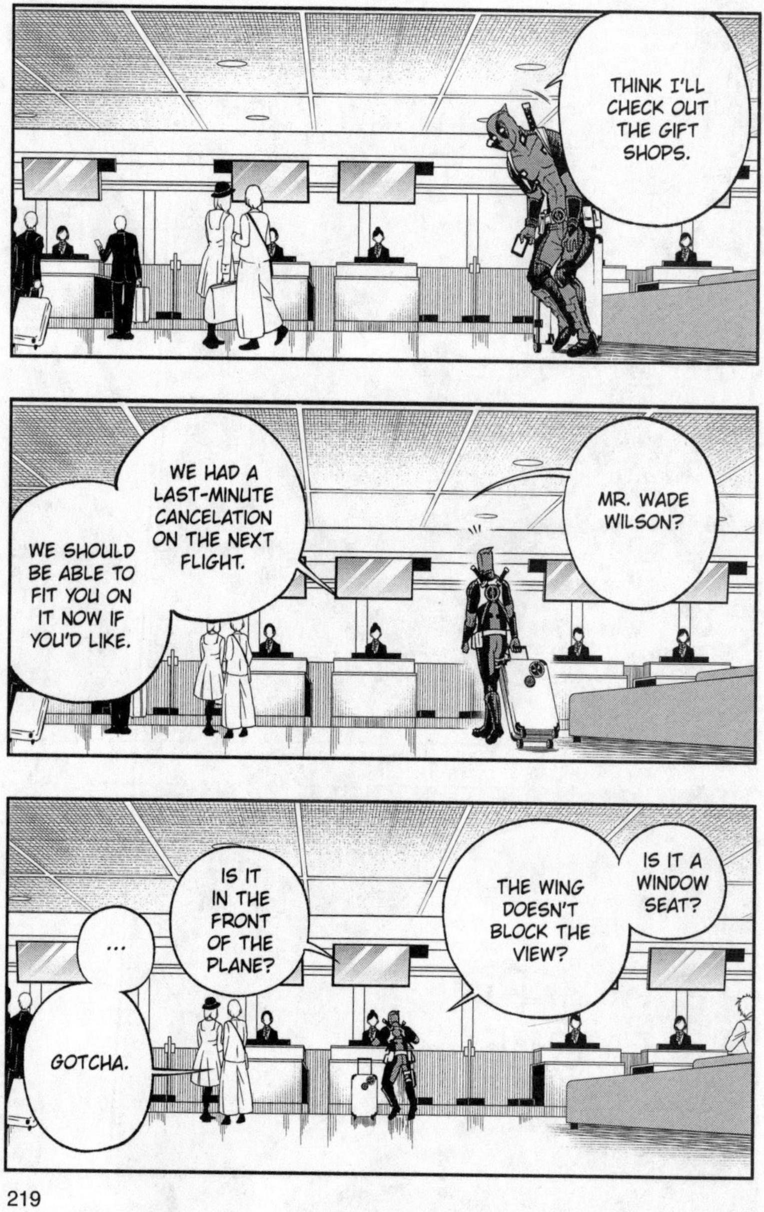
THINK I'LL CHECK OUT THE GIFT SHOPS.
MR. WADE WILSON?
WE HAD A LAST-MINUTE CANCELATION ON THE NEXT FLIGHT.
WE SHOULD BE ABLE TO FIT YOU ON IT NOW IF YOU'D LIKE.
IS IT A WINDOW SEAT?
THE WING DOESN'T BLOCK THE VIEW?
IS IT IN THE FRONT OF THE PLANE?
...
GOTCHA.

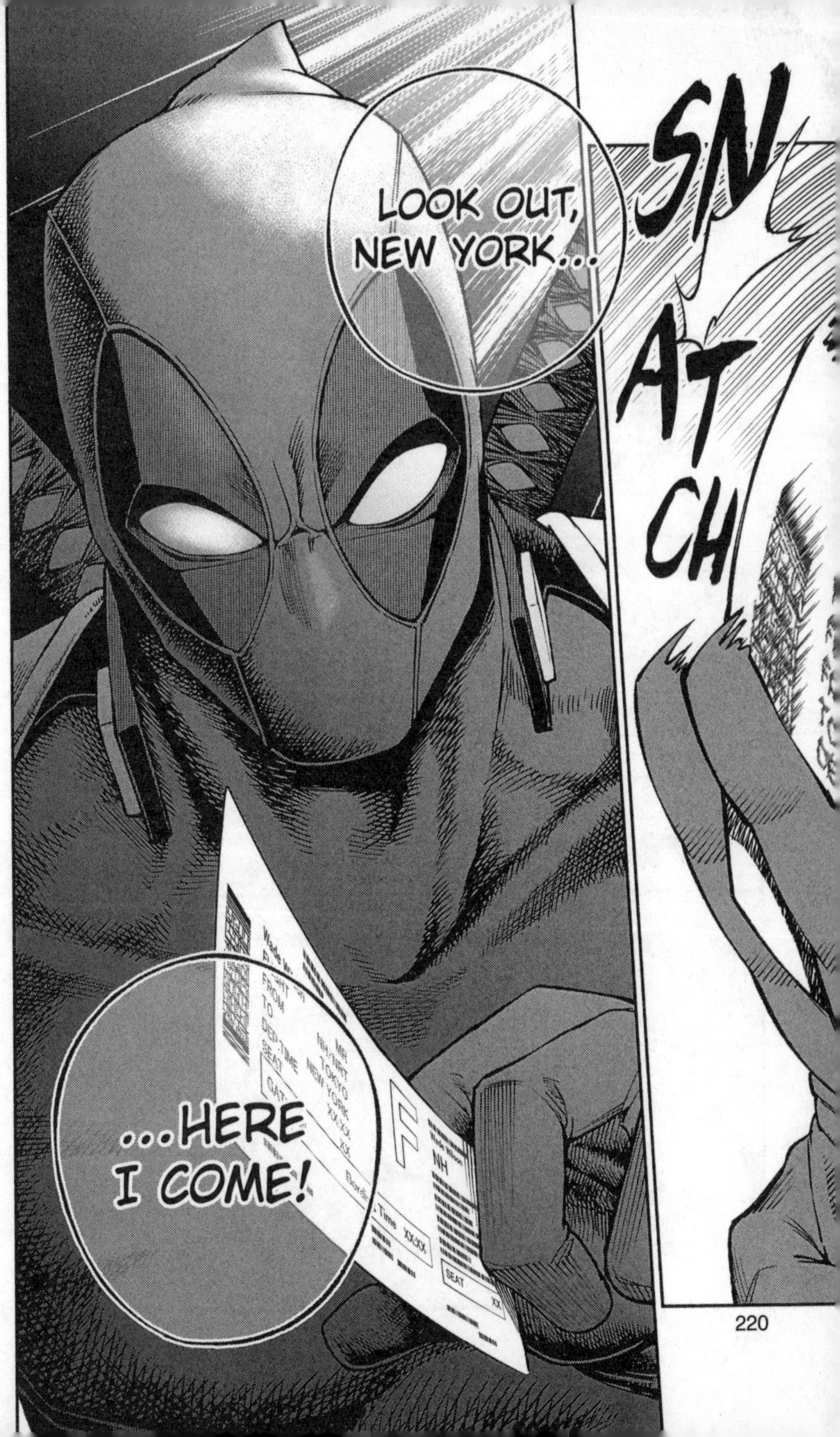
SNATCH
LOOK OUT, NEW YORK...
...HERE I COME!

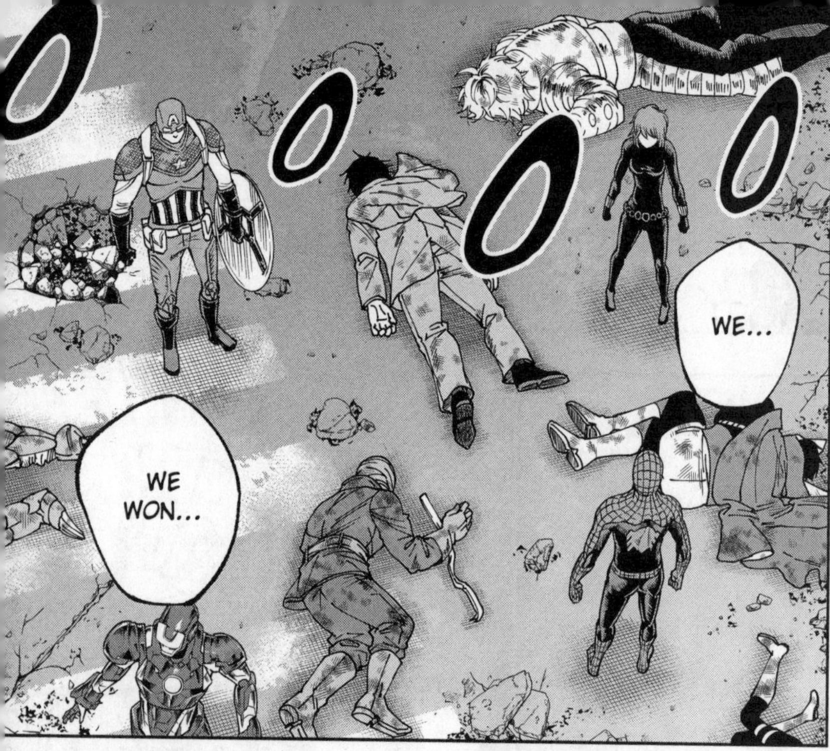
WE...
WE WON...

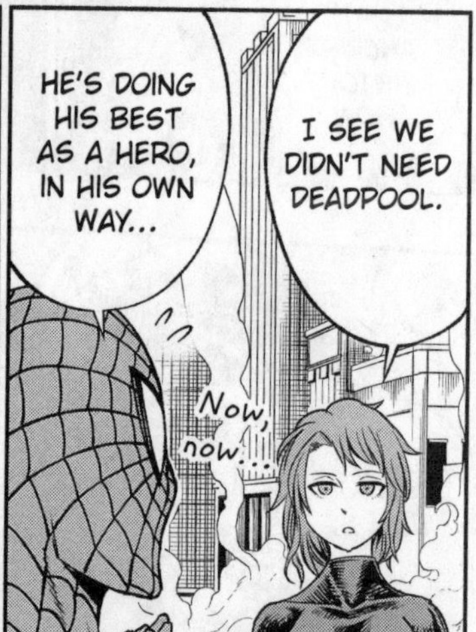
I SEE WE DIDN'T NEED DEADPOOL.
HE'S DOING HIS BEST AS A HERO, IN HIS OWN WAY...
Now, now...

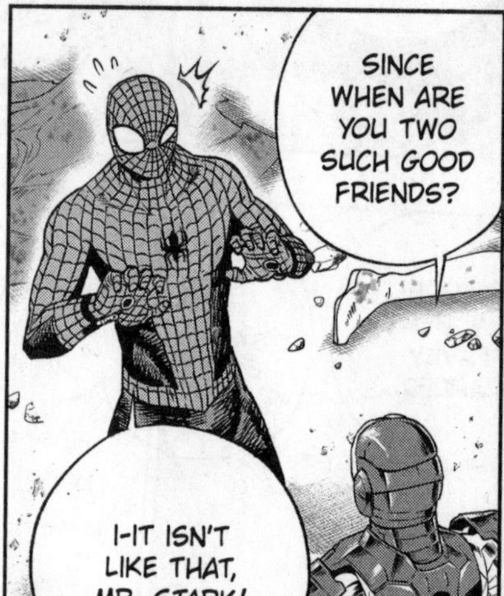
SINCE WHEN ARE YOU TWO SUCH GOOD FRIENDS?
I-IT ISN'T LIKE THAT, MR. STARK!

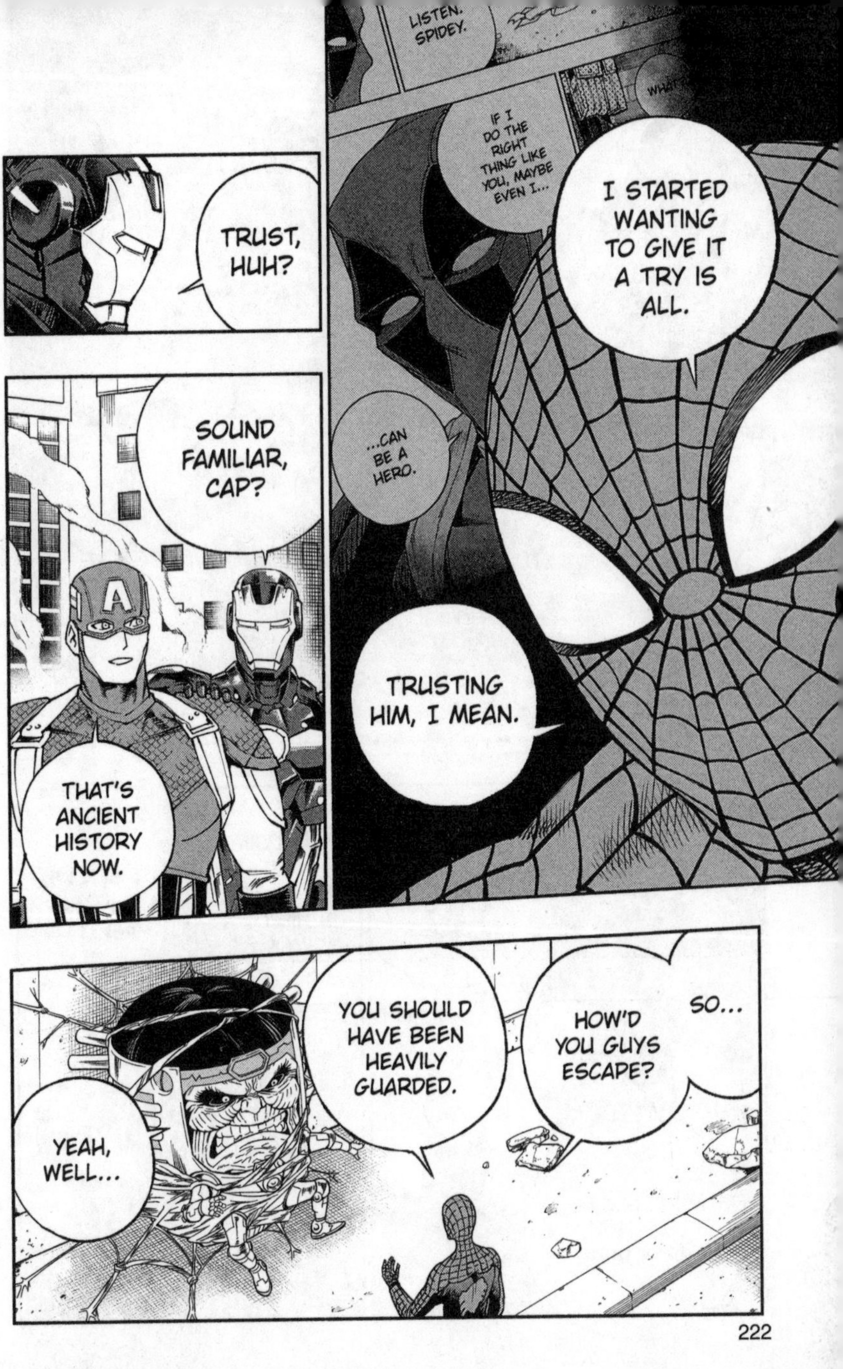
LISTEN. SPIDEY.
WHAT?
I STARTED WANTING TO GIVE IT A TRY IS ALL.
IF I DO THE RIGHT THING LIKE YOU, MAYBE EVEN I...
...CAN BE A HERO.
TRUSTING HIM, I MEAN.
TRUST, HUH?
SOUND FAMILIAR, CAP?
THAT'S ANCIENT HISTORY NOW.
SO...
HOW'D YOU GUYS ESCAPE?
YOU SHOULD HAVE BEEN HEAVILY GUARDED.
YEAH, WELL...

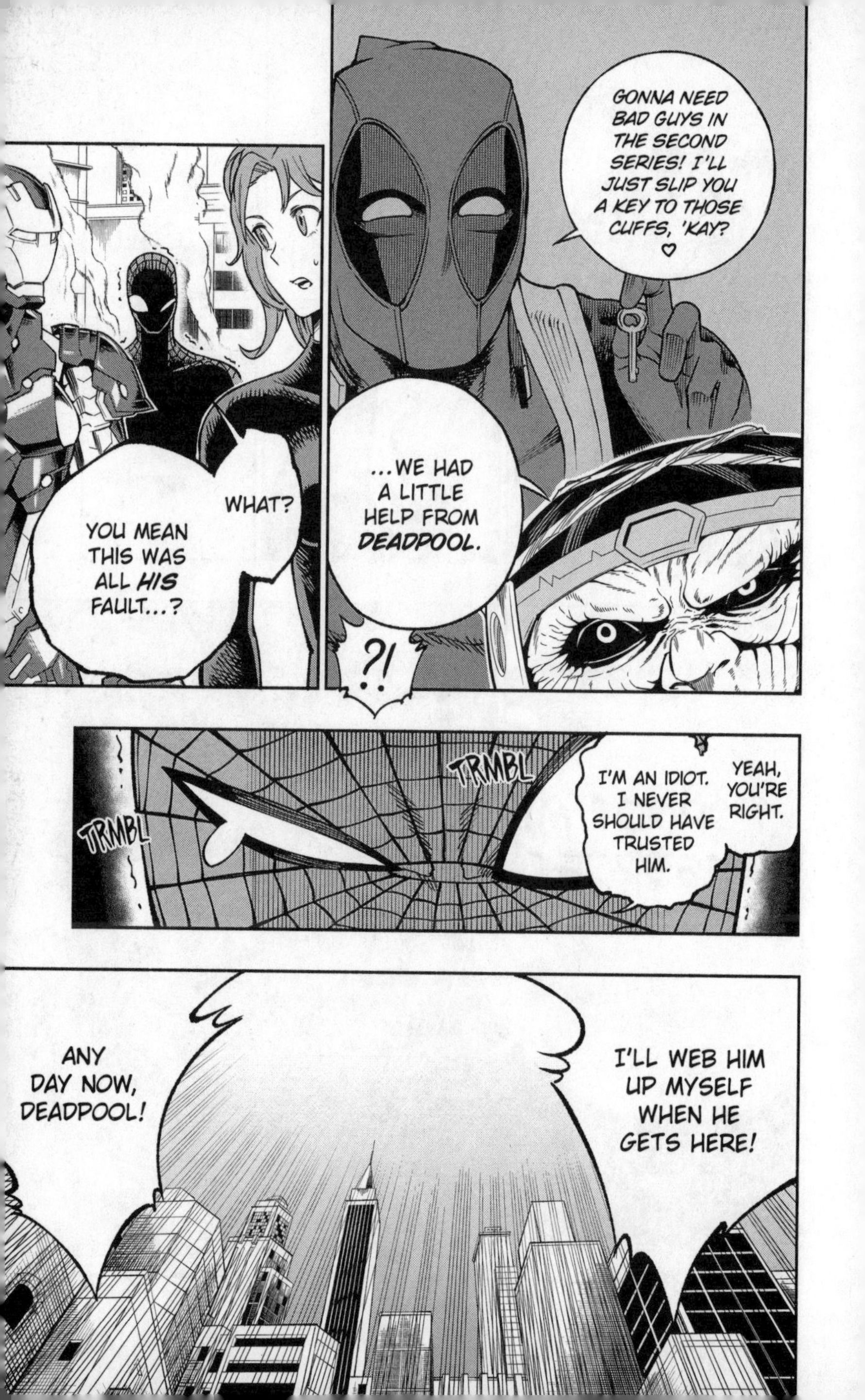
GONNA NEED BAD GUYS IN THE SECOND SERIES! I'LL JUST SLIP YOU A KEY TO THOSE CUFFS, 'KAY? ♡
...WE HAD A LITTLE HELP FROM DEADPOOL.
?!
WHAT?
YOU MEAN THIS WAS ALL HIS FAULT...?
TRMBL
YEAH, YOU'RE RIGHT.
I'M AN IDIOT. I NEVER SHOULD HAVE TRUSTED HIM.
TRMBL
I'LL WEB HIM UP MYSELF WHEN HE GETS HERE!
ANY DAY NOW, DEADPOOL!

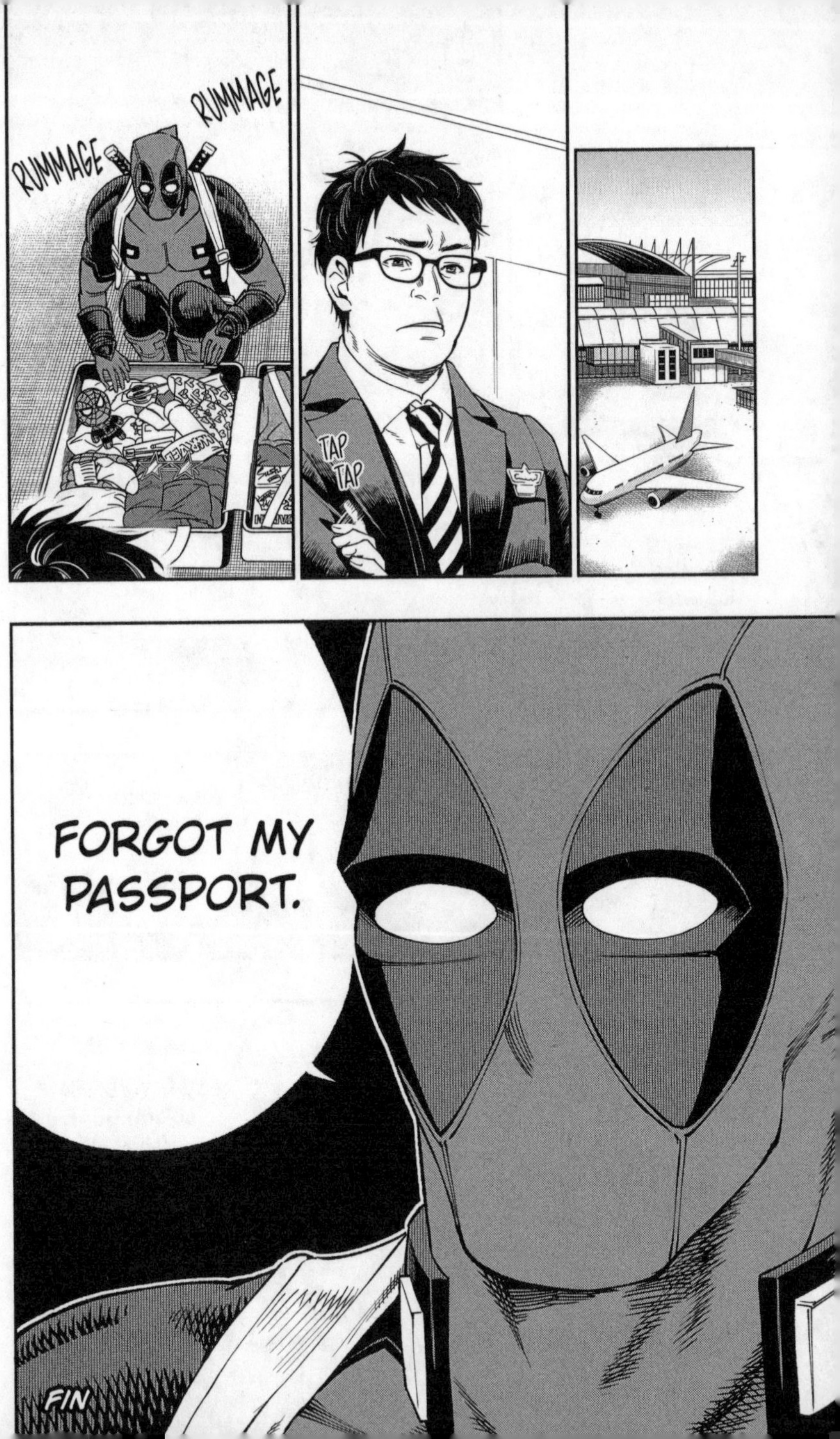
TAP
TAP
RUMMAGE
RUMMAGE
FORGOT MY PASSPORT.
FIN

DEADPOOL

SAMURAI

DEADPOOL SAMURAI

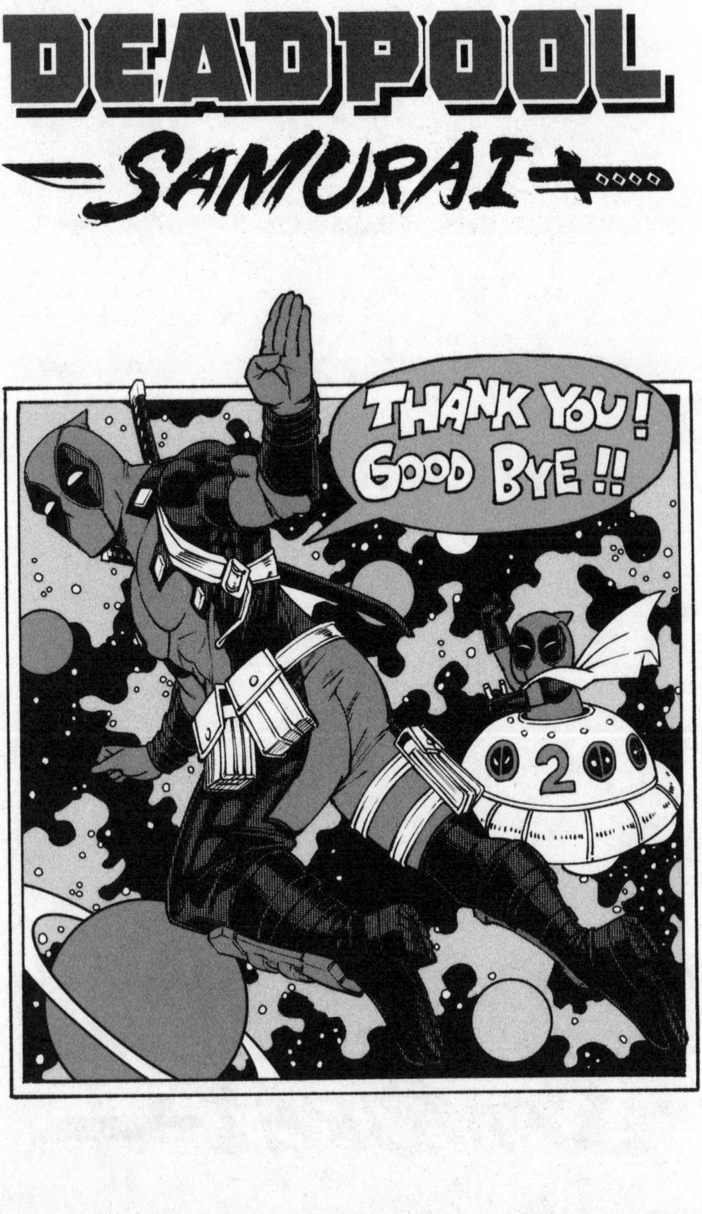
THANK YOU! GOOD BYE!!

Afterword

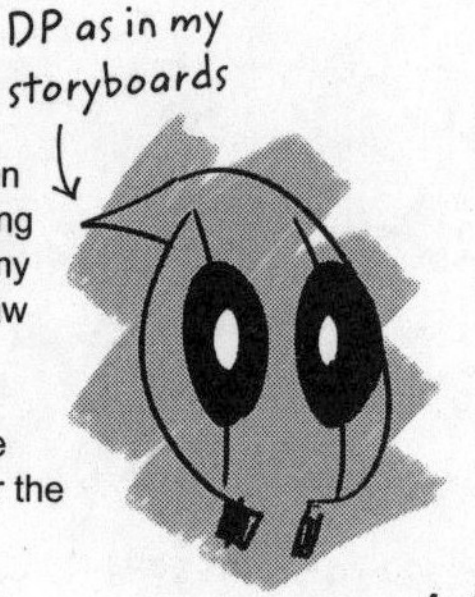
DP as in my storyboards

Writer Kasama here. Thank you for buying *Deadpool Samurai* volume 2. The Deadpool movie hooked me on him immediately. I worked on my manga while dreaming about depicting a character that absurd, but never in my wildest dreams did I think I'd get the opportunity to draw Deadpool himself.

Thank you so much to those who supported me, to the manga creators who graciously gave their approval for the references, and to everyone involved in the making of this manga.

Also, I'm pretty sure this manga's MVP was our editor, who handled the back-and-forth with Marvel, got permission for an enormous number of references, and more, so please give the editor some appreciation.

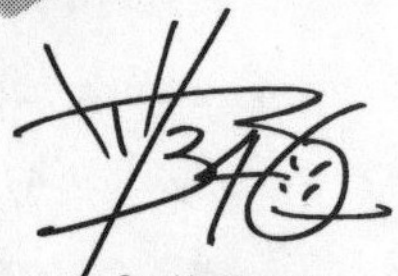

Sanshiro Kasama

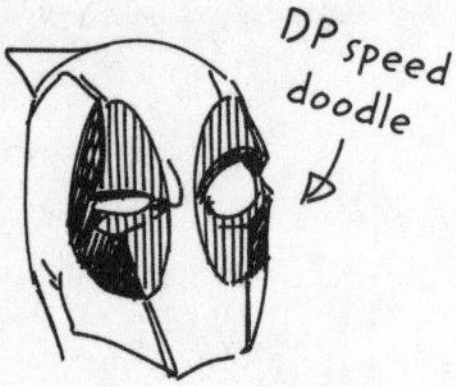
DP speed doodle

Artist Uesugi here. Thank you for not only buying this book but also reading it all the way to this page. I feel my art is crude compared to the American comic books, but I hope you were able to enjoy it anyway. Deadpool's design is my personal favorite of the Marvel characters, so I had a lot of fun drawing him. There's something moving about seeing the differences in the art between the one-shot, the first chapter, and now.

I was struck by how well the character combines both action and comedy. On top of that, I have to admire a design so strong that a character can be that expressive while *masked*.

Finally, getting to have my art next to Horikoshi Sensei's, getting to see Superlog's art from the closest distance possible… This was a once-in-a-lifetime experience.

Thanks, DP!

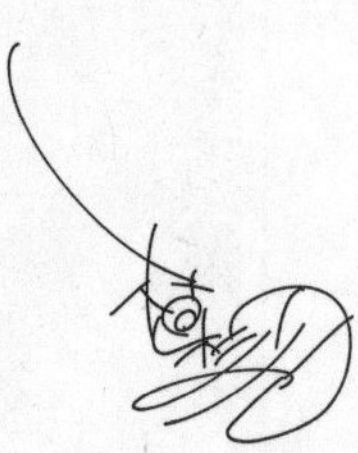

Hikaru Uesugi

Special Thanks

C. B. Cebulski (Marvel)

Kusano-san (Disney)

Sakakibara-san (editor)

Kohei Horikoshi Sensei

A bunch of bigwigs

Jake Thomas (Marvel)

Miho Matta Takahashi
(translation assistance)

Kamei-san (designer)

Superlog Sensei

Yumi Yaoshida (Superlog Sensei's Colorist)

All our readers

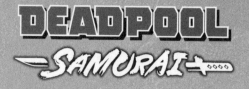

DEADPOOL SAMURAI

Volume 2
VIZ MEDIA Edition

STORY BY SANSHIRO KASAMA
ART BY HIKARU UESUGI

Translation: Amanda Haley
Touch-Up Art & Lettering: Brandon Bovia
Design: Francesca Truman
Editor: David Brothers

MARVEL Publishing
VP Production & Special Projects: Jeff Youngquist
Associate Editor, Special Projects: Sarah Singer
VP, Licensed Publishing: Sven Larsen
SVP Print, Sales & Marketing: David Gabriel
Editor in Chief: C.B. Cebulski

First published in Japan in 2018 by SHUEISHA Inc., Tokyo.
English translation rights arranged by SHUEISHA Inc.

Printed in the U.S.A.

Published by VIZ Media, LLC
P.O. Box 77010 | San Francisco, CA 94107

10 9 8 7 6 5 4 3 2 1
First Printing, June 2022

MARVEL VIZ MEDIA
viz.com

ratings.viz.com RATED T+ OLDER TEEN

PARENTAL ADVISORY
DEADPOOL: SAMURAI is rated T+ for Older Teen and is recommended for ages 16 and up. This volume contains violence and gore.

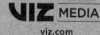

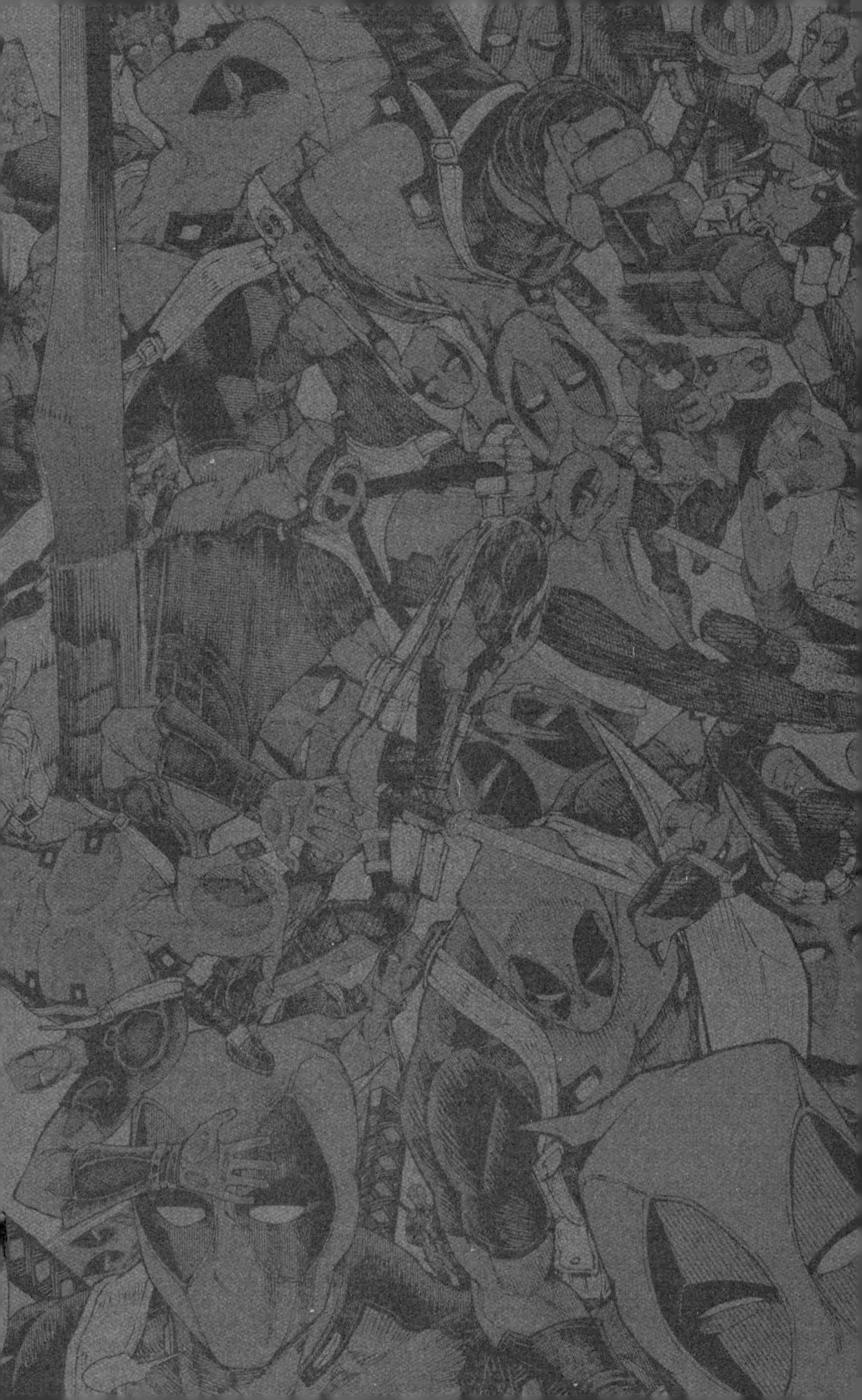

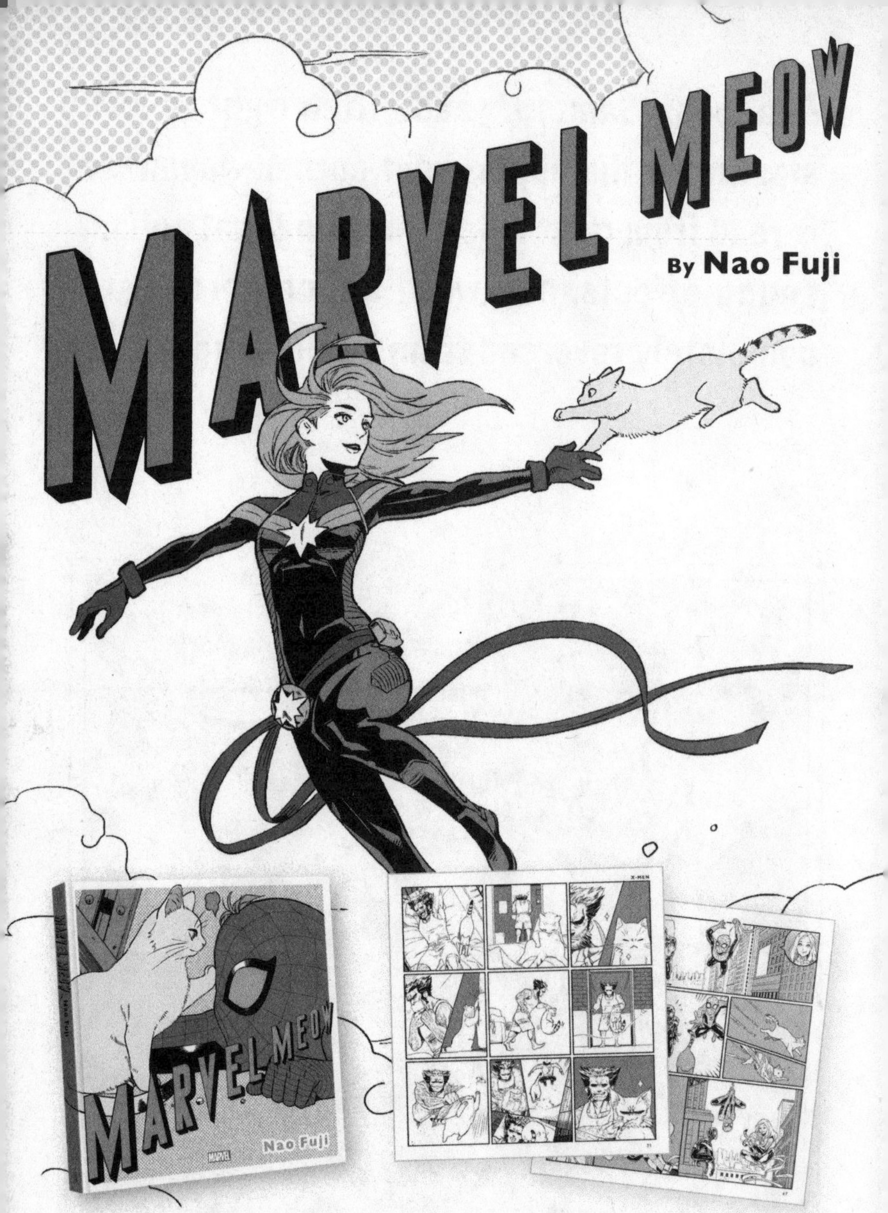
MARVEL MEOW
By Nao Fuji
MARVEL MEOW
Nao Fuji

***Deadpool: Samurai* reads from right to left, starting in the upper-right corner. Japanese is read from right to left, meaning that action, sound effects, and word-balloon order are completely reversed from English order.**

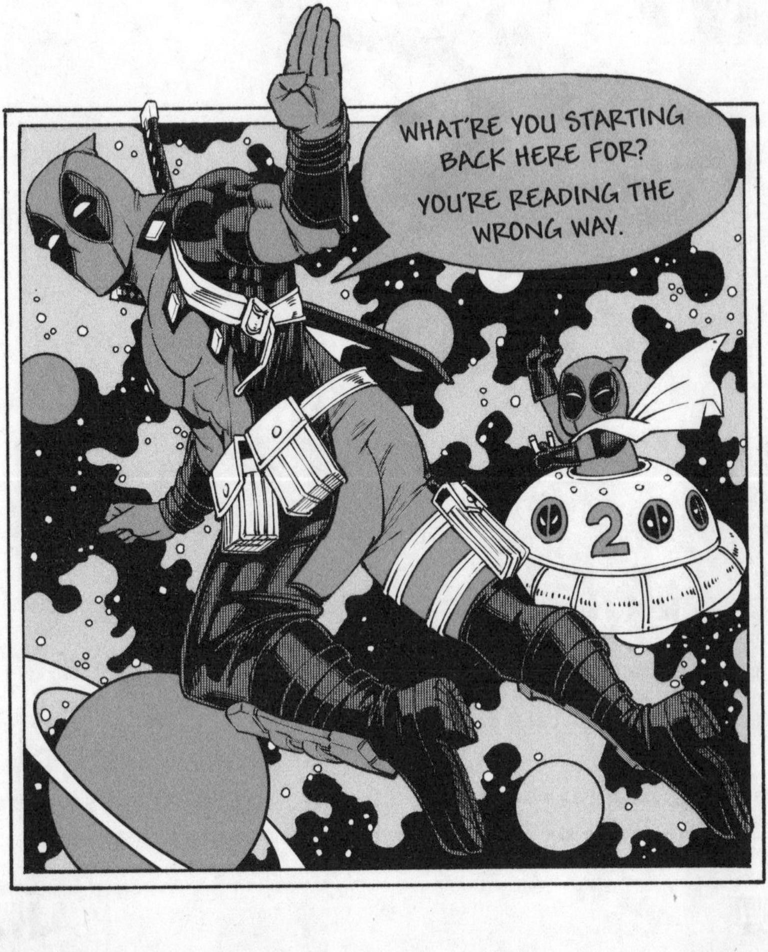
WHAT'RE YOU STARTING BACK HERE FOR?
YOU'RE READING THE WRONG WAY.
2